GHOSTS AND SHADOWS OF ANDERSONVILLE

The publication of this book is due in part to a generous gift by the Watson-Brown Foundation.

Mercer University Press
1400 Coleman Avenue | Macon, Georgia 31207 | www.mupress.org
MUP/H703 |
ISBN-13: 978-0-88146-012-4 | ISBN-10: 0-88146-012-5 (hardback: alk. paper)

First Edition | Printed in the United States of America

Library of Congress Cataloging-in-Publication Data
Davis, Robert Scott, 1954-
Ghosts and shadows of Andersonville:essays on the secret social histories
of America's deadliest prison
by Robert Scott Davis–1 st ed.
p. cm. | Includes bibliographical references and index

1. Andersonville Prison–History 2. United States–History–Civil War,1861-1865–Social aspects
3. Andersonville Prison–Biography 4. United States–History–Civil War, 1861-1865–Biography
I. Title

E612.A5D158 2006
973.7'7109758913–dc22

2006017047

GHOSTS AND SHADOWS

IIIIIIIIIIIIIIIIIIIIIII OF IIIIIIIIIIIIIIIIIIIIIII

ANDERSONVILLE

ESSAYS ON THE SECRET SOCIAL HISTORIES OF AMERICA'S DEADLIEST PRISON

ROBERT SCOTT DAVIS

MERCER UNIVERSITY PRESS

MACON, GEORGIA

Mr. Davis directs the Family & Regional History Program, Wallace State College, Hanceville AL. He has published dozens of articles in professional journals. His books include *Encounters on a March through Georgia in 1779: The Maps and Memorandums of Lt. John Wilson, 71st Highlanders; Cotton, Fire & Dreams: The Robert Findlay Iron Works and Heavy Industry in Macon, Georgia, 1839–1912;* and *Requiem for a Lost City: Sallie Clayton's Memoirs of Civil War Atlanta.*

For Ted Key,
the teacher who introduced me to Georgia history,
Andersonville, MacKinley Kantor, and the one
hundred-page term paper.

"Writing...has developed in me an abiding respect for the unknown in a human lifetime and a sense of where to look for the threads, how to follow, how to connect, find in the thick of the tangle what clear line persists."

—Eudora Welty

ACKNOWLEDGMENTS

We owe respect to the living but to the dead we owe only the truth.
—Voltaire

Writing in English is the most ingenious torture ever devised for sins committed in previous lives.
—James Joyce

At least one author has rightly complained about the extraordinary number of instances where persons with Andersonville material failed to fulfill promises to share. This project, however, owes so very much to so many. Specifically, I would like to acknowledge the help provided by Jane Singer, Bruce Allardice, Elizabeth Willauer, Jack Lundquist, Richard Sauers, Kenneth H. Thomas Jr., William Marvel, Carl A. Anderson, Greg White, Farris Cadle, Linda Aaron, and Michael Musick, in too many instances to remember and record here. The staff of the Andersonville National Historic Site have repeatedly helped me, on site and at a distance. Brenda Scott, Dan Scott, Jess Shelander, Richard Smallwood, and Dr. Karen S. Walker proved their friendship, beyond the call of duty, by reviewing this manuscript and making many helpful and sometimes imaginative suggestions. Where even they failed speaks more as to my insurmountable shortcomings with grammar than to their considerable skills as critical readers. To people who reviewed this manuscript and claimed to see poetry in my prose, may I recommend a good optometrist and a basic writing class?

Individual chapters received special attention and help. Dr. Edwin C. Bridges, David M. Sherman, Doug Carter, Charlotte Marshall, and Jane Benson kindly shared with me the experiences of their respective Georgia families with a place called Andersonville. Historian Dr. Keith Bohannon provided me with information on a number of sources but, more importantly, of news of the recent emergence from private ownership of the diary of prisoner William H. Smith. Although this document turned up at the last moment in the preparation of this manuscript, it proved a valuable source in a number of chapters here, as did the Benjamin B. Dyke court case found for me by Farris Cadle. Robert Hewson (also known as novelist Henry Nary) brought the memoirs of Daniel Bond to my attention, and the late David T. Thackery kindly provided me with a copy. Brenda Dye joined with me in the quest for her mysterious ancestor George W. Fechter. Similarly, Jan Botkin Therkildsen found for me the diary of Jasper Culver. The search for the saintly Father Hamilton called upon the services of Colm McQuinn of All Hallows, Muriel Jackson of the Washington Memorial Library, and Karen Smith. Joe Lee, Don Brown, and Mike Griffith proved to be a tremendous help in putting together a life picture of photographer Andrew J. Riddle. An epic like the story of the Spencer family needed the equally grand efforts of Erick Montgomery, Roger Bristow, Rebecca A. Livingston, William Elliott, and Philip Bye. DeAnne Blanton provided advice on women in the Civil War, based upon her research for her book on that topic. John Lundstrom of the Milwaukee Public Museum provided valuable information from the lost memoirs of Henry W. Miller. Sylvia M. Rowan and Jeff Steele of the Office of the Herkimer County Clerk provided copies of the court cases on John H. Morris. The Herkimer County Historical Society provided background material on Morris. Suzanne Dewberry, Mary Ladner, and Mary Anne Hawkins searched the Confederate court records for this project. Many other people also contributed to this work. For not acknowledging their contributions here, I sincerely apologize.

Like many of the people discussed here, often I have wished that I could escape from Andersonville. I had so many adventures in preparing this work that I could have been a chapter in my own book. With the help of my Internet research buddies and a cyber detective agency, for example, I located the last living descendent of lawyer O. S. Baker in Seattle. He knew nothing of his fascinating ancestor and could offer no hope of help. Within a few weeks, however, he sent me copies of letters and original photographs that he had not known he had. A similar search for Harkness Lay's diary of his time at Andersonville did and didn't end so well. The part of the document about the escape by Harkness that I wanted so much did not survive. The manuscript, a copy of which was generously provided for my use by Richard D. Goff after many adventures, however, did include a one-of-a-kind map of Sapelo Island, Georgia, that allowed me to reward Kenneth H. Thomas, Jr., for his help with a boon to his own research.

The manuscript did reach a point where I feared that this research would go on forever, to the detriment of my other projects, and to the point I risked failing to go to press at all. My finding and use of newspapers that have never even been microfilmed, in various libraries and museums, and my searches in the new computer programs that read millions of pages of newspaper text illustrate something of the breadth of my research. Friends Beth Willauer and Jane Nardy, among others, inquired where I would finally set the limits on this research. I responded that I had decided not to fly to San Francisco in search of the tombstone of O. S. Baker. This incidental record of his death likely lies with the other markers of the Golden Gate Cemetery that were dumped in the bay. Seeking this record would require my learning to scuba dive.

I do feel that this journey has been worthwhile. Along the way, many of the worst kind of mysteries, the secrets hidden not by deceit but by historical accident, have been solved. D. W. Vowles, for example, would have remained a shadowy figure who walked away from his last assignment and vanished until, as with the lawyer O. S. Baker, a search found him in places previously overlooked. Historians previously did not even have Baker's correct name. On the other hand, maybe the identity of Limber Jim and the truth about the women of Andersonville have now been found—or maybe not. With Andersonville, answers only come with more questions.

INTRODUCTION

Search then the ruling passions there alone,
The wild are constant, and the cunning known,
The fool consistent, and the false sincere,
Priests, princes, women, no dissemblers here.
This clue once found unravels all the rest.

—Alexander Pope

The tone in which topics connected with our late civil war are discussed has undergone a great change within a few years. The great body of pen-fighters who came forward on each side as soon as the clashing of battle died away, waging a fierce though bloodless fight, resembled the first troops who reached the seat of war, both in abundance of zeal and lack of knowledge. It was impossible for them to write the true history of the war.... Even the North itself could not long remain content with its own polemical histories.... And, now, we are willing to admit that, in many cases the truth lies at the half-way point between these accounts and those to which we formally trusted

—Rufus B. Richardson (1880)

This work seeks to build upon the earlier scholarship on Andersonville by Futch, Marvel, Lynn, and Roberts—to explore the most famous and controversial questions that arose in their comprehensive histories of Confederate Camp Sumter, the infamous Civil War prison that became popularly known as Andersonville.[1] The resulting eclectic collection goes to many very different places by many curious routes.

This journey for me began when, working on other projects, I found in the National Archives miscellaneous information on men who had successfully escaped from Andersonville. Somewhere I thought I had read, perhaps as was implied in MacKinley Kantor's novel *Andersonville*, that the guards had successfully kept in all of its victims. I later read that 328 men had, officially, escaped never to return as prisoners. (I subsequently learned, as explained in chapter two, that even that number proves inaccurate and for historically significant reasons.)[2] Initially, I felt proud to have found an interesting and unexplored topic, the story of the escapes from an infamous prison. In researching that essay, as in so many other places in this work, I discovered that the Civil War still has many secrets and stories yet to tell. I also learned, on many different levels, that the story of any prison centers more on freedom than captivity, as shown in the famous Winslow Homer painting *Near Andersonville.* Homer depicted a slave woman watching the recapture of a federal soldier. The soldier suffered imprisonment so that the slave woman would eventually receive freedom. Slaves, however, would help earn their own emancipation by aiding prisoner escapes from Southern prisons.[3]

From that first glimpse of something greater than the obvious, ideas for other essays followed, each as an exploration of the American Civil War era as social history. The studies of the greatest American conflict have heretofore been almost exclusively in terms of the military and emancipation and have been devoid of social history. In this collection, the purely military takes a role as only one of many aspects of this story. Before the 1960s, it was common to study a historical period or place by dividng that time or place into chapters by subjects such as women, religion, and the military. This practice largely disappeared after the 1960s but has been revived here to answer specific questions and issues and to combine several themes at once. This book presents lives that share experiences of Andersonville. Exploration of an era through biography is a form of *Annaliste* social history. When a writer lacks such sources as comprehensive statistics for such topics, this method allows for the study of the whole by looking at its people, parts, or images.

The inspiration for researching Americans through connections to this infamous prison camp came to me from MacKinley Kantor's Pulitzer Prize-winning novel, *Andersonville.*[4] Kantor succeeded so well not only because he impartially used the best nonfiction resources available to him but also because he chose that place as the stage rather than as the story; as a common starting point for observing the varied lives of nineteenth-century Americans. He gave his characters depth through the literary device of their looking out, from a unique place in the world, at their roles in a changing America, both in the North and in the South. Novelist Dennis Lehane has pointed out that such great literature allows for the exploration of broader meanings through the experience of the characters, the same aim of historians in nonfiction.

My work now uses Kantor's perspective but in a nonfiction work of history to make Andersonville again as a center point for studying broader issues in a way similar to how Michael Golay explores the end of the Civil War in *A Ruined Land.* Father Peter J. Meaney first so specifically used Andersonville for this theme in his 1987 article on Father Peter Whelan and William Marvel similarly used the camp as a vehicle to explore the past of the prison's most controversial character, Henry Wirz, in his *Andersonville: The Last Depot* (1994).[5] In this new work, I look at such persons as Ambrose Spencer, likely the real life model for Kantor's fictional planter Ira Claffey. Whatever the truth about Spencer, his resulting notoriety serves as a beginning for exploring the nationwide Edgar Allen Poe like saga of the fall of his prominent family. Beyond Andersonville, this generational tale documents much about the beginnings of scandal and the national media in America.[6]

Spencer, and many other travelers found in the following pages, represents much of the social history of America at that time. Attorney O. S. Baker, for example, publicly exposed Spencer's perjury. Baker determined to fight for the right of due process and justice, even for the "Demon of Andersonville," despite his support of the federal cause and the public passions of his times. A fictionalized version of Baker's struggle would become the basis of Saul Levitt's Emmy winning drama *Andersonville Trial.*[7] As a life long idealist, he represented much more.

My research also brought me to "Limber Jim," a famous example of the players in the greater drama. As portrayed in John Frankenheimer's 1996 movie *Andersonville,* he organized the prisoners to stop banditry, try miscreants, and execute the leaders of the inmate criminal gangs. The reality behind the myth of Limber Jim reveals much more complex issues than merely good triumphing over evil but explores even deeper and darker matters concerning the timeless economic and social clash between the "Over world" and the "Underworld" more commonly understood in our own time.

The American Civil War needs exploration from the study of the personal lives of such intriguing characters. It became the greatest war to that time and it was fought by armies, navies, and even civilian bureaucracies created almost entirely from scratch, and largely led by amateurs. More than the "Captains and the Kings," however, the passions of millions of ordinary Americans created the war and its aftermath. Complete accountings of the lives of such people seldom appear in print, even in their own time. Without modern research libraries and tools like microfilm and the Internet, writers would have a difficult time putting together the details of such lives. Few such detailed and personal works as the biography of the colorful (but now forgotten) Andersonville contemporary W. W. Pancoast exist.[8] We now have the means, and Civil War history has achieved the maturity, to tell the stories of these people.

Andersonville also became one of America's greatest man-made marvels. The many different American populations that had developed by 1864 came together in this artificial city that had been built as a prison. Two great truths about prisoner of war camps in general largely began here. Prisoners almost never try to overwhelm their captors, no matter how good the odds for such a successful rush, and a nation will go to any extremes, no matter how impractical, to hold on to POWs to the very end. As a consequence of these strange truths, the Yankees held at Andersonville came to interact with the guards to such a degree as to sometimes develop life-long friendships. At the time, for most of these men, Andersonville became their first real personal encounters with the "enemy." As with the issue of slavery and freedom, the story of the guards and their charges at Andersonville highlights the many divides of a nation that existed as very different cultures.[9]

In this new America, people could acquire new lives in a new world. They took advantage of the grand new limitless horizons introduced with the steam engine, the telegraph, and cheap newsprint to leave their pasts but with a better idea of what they wanted to leave behind them than of what they had to gain. Andersonville stood as a strange and unintended crossroads for this generation of Americans newly freed from ties to land, family, and profession. Persons like Limber Jim could reinvent themselves by changing locales. A person with little more than an education could find work in a universally accepted profession such as a lawyer, physician, teacher, newspaper editor, or even as a soldier of fortune. Ambrose C. Spencer worked as each at different times. Usually, only when they became merchants who required solid references for credit did they have problems with their pasts. Poe, Twain, Melville, Henry, and other writers of this period sought to find fictional plots for the "great American novel," while ignoring that people then living around them—and they themselves—often lived sagas as dramatic and as grand as any plot to any novel that they could have invented.

This lifestyle had special dangers. Mobility without societal restraints heightened the incidents of disease, psychological dysfunction, alcoholism, drug abuse, and even bigamy to the level of national epidemics, a fact hidden by the even greater levels of these excesses brought about by the Civil War.[10] Syphilis and other dangers of the times also became a cause as well as a result of the course of some of the lives described in this book. The greater risks, however, came from emotional intangibles that included loneliness, depression, and self-destruction. Such people begot later generations even more mobile and invisible but frequently without ties to spouse and children. This new class of American "Gypsies," had deaths that equally went without note, fill unmarked graves, and today have few, if any, known living descendants. Social class, as a factor in peoples' lives, however, could catch up with a person. People like Ambrose C. Spencer and William T. Sherman found themselves having to depend upon personal connections to the very pasts that they sought to escape.

History, at its best, as with prose, poetry, and art, helps us to find such intangible truths. Survivors of Andersonville, the world's first modern concentration camp and the Civil War's most notorious prison facility, tried to find meaning for their often-deadly experiences through newspaper articles, lectures, prints, and memoirs. As historian Lonnie R. Speer wrote:

> For many of both sides who had survived the prisons, the experience continued to be a devastating factor in their lives. Those who had endured long periods of confinement often remained humiliated and bitter. They, their families, and families who had lost love ones in the various facilities accused one or both governments of being deceitful or incompetent. The blame, lies, accusations, vindictiveness, and propaganda as to who or what was responsible for the starvation, cruelty, and prison deaths continued for many years.[11]

Maybe Clio, the Greek muse of history, could find the truth in a subject as controversial as Andersonville Confederate prison—but even she would only succeed after a great struggle. Sensationalism and differing prejudices about the prison encouraged misinformation and myth rather than credible research. Over time, these distortions of facts became misunderstandings accepted as truth—what Dr. Jan Assmann has termed "mnemohistory." For example, although Camp Sumter (Andersonville) operated only in the last fourteen months of the Civil War (24 February 1864 to 4 May 1865), and as only the largest of 117 Confederate prisons of all types, it achieved such notoriety that many people today believe that it was the only Confederate prison camp and even the sole prison during the whole war for either side! From such "well known facts," many other myths emerged, so many in fact, that the truth has become the last prisoner of Andersonville. It too deserves a parole.

Sensational prisoner memoirs first generated such myths. The often lurid retelling of the story of being a federal soldier held by the Confederacy answered the peculiar curiosity of an interested public; helped the individual prisoner to refute that he had been a coward, shirker, or otherwise less of a soldier than other members of the victorious federal armies; pressured Congress for special veterans' benefits for former prisoners of war; and defined personal or divine meaning for what had happened, and, thus, resulted in closure. Most of these works appeared in only limited printings, but former Andersonville alumnus John McElroy wrote a 650-page collective memoir of the prisoner experience that sold 600,000 copies.[12]

These memoirs failed as important literature although John Worrell Northrop did try to use anthropology, literary allusion, and poetry to explain his Andersonville experience in his 1904 *Chronicles from the Diary of a War Prisoner.* The fiction about the prison, even when presented as fact, did not result in great writing. Then and now, the authors likely had a subject of too much partisan feeling, created in an era of notoriously excessive sentiment, to achieve anything of lasting literary merit.[13]

Non-participants later did better with the subject. In time, meanings drawn from the saga of this Civil War prison became the basis for a notable painting, unprecedented legal proceedings, a popular novel, a well-received drama, and even a widely viewed television movie. However, scholarly histories of the camp came relatively late in its genre. The first of these, Ovid Futch's *History of Andersonville Prison* (1968), finally appeared, in part, as a response to MacKinley Kantor's novel *Andersonville* (1955).[14]

But the reality of Andersonville lacked nothing in drama, in fiction and nonfiction, even as part of America's greatest war, racial strife, and societal changes. Begun as little more than as an unfinished stockade wall and a cleared piece of ground, it eventually had a population of as many as 33,006 prisoners and became the largest prison up to its time and for generations to come. Statistically, it would have been the fifth-largest city in the Confederacy. Of the roughly 800,000 Americans held in prison camps in all of the nation's wars, some 40,000 were inmates of this camp.

Men, crowded into this open-air stockade of less than thirty acres, starved, sickened, and died. Of those who entered its gates, almost 13,000 remain forever in its cemetery. Thousands more of the prison's victims failed to recover fully from the physical and mental effects of their ex-perience. The horrors of the camp proved so bad that D. W. Vowles would hide his service as an officer at Andersonville up to his death in 1919.[15]

Andersonville also became the first great example of bureaucratic collapse due to an administration that was unable to manage the modern forces that, uncontrolled, create such horrors. For the first time, mismanagement of transportation and resources proved fatal for thousands of men. While civilians and soldiers also went hungry throughout the war-time South because bureaucrats and railroads failed, those victims could forage and, thus, stay alive. Few prisoners had that opportunity. The North had a comparable level of administrative incompetence and inexperience. (Before the Civil War, the only true experience with a nationwide bureaucracy in the United States had been the post office.) The Civil War United States government, however, had so much more in resources of all types that waste would not prove to have such fatal consequences.[16]

For most of the last months of its relatively short history, Andersonville served as hardly more than a hospital. With a then manageable number of prisoners, very close to the intended capacity of the camp, the prison's staff finished a bakery, barracks for the inmates, and a hospital, hardly the actions of officers whom critics would claim conspired to systematically murder helpless Union soldiers, sailors, and civilians. Prisoners transferred from Andersonville went to Camp Lawton in Millen, Georgia, a prison designed specifically to avoid the fatal defects of Camp Sumter.

Similarly, defenders of the Confederacy have made their own misstatements about Andersonville. They argue that the guards died at the same rate as the prisoners. In fact, only 225 of the some 5,000 members of the garrison and staff died at this Camp Sumter, a mortality rate of only some 4.3 percent, compared to a prisoner death rate that, just within the prison, must have at least approached 33 percent.

People trying to excuse the mortality of the prison at the simple whistle stop of Anderson state station, Georgia, also perpetuate the myth that with the

North's greater resources, a greater disparity should exist between the rate of death in the United States' and in the Confederacy's prisons. This claim usually focuses specifically on Elmira, the worst of the federal camps (24 percent death rate) compared to Andersonville's mortality (33 percent). Proponents of this claim charge federal officers with deliberately having operated death camps instead of inventing and then adhering to a policy of providing for prisoners on a level equal to that supplied to the federal soldiers.

To have categorized any federal prison as the "Andersonville of the North" would be an exaggeration. The resources of the North proved so great that, even within its relatively lack luster war effort, only a well managed, institutionalized program dedicated to the murder of captive Confederates could have matched the wartime fatalities caused by the South's poverty, technical backwardness, and administrative incompetence. The great wealth of the Union overwhelmed whatever problems resulted from the effects of any cruelty, ineptitude, and waste of depraved, indifferent, or vengeful federal officers. Typically, many of the federal prisons formerly were barracks while, in the South, the holding areas had formerly been old tobacco warehouses or, as at Andersonville, simply cleared ground. Just as stopping massive systems failure in the blockaded wartime South proved beyond the powers of any individual, so too did the excess of the prosperity of the North prove unstoppable and uncontrollable, even in affecting prisoners of war.

Factors other than a murderous conspiracy drove up the numbers of Confederate dead at Elmira and elsewhere, such as the generally poor physical condition and malnutrition of Southern soldiers before capture. Typically observers would remark at how, on a battlefield, the corpses of Confederates would keep a natural color while those of the Union soldiers turned purple, the difference due to the malnutrition of the Southern soldiers. Some Confederate soldiers even preferred to remain prisoners of war in camps like Elmira rather than return to the starvation and other hardships of service in the butternut and gray armies. The intense and prolonged cold weather of the North could also kill Southern prisoners, even if they had adequate clothes, fuel, and blankets. The hellish conditions at Andersonville caused men to suffer from the effects of exposure, malnutrition, emotional breakdown, infection, and insect infestation on an industrial scale, but the medical sciences of the era, everywhere, failed to effectively treat such diseases as dysentery, diarrhea, and pneumonia that created a high level of mortality for any concentration of men, whatever their otherwise condition or treatment.[17]

Origins of such stories have received study. The prejudices generated by the misinformation about the camp received encouragement from the trial and execution of Andersonville functionary Henry Wirz in 1865. In some ways, Wirz became as much a victim of the prison as any of the federal dead. He went to the gallows, both as monster and martyr, to satisfy a public need for retribution. During his trial and in the writings about him, myth and falsehood about Andersonville would be mixed into an almost inseparable mass. Photographs were even sold that falsely showed him as a hideous dwarf. His champions, however, would later go so far as to doctor photographs to award him the rank of major that he never received or claimed. In the decades that followed, prisoner memoirs appeared that defended or attacked Wirz as the symbol of the prison, again reflecting partisan opinion, rumor, and speculation rather than reality.

The ghosts and shadows of Andersonville remain, made worse by the bizarre but steady modern movement toward more interpretation based in secondary sources, political correctness, and regional prejudice instead of records. Even discussing the facts sometimes proves problematic. Some readers will challenge this book's conclusions. Other readers will be disappointed that some aspects of Camp Sumter's history will have to wait to be explored elsewhere.

Andersonville as depicted in one of the popular post Civil War prints.

WHEN HELL HAD A POST OFFICE

The people told us that we were going to Andersonville, but they said it was a fine place; they represented it as a pleasant shady grove, with a fine stream running through it, with barracks enough to accommodate all of us.

—Corporal Alexander McLean (1866),
USA 117th New York Infantry

The condition of the prison at Andersonville is a reproach to us as a nation.

—Colonel Robert H. Chilton (1864),
CSA assistant adjutant and inspector general

So much misinformation and legend surround Andersonville that any work about the prison should begin with at least an outline of the facts about the real place. A look at the basic history of this, the Civil War's largest prison population and most infamous prison camp, also provides one of the best case studies of the many examples of how the aspirations of a society deteriorated over four years into a nightmare that imprisoned all of its members. It demonstrates how even a place, in legend and reality, comes to have identity issues.

No one deliberately conspired to murder an imprisoned enemy at Andersonville, but too few people offered any sympathy, either. Such tragedies often come about not from organized conspiracies but due to unorganized combinations of individual actions, fear, and indifference encouraged by widespread prejudice generated by the public's conceptions and misconceptions. Southerners, of all classes, increasingly wanted to believe in the sufferings of federal prisoners as the deserved fate of invaders. This feeling grew as their own suffering increased and as lurid tales of the terrible conditions of the Confederates in federal hands appeared in print. Andersonville also became the classic example of fatal consequences derived from long-distance indifference and mismanagement in a place where the local command fell to several people who had official responsibilities but no authority. System failure under wartime stresses proved fatal for a great many people in the Confederacy but especially for men such as these, the people least able to provide for themselves.

The South's lack of experienced administrators repeatedly receives the blame for Andersonville and other such disasters. Confederate clerks lacked, more than just paper and ink, training and experience. Even as late as 1860, however, the United States had almost no experience with any sort of effective, nation-wide administration beyond the postal service.[18] Federal officials too had their share of massive system failures in 1861–1865, but the North's much greater resources, relatively well-distributed among its population, prevented widespread and, usually, even localized suffering. Indeed, many people in the Northern states prospered as a result of economic expansion brought about by the war. Their Southern counterparts, conversely, struggled with highly segmented and localized transportation systems designed principally to haul cotton to the sea, a lack of manufacturing facilities due to the huge investment in cotton, and a hostile captive labor force consisting of largely uneducated agricultural workers who required constant supervision. As the war continued, the declining transportation network failed to provide the internal communications once provided through the now blockaded or captured harbors; factory production slowed for lack of fuel and raw materials; scarce regional resources steadily fell to advancing enemy armies; and hundreds of thousands of the South's workers escaped to the Union lines or left agriculture and manufacturing, often involuntarily, to go off to war.

During the Civil War, the federal military may have outnumbered its "rebel" foes by only a ratio of as little as 3:2, and the South likely could have fed its soldiers, civilians, and prisoners. The South lost its war for independence for many reasons but, among the most important, were failures to properly manage

Places related to Camp Sumter (Andersonville) Prison

its limited resources and move men and material by railroad. Starvation consequently became widespread. Hungry housewives rioted in the Confederate cities as early as 1863. From Vicksburg to Fortress Monroe, the United States government found itself feeding tens of thousands of Southern refugees. After four years of almost continuous success everywhere but in Virginia, the United States, even with less than a full popular commitment to the war, successfully conquered the Confederacy. Conversely, critics, inside and outside of the South, would claim that the tiny minority that made up the Confederacy's upper class and governmental leadership had more interest in exploiting the South's suffering through profiteering than in sharing resources with the general population. The members of the planter elite often appeared as indifferent to the

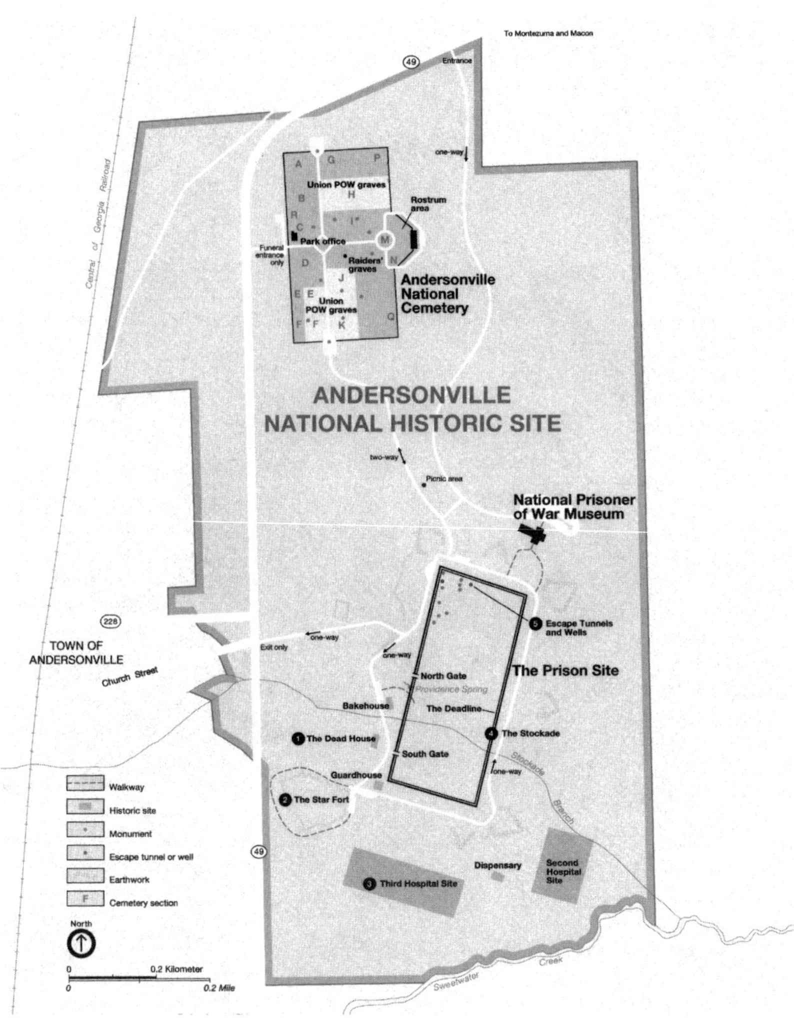

Courtesy Andersonville National Historic Site

needs of tens of thousands of federal prisoners as they were to the suffering of hundreds of thousands of Southerners fighting and dying to prevent the emancipation of the planters' slaves.[19]

Beyond differences in amount of and distribution of resources, both sides failed to look for or find any "moral high ground" on the issue of prisoners of war. Just as voices in the Confederacy didn't call for merely releasing these starving and sick men back to the federal lines, after 1863 the Union seldom allowed for the exchange of prisoners, even on purely humanitarian grounds. Each side excused or committed atrocities upon reports—sometimes only rumors—of the sufferings of its own men in captivity.

The hardships of the captive federals began with the breakdown of that prisoner exchange. From 1861 to 1863, the opposing sides had dealt largely with the problem of prisoners by regularly releasing the captured by rank, through established internment camps. During that time, the Confederacy operated such detention camps as Belle Island, Cahawba, Danville, Libby, and Salisbury. Following the huge defeats suffered by the Confederate armies in the Gettysburg, Vicksburg, and Port Hudson campaigns in July 1863, the general exchange of prisoners broke down although some local exchanges by individual commanders continued. Rebel armies would now not only waste away from casualties, sickness, desertion, and draft evasion but also from capture.

By the last months of 1863, the thousands of federal prisoners now held indefinitely in Richmond, Virginia, had become a particular liability for the Confederacy. The Yankee captives consumed precious rations at a time when the civilian residents of Richmond had to eat household pets to keep from starving. Hunger among the inmates of Richmond's Belle Island prison drove the men there to capture and eat any dog that came near. A mass escape from Belle Island and Libby, aided by Union cavalry, could overwhelm the garrison of the Confederate capitol and then attack the civilian population, thus taking a decisive step towards a Union victory that the Northern armies repeatedly failed to achieve on the Virginia battlefields. Federal officers, as a group, did stage a mass escape from Libby prison on 9 February 1864.

In November 1863, Confederate Captain W. Sidney Winder received orders from the War Department to solve these problems by finding a location for a prison for civilians, privates, and non-commissioned officers in the area of Americus or Albany, in deep southwest Georgia. Richmond insisted that the immediate area around the prison be able to produce abundant foodstuffs for the prisoners. The Southwestern Railroad would support such a site, hundreds of miles from any federal forces. In theory, the region could provide prisoners and guards with ample provisions. Winder enlisted the help of Uriah Howard, Confederate commissary for the region, to find the best location for the prison.[20]

Winder and Howard considered several specific sites but rejected each due to local political opposition. Finally, Benjamin B. Dykes, formerly of Wilkinson County, persuaded Winder to lease land owned by Deputy Sheriff William Wesley Turner on a tributary of Sweetwater Creek in Sumter County for thirty dollars per month. (The county line later moved, and today most of the site lies in Macon County.) Dykes, having taken over his father's job as the local railroad agent in 1861, owned the adjoining lands that would include the town that subsequently grew up around the prison. He would soon earn fifty dollars per month for leasing various buildings to the Confederacy, while working as station master until 1864.[21]

In 1853, George W. Adams, superintendent of the Southwestern Railroad, had named this seldom-used railroad siding and platform "Anderson Station," after prominent Georgia entrepreneur John W. Anderson of Savannah. Local people continued to call it by that name as late as 1894. The United States Postal Department, however, designated the post office there as "Andersonville" because an Anderson post office already existed in Whitfield County, Georgia.[22] By the time that the prison opened in February 1864, this isolated and impoverished crossroads of Anderson Station consisted only of one log building used by the railroad. Between one and four families lived nearby.

The Confederate government had ordered that the prison be built in an area of ample provisions but, in reality, the area immediately around this lonely whistle stop was almost as uninhabited as it had been in 1540 when Spanish explorers called it a desert. A writer from the nearby community of Plains wrote in 1859 that the ground was so flat that on one large plantation he had failed to find a variation in elevation in the area of more than twelve inches, that the whole area hardly rose above the river bottoms of the Chattahoochee River. The people "of this primitive, rural district," he claimed, were "of very simple character and wholly agricultural."[23]

With the arrival of the Confederate government, however, Anderson Station finally became the success that Dykes had envisioned. The prison covered less than thirty acres, but the adjoining area became a western-style boom town complete with mining (the prisoner escape tunnels); the personal belongings that the prisoners brought into the stockade became the "gold" that the "miners" traded to the locals for provisions. The community quickly grew to include two saloons, a blacksmith shop, a Methodist church, a couple of general stores, and a dozen houses, but all with a resident, non-prison related population of less than twenty. Only about seventy people lived in the immediate area. One prisoner remembered the greatly expanded Anderson Station as still consisting of only "four or five straggling rough board structures resting drowsily on the yellow sand west of the railroad; twenty or thirty people as vapid and rickety as the buildings...."[24]

Station agent Dykes claimed that as practically no one lived at this whistle stop, who would oppose the prison? Local people did protest, however. The people of Sumter County voiced fears about potential mass prisoner escapes, bloody slave revolts organized by the Yankees, and the looting of their farms by hungry guards. Sawmill owners refused to sell their products to Winder at the government rate. Personal visits by both Governor Joseph E. Brown and his opponent, popular former governor General Howell Cobb, failed to change minds. Finally, Winder received orders from Richmond that, for a sixty-day period, he could commandeer whatever labor and materials he needed to build the camp and at the government's prices. Construction of "Camp Sumter," the official name of the prison began on 10 January 1864 under Quartermaster Captain Richard B. Winder, Sidney Winder's cousin. He employed local English-born carpenter Samuel Leach Heys to build the stockade and administrative buildings. The Confederacy seized the unpainted Methodist church for use as a warehouse. C. C. Sheppard and J. M. McNealy supervised nine hundred male and female slaves impressed as laborers from plantations in Sumter and Dougherty counties.[25]

The new construction added to the area's other defects. Workers cut down the pine trees from the interior of the prison to build the stockade wall, thus depriving the future prisoners of that protection from the elements. Camp officials intended from the beginning to build barracks, but tens of thousands of prisoners would arrive and leave for other camps months before any permanent prisoner housing was constructed. Supplies of cut lumber and nails varied between scarce and non-existent in the blockaded South.

Slave laborers building a Confederate stockade. (Library of Congress)

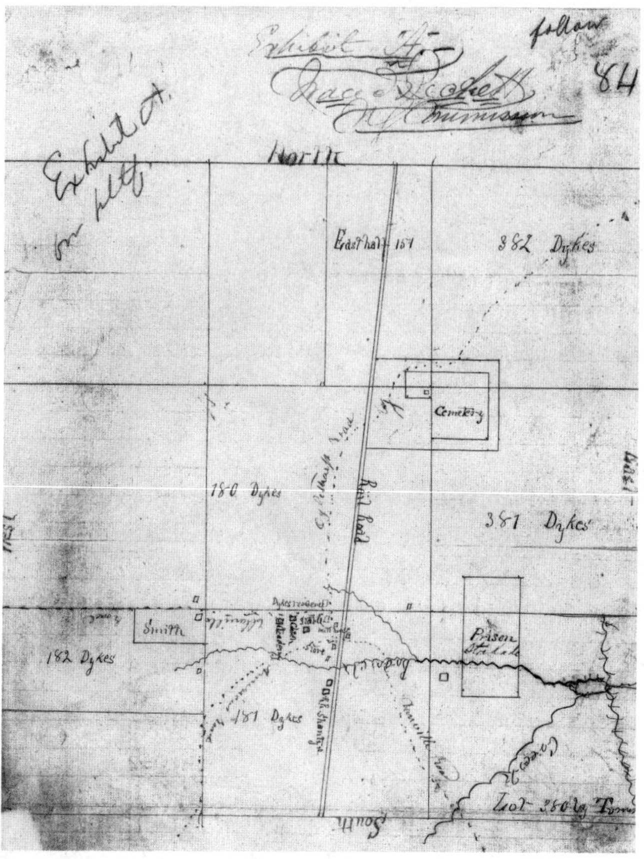

Andersonville neighborhood as depicted in the claim of Benjamin B. Dykes. (National Archives and Records Administration)

On 24 February, Sergeant J. S. McGinley became the camp's first prisoner. He saw slave women setting logs for the still-unfinished north wall of the stockade. Over the months that followed, McGinley would witness all of the problems as they developed, prison train after prison train. Inmates began arriving at a rate of as high as five hundred or more per day, as camp surgeon Isaiah White set up an ad hoc hospital and Richard Winder chose a site for the cemetery on Dyke's land.[26]

Prisoners at Belle Island fought for the chance to leave the hunger and brutal conditions there for this camp at Andersonville. Positive reports appeared in the Southern press about the new prison. Reporters praised the Yankee ingenuity employed by the prisoners in building their own shelters. McGinley and others of the first prisoners remembered better rations and conditions, initially,

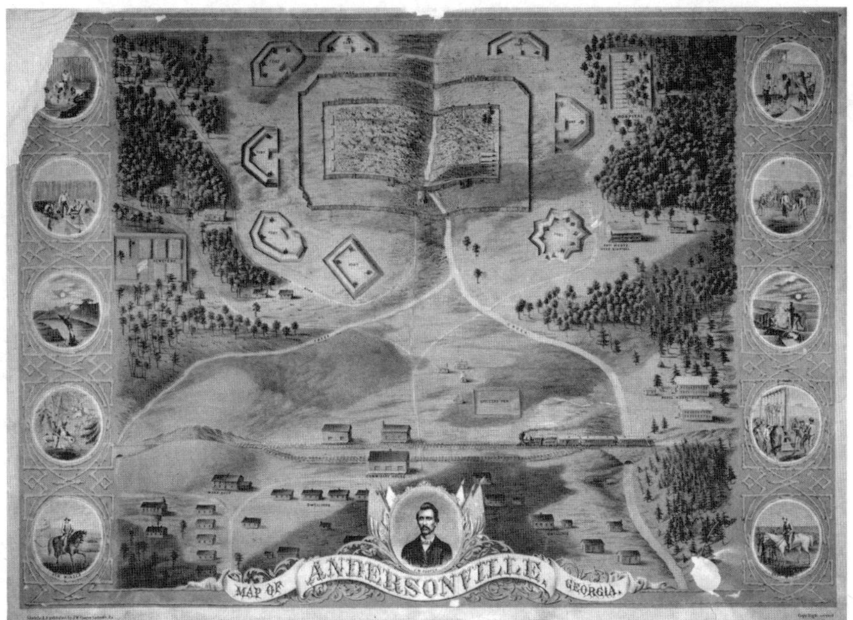

The Civil War town of Andersonville at its height, and the prison, appears in this post Civil War print. (Library of Congress)

at Camp Sumter than they had experienced at other prisons. Inmates, for example, at first found the climate in Georgia as a pleasant change from the often bitter cold of Richmond. Quartermaster Richard Winder expanded the stockade beyond the original plans for six thousand inmates so that it could hold nine thousand men.

The favorable reports, however, appeared before the overcrowding and the mortality reached extraordinary heights. Richmond's orders that the site be chosen because of proximity to abundant foodstuffs had been sacrificed for political expediency. Winder consequently had to scrounge for food for the prisoners even as Camp Sumter became operational. Shortly afterward, an act of the Confederate Congress transferred his responsibilities to Commissary Lieutenant John H. Wright of the 55th Georgia Infantry. Wright only had authority to make requisitions for corn meal and salt pork from the distant military depots at Columbus, Albany, and Macon.[27] The prisoners of war illegally traded with the guards to acquire food locally. While the illegal trading saved thousands of prisoners from starvation, it gradually depleted the surrounding area of its limited food resources and further drove up the already-inflated prices for the Confederate military and civilians. Prisoner Jerry Foley of New York found that even used tobacco came to have great value among the desperate men. He would dry out the cud of his chewing tobacco and make snuff from it. If he dropped it on the ground, another prisoner would seize it.

Similarly, medical care often existed more as an ideal than as a reality. B. H. Baldwin remembered the daily sick call in the stockade for the men fortunate enough to get attention before the medicines ran out: "The rebels came in with two buckets and the men suffering with bowel trouble lined up in one row and those with scurvy in another, with the "rebs" and their pails or dope at the end. Then the boys would get their medicine. It was dished up in a little tin dipper."[28]

Originally, the hospital consisted only of a single tent in the stockade. On 21 May, the camp administration erected a new enclosure for the sick outside of the walls, but it was next to a swamp and the sinks that the prison population used a latrine. Even this arrangement failed to create enough space for the thousands of prisoners who needed it daily. Patients lay on the ground, in the open air, with only what blankets they provided for themselves. By the Spring of 1865, sheds existed for the sick, but by then most of the prisoners had left for other camps, and the whole prison existed largely as a giant hospital for men too sick to leave. Investigations of Andersonville's medical department found typical Confederate incompetence and inefficiency. At the end of the war, Dr. R. Randolph Stevenson, director of the camp's hospital, also faced charges of embezzling one hundred thousand dollars.[29]

Richard Winder's uncle, Sydney's father, and commander of the prisons east of the Mississippi River, Brigadier General John H. Winder, had planned to avoid such problems by constructing a number of secure and supportable prisons in remote areas of Georgia.[30] Even before slaves finished constructing the walls at Camp Sumter, however, Richmond authorities began transferring prisoners to Anderson Station. A federal cavalry raid, coordinated with the prisoners in early February 1864, almost made the long-feared mass prisoner release in Richmond a reality. Because of this near catastrophe, Confederate officials rushed more and more captives to the stockade at Camp Sumter, just as the campaigns in Georgia and Virginia heated up in the late Spring of 1864. The bureaucrats in Richmond, ignorant or indifferent to the situation at Camp Sumter, preferred shipping captives to it rather than keeping thousands of men at the increasingly vulnerable rebel capitol. They blindly sent prisoners of war to whatever fate awaited in far-off Georgia.

Survivors of Andersonville put their impressions of being there in drawings such as these, as well as words. In the bottom engraving a prayer meeting is being held. (R. S. Davis)

These transfers created the nightmare that became synonymous with the name "Andersonville." Advances in transportation, even in the South, allowed for the shipment and concentration of large numbers of prisoners at an isolated whistle stop in deep South Georgia. A corresponding lack of progress in management, medical knowledge, and food production, however, guaranteed that the resulting prison would become a death camp for prisoners and guards. By August, the prison population reached a high of 33,006 men, the most for any Civil War prison and for any prison of that time. Statistically, Anderson Station came to have enough people to qualify as the fifth-largest city in the Confederacy.

The weak security and problems of lack of food, clothing, and shelter at Belle Island and other prisons had only been moved to and made worse in Georgia. In some ways, the Confederate government created a problem as great as if it had opened a critical new battle front in the war. It is symbolic that the embattled nation even failed to provide Camp Sumter with a flag. That the horrors of Andersonville existed without anyone's deliberate malice made its situation even worse. When a system, rather than an individual, fails, then alleviating the crisis frequently goes beyond the power of any individuals.

To the myriad other sufferings that the Confederate States of America imposed upon the Southern people now there arose the threat of a pen where a relatively few guards held back tens of thousands of desperate men. The garrison of Andersonville essentially went from guarding a military commodity (the prisoners) to protecting the defenseless population of the South from this enormous hazard created by its own government. When a month later a group of prisoners tried to undermine the stockade for a mass escape, construction began on sentry posts—called "pigeon roosts" by the prisoners—on top of the wall to detect and try to stop any rush on the palisades. (The concept of trying to shoot individual prisoners who tried to scale a wall largely began with the Civil War.) On 17 April 1864, the camp administration created the "dead line," a railing three feet high that marked off an area that extended fifteen feet from the stockade into the prisoner area. General Winder ordered it established to copy the same security measure found in northern prisons. It used the threat of shooting any prisoners within that zone to keep the inmates from massing against the wall or slipping through it undetected. Prior to that time, the prisoners could lean against the stockade and even talk through it to people on the outside.[31] The garrison also positioned cannons to sweep the stockade with shot, should the prisoners rush the wall, or if federal cavalry approached. When heavy rains undermined a part of the twenty-foot-high wall in early August, a second wall (sixteen feet high) and a never-completed third wall (twelve feet tall) went up around the original prison pen. The respective heights of the walls turned the prison pen into a fort for repelling outside assaults. The second wall, 150 feet from the original stockade, made breathing while digging a tunnel long enough for an escape almost impossible.[32]

The Andersonville guards only used demonstrations of force to squelch planned mass escapes by the prisoners in April, May, and July.[33] Workmen physically strengthened the stockade to prevent the prisoners from pushing it down. On 28 July the camp gunners fired a cannon shot into the marsh in the middle of the camp as a warning to the prisoners. The next day, additional areas within the stockade were marked with white flags to indicate where artillery would disperse any large gatherings of prisoners. When a severe thunderstorm on 9 August created gaps in the wall, General Winder flew into a panic and called out the militia. By then, the inmates were in such a weakened condition, however, that they made no effort at an escape. They instead huddled together and pleaded with the garrison not to open fire.[34]

Prisoner Robert Knox Sneden made a series of post war drawings of Andersonville based upon sketches that he smuggled out of the prison, including of his "shebang." This drawing and those that follow are from his papers in the Virginia Historical Society. (Virginia Historical Society, Richmond, Virginia)

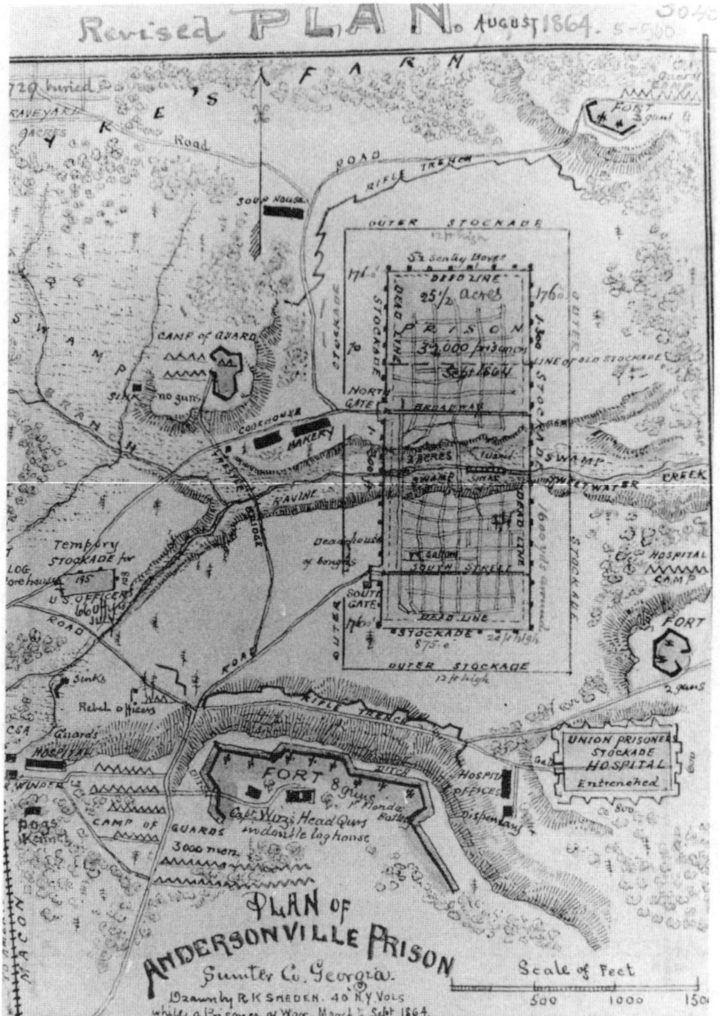
Revised PLAN. AUGUST 1864.
FARM
Road
ROAD
RIFLE TRENCH
FORT
SOUP HOUSE
OUTER STOCKADE
DEAD LINE
25 1/2 acres
PRISON
32,000 prisoners
Sept 1864
LINE of OLD STOCKADE
CAMP of GUARD
no guns
NORTH GATE
BROADWAY
COOKHOUSE
BAKERY
SWAMP
SWEETWATER CREEK
RAVINE
Tempory STOCKADE for U.S. OFFICERS
SOUTH STREET
SOUTH GATE
STOCKADE
HOSPITAL CAMP
Rebel officers
Guards HOSPITAL
UNION PRISONERS STOCKADE HOSPITAL Entrenched
FORT 8 guns
Capt. Wirz's Head Qurs in double log house
CAMP OF GUARDS 3000 men
Dispensary
Dogs Kennel
MACON
PLAN OF ANDERSONVILLE PRISON
Sumter Co. Georgia.
Drawn by R.K. SNEDEN. 40 N.Y. VOLS
while a Prisoner of War. March to Sept 1864.
Scale of Feet
500 1000 1500
in August the Union Prisoners numbered 31.678. of whom 1693 were in

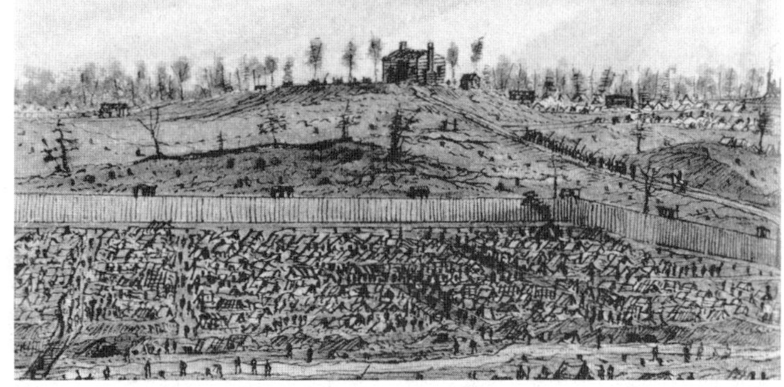

Sneden drew the south gate of the prison from outside and the cook house (above) that was built too late to have fed many of the prisoners. (Virginia Historical Society, Richmond, Virginia)

The security measures had a basis in more than paranoia. Rebel leaders believed that Rousseau's cavalry had intended to release the Andersonville captives in July 1864. General Sherman's horsemen later made a failed effort to rescue the prisoners at Macon and Andersonville. The women around Andersonville were evacuated.[35] Federal officers held at Camp Oglethorpe in Macon planned to rescue the prisoners at Camp Sumter. They intended to tunnel out of their prison, overcome the guards, seize weapons in the Macon

Barber's Shops in the Stockade.

Just near my tent is a barber shop - the owner lives, or exists in a sunken shanty. he has a barber pole too - made of a long stick with the bark cut out in Serpentine shape like any barber pole in a City -

A Barber's Shop.

Some of the prisoners who last came in managed to secrete the razors somehow - everything else was taken from them by Wirz at his headquarters on the hill before they were marched in the Gate. — The barbers do a good business on fine warm days only. We have been having very Cold blustry weather for nearly a week - Several have died from hunger - and exposure - as hundreds have <u>no shelter at all</u> only the ragged clothes on their backs - They mope all day and night over little fires - all are woe begone - ragged, dirty. and black with pitch pine smoke

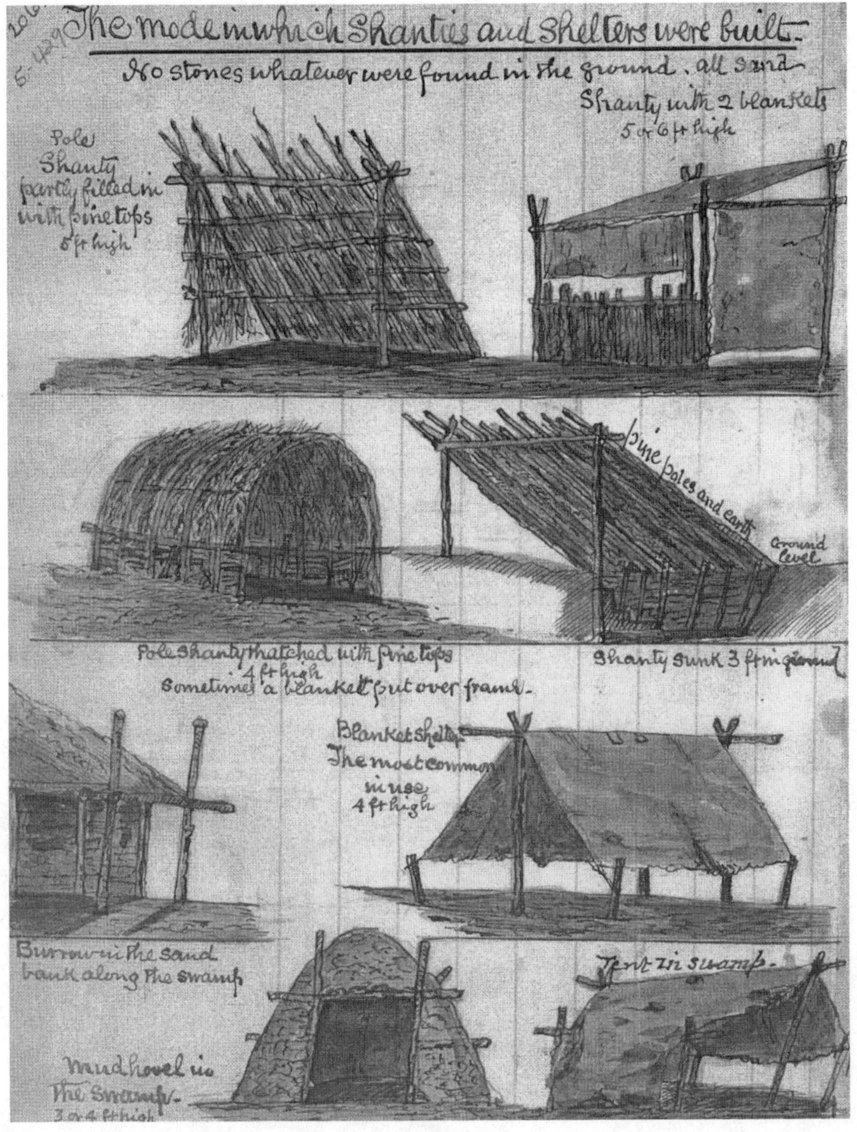
The mode in which Shanties and Shelters were built.
No stones whatever were found in the ground. all sand
Shanty with 2 blankets
5 or 6 ft high
Pole Shanty partly filled in with pine tops
5 ft high
pine poles and earth
Ground level
Pole shanty thatched with pine tops
4 ft high
Sometimes a blanket put over frame.
Shanty sunk 3 ft in ground
Blanket shelter
The most common in use
4 ft high
Burrow in the sand bank along the swamp
Tent in swamp.
Mud hovel in the swamp.
3 or 4 ft high

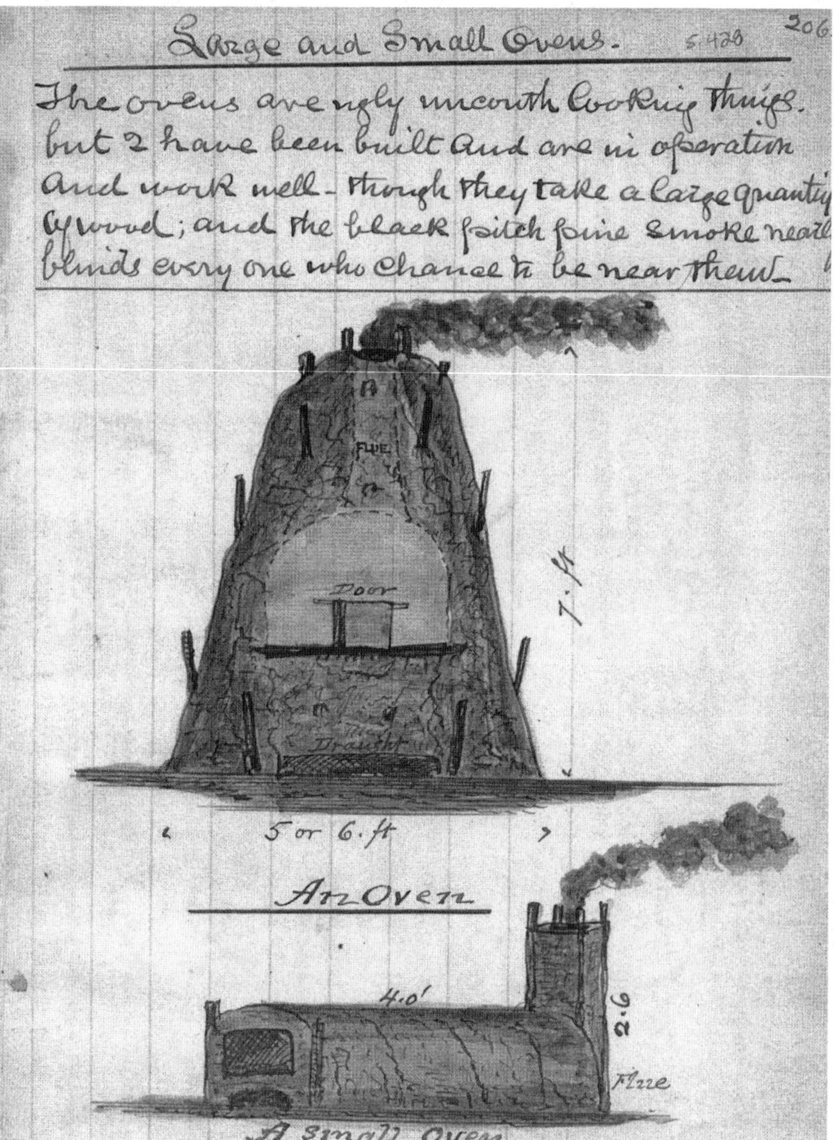
Large and Small Ovens.
5.428
206
The ovens are ugly uncouth cooking things. but 2 have been built and are in operation and work well - though they take a large quantity of wood; and the black pitch pine smoke nearly blinds every one who chance to be near them
Flue
Door
Draught
7. ft
5 or 6. ft
An Oven
4.0'
2.6
Flue
A small Oven

Arsenal, and then steal a train to Andersonville. An informant betrayed the scheme to the guards before it could be attempted.[36]

This huge population at Anderson station that the Confederate government created and now worked so hard to contain rather than maintain had all of the characteristics of a major city except for women and children. It had small merchants, thieves, gamblers, smugglers, watch repairmen, and at least one counterfeiter. (John B. Vaughter remembered that the counterfeiters "raised" the value of the virtually identical Confederate notes.) Inmates rented and sold space just as they would have dealt in real estate in their former lives. The newcomers would trade, lose in gambling, or have stolen from them goods that then passed in an illicit trade through the guards to farmers outside of the camp. Until the goods and federal greenbacks ran out, the prisoners and the guards could thus sustain themselves. Henry W. Miller wrote of a trade he made in this bazaar:

> I continued selling molasses until I had seven dollars, then went down on Broadway, as the street was called that ran from

> the northwest gate through the prison. On this street you could buy dead men's clothes or most any old thing—some of the finest bone rings and ornamental carvings made from bone and wood, if you had the money. Not being on the street long one of our boys came along with an artillery jacket nearly new; he had taken it from the body of one of his boys who had just died. He wanted $20 for it and I told him I would gladly give $50 if I had the money, but only had $7. He said, no, he must have $20 and it was cheap at that. Following him all day I saw he did not get another offer. He returned to me and said 'I will take your $7, for I must have some money to buy something to eat for sick comrades.' When I put on the jacket it lacked two inches of reaching the waist of my pants, so it left a space two inches wide around my body that was exposed to the hot sun or chilly wind, but it seemed so warm and comfortable that I could shout with joy, and then how sad it made me feel when I thought of the man that has sacrificed his life in such a place and the many comrades around me who had scarcely any clothing on their bodies.[37]

Prisoner Solon Hyde of the 17th Ohio Infantry made exploring this prison and understanding these men his pastime. Among the prisoners, he found all types of characters as well as communities of all races, languages, and nationalities serving in the federal military. The prison population included some of the first Italians, Slavs, and Portuguese to arrive in America. All states had representatives, including at least one Georgia soldier. Even California had soldiers who had come east and enlisted in the 2nd Massachusetts Cavalry. Hyde found that the single men tended to last longer than did husbands and fathers. The latter worried about the future of their families, often with fatal consequences. The naturally large, stout, and robust inmate died sooner than the small and wiry soldiers. Members of the Odd Fellows and Masonic fraternities received special aid from their respective brothers inside and outside of the prison.[38]

Conditions inside the stockade killed. Prisoner James Barton Adams, later a famed poet, wrote, based upon a children's rhyme and (likely) his experience at Andersonville:

Fainter grows the flickering light
As each ember slowly dies;
Plaintively the birds of night
Fill the air with saddening cries.

Over me they seem to cry:
"You may never more awake."
Low I lisp: "If I should die,
I pray Thou, Lord, my soul to take."

"Now I lay me down to sleep,
I pray the Lord my soul to keep.
If I should die before I wake,
I pray Thee, Lord, my soul to take."[39]

The sergeants among the prisoners would sign a petition to President Lincoln in which they stated that twenty thousand of their fellow prisoners lacked any shelter at all and that a few men did not have even a blanket. Within the crowded stockade, they claimed that the "mass of men jostle & crush each other up and down the limits of the enclosure."[40] Captain Richard B. Winder, the quartermaster, failed to obtain sawed lumber for barracks. Lieutenant Colonel Alexander W. Persons of the 55th Georgia Infantry, the first commandant, searched across Georgia unsuccessfully for the materials needed to finish and equip the prison. Lumber for prisoner housing finally arrived in early June, by which time he had been relieved of duty. He soon saw the guards appropriating the precious boards for their own use. James Burton wrote in his diary of how he and his fellow first prisoners survived the cold nights by huddling around any embers they had burning. They slept during the blazing hot days in holes in the ground, the only shelter most of them had. As prisoner Alexander McLean wrote:

> During the day the sun would pour down scorching hot, and, owing to the lowness of the ground where we were, and our nearness to the stockade, not a breath of air could reach us; when night came, the men would stretch themselves on the ground where they would soon become stiffened with the cold, and, during the night would be so tormented by vermin and worms, with which the ground was perfectly alive, that

> they could get no sleep till their strength was completely exhausted. Oh! how we would long for the dawn.... Some days there would be a slight thunder shower, and immediately after, the sun would come out so hot that it would be almost impossible to endure it. I hardly know which we most dreaded, the clear noon-day, the chilly and dewy nights, or the passing shower.[41]

The inmates needed protection from their environment. Without adequate cover, men died from exposure. For an entire month in the summer of 1864, rain fell every day. Uniforms deteriorated to rags, and thousands of the Yankees had to go nearly naked while suffering from the bites of lice, flies, and fleas. Maggots became as numerous as to make the ground appear to move. Survival often meant still having the strength and the will to stay clean from ticks. Clouds of flies and mosquitoes swarmed over the camp.

Overcrowding and the effect of the stockade walls blocking any breeze made conditions even more difficult. Several inches of human excrement covered the marsh that occupied a quarter of the ground in the center of the stockade. Visitor Ambrose C. Spencer claimed that when the wind cooperated that he could smell the camp for two miles before reaching the stockade. The swamp in the camp's center spread disease from sick prisoners. Insects infested its dank, muddy waters, and bathing became almost intolerable. The prisoners would skim insects off the creek just to have water to drink. After the railroad had stripped the area of almost all hard wood, prisoners used pine in their cooking fires. As a result, a smoky haze from the burning green wood permeated the camp and added black soot to the dirt and grime that already covered the prisoners. James Burton arrived at the prison just as it became overcrowded. Alternatively, in his diary, he described the stockade as nothing more than a hog, sheep, and bull pen. Burton found it a "hard place for a white man or any other human being."[42] When the new addition to the stockade opened on 1 July, he wrote that at least the men now had room to breathe.

New arrivals, "fresh fish" in prison jargon, would become sick just on their first sight of the interior of the stockade, as the guards forced them into the enclosure and tried to prevent a riot by inmates trying to rush through the gate. Men fought for or bought the chance to carry out the dead just for the opportunity to get fresh air or to gather firewood.[43] Confederate Dr. Louis Manigault claimed that he witnessed the horror of suffering and dying on a greater level at

Anderson Station than anything he had witnessed in China and other foreign lands.[44]

Historian Edward F. Roberts blamed the massive human tragedy at Andersonville on the cumulative effects of the South's inadequate railroads, drought, the federal blockade, widespread corruption in the besieged South, local politics compelling an unhealthy choice of a site for the prison, and entrusting the often ineffective rebel commissary to feed the prisoners. Many studies attribute the horrors that these men faced to administrative failure. Whole books about general organizational collapse use Andersonville as a case study. Supplies could only arrive from outside of the camp. Officers far from Andersonville and beyond the authority of anyone in the conflicted organization at the prison made life and death decisions on its provision. Failure to provide Camp Sumter's officers with funds for needed purchases made even obtaining local supplies difficult or impossible.[45]

This Andersonville prison also illustrated two major truths that came to be common in prisoner of war camps thereafter—that prisoners almost never rushed the guards, even when the POWs outnumbered the guards by a wide margin, and that a government will do almost anything to avoid releasing prisoners, no matter how impractical maintaining the inmates has become. The Confederate bureaucracy, when facing an emergency, could make extraordinary efforts, such as moving tens of thousands of prisoners over hundreds of miles by scarce trains to isolated Anderson Station. Later, this same bureaucracy, when facing a threat called "Sherman," would hastily construct, at Millen, Georgia, a prison that had almost all of the amenities that Andersonville fatally lacked, and would then transfer tens of thousands of the prisoners to this new camp. This same government, however, failed on a regular basis, to send adequate supplies over those same rails to Anderson Station, even from nearby Albany, Georgia, or to even provide adequately for its own soldiers and civilians. Shortages and living conditions in both armies could prove deadly. Soldiers, however, by being in a free and open environment, could at least forage (steal) from civilian farms and businesses although the few farms near Anderson Station lacked the crops to have fed even the guards adequately.[46]

Food did become scarce as it also declined in quality. Almost immediately the district commissary, Captain A. M. Allen, found the supply of beef in Georgia so scare that pork assigned to the army had to be sent to Andersonville instead. Pleas went to Florida for cattle but the depleted wild herds there were malnourished.[47] Captain Richard W. Winder began a prison bakery, but his clerk and baker, Private James W. Duncan, never had the facilities to provide cooked rations for all of the inmates at any one time. Each day half of the camp's population received prepared meals; the rest had to accept uncooked rations. Duncan often served corn meal that proved to be coarse and inedible. Inmates dug for roots in the swamp, killed swallows on the dead line at dusk, and ate rats to prevent starvation. Men without the means of obtaining extra rations by theft, labor detail, packages from home, or trade would starve and die. Survivors would write of individuals losing sixty pounds or more before dying on the little corn meal, beans, rice, and meat rations that the Confederacy provided. Captain Henry Wirz, commander of the prisoners, complained of the almost inedible quality of the food and the lack of utensils with which to serve it. Too often, the arrival of a single provision train proved the difference between everyone going hungry or anyone getting a meal for one more day. Prison officials at Camp Sumter, as at other camps, ordered passing trains seized for food consigned to the army. On 25 July 1864, General Winder, as commandant of Andersonville, wrote to the Confederate Adjutant General that Andersonville had 29,400 prisoners, 2,650 soldiers, and 500 black laborers—but not one ration.[48]

The Confederacy had begun the war with adequate, internal sources of meat and grain but under wartime conditions lacked the ability to transport and consolidate those resources to feed soldiers, civilians, and prisoners. Throughout Georgia, administrative and transportation failures allowed supplies to pile up at railroad stations that would later, in many instances, unintentionally become captured supplies that fed advancing federal armies. As those enemy columns advanced, even what did function in the Confederacy's supply system collapsed. Corrupt suppliers also kept all but the poorest quality of foodstuffs from the government.[49]

At the same time, starving prisoners obsessed about food until they lost the will to live. Hunger became the chief subject of their dreams and conversations. Aaron Bachman remembered a prisoner receiving a package from home and then stuffing himself with the food until he died. He gorged himself, as he told his comrades, to commit suicide with a full stomach.

Traditionally prisons use authority imposed by fear of force to contain prisoners but, at Andersonville, its location became its greatest barrier to escape and one of its worst punishments upon the inmates and the guards. Isolation as a tool of imprisonment began with Camp Sumter and Anderson Station. Federal authorities tended to use old forts and barracks as prisons. The Confederacy originally chose tobacco warehouses and like structures in populated places for its prisoners. Even the warehouse that served as Cahawba Prison in Alabama adjoined a town with, then, a population of two thousand. Prisoner Ransom T.

Powell wrote that even at the South's largely open-ground Belle Island prison, the inmates could at the least watch the world outside as people moved about, and see that life went on. They imagined meanings for the events that they saw and could take cheer in hearing the sound of federal cannons.

In the empty wilderness around Andersonville, however, life took on a special hellish quality because of the emptiness of the area. Some of the federals, according to Thomas Hinds of the 1st Maryland Infantry and others, became "idiots and were peevish and childish." Prisoners would give up and lie down to die by the marsh that filled the center of the pen. Inmates received punishment for even talking to slaves and prisoners paroled to work outside the stockade. For this reason, Catholic priest Peter Whelan avoided sharing news with the men he came to help. Some information on the war did come in with new prisoners and from newspapers smuggled into the camp by Ransom "Little Red Cap" T. Powell, a drummer boy allowed to work in the camp's headquarters. Within the closed society held captive at Anderson Station, however, its members could come to feel as if the world only existed within the misery of their confinement.

Men broke under this stress. They would announce that the next time they passed through the gate it would be on the dead wagon.[50] Andrew McLean remembered that the cumulative effects of these conditions in the camp wore his fellow inmates down until they finally gave out and died. John Burton referred to the "Plenty of sameness" and "tough times in old Georgia" in his diary.[51] One soldier remembered how inmates would help anything green to grow in the stockade, even individual blades of grass, so as to encourage any life.

Death proved as inglorious at Andersonville as life. Inmates stripped the dead for clothes and even gold fillings. The first three hundred corpses received coffins, and the next nine hundred dead received boards and boroughs. For the thousands of men who followed them, however, the Confederacy could often provide for each man only an incomplete record of burial and a tight place in a shallow ditch. The dead had neither boards for coffins, logs for a crypt, or even sheets for shrouds. Vultures preyed upon the poorly covered bodies in the shallow trenches of the camp cemetery. McLean wrote:

> The rebels had built a dead house of boughs, near the south gate. Into this the dead were carried; it was open at the front and faced the prison, so that we could look into it from the north hill, and see the long rows of dead that accumulated there each day. It kept from one to two wagons carrying them off all the time. Two men would take hold of a dead body, one

> on each side, by the arm and leg, and throw it into the wagon as men would a log; when they had piled in as many as the wagon box would hold, they would jump on the top and drive off. They were digging trenches all the time; into these trenches the dead were laid side by side.[52]

Confederate Dr. Louis Manigault also witnessed a burial and added:

> The numbers are noted in a small black book kept by a Yankee white man, paroled prisoner, who remained there each day until the last wagon has left, when he repairs with his list to the Bureau, where the statistics of the stockade are kept, and the numbers are recorded in a large volume, together with the Name, Rank, Regiment &c, of each man, I have no doubt in the least that errors occur in which the numbers do not indicate the correct names... The very first impression made upon me was the astonishment to think of the small area required for the burial of so great a number of human beings.[53]

Prisoners principally avoided the above fate by refusing to give up. Already mad, hat maker and sergeant Thomas H. "Boston" Corbett of the 16th New York Cavalry had a history of acts as a religious zealot that included self-castration and, much later, the killing of assassin John Wilkes Booth. Fellow prisoner Richard Thatcher remembered that Corbett lived without any kind of shelter, simply finding a few feet of open ground between tents upon which to lie down at night. At Andersonville, he found a place otherwise missing in his life. In an environment that encouraged hostility among the prisoners, he, Sergeants Benjamin N. Waddell and Thomas J. Sheppard, and others, led prayer meetings and patriotic rallies that raised morale and thus saved lives.[54]

A few prisoners more than survived and even did relatively well compared to their "free" comrades serving on battlefields. William H. Smith entered the stockade on 27 February 1864 as just another starving prisoner from Belle Island. He added nothing to his diary from 1 March to 8 May. When he began writing again he had obtained a job on the outside helping to feed prisoners in the hospital. Now Smith lived in a cabin, had taps added to his boots, read newspapers, had access to books, made a chess set, played baseball, secured his goods with the help of the prisoner police, baby sat as a favor for a female prisoner, and socialized with local ladies. With the permission of Captain Henry

however, would leave Wirz, when his frail health allowed, the highest ranking officer of the administration present. The emaciated captain, in a white suit, rode about the interior of the prison "protected" by only two inoperative pistols. He gave the bizarre appearance, to some of the soldiers, of the jailer of Hell as he rode about on a large grey mare, cursing his charges. He would leave the post on extended medical leave, and the inmates would hear rumors that he had died. Confederate inspectors, however, praised Wirz for his energy and efficiency, while recommending him for promotion to help him to do more for the prisoners.

Other staff members had worse situations. James W. Duncan, as one example, had the thankless job of feeding the tens of thousands of prisoners each day despite the fact that he held only the rank of private. Similarly, responsibility for the packs of mongrels that served as the primary means of tracking fugitives fell to Private Edward C. Turner. Seventeen-year-old Private Lemuel Madison Park worked as a clerk for the commissary. Aside from their rank, these latter two men lacked even the prestige of being in the regular regiments. They came from among the old men, boys, and cripples of the 1st Georgia Reserves.

The inmates also had some of their own to blame for their circumstances, the few bringing down the many, according to several sources. Joseph Ferguson, in his early history of Andersonville, had little sympathy for the rebel prison authorities, but he also wrote of the comrades at Andersonville: "There were desperate characters in the prison, who committed acts of violence, outrage and murder. Men, who never were honest or good in their manhood, became devils in this pandemonium. Surrounded by no moral or restraining influences, their natures became hardened to vice and crime."[59] When Soren Peterson bought extra food from camp sutlers, he had to take precautions to keep bandits from following him and robbing him where he slept. An anonymous federal officer claimed, as did some of the guards, that the habits of some of the prisoners defeated all efforts by Wirz at organizing the camp's stream as a sanitary source of water. This same officer pointed to the "filthy" habits of the soldiers as making the food unhealthy. The prisoners might have made adequate shelter for themselves if so many of them had not violated their paroles by escaping on wood-gathering details. Prisoners detailed as bakers stole salt to sell to comrades. Finally, the officer agreed with witnesses at Wirz's later trial that prisoners detailed to work in the hospital often robbed the sick of "food and delicacies." Wirz tried to have a stockade built around the hospital to keep prisoners from stealing hospital property to sell to the guards and to keep men paroled to work in the hospital from escaping. He also initially allowed tools to the prisoners with which to dig wells. When they used this opportunity to create escape tunnels, however, Wirz collected the implements and had the wells filled in.[60]

Numbers illustrate the effects of the shortcomings of the prison and paint a picture of a humanitarian disaster on a scale that would appall even twentieth-century sensibilities. In the American Civil War, only Andersonville prison held as many prisoners or still holds as many dead. Almost all of the 12,949 Andersonville inmates buried in its cemetery died from the effects of exposure, malnutrition, disease, and declining morale. For both armies during the war, deaths reached twelve to fifteen percent, close to the same percentage overall for men who died in captivity. Calculations of Andersonville's mortality rate, however, range from an official 28.12 percent to a more credible 31.58 percent, to as high as 35 percent. By means of contrast, Elmira, the worst federal camp, reached a mortality rate of only 24 percent, while the average death rate for the allies held in the Japanese prison camps in World War II stood near 40 percent. Some sources credit the Confederate prison at Salisbury with a higher mortality rate (34 percent), for a brief time, than Andersonville. More likely, Salisbury came in at only 25 percent overall, but whatever its death rate, it counts among its burials sick and emaciated transfers from Camp Sumter, some of the thousands of men who later died from their time at Anderson Station. According to one estimate, by 1890, only some eight hundred to nine hundred of the almost forty thousand individual prisoners who entered Andersonville still lived.[61]

There are many tragic anomalies and coincidences among the victims buried in shallow graves at Andersonville. Of the several men from Pittsfield, New Hampshire, who passed through the gates of Andersonville, none lived to see freedom. Teenager Michael Dougherty of the 13th Pennsylvania Cavalry only barely survived sickness at Andersonville and the explosion of the troop ship *Sultana* on his return home. The other 126 members of his regiment who entered Andersonville, however, died in rebel custody. James M. Emory of the 3rd Pennsylvania Heavy Artillery entered the camp with fifteen comrades. Only he and one other of these men lived to leave. William O. Washburn entered the prison with almost three hundred other members of the 16th Indiana Cavalry. Of that number, 180 men died there, including 32 of the 53 men in his company. Everyone who survived from his Company M became seriously sick. Fourteen men survived the confinement only to later receive discharges as permanently disabled. Perry E. Carlton had three brothers held at Camp Sumter. Two of his siblings died in rebel captivity and one escaped. John

Northrop wrote of three Tennessee brothers who, one by one, died in the same spot.[62]

Such Southerners as the Tennesseans drew special abuse from the guards and died at an exceptionally high rate. Confederate official H. A. M. Anderson urged Captain Wirz to hold back from exchange any men who had deserted the Southern army to join the federal service. When Confederate soldiers surrounded Colonel James P. Brownlow and his 1st Tennessee Cavalry (USA), he determined that he and his men would risk their lives trying to break out rather than become prisoners at Andersonville. He and his men succeeded in their escape. Prisoner poet John W. Northrop memorialized the service and sacrifice of the Tennesseans at Andersonville. Prisoner John McElroy would survive to write a prison novel with Tennessee Unionists as the heroes. Deaths from their regiments propelled the 2nd Tennessee Infantry and the 7th Tennessee Cavalry into the positions of having the third- and fourth-highest mortality rate, respectively, of any federal units in rebel captivity. They only ranked behind two more unfortunate New York regiments.[63]

Other Southern unionists, or "Tories," also especially suffered for their cause. Comparing the number of identified dead at Andersonville to the total number of men enlisted in the army by state shows North Carolina had the worst mortality rate, followed respectively by the Southern states of Tennessee, Alabama, and Virginia-West Virginia. Robert H. Kellogg remembered the exceptional sufferings of white North Carolinians, or "buffaloes" as the guards called them (for reasons unknown), many of whom had previously deserted the Confederate army. He and his comrades helped the men from the 2nd North Carolina Infantry to hide their identities and unit from the guards. Of the thirty white men of the 1st Alabama Cavalry (USA) known to have found themselves in Andersonville, at least eighteen of them died there.

Former Virginians (West Virginians after 1863) captured in federal service also suffered terribly. Of the twenty men in Company I of the 10th West Virginia who entered Andersonville, only Ransom T. Powell survived to go home. This thirteen-year-old boy believed that he lived because a Confederate officer took pity on him and removed him from the inside of the stockade for use as a drummer boy.

If white Southerners in blue drew sometimes fatal treatment from their captors, they also became especially attractive, because of their nativity, to Confederate recruiters. Few of them joined, or rejoined, the Confederate army, however.[64]

Another group also received special notice. The guards placed black soldiers on work details that brought them extra physical labor and punishment but which, incidentally, allowed them better rations and thus a better chance at survival. Prisoner Reuben C. Griffitt believed that the guards at Camp Sumter shared wider Southern fears of violent slave revolts and of the perceived loss of social status that would come with granting African Americans any rights at all. He felt that this fear inspired a particular hatred of Yankees, black soldiers (many who had been slaves), and their white officers. Memoirists wrote of the denial of attention by Confederate medical personnel to African-American soldiers and to their white officers. Rebel leaders sent the latter to Andersonville, despite their rank, rather than hang them, as prescribed by Confederate law, to block any exchange of the white officers of black soldiers. Planters came to the stockade to claim black soldiers as escaped slaves.[65]

Two different views of the treatment of the black prisoners at Andersonville survive. White sergeants, in unsuccessfully petitioning President Lincoln for a resumption of the exchange of prisoners, wrote the following about the African Americans captured by the Confederates:

> The 2 classes are treated differently by the enemy. The white are confined in such prisons as Libby and Andersonville, starved and treated with a barbarism unknown to civilized nations. The black on the contrary are seldom imprisoned, but are distributed among the citizens or employed in government works, under those circumstances they receive enough to eat and are worked no harder than [they are] accustomed to. They are neither starved, nor killed off by the pestilence in the dungeons of Richmond and Charleston. It is true they are again made slaves, but their slavery is freedom and happiness compared with the cruel existence imposed upon our gallant [white] men.[66]

The white men who signed the above, however, believed rumors that the exchange had ended because the United States government refused to participate in any prisoner trade that failed to include African-American soldiers.

Andersonville survivor Robert N. Sneden, however, remembered a very different treatment of the black soldiers and laborers. He wrote:

> They [black soldiers and impressed slaves] often get lashed by their masters or overseers, as we can hear their cries of pain plainly over at the log house village of Andersonville on still nights. When the Rebels acquire a Negro soldier, if he is already wounded they either shoot him instantly [or] if not badly wounded they capture him so that he may work for them when he recovers. All of the others have to work, on fortifications, felling trees, making roads, etc.[67]

Brigadier General John H. Winder, the prison commandant, made a number of efforts to end the tragedy at Andersonville for all of the persons involved. He answered the failures of his government to improve the prison's security and to reduce the staggering mortality rate by recommending an end of transferring prisoners to Andersonville and by urging the construction of new prison camps. In August 1864, he allowed prisoners Henry C. Higginson, Edward Bates, Sylvester Noirto, Abraham Barns, W. H. Bynon, Jacob Harbauer, and Prescott Tracy to return to the North with the petition signed by the camp's sergeants that pleaded for the resumption of the exchange of prisoners as a means of saving the inmates of Andersonville.[68] They met with President Lincoln, and the long process began that eventually resulted in an exchange of the prisoners.[69]

The Confederate government that failed to adequately provide for its soldiers, sailors, and prisoners, on a day-to-day basis, did make a final, Herculean effort to keep the population at Anderson Station from another form of liberation. As Sherman's armies prepared to move into central Georgia in September 1864, the Confederate government quickly evacuated most of the prisoners by train to newly built Camp Lawton at Millen, and still later to Savannah, Charleston, Blackshear, Florence, and Salisbury. At the last three prisons, the men found conditions and rations even worse than at Andersonville. Rebecca Latimer Felton saw a train load of these men being moved:

> On that trip we passed car-loads of Andersonville prisoners being removed to another camp as it was expected that Sherman would strike for Andersonville. The night was gloomy and the torch fires made a weird scene as our train rolled along beside passing flat cars on which those Federal prisoners were guarded, with torch lights illuminating the faces of those ragged, smoke begrimed, haggard and miserably

> filthy men. I had a glimpse of war conditions that was new to me. Prison treatment of such men has always been a disgrace to Christianity and civilization. I had read of Camp Chase and Johnson's Island and been angered at the treatment accorded to our Confederate prisoners, but the sight of trainloads of Federal prisoners on that wild night in Southern Georgia, when I could look into their faces within a few feet of the train I became an eye witness to their enforced degradation, filth and utter destitution and the sight never could be forgotten.[70]

The balance of the remaining Andersonville survivors on the move went to Savannah for parole and release. That moving these sick and starved men became more important than using this same transportation to feed starving soldiers and civilians reflected the strange priorities of a failing bureaucracy. Similar to other such collapsing organizational systems throughout history, the Confederate government now only survived in order to continue to exist beyond any practical benefit to its people or credible hope of success. Some prisoners survived Belle Island, near Richmond, and even Andersonville, to travel on to such places as Salisbury and Vicksburg. They thus traveled over more of the Confederate nation than the almost any free member of any of the armies.

The inmates too sick to survive transfer remained at Camp Sumter. They numbered so few that the prison finally had a supportable population. Eventually a hospital, a bakery, some barracks, and other amenities went up. The camp administration even abolished the dead line. General Howell Cobb tried to confiscate the prison's newly acquired lumber for the Confederate hospitals in Macon but Wirz managed to keep the boards for prisoner housing. Cobb, however, praised the Andersonville captain for his efficiency, as did other inspecting officers. After the federal army moved on from Georgia, the Confederate government returned several thousand of the captive federals to Andersonville from the open ground prison at Blackshear, Georgia.[71]

As 1864 became 1865, the two warring governments moved towards a general exchange of prisoners although this effort came too late for most of the captives of Andersonville. On 31 December 1864, General John H. Winder urged his Confederate superiors to release any federals who agreed to abstain from military service until exchanged and also those men whose enlistments had run out. General Grant wrote of releasing healthy Confederates to fight again as inhumane to the soldiers they could now kill, but at the same time in February 1865, he authorized the exchange of prisoners as quickly as possible. By March

1865, Andersonville's administration could begin returning its almost five thousand remaining prisoners to the federal lines.[72]

The same kinds of bureaucratic incompetence, societal indifference, and transportation problems that had made the prison such a place of misery now worked to force these men into two last nightmares that would include further confinement and more Andersonville-related deaths. An agreement to dispatch the western soldiers to Camp Fisk, four miles from Vicksburg, and the easterners to Baldwin, near Jacksonville, Florida, broke down as the garrison auctioned places on the first trains (those cars that took men to the West). The "fortunates" who "won" this chance of first release then took a complex odyssey along the Civil War South's often different gauge and worn out railroads. After traveling by train, foot, and water, they finally arrived near Vicksburg. By that point, they had gone without a meal for three days. Even then, they had to wait at Camp Fisk with thousands of their comrades until, at last, the opposing sides could arrange for their final release. In one of the final ironies, on a long list of bizarre circumstances, the last prison camp for holding Union soldiers, sailors, and civilians was thus officially operated by Confederacy but supplied by the Union and was just outside of the federally occupied Confederate city of Vicksburg, a city whose Confederate garrison had been allowed to go home upon surrendering in 1863! At least 386 of these Andersonville survivors subsequently died in the explosion of the overcrowded troop transport *Sultana* on 27 April 1865.

Back at Andersonville, on 6 April, Wirz sent 3,424 of his remaining inmates to Albany, Georgia, for later release in Florida. They took what they could carry of their personal belongings and burned the rest. At Albany, the mayor used sentries to keep the guards and the prisoners out of the town. He did present each guard with a Confederate uniform, however, likely the only uniform most of the men of the garrison ever received. Unfortunately, they all soon found themselves where they had started. Lacking any orders about a prisoner release, federal General Quincy A. Gilmore declined to accept the long-suffering prisoners. Wirz had no authority to just let the men go and doing so might have negatively affected the release of Confederates. (Had Wirz taken that personal initiative, however, he might have later avoided the gallows.) The prisoners next went to Macon, from where Wirz planned to transfer them to the Central Railroad for shipment to the federal garrison at Savannah. The arrival of Wilson's Union cavalry caused Colonel George C. Gibbs, Andersonville's new commandant, to order the prisoners back to Anderson Station, even as reports arrived of sightings of federal cavalrymen only one mile away. In the rush, Captain Wirz found himself left behind. Finally, Gibbs and Wirz personally escorted their charges back to Albany. They then led them and the guards on a three-day march to the railhead at Thomasville, Georgia. From there, they took a train and then made a march to Baldwin, Florida, where Wirz finally released his prisoners.

The sufferings of these men did not end, however. These survivors of Andersonville had to walk still another twenty miles through jungle and swamp to reach the federal garrison. Some of these ragged, starved men didn't survive this last leg of the journey. On 4 May 1865, the last prisoners died at Camp Sumter. The next day, only five sick men and seventeen other Yankees remained in the otherwise abandoned stockade. By then, the guards and local families had looted what military stores that remained in the camp.[73]

In the interim, other prisoners went to special federal camps for rehabilitation. One of their nurses wrote a particularly grim account of their arrival:

> The hair of some was matted together, like beasts of the stall which lie down in their own filth. Vermin are over them in abundance. Nearly every man was darkened by scurvy, or black with rough scales, and with scorbutic sores. One in particular was reduced to the merest skeleton; his face, neck, and feet were covered with thick, green mold. A number who had government clothes given to them on the boat were too feeble to put them on, and were carried ashore partially dressed, hugging their clothing with a death-grasp that they could not be persuaded to yield. It was not infrequent to hear a man feebly call, as he was laid on a stretcher, "Don't take my clothes," "Oh, save my new shoes," "Don't let my socks go back to Andersonville." In their wild death-struggle, with bony arms and hands extended, they would hold up their new socks, that could not be put on because of their swollen limbs, saying 'Save'em till I get home.' In a little while, however, the souls of many were released from their worn-out frames, and borne to that higher home where all things are registered for a great day of account.[74]

* * * *

> I do not think the land should be allowed to revert to the former owners, some of whom it has been stated have boasted that the soil, enriched by the bodies of our martyrs, would produce excellent wine, and should be converted into vineyards. These people should not be allowed to make themselves drunk on the blood of their enemies,—our friends. It ought to remain desolate forever in respect to the memory of the martyrs who suffered and perished on it.
>
> —Montgomery C. Meigs
> Quartermaster General of the US Army

Andersonville also had a significant history after it closed as a prison. It became a symbol of the remembrance of the Civil War but also, eventually, of the sufferings of all prisoners of war. Its history took a positive turn toward redemption on 29 October 1866 when Northern missionaries opened a freedmen's school for blacks and whites in Camp Sumter's buildings, inadvertently giving to the local African Americans something in return for the aide they had so often given to escaped prisoners. The Ku Klux Klan, led by Benjamin B. Dykes, however, drove the freedmen from the buildings and from houses they had built for themselves in 1868–1869. Despite such opposition from local whites, the school would continue into the first decades of the twentieth century.[75]

Joel R. Griffin, a former Confederate colonel who lived at nearby Fort Valley, started the second phase of the prison cemetery's history, under orders from federal General James Wilson. Griffin prevented Dykes from taking the stockade walls and growing grapes over the remains of the soldiers. The colonel reburied some of the corpses at Andersonville and started a fence for its cemetery. Prisoner Dorence Atwater had smuggled out a grave register of his fallen comrades. He used this record to help Clara Barton organize an expedition to mark the graves in the camp cemetery in July–August 1865. On 25 July 1865, Major James M. Moore, with two companies of troops, arrived at Andersonville to take charge of the cemetery. He began cleaning up the cemetery. Ironically the hospital buildings were taken over for use by sick ex-Confederates employed by Moore to supervise the laborers who cleaned up the grounds and covered over the constantly exposed bodies. Some bodies were interred and sent to their home towns at the request of their respective families. Moore started a fence around the graveyard from boards found inside and outside of the stockade. On 17 August 1865, his troops raised the first United States flag at the site. Lieutenant C. E. Moore and Captain A. W. Corliss later took over the work. Corliss would employ from some fifty to two hundred workers, but he would have no more troops than a corporal and six soldiers. The War Department debated whether to move the bodies to new national cemeteries in Chattanooga or Marietta, places with facilities for visiting families, or to build a much larger and more appropriate cemetery at Andersonville. In the end, the bodies remained where their comrades had originally laid them in 1864–1865.[76]

Congress made the graves a national cemetery, with a permanent, paid government superintendent, on 11 November 1865. (One of the first superintendents even chose to have his interment there.) By 1868, 868 corpses of federal soldiers received relocation to the Andersonville cemetery from Americus, Columbus, Eufaula, Macon, and other places. In 1869, when a federal contractor removed the Andersonville alumni buried at the site of Camp Lawton in Millen, Georgia, however, he reburied them in the national cemetery at Beaufort, South Carolina, as if returning them to Camp Sumter's cemetery might have been seen as an indignity. The Women's Relief Corps, formed in 1869 under the local leadership of Elizabeth Ann Thompson, did most of the major maintenance for the Andersonville cemetery for many years. In 1875, the United States government finally officially purchased the cemetery property from Benjamin Dykes, the man who originally persuaded Confederate officers to locate the prison at such a grossly inadequate site. Two years later, tombstones of Georgia marble replaced the wooden grave markers. Family and friends of some of the deceased provided some special tombstones. The Women's Relief Corps erected a fence around the graves in 1878.

The Andersonville cemetery immediately after the Civil War. (Library of Congress)

Andersonville survivors at the Providence Spring at a post war reunion. (Library of Congress)

Andersonville had drawn tourists, even during the war. Southern women would stand in the guard towers to see the captive Yankees. Some of these female rebels would throw food to the prisoners, but others would jeer. The curious continued to journey to the ruins of Camp Sumter long after it had closed as a prison, joined by survivors and family members of deceased prisoners. In the first year after the fighting ended, the prison site allegedly drew some ten thousand visitors, undoubtedly making it the devastated state of Georgia's principle tourist attraction. They came in especially great numbers, in later years, for the

These views of Andersonville were taken by John F. Engle and James Furlong for the federal government after the Civil War. (R. S. Davis and National Archives and Records Administration)

dedications of the various state monuments at the site. For decades, visitors could still collect souvenirs from the piles of scrape and junk strewed across the prison grounds. An anonymous writer wrote of the many alumni who returned, "These men, whatever their natural temper, the superintendent says, can almost be distinguished by the effects of fear, dread, and vivid recollection which come back like a shock into their faces as they again stand on the now quiet and sunlit scene of their experiences."[77]

Local people also scavenged the prison site but in hopes of finding buried treasure. Some of their neighbors, believing rumors of strange noise, flying swords, and unexplained fires, however, avoided the site. Most of two complete stockade walls still stood for visitors to inspect as late as 1873. Ten years later, only one wall remained. The swamp through the middle of the grounds and the Providence Spring also disappeared. The latter held a special place in the memories of the old soldiers. They argued endlessly in their veterans' newspapers about the location and the lightning strike that led to the creation of that source of badly needed clean drinking water in August 1864. In 1883, H. S. Beaman of Beaman, Iowa, paid to have what he remembered as the spring cleared out and walled. Later visitors would frequently picnic by its waters.

Five years later, only one pole of the wall remained standing, and all of the prison buildings had disappeared although the stumps of the rotted palisades still indicated the location of the walls. Holes that had once been the homes of the prisoners, some cannon barrels, and the earthen walls of the forts also remained. The open wells became a death trap for livestock. The famous Providence Spring turned into a fishpond that deer and other wild animals frequented.

Visitors saw little more. As late as 1888, the community had only added a depot building to stand with the "squalid" three or four old houses. M. P. Suber, depot manager since 1857, still held that position. Anderson Station lost a chance of becoming a substantial town when the Buena Vista Railroad bypassed it in 1886. When former prisoner Samuel Creelman returned to the state of his imprisonment in 1889, he found the civilian community there, now incorporated as the town of Andersonville, as still unimpressive, consisting of only some eight or ten dwellings and a hotel.

In the 1880s, K. G. Kennedy, a former slave, owned the site of the stockade and grew cotton there. Some individuals suggested rebuilding the prison pen as it appeared in 1864–1865 as a money-making venture. The stockade had completely vanished by 1890, when a committee of the Commander E. S. Jones Post number 5 of Georgia Department of the Grand Army of the Republic

(GAR) visited the site. Captain I. D. Crawford, commander of that GAR post, and Dr. J. W. Stone of Atlanta bought most of the prison grounds on 30 December 1890 from freedman George W. Kennedy. Under public pressure, they abandoned the idea of making it into a money-making venture. They now proposed to clear the last remains of the prison for a public park.[78]

With the encouragement of Crawford, the Georgia Division of the GAR formed in 1889 and almost immediately began efforts to acquire the site of the Andersonville stockade to protect it from development. The GAR had problems with raising funds and formally incorporating, however. Dr. Stone traveled to the North to find donations for the prison project. Crawford and Stone served on a Board of Control connected with the GAR to oversee clearing the brush and restoring some of the parts of the prison. The Board even planned to build a museum, supported in part by accommodations for visiting veterans. The Georgia GAR finally purchased the seventy-one acres that included most of the rest of the prison site on 19 September 1892 for $1,550. The GAR hired George W. Kennedy to mark the lines of the old stockade with posts and to build a cover over the Providence Spring. The National Cemetery superintendents, starting with J. W. Bryant, helped the GAR to lease the grounds that lacked historical significance to farmers including Kennedy.[79]

Controversy surrounding such commemorations of the prison began by 30 May 1870. On that day, Georgia's widely despised Reconstruction governor Rufus Bullock gave a public address from a wagon at Andersonville. He raised a great deal of ire when, in reciting the horrors of the prison camp, he claimed to have witnesses present to testify to six prisoners being taken out of the camp, tied up, and then eaten alive by the camp's dog packs. General Phil Cook of Oglethorpe refused to tolerate this tirade. He mounted another wagon and challenged the governor to produce the witnesses. No one came forward.[80] Southern opposition to the commemoration of this Confederate-operated prison persisted even more than a century later. Some Georgians also resented the reunions held at Andersonville by various federal veterans groups, especially when the old soldiers became drunk and rowdy, or when these gatherings involved African Americans. The latter had begun conducting Memorial Day services at the cemetery after the war. The Georgia Division GAR made the services a formal annual event, starting on 30 May 1889. The ceremony drew crowds of thousands of visitors, including hecklers from outside of the Andersonville community. Troops from Fort McPherson began providing security.

In 1896–1897, the GAR gave the prison site to the Women's Relief Corps (WRC), an auxiliary of the GAR. The WRC acquired an additional fourteen and a half acres of the prison site property from local landowners. The women also had the grounds cleared, bridges erected, and a driveway graded. For the caretaker and visitors, the WRC erected a nine-room house with a view of the grounds, north of the site of the stockade. In 1901, the WRC erected a white marble springhouse over the Providence Spring, to which the National Association of Union Ex-Prisoners of War added a fountain dedicated to all of the Andersonville prisoners.

A new storm of controversy about the prison began with the United Daughters of the Confederacy's (UDC) plans to erect a monument to Captain Henry Wirz. The federal government hanged Wirz in 1865 for war crimes and had sentenced baker James W. Duncan to fifteen years in prison for murder, the only Confederates ever tried for the atrocities at Camp Sumter. To Southerners, Wirz had been a martyr to Northern passions against the Confederacy. Negative public reaction to a memorial to Wirz proved so severe that the UDC failed to have the monument erected in Andersonville or even in Atlanta. Macon, Richmond, and Savannah wanted the memorial, but it finally went up in Andersonville in 1909. Critics called it the only monument on American soil erected to brutality. Vandals attacked it in 1919.[81]

The modern history of Andersonville began when the Women's Relief Corps turned control of the site over to the War Department, under an act of Congress of 2 March 1910. The federal government and former prisoners had already marked the major sites in the stockade with signs and posts.[82] On 10 August 1933, Andersonville Prison Park and other federal Civil War sites came under of the Office of National Parks (returned to its earlier name of the National Park Service in 1934) in the Department of the Interior. The Civilian Conservation Corps (CCC) filled in the post-war gullies and did ditching necessary to prevent further erosion. The CCC also replaced the wooden markers in the park with stone. On 16 October 1970, the Andersonville National Cemetery also became a national historic site and, in 1998, the National Prisoner of War Museum opened there. Andersonville National Historic Site formally came into existence on 1 July 1970 and today includes the site of the prison, the still-active national cemetery, and a research library.[83]

During those years, the countryside around Andersonville earned notoriety beyond the fame of the prison. Charles Lindbergh bought his first airplane and made his solo flight near the prison site; bauxite and kaolin mining became a major industry; and Reverend Clarence Jordon started the international bi-racial farming cooperative of Koinonia in nearby Americus.[84] In 1976, native Sumter County resident Jimmy Carter became the thirty-ninth president of the United

States. His kinsmen included at least one Andersonville guard, Jesse Taliaferro Carter of the 3rd Georgia Reserves. Today, tens of thousands of people from around the world come to the park each year. Many of them descend from men once held there and others who remain in the cemetery. Some visitors (the author included) have guards as ancestors, and still other people come just to see what still remains as one of the world's most notorious places.

The Wirz Monument, Andersonville, shortly after its erection. (R. S. Davis)

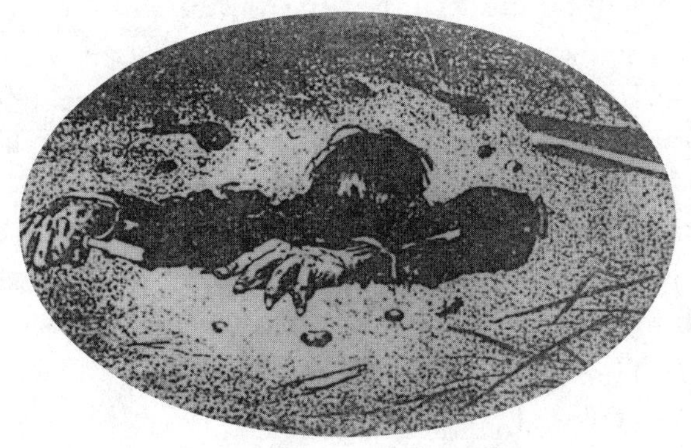

Engraving from a prisoner memoir. (R. S. Davis)

BARBED WIRE DISEASE[85]

To prevent them from escaping—to report in writing the attempted escapes—that was my responsibility. Isn't that clear? Even though I did not have enough men.... So it went, I preventing, they trying. And no move to stop them completely successful. Nothing, nothing could stop them.

—Fictional Henry Wirz
in the play *Andersonville Trial*

1

Private Henry Clay Damon of the 11th Michigan Infantry Regiment escaped from Andersonville in early July 1864. The Confederates had captured him during the Battle of Chickamauga in 1863, and he then spent time incarcerated in Virginia before finding himself transferred to Andersonville. The staff of federal General George Henry Thomas would record Damon's subsequent description of the strength of the stockade's defenses and his claim that the prisoners had three hundred concealed pistols. The former prisoner of war also told of the unsanitary conditions that the nearly naked inmates had to endure while being held in an open stockade. A single marshy creek that passed through the middle of the prison acted as both a water supply and a sewer. With little shelter, the inmates had to endure twenty-two continuous days of rain in June.[86]

Damon represented many curious aspects of the Andersonville story. Like the majority of the some two dozen men known to have successfully escaped from that place of confinement, he lived for many years after the war. (DeLayvan R. Streeter, perhaps the first man to successfully escape Andersonville, for example, lived until 22 March 1932.) By contrast, only an estimated eight hundred to nine hundred of the thirty-nine thousand men who entered Andersonville reportedly were living as late as 1890. In addition, as common with those comrades, Damon declined to write a book about his escape, or even to find a reason to mention it in his federal pension claim.[87] Details of most of the successful escapes, however, do survive in obscure regimental histories, local studies, newspapers, and unpublished memoirs.

Information on escapes also appeared in contemporary newspapers, reports which helped to create Andersonville's infamous reputation. Some of these men even met with General William T. Sherman to plead for the release of their comrades by any means.[88] Escaped soldiers certainly contributed to the respective reports on conditions in Confederate prisons published by a joint congressional committee and by the United States Sanitary Commission. The six hundred Confederate officers used by the federal military as human shields in the siege of Charleston, South Carolina, had their rations reduced to what fugitives from Andersonville claimed they had received.[89] A number of the escapees would also serve as witnesses in the post-war trial of Captain Hartmann Heinrich "Henry" Wirz of Andersonville, although only one of them, Jasper Culver, mentioned his escape. The experiences of this Jasper Culver of the 1st Wisconsin Infantry in his escape proved all too typical of his special class of comrades. He tried unsuccessfully to flee captivity in Virginia before receiving a transfer to Andersonville. Once there, Culver, along with Lewis Trowbridge and Thomas D. Mason, escaped and, with the aid of slaves, joined Sherman's army near Atlanta. Despite having kept a diary that he later edited into a memoir in 1923, the few published details of his escape only appear in his regiment's history.[90]

This almost universal silence on the subject of escapes from this prison, by men with such interesting tales to tell, represents an enigma within a significant body of historical literature. More works about Andersonville have appeared in print than any other prison of the Civil War, if not the world. Books about escapes from Confederate prisons became and remain popular reading. Escape legends enhanced the notoriety of Andersonville. Personnel at the Andersonville National Historic Site have heard thousands of family stories about ancestors who fled from confinement there. Descendants tell of federal soldiers escaping from Andersonville, even months before this prison actually existed.[91] Because no one wrote a nonfiction book about successfully escaping from this prison, however, the four general histories of Camp Sumter omit any significant discussion of the successful escapes.

What kept these escapees from going to the public with their special experiences? Andersonville alumni certainly had the motivations to tell their stories and had a receptive audience. Other former prisoners of war could and did write of their experiences. Tens of thousands of literate men, consumers of the North's burgeoning publishing industry, survived Andersonville, including the escapees. Many of these former prisoners became publishers after the war or had family members in the printing business.

All Andersonville prisoners, but especially the escapees, had incentives to tell their stories. William N. Tyler of the 95th Illinois Volunteers wrote that the inventor of forgiving and forgetting never spent time at Andersonville. Even before the war ended, Camp Sumter had such notoriety that a survivor of that experience, such as Austin Carr, could return home as a hero who drew large crowds that demanded to hear a description of his experience. Numerous campaigns from the end of the Civil War to 1900 sought to procure extra veteran's benefits for survivors of Southern prisons.[92] In support of these efforts, dozens of books, prints, and lectures about Andersonville appeared to remind the public of inmate suffering. Former prisoners formed special Prisoner of War survivor societies. Pension attorneys, such as George E. Lemon, founder of the veterans' newspaper the *National Tribune* (predecessor of today's *The Stars and Stripes*), widely promoted these efforts to increase business for their practices. John McElroy, Andersonville survivor and author of the major memoir of the prison, became editor of the *National Tribune* and something of a professional prisoner of war. Eventually, he even wrote a novel and a humorous satire about the prison.[93] Charles Mather Smith's account of his escape received nationwide attention in the 1890s. He even went on tour as a speaker, wherein he displayed artifacts from his escape. A Rhode Island officers' organization of veterans later published an expanded account of Smith's escape.[94] Each new work on this prison would build upon the facts, rumors, and exaggerations of earlier works to create a greater body of Andersonville lore.

Failing to escape from Camp Sumter—or even not having been there at all—proved no hindrance to publishing a personal escape memoir. Joseph Keen,

Hiram S. Daskam, and Thomas H. Howe wrote their respective books with "escape from Andersonville" as part of the titles. These books, however, actually dealt with their adventures after jumping from trains that had taken each of them away from Andersonville. Morgan E. Dowling took advantage of this same market to write romantic historical "escape" fiction around his real experiences as a prisoner. This tale, which he promoted as factual, even had a heroine who follows (stalks?) him to the prison. Englishman James Gillespie's account of his various escape attempts suspiciously resembles the known experiences of other prisoners. Similarly, Ralph O. Bates toured the country giving lectures about what he claimed was his service as a teenager in the 9th Ohio Cavalry, his imprisonment in Camp Sumter, a daring escape with a friend, an interview with President Lincoln, and his testimony in the trial of Captain Wirz—none of which actually happened! His widow later published his purely imaginary memoirs in what amounted to a novel that a critic described as expounding "bad fiction as fact."[95]

Places in Georgia related to escapes from Camp Sumter (Andersonville) Prison

The few men who did successfully escape had a greater story to tell than just the details of fleeing from a notorious prison. They often led lives of escapes in which the brutal confinement at Camp Sumter became only one, almost incidental, stop. People write about what matters in their lives and, for this group and in that era, freedom, rather than any single experience, drove them. To write about being a prisoner likely proved beyond their words or too personal to make public, as illustrated by Robert Sneden's heavily illustrated and extensive manuscript on his Civil War experience, a document only recently published.

Historian Robert Doyle suggests other psychological "fire walls" to publicly sharing escape adventures. He wrote that the American prisoner of war seeks first survival, then resistance, and finally escape, if possible. For most of the prisoners at Andersonville, achieving even the first priority proved extremely difficult, if not impossible. This last point especially proves worth noting. Aside from some pathological need to escape despite any obstacle, opportunity and the perception that escape meant avoiding certain death most often created the circumstances that pushed men to attempt to get away.[96] No prisoner account

Places in Florida related to escapes from Camp Sumter (Andersonville) Prison

lists patriotism as a reason for escape from Andersonville, quite possibly because the horrible conditions of the camp were incentive enough. Unlike in other wars, many of the Yankee prisoners failed to see the Civil War as a mortal threat to their homes and way of life. Many of these men even blamed the United States government for an unnecessary war and their continued imprisonment to questionable social causes. The inmates of Andersonville found themselves caught in the classic paradox of finding themselves trapped between "heaven" (hope of salvation in some form by divine or other intervention) and earth (awaiting death as an inevitable outcome). In this situation, few men ever realistically make the third choice, to explore escape as the unknown alternative to reality and faith.

Geography did make the chances of reaching federal lines poor. Most Civil War prisons stood close enough to safe refuges for escaping prisoners to have a reasonable hope for success. Camp Sumter, however, went up as an open pen hundreds of miles from federal lines. The several days' journey by railroad to reach the camp took the federal prisoners through a largely uninhabited, vast and impenetrable pine forest. This trip not only discouraged planning for an escape but could also instill in the inmates the idea that the sheer size of the Confederacy made it physically unconquerable. The failure of Sherman's later, relatively close, advance to reach even the neighborhood of the prison confirmed distance and isolation as two of the prison's greatest defenses.

Andersonville's administration also effectively used rumors of pending prisoner exchanges to discourage breakouts. Diaries of prisoners such as Henry B. Sparks show that the inmates believed every report of eminent release. The nearby Sumter County newspaper encouraged these hopes with stories that the warring sides had revived the prisoner exchange. Federal prisoners even made up a song about wanting to hear news of exchange. Jesse Altom's hopes for release rose and fell four times. At the end of the war, he and his companions finally found themselves abandoned to find their own way, over hundreds of miles, to the federal lines. Warren Lee Goss saw only two options for a prisoner of Andersonville, "to die without an effort, amid all of the misery of the prison pen, or to die with our hands uplifted to strike one blow at our enemies,"[97] but he and Amos Stearns of the 25th Massachusetts found most of their fellow prisoners had "exchange on the brain." Thousands of these men, however, found release only in death. They dreamed of feasts and talked of exchange and escape, while sharing in the dying words overheard by John Northrop, "could I be at home!"[98]

The small garrison also used all physical means available to them to protect the people of southwest Georgia from tens of thousands of hungry, uncontrolled men breaking out. The prison began as hardly more than an open field surrounded by a simple, unfinished log wall with two gates. The camp's administration eventually added a dead line and towers for firing over the wall as a desperate ploy to stop the front rank leaders of any mob that tried to rush the wall. (The concept of firing upon single prisoners only developed during the Civil War.) Almost the entire garrison would line up to stop any mass escapes when the gates opened to allow rations or new prisoners to enter the stockade.[99]

The camp administration also saw that recaptured prisoners received such punishments as "buck and gag" (tied by ankles and wrists around a log), stocks, and chains. Comrades left behind also could suffer. Henry B. Sparks of the 3rd Indiana Cavalry wrote in his diary of three such men. After their comrades escaped by tunnel, the men had balls chained to their legs.

These punishments could last for a matter of hours and without serious harm to the prisoners. In early May 1864, a man named Connally made one of the first successful escapes, and by tunnel. With only one of the men who helped him, he escaped before the guards moved in. He succeeded despite having a ball and chain attached to his leg in punishment for having tried to escape the previous April. Like other prisoners so afflicted, he had filed the head off the bolt that held the bracelet to his ankle. Before roll call each morning, he put the shackles back on with a blackened piece of lead shot made to look like the bolt. Once outside of the prison, Connally reached a boat on the Flint River and sailed to freedom, using a stick to kill the dogs who tried to reach him.[100] The guards later learned of the ploy to defeat the ball and chain; they then began chaining men in gangs to make them easier to observe.

As more men escaped, punishments and threats did become more severe. The first inmates arrived in February 1864. By early May, the garrison had an artillery battery of four cannon and earthworks set up to stop any massing of the prisoners. The inmates responded by digging a series of tunnels to undermine the stockade and bring it down. The Union soldiers intended to seize the prison's artillery and then shell the camps of the guards, prior to escaping en mass to Pensacola. An informer betrayed the plan to Captain Wirz before the prisoners finished the tunnels. By 1 August, the garrison had positioned eight of the camp's sixteen heavy guns to fire on the inmates in the stockade.[101]

Outside the stockade wall, pine knot fires burned all night to illuminate the outside of the wall as sentinels called out to each other to assure the inmates of their vigilance. Dog packs and mounted guards regularly circled the stockade.

Once past these obstacles, escapees would still have to evade slave patrols, home guards, militia, posses, and Confederate troops, while fighting exposure and hunger.[102] Aside from his fear of "crocodiles" and lizards, Samuel E. Preston wrote of the struggle to escape, "Imagine yourself in a strange land, enemies on every hand, Rivers to cross, Large forests to pass, through Incessant rains by night & day, shivering in our wet garments, such as we had after living with the Johnnies so long."[103] Many men found themselves outside of the stockade without any idea of what to do next.

Few men knew more about the problems of escape and recapture than did Henry Clay Hartwell. He arrived with the first of the prisoners in February and remained until September 1864. He first scaled the wall, but the guards apprehended him the next morning. Next, he worked for several weeks on a tunnel, but his fellow diggers were captured. He was not captured as well because he had been placed in chains as punishment for his earlier escape. Finally, as the Andersonville records show, Hartwell and seventy-four of his comrades fled on the night of 10 September, with little or no resistance from the guards. Local people eventually captured of the fugitives, including Hartwell, whom they found forty miles from the prison. These prisoners had the consolation of being sent to the new and better prison at Millen, Georgia, rather than being returned to Andersonville. News of their recovery failed to reach Andersonville and, therefore, into the camp's records and statistics of men recaptured.[104]

Nevertheless, prisoners did have strong encouragements to try to escape. Many survivors of Andersonville would try to describe the horrors they remembered from their stay in the prison. Henry E. Ollinger of the 20th Indiana, for example, wrote upon his arrival, "I am tolerably well But find this the most miserable place man ever conceived of."[105] James Jennings of the 20th Illinois Infantry, at least as well as any, wrote one such account:

> Around us on every side lay the poor wretches who had been there six or eight months, men afflicted with all manner of disease; teeth dropping out from the effects of scurvy. Those that were able to walk were mere skeletons. You could almost hear their bones rattle as they walked around and were being eaten alive with gray-backs [ticks]. Some of these poor fellows were so covered with lice and nits that their hair would be matted tight to their heads; and their hands and faces and bodies almost as black as a negro from the dirt and smoke of pitch pine fires as they huddled over [them] to keep warm.

> [Even] Students and college graduates had become so discouraged by disease and the treatment they received, and the long confinement that they had lost all sense of pride and decency, and certainly it is no wonder.[106]

Magnus Tait survived a long captivity at Andersonville and other prisons although he never completely recovered emotionally or mentally. He told of a job he took outside of the camp and around women. Tait had to get his hair cut with shears, layers of soot washed off with the only soap he had used in months, and the meal sacks he wore replaced with clothes, in order to appear presentable for polite society. On his way to Andersonville, Reuben C. Griffitt of the 22nd Indiana Infantry had a preview of what this confinement at Anderson Station meant. He encountered a New England soldier recaptured after fleeing the prison. The fugitive still wore the tin star given to inmates paroled to work outside of the stockade. Such prisoners received double rations and left the prison's smell and filth to live outside of the stockade. "Star," as Griffitt called him, however, declared that he would die rather than return to Andersonville. The guards later shot him dead when he tried to escape on the way back to the prison.[107]

To many of the prisoners, escape came to mean just leaving the camp briefly to find green leaves and weeds to eat, or to get away from the almost overwhelming stench and swarms of insects. John Northrop wrote of men getting out of the stockade, spending a few days being fed and hidden by slaves, and then giving themselves up to the nearest authorities. John Ransom worked for months with his comrades on a tunnel. When he finally escaped, however, he only hoped that he would reach a house and food before the guards returned him to the prison and punishment on a chain gang in the stockade. After his recapture, he discovered that he received better treatment and more rations while on the camp's punishment detail than when he was not being "punished." Prisoner Robert Sneden wrote that less than one in twenty of the inmates who volunteered to work on building the camp cookhouse knew anything about carpentry or bricklaying. They lied just for the chance to leave the stockade and to get extra rations.[108]

More ambitious escape efforts required some knowledge of direction and navigation. Andrew J. Spring of the 16th Connecticut and two comrades likely set some sort of a record for narrow escapes by passing through three enemy picket lines in just five days to reach federal lines. They subsisted on sugar cane, green corn, and persimmons while looking for the tree moss that allegedly grew on the north side of trees to keep their direction. Joseph Keen, however, found that, due to the South's warm climate, moss in its wet areas grew on all sides of the trees. Other prisoners believed that trees and bushes grew larger on the south side of hills and fences. Jasper Culver and his two fellow fugitives failed to agree on the direction to go. When Tom Mason declined to lead and told Culver to go to Hell, Culver cynically responded that to do that would mean returning to Andersonville, which he refused to do. The group finally saw the sun and used it to determine north.[109]

If the prisoners did get out, they had to evade not only the camp's patrols but also its infamous dog packs. Failure to appear at morning roll call resulted in pursuit by some seventy canines. Every morning at six o'clock, handler Edward C. Turner, formerly of White County, Georgia, also released the camp's dogs. His pack included any available mixture of breeds. The dogs had received training in hunting raccoons, opossums, and escaped slaves. Turner led them on a circuit of the camp searching for the scent of Yankees. Packs of some five animals each had at least one "leader" or "catch hound," a canine at least a part blood hound. The prisoners never determined how the pack distinguished them from the guards. Joseph R. Achuff and two comrades bribed a guard with brass buttons to take them out on a wood detail. They then jumped him and escaped, "mugging the guard" being a common practice. In their trek, the fugitives crossed the Flint River three times and went down the river in a boat. The dogs

These engravings and those on the following pages, from prisoner memoirs, tell the story of the typical escapes—leaving Andersonville, being chased by hounds, traveling through an unknown land, receiving help from sympathetic Southerners, and finally, finding recapture or success. (R. S. Davis)

still found them, however, and a group of citizens turned them over to the guards. Other prisoners tried red pepper to defeat the pack. The mongrels and hounds, however, frequently failed at tracking prisoners. Some accounts have the dogs running past concealed prisoners, completely oblivious to the Yankees.

No contemporary account by a witness mentions these mongrels biting prisoners although such tales frequently found a place in memoirs written many years after the war and in the testimony submitted against Captain Wirz. When the dogs did stumble onto a fleeing man, they acted more like harmless pets

playing a game than vicious monsters. Boston Corbett of New Jersey, for example, tried to escape while outside the stockade on a work detail. The dogs tracked him down, but Corbett returned unharmed. He had received kind treatment by the pack and its handler, as other prisoners also claimed.[110]

Accounts exist, however, of men overcoming these problems of escape and all but reaching federal lines before suffering recapture. One veteran remembered two of Sherman's men brought back to Andersonville after being gone seven weeks. The prisoners had escaped by running off from one of

Andersonville's grave digging details. The men had eluded the dogs by crossing the Flint River. A bear chased them through a canebrake and they nearly drowned when rapids tore apart their raft. The soldiers lived in a cave for three weeks, receiving food from a sympathetic slave. The Confederates, however, recaptured them almost within hailing distance of the federal lines.[111] Tom Williams and two comrades from the 20th Indiana Infantry jumped a guard while on a detail to build the camp cookhouse. They escaped after leaving their captor gagged and bound to a tree. The guards soon captured his comrades but Williams evaded pursuit by hiding under logs in a millpond. He almost reached the mountains of north Georgia when the men and dogs of a patrol looking for deserters and escaped slaves caught him. His return to Andersonville provided an example to other prisoners of the futility of trying to escape. Joseph Lopez of the 99th New York and Frank Patrin, an Indian in the 4th Minnesota Infantry, escaped together from the stockade. They too returned after hiding out for weeks. Captain Wirz dubbed them the "swamp angels."[112]

The scheme devised by Henry M. Davidson of the 1st Ohio Light Artillery and two comrades, Hudson of Maryland and Beach of Wisconsin, proved that even careful planning only took one so far in an escape. Davidson found a small map of the southeastern states among the ashes of a fire left by a guard. Hudson stole a compass from the chief surgeon's office. The men secreted food in a nearby swamp and then made their exodus from the prison hospital. They took a circuitous route south before turning north, guaranteeing that the pursuing dogs would begin searching for them in the wrong direction. The escapees avoided houses and the often guarded roads while covering their scents by traveling through swamps. When they accidentally encountered Confederate soldiers, they explained their blue uniforms with the story that they were guards from Andersonville wearing clothes traded from the prisoners. On cloudy, starless nights, the fugitives used fireflies in a matchbox to illuminate their compass. With all of their preparation and care, they had almost reached General Sherman's federal lines near Atlanta when they blundered into recapture by the Confederate army.[113] Hugh R. Snee of the 39th Illinois would eventually escape, but after his first attempt, he came to a negative opinion about fleeing the stockade and traveling over land: "I will say right here that there was not at any time the remotest chance of escape from that prison any and all of such attempts were only a dangerous waste of energy that brought only punishment and despair."[114]

2

Despite the deplorable conditions and the weaknesses of the camp's security, the prisoners planned but failed to carry out a mass escape, a situation common in almost every prisoner of war camp that followed. The prisoners did form a secret organization, called the "liberators" or "Union League," to take over Andersonville. The conspirators received encouragement from reports of approaching federal cavalry and hoped that the guards would flee in the face of a resulting stampede by the tens of thousands of inmates.

Later, they came to see the rumors and newspaper reports of pending exchanges as false hope. The inmates then plotted to tunnel out of the stockade, overwhelm the guards, and seize local civilians as hostages. An informant reported the plan to the guards. On 20 April, the prison authorities called up the local militia to stop this scheme.[115]

Something else also prevented the greatest of Civil War breakouts from occurring. The garrison of Camp Sumter learned, as many guards have over time, that terror to the individual contains the masses even against the best of odds. An occasional show of force, such as parading the troops, the calling out of the local militia, or firing a cannon or two, reinforced the perceived threat of the garrison's ability to kill at least some of the inmates in any mass escape.

On 24 June, Andersonville commandant and Brigadier Confederate General John Winder wrote that white sympathy for the prisoners at Andersonville had grown so strong that even the local people plotted with General Sherman to organize the greatest escape of the war. Winder believed that people in nearby counties had stockpiled arms for the prisoners in preparation for the greatest of mass prison breakouts.

He had reasons for his concerns. A letter from a civilian at Anderson Station warned that the some three hundred prisoners allowed to live and work outside of the stockade had the potential for organizing such a plot. A report appeared in the Southern press that a mysterious group of horsemen, suspected of being federal spies posing as Confederate guerrillas, had appeared in the Andersonville area. In an incident described at Wirz's later trial, Winder turned back women claiming to bring a few wagon loads of provisions to the camp for the tens of thousands of prisoners. Likely, the general believed that he stopped some plot to release the prisoners.[116]

People of questionable motives and loyalties frequently drew the attention of camp officials. Captain Henry Wirz, for example, had an Ann Williams from federally occupied Liberty County, Georgia, arrested. She had come to the camp to have sexual relations for free with the prisoners. Wirz reported that Williams had carnal knowledge of at least seven of the inmates. Rhode Island-born, Charleston, South Carolina, merchant Lorenzo T. Potter, on behalf of his wife, Eliza, bribed Confederate officials to ship supplies to the prisoners at Andersonville.[117]

Local residents did have mixed feelings about the prisoners. They helped to build the prison, under protest, while fearing for mass prisoner escapes and looting by the guards. They could smell, if not see, the conditions there. Ambrose Spencer lived nearby. He claimed that some of his neighbors felt that escaped prisoners should be shot, mutinous prisoners hanged, and sick prisoners poisoned, to save rations for the starving Confederate soldiers. His neighbor, Mrs. Cunningham, routinely fed escaped prisoners but only out of fear that they might otherwise harm her.[118] Contacting the local people could prove dangerous. One fugitive reached a house and compelled the woman there to cook him breakfast. While preparing the meal she grabbed a gun and then marched her prisoner seven miles back to Andersonville. In Monroe County, Georgia, north of Macon, two men suffered recapture while trying to force a family to feed them. Citizens of Chattahoochee County, using dogs, captured two other men.[119]

Many white Southerners did pity the Andersonville prisoners. John R. Tate owed his successful escape to a small boy, Z. T. Walker, and the child's brother and sister. They lived six miles from the prison and nursed him back to health before sending him on with a sack of food. George W. Bailey escaped en route to Andersonville. Several white and black families in the Conyers area helped him, including one household with a crippled Confederate veteran and a family with a son who served as a guard at Andersonville. Aaron Bachman, during his escape in the last days of the war, discovered that almost everyone he encountered wanted to help him, including two men who fired guns in the air to pretend to have killed him and his comrade.[120] Prisoners Brumer and Hoyt escaped and traveled for three weeks to reach the swamps of North Carolina. A community of Southern Unionists and deserters hiding in "Devil's Swamp" took them in and treated these fellow refugees well.[121]

Other prisoners had similar experiences but with particular twists of irony. Joseph S. Keen and two other escapees encountered six armed Confederate deserters in a cornfield near Atlanta. The two different groups of fugitives got along well and discovered that they had Sumter County in common. The Yankees had fled from a prison camp located near the homes where these deserters sought to return! Joseph Lopez had received a coat from a sympathetic

Confederate colonel who heard that he would go to the infamous prison. During his escape, recapture, and return to Andersonville, the Yankee soldier received aid and sympathy from a Southern deserter, a white woman, the Confederate captain who recaptured him, and even from Captain Henry Wirz![122]

Some women in the neighborhood of the prison tried to ease the suffering in the camp, such as Lucy Herrington who carried food to the sick prisoners.[123] In January 1865, Wirz wrote of a suspicious Mrs. Spaulding from Americus whose husband played a prominent role in a local Unionist meeting. She came to visit a federal soldier from nearby Americus who had traveled north at the beginning of the war, married there, and enlisted from Dubuque in an Iowa regiment. He had smuggled a letter out of the prison by way of a friend among the guards. Mrs. Spaulding had been in the North. She brought back the reply as a family friend, while also inquiring about buying federal currency from the prisoners. A Mary Rawson of nearby Plains also regularly visited a Peter Kiene of the 16th Iowa and brought him food baskets.[124]

An unknown soldier from Lexington, Kentucky, received aid from Agnes Spencer, Ambrose's wife and likely the "Mrs. Spaulding" referred to by Wirz. This prisoner had fled on a freezing cold day in January 1865, apparently without further thought as to how he would escape. Recaptured, he made a rare escape directly from the guards. With only rags for clothes, he hid for three days in the winter weather. A sympathetic slave found him and directed him to the Spencer home. Agnes fed, clothed, and sheltered the fugitive until he could safely move on to rescue at St. Marks, Florida. The soldier had lived so primitively for so long that he had to relearn how to use of eating utensils.

Adam E. Head of the 12th Ohio Heavy Artillery had made a similar escape to Tennessee the previous July. He and a friend fled while taking a corpse out of the stockade. Guards killed his comrade but Adam succeeded in escaping from pursuing dogs because a providential rain covered his scent. Slaves found him sick. They took him to Unionist Emily Karnes of Talbot County. She nursed him back to health over three weeks and then set him on the road to freedom with five days' supply of rations.[125]

Three other escaped prisoners unintentionally found very different, sympathetic white Southerners. Charles Mather Smith of the 1st Massachusetts Cavalry, with Dr. Ashley W. Barrows of the 27th Massachusetts and Allington A. Crandall of the 53rd Pennsylvania, sought to avoid the obvious in their escape. Barrows worked as a doctor in the hospital and managed to slip Smith out of the stockade as his assistant. Crandall simply walked to the hospital. He gambled on the good fortune of the guards ignoring what appeared to be normal activities. As most escapes occurred at night, they took the unexpected risk of fleeing during the daylight of 9 October 1864 with their clothes filled with biscuits made at the hospital as well as medicine, matches, salt, and bacon. They used turpentine to hide their scents from the dogs.

They had a curious odyssey by any standard. Deciding that reaching Sherman's army posed too many risks, they sought the ocean, using a crude map and the stars for guidance. To determine their location, they questioned elderly women they found at home alone. At night, the fugitives had to evade raccoon hunters. On foot and using six different boats, they passed through Alabama to reach the Florida coast at the mouth of the Choctawhatchie River, near the present-day Eglin Air Force Base.

After taking twenty-five days to cover four hundred miles, these refugees discovered that they had no idea of how to reach the federal fleet. In desperation, they sought advice from Thomas Reddick, a local Southerner they had met and who had mistaken them for Confederate deserters. Unbeknownst to the Yankees, however, four of Reddick's sons had died in the Confederate army, ninety of his slaves had abandoned him for the federal lines, and the United States Navy had destroyed his $1,500 sloop. Although he had little regard for Yankees, he refused to turn away men in such a desperate need of help. Reddick took them to Eli Wright, a nearby Unionist. Fearing retaliation by one side or the other, Eli initially declined to help. With great reluctance, the Wright family finally agreed to provide for the fugitives for a few days until a federal ship arrived. When a vessel failed to appear, Wright directed the fugitives to George Brown, a pro-Secessionist local bandit with an arm paralyzed from a fight. Brown had a boat that could take them to the blockading federal fleet. Using guns loaned by Wright, the Yankees removed Brown's revolver and Bowie knife before forcing him to take them all to his vessel. After an opossum and potato dinner, the escapees and the pirate set sail. Thirty miles out to sea, the fugitives found a federal warship and safety. Smith wrote of the ship's flag, "No one except the man who has been a prisoner of war can understand my emotions.... Its red never appeared so red, its white never so white, blue never so blue and its stars never shone with such a luster to my eyes as on that 11th day of November, 1864!"[126]

3

Determining even how many men escaped from Andersonville may never be possible. Some lists of the names do survive. Two volumes, begun at the prison as a death register, also include incomplete lists of escapees. The federal Commissary General of Prisoners also maintained lists, for purposes of paying these men for rations owed to them during their captivity by the United States government. Many prisoners did not know to apply for this benefit, however.[127] In the more than a century since the establishment of a national cemetery at Andersonville, the staff has compiled a database of some thirty-seven thousand names of the almost forty thousand prisoners.[128] The current version of the Andersonville database, prepared by Jack Lundquist, includes information copied from the Confederate registers with supplemental information from visitors and federal rosters published after the war.[129]

Many of the men now remembered as having escaped from Camp Sumter, however, actually escaped from other prisons. Hundreds of these federal soldiers successfully fled from Confederate confinement in Atlanta, Blackshear, Charleston, Columbia, Dalton, Florence, Macon, Salisbury, and elsewhere, or they jumped through holes cut in train cars while being transported between prisons. Also, contrary to many family stories, the only officers who spent any lengthy time at Andersonville commanded black troops.[130]

Statistics from the contemporary sources fail to accurately answer the question concerning the true number of escapes. The first prisoners arrived in February 1864, but morning reports survive only from the following 1 April, when the prison already had a population of 7,106 and the cemetery held 304 of their comrades. Prisoners had already successfully escaped by that time, according to Confederate sources, and newspaper accounts reported two or three men as still out in late May. Guards also declined to record escapes foiled before the compiling of each morning's roll call. For example, the morning reports for August 1864 show thirty men as having escaped and four as recaptured. Captain Wirz, however, estimated that another twenty-five prisoners had escaped but the guards had them recaptured before the morning roll.[131]

Prisoner memoirs also fail to provide an answer to the number of escapes. Some of the survivors wrote that no one successfully escaped from Camp Sumter.[132] Ransom T. Powell, the Yankee drummer boy who worked as an orderly for Captain Wirz, believed that only DeLayvan Streeter successfully fled from the prison. George W. Rumble claimed his as one of only seventeen successful escapes from Andersonville. W. F. Lyon of the 9th Minnesota wrote that twenty-five escapees reached the federal lines.[133] Popular accounts of Andersonville give the percentage of these special men as one percent of the total number of prisoners, or approximately 390. That number seems too high, even if it included the 338 men who, according to the Commissary General of Prisoner records, enlisted in the Confederate army and others who left to work for the Confederacy as skilled craftsmen.[134] A chart, based on Wirz's morning reports and published by Ambrose Spencer in his 1866 book, shows that 328 escapes occurred from Camp Sumter, a minuscule number of the 2,696 men estimated to have gotten away from Confederate imprisonment for the whole war. Spencer, however, did not deduct the official number of prisoners recaptured—181 men—from Wirz's official morning reports. Subtracting that number from the escapes gives an official total of 147 inmates (44.82 percent of 328 recorded escapes) who escaped without return.[135]

The previously mentioned Andersonville database, based on surviving Confederate registers, identifies 169 men as having escaped, something close to the previous figure of 147. Even those numbers prove suspect. Captain Wirz wrote, for example, that from 1 April 1864, when he began his reports, to the end of the following July, that only twenty-seven men escaped without recapture. His morning reports for this period, however, show thirty-four more prisoners having fled than those recaptured. Similarly, Wirz reported thirteen men as having escaped on 18 October 1864, but diarist William H. Smith claimed that eighteen men actually fled. He added that three men gave up when a guard snapped a gun at them, and eleven more of the group were immediately tracked down by the dogs. The returns also fail to count as recaptured the more than one hundred men who escaped in September 1864, and who later, after recapture outside of the camp, went to other prisons without any report sent to Andersonville. Wirz's numbers of escapes are further inflated by including some men like Josiah J. Morefield and his comrades who freed themselves by jumping from trains, sometimes by cutting holes in the bottom of the cars, en route to or from the camp.[136] Some of the men on those lists and returns succeeded in fleeing the stockade, but as historian William Marvel wrote, only found "a quiet end in some Georgia swamp or forest."[137] Captain F. J. Browning of the 28th Georgia Confederate Cavalry told Joseph Lopez, whom he both recaptured and rescued, that several Yankees had been found dead in south Georgia after escaping. They had starved to death from trying to subsist on weeds and roots.[138]

Part of the problem of determining the number of successful fugitives has been in defining a meaningful escape from Andersonville. For example, Richard Thatcher proclaimed his leaving Andersonville with his comrade Harris P. Weir as "a successful escape," when they were actually only exchanged. Private Adam Fornof of the 37th Ohio Volunteer Infantry left the prison with them on 19 September 1864. Rejected as qualified for parole by federal officers, he later escaped from a train near Macon, Georgia, en route back to Anderson Station. By crawling through a ditch on all fours for a mile and a half, as well as by "constant running and dodging," he survived "the terror and excitement of such an escape."[139] Similarly, William Morgan Davies also slipped in among these men and escaped. Along with Wakeman Bell, Davies escaped on the march to the exchange and traveled fifteen miles to the federal lines.[140] They had harrowing adventures, but they fail to qualify as escaping from Andersonville as they did not flee directly from the prison. Similarly, Thomas Hinds would survive to publish a lengthy account of his adventures from starting with his confinement at Andersonville to reaching the federal lines. Between those two points, however, he suffered recapture and, technically, he made his successful escape from the Bibb County jail.[141]

Many of these fugitives trekked across a hostile landscape inhabited by desperate deserters, refugees, fugitive slaves, and bandits. Henry McKinzie of the 14th Illinois escaped to federal lines at New Orleans. A group of Andersonville escapees reached safety in coastal North Carolina in October 1864. Although certainly former Andersonville prisoners, however, they likely actually fled from a train near the prison at Florence, South Carolina.[142] Harkness N. Lay escaped from a train while being transferred from Andersonville. He traveled hundreds of miles to Georgetown, South Carolina, before suffering recapture.[143]

To have escaped officially from Andersonville also required having someone seeking to return the fugitive to confinement in the prison. Jesse Altom, W. T. Ziegler, and fifty of their fellow prisoners signed a parole on 18 April 1865, and took a train to Albany, Georgia. From there, they began a long odyssey by train and on foot that brought them back within sight of the prison before, abandoned by their guards, they finally reached federal lines near Jacksonville, Florida, on 28 April. This trek cost at least one prisoner his life and constituted a harrowing escape although technically these men fail to count as either prisoners or fugitives. Michael Heiman and several other men similarly escaped from the prison late in the war. Local people rounded them up and sent them back to Andersonville. With the stockade all but abandoned, they took a train to the federal forces in Macon. Strictly speaking, they left the prison unopposed rather than escaped.[144]

Accepting the narrowest definition of escape and the lowest numbers, perhaps W. F. Lyon was correct in claiming that only twenty-five men succeeded in obtaining their freedom from Camp Sumter and returning to "God's country," prison slang for the federal lines. Statistics of successful escapes from other Confederate prisons prove equally murky, but considering Andersonville's much greater number of inmates, any number given for its successful escapees appears minuscule compared to the three hundred or more men who escaped permanently from just Salisbury prison in North Carolina.

The adventures of these men from Andersonville appear all the greater because they numbered so few. Memoirs of survivors imply that almost everyone in the stockade tried to help themselves and their country by considering escape. Reuben C. Griffitt claimed that ninety-nine percent of the prisoners looked for a chance at escape, each man making plans and considering risks by methods that reflected his own character and background. Statistics paint a very different picture, however. The 328 recorded escapes out of some 40,000 prisoners came to only 1 escape per 119 men. As some inmates, such as Warren Goss, made more than one attempt, the number of individual prisoners who made a serious effort to get out must have been far less, perhaps only 1 man in 230 prisoners of war.[145]

4

With so few men successfully making escapes and limited information concerning their journeys, credible generalizations prove difficult to make. Records seldom survive to confirm the details in the escape accounts or to expose exaggerations and misinformation. Existing information supports some conclusions however.

Men with the shortest time in captivity would logically seem to be the best candidates for successful escapes due to their better physical condition and morale. Available information, however, suggests that opportunity rather than time in captivity had the greater bearing on escape attempts. Many escapees spent nine months or more as prisoners before making their own release. Lawrence LeBron would suffer from scurvy so severely at Andersonville that he gave away his belongings and prepared to die. He lived to escape, however.[146]

Also, when prisoners fled in groups (usually no more than three men), they often hailed from different regiments and even states. Men who thus tried to break out banded together primarily out of a mutual desire to escape, not from some unit camaraderie. Aaron Bachman claimed that the inmates came together in groups based upon common interests, from church groups to robbers. The serious and determined escape risks apparently organized in the same way. Private Alphonso Barrows of the Vermont Cavalry serves as such an example. He had been a prisoner since October 1863. Eleven months later, he and John Wolcott of the 5th Michigan Infantry ran off from a work detail for gathering wood. They bluffed their way through a patrol by Wolcott claiming that they were guards from the 55th Georgia. The two fleeing Yankees had carefully planned their escape. With previously concealed onions, turpentine, and skunk odor obtained from slaves, they defeated the camp's dog pack. They had also squirreled away biscuits and a compass. Like many other men from Andersonville at that time, they traveled "day and night, through cane brakes and swamps and over rivers, and through thick woods, for eight days and nights," to reach the safety of the federal lines north of Atlanta. Barrows had been captured serving under General Kilpatrick in Virginia. He happily received his general, now serving under Sherman, as a guest.[147]

Psychological studies have suggested that such escapees from prisons do so out of a personal nature to leave confinement, coupled with a love of adventure. Modern military critic Shimon Tzabar wrote of this "barbed wire disease," as a psychotic form of boredom that results from more than maltreatment and which reduces individuals to a level of idiocy. The victims recover by working at escape or taking dramatic physical risks such as fleeing guards. The Civil War era produced a number of such persons, including spies and "conductors" (white persons who helped escaped slaves in "free states" to reach Canada through the legendary Underground Railroad). A New Orleans physician diagnosed this malady, when it appeared in slaves, as "drapetomania," from the Greek words for "enslaved" and "insane." Even today, many career criminals, journalists, missionaries, entrepreneurs, soldiers, and explorers suffer from the same compulsion. By this definition, the more the guards did to keep such men in Andersonville, the more the guards unintentionally encouraged this particular type of prisoner to escape.[148]

Barbed wire disease achieved epidemic status during the Civil War. Federal Fort Delaware, for example, held roughly as many men as Andersonville although the inmates lived in much better and far less isolated circumstances. Understandably, considering the closer location to safe refuge, twice as many men escaped from the former as the latter. Of the escapees, however, the two camps had the same ratio of completely successful fugitives to failures, roughly one man in seven who fled.[149] Simon Dufur saw the same malady in a particularly fatal form. He witnessed ten to fifteen Indians from a western regiment enter the prison and all die within less than three months. He wrote that they found the confinement intolerable.[150]

Some prisoners did illustrate "barbed wire disease" in the extreme, such as George R. Barse of the 5th Michigan Cavalry. He escaped from prison trains three times just on the trip to Georgia. Thomas Boyle escaped and suffered recapture three times before he, after "many hairbreadth escapes and thrilling adventures," reached the federal lines near Atlanta without having learned the name of the prison, or where it stood, near Americus.

DeLayvan Read Streeter of the 100th Ohio, on 3 March 1864, probably became the first man to successfully escape from Andersonville and represents a particularly strong case of barbed wire disease. He had tried to flee from Belle Island near Richmond, Virginia, twice before receiving weeks of solitary confinement. He survived by breaking into the adjoining commissary building every night before returning to his pen undetected. Andersonville had been open less than a week when Streeter arrived there. Initially, the prisoners at Andersonville had more rations, better shelter, and much more space than at Belle Island, although they found themselves almost one thousand miles deeper into the Confederacy. Almost immediately, however, Streeter prepared for his escape and left without leaving a record with the camp authorities that he had even been there. He and Ira Beverly went out on a wood detail and brought back a pole they had made from a tree. On the first stormy night, they used it to scale the unfinished stockade and then, using a rope made from strips torn from a blanket, climbed down the wall. When they heard the camp's dogs pursuing them, they split up. Beverly followed the railroad tracks only to suffer recapture. Streeter knew the camp dogs received training in chasing escaped slaves. He deliberately crisscrossed slave trails to confuse the dogs. At the Flint River, he crossed a bridge, while slipping past a sleeping guard. Streeter then built a raft that eventually wrecked on rocks. Using a canoe, he continued his journey until thrown into the river by a collision with an unforeseen ferry rope. Later, rescued by slaves, he eventually reached a federal gunboat that took him to New York and a thirty-day leave before he returned to his regiment near Atlanta. Captured again, he had the unique distinction of having been captured in battle twice and sent to Andersonville both times. He returned to a very different prison camp, one now grossly overcrowded, more heavily guarded, and packed with starving, desperate men. Streeter and many of his fellow inmates soon received transfers to Savannah, where he escaped once again and hid out with a German family until Sherman's army arrived.[151]

Other soldiers made numerous escape attempts. John R. Tate suffered recapture twice before he made his successful escape. Even then, he accidentally found himself surrounded by the Confederate Army withdrawing from the Battle of Jonesboro. Mistaking him for one of their own, the Confederacy conscripted him as an ambulance driver. Near Newnan, he abandoned the vehicle and its ailing passenger to reach the federal lines.[152] John R. Porter failed to arrive at Andersonville because he escaped twice en route to the prison. He also used an assumed name because he had escaped after his capture in 1862 as one of the federal soldiers involved in the clandestine Andrews Raid or "Great Locomotive Chase." He feared the Confederates would hang him as they had some of his fellow saboteurs. Andrew J. Arnold left Andersonville repeatedly only to suffer recapture every time.[153]

George Mussen of the 2nd Ohio Cavalry had experiences that represent an obsession with the great journey of escape. He failed in his escape attempt while traveling between Andersonville and another prison. When the inmates on the island prison at Blackshear found themselves ordered back to Andersonville, he and a friend tried to hide in a hole in order to escape after the guards abandoned the area. The guards found them while burning out the camp. Members of the 4th Georgia militia caught him and his comrades after they subsequently jumped from a train. The railroad line ended at Thomasville, and during the march back to Andersonville, Mussen and his comrades again escaped. They assumed an identity of paroled prisoners. In this guise, they deceived soldiers, deserters, and civilians who often gave them food. The Confederate provost marshal in Thomasville, however, saw through their tale and again they found themselves back in Andersonville. At the end of the war, Mussen failed to appreciate that he had received an exchange. He and friends "escaped" one last time, and with fellow inmates, reached the federal lines in Macon. Mussen arrived in time to save a former slave from the federal provost by supporting the black man's story that he had helped a wounded Yankee named Pete Barringer, an escapee from Andersonville. Unable to find transportation beyond the ruins of what had been the city of Atlanta, Mussen and his friends risked their lives by passing through guerrilla-infested north Georgia in their hurry to get home.[154]

5

"Barbed wire disease" explains the persistence that often resulted in success for the prisoners determined to be free, but it fails to account for all escape attempts from Andersonville. The morning reports, for the spring of 1864, show that as the camp became more overcrowded and conditions correspondingly deteriorated, the number of escapes increased rapidly. Only eight men officially fled in April 1864, with seven of them quickly recovered. The remaining man, Tom Williams, also eventually found himself returned to the stockade. (Another man, Peter Bateman of the 14th Ohio Infantry, however, reportedly successfully escaped on 1 April.) The first men recorded as having escaped without being returned, according to Confederate records, left during the first week of May. The number of fugitives "out" jumped to thirty-one prisoners following the first major escapes on 23–24 May. Of thirteen of these escapees, seven became immediate returns. The successful included William Dickerson Freeman and Francis J. Liggett of the 112th Indiana. After suffering "untold hunger and fatigue," they became among the first men to reach Sherman's approaching armies.

In the summer of 1864, historian Robert Doyle's most important condition for the traditional American escape—opportunity—especially when organized in groups finally occurred. With the proximity of Sherman's army, most of the prisoners of war believed that they finally had a real opportunity for a successful escape. In June 1864, thirty-seven men left during just a ten-day period. By the middle of June, Henry B. Sparks wrote in his diary that many men had escaped, and the guards could do little to prevent more from leaving. In August, the prison population reached its greatest number of 33,006. The mortality number rose to 2,992 men for that month, an increase in deaths by 58 percent despite a population increase of less than 4 percent. The number of escapes increased from twenty in July to thirty in August, but both months saw fewer than the forty-seven escapes in June.

Because of the deteriorating conditions, the abandonment of hope for exchange, the proximity to Sherman's army, fear of violent action by the guards in response to a perceived threat of federal cavalry, or a combination of these factors, in September, the number of escapes soared to the prison's official high of eighty-four. Only thirty of these men suffered immediate recapture and return to the prison. Sixty-six men left between 9–13 September; following the wild celebration of the prisoners to special news from the sentinels. The veterans would long remember the call from the guard stations: "Post number four, nine o'clock, and Atlanta has gone to Hell" and to capture by General Sherman. The escape accounts that survive, however, come from only from the periods before and after the September exodus from the prison. Private Josiah Dye of the 52nd Ohio, for example, fell into Confederate hands during the fighting around Atlanta on 19 July 1864; he and G. F. Rothrock of the 20th Ohio escaped on 17 October and, undoubtedly with great effort, succeeded in contacting the United States bark *Ethan Allen* off Dobey Island near Savannah on 22 November. They arrived there just in time to witness the surrender of the city to Sherman's troops![155]

These later escapes from Andersonville inadvertently worked against their chances for success. By September, in the wake of Sherman's advance, the Confederacy had begun evacuating prisoners from Andersonville, shipping them to other camps. Prisoners escaped from the trains transporting them, usually through holes made in the car floors. Posses and militias, called out to defend against the federal invasion and the related attempts by slaves to escape, quickly formed and proved effective in recapturing both these prisoners and the men who escaped directly from Andersonville. The captured men went to new prison camps.

Only 8,218 soldiers remained at Andersonville at the end of September; half of those men remained in the prison at the end of October. Thirteen men still escaped on 18 October. Among the few thousand, largely sick men left in the camp, the number of escapes per month remained in the double digits until March 1865. All but a few of these men were returned to the prison.[156]

6

Legend wrongly credits tunnels as the most frequent means of secretly fleeing Andersonville. Most family stories of escape tell of leaving from Andersonville by this means. One guard even attributed the Providence Spring (the source of badly needed fresh water in the stockade that originated with a lightening bolt) to depressions caused by so many tunnels.

Many inmates did try to escape by going under the wall. The men at Camp Sumter had an advantage over prisoners in some other prisons. With no river around them, they avoided the danger of drowning. Typically some one hundred men, called "shareholders," would form a [mining] "company" to do this clandestine work. Men would shift from one tunnel project to another, more promising effort. Even participating in failed tunneling projects could earn prestige for an individual. Men whose efforts earned them some notoriety could share such acquired knowledge as exiting the tunnel in the dark when the noise of the insects could cover the sound of fleeing feet.

In theory, tunneling allowed prisoners to escape in secrecy and at a time largely decided by the digger. They did have to hide tunnel entrances inside wells and shelters, as well as under blankets, litter, leaves, and even sick comrades. Diggers disposed of removed dirt by scattering it around the camp or putting it in with the earth turned up by digging wells. Tunnelers used anything with a sharp edge as a digging tool. Halves of tin canteens often served for shovels. Old bootlegs and split pieces of pinewood became buckets. Tunneling typically required five to seven weeks. Diggers worked at night to avoid capture during the daylight searches and used small amounts of water as a level to keep the tunnels horizontal. Tunnels frequently extended from ten to five hundred feet long and as much as twenty feet below the surface.[157]

Few tunnelers, however, succeeded in digging out. From 1 April through the end of July, Wirz reported that of eighty-three excavations found and filled in, only one man succeeded in leaving by tunnel. One survivor agreed, claiming that only one digger ever escaped. Another memoirist wrote that only three men successfully went out. Prisoner George W. Fechter kept track of much of what went on in the stockade. He remembered that few of the many tunnel projects succeeded. When anyone did escape, rumors would fly around the camp greatly exaggerating the number of men who escaped. Henry B. Sparks, for example, wrote of thirty men or more leaving in early May when, in fact, only five made it out and at least three of them soon found themselves back in custody. Another diarist wrote that at least one hundred men dug their way to freedom in late July 1864. If that escape did occur, anyone who made it to the outside found himself recaptured so fast that his escape would fail to even register on the morning report. Some forty men, however, had at least a brief stay outside the stockade in late August, after escaping through a five-hundred-foot tunnel.[158]

Too many obstacles stood in the way of a successful tunnel. Seemingly as fast as an excavation began, paid informants, or "tunnel traitors," reported the new project to Captain Wirz. Allegedly, an individual reward might be as small as a plug of tobacco. Wirz also disguised guards as prisoners to learn of escape plans. The often-told story of the death of "Chickamauga" (Thomas W. Hurlbut of the 84th Illinois) came about because of a tunnel. A guard shot him on 16 May 1864, when he refused, after repeated warnings, to leave the dead line area.

The one-legged prisoner had fled there to escape from angry inmates who believed that he had reported a tunnel attempt. Had he actually done so, he could only have informed on one of the first tunnels attempted.[159]

Discovery of excavations occurred by many means. Guards located one tunnel when they noticed five hundred men gathered around a hole awaiting their chance to escape. An effort to leave this "Eve-less Eden" by the ever sarcastic Charles Richardson of the 76th New York ended when a guard caught him discharging dirt hidden in his shirt. Excavations in the sandy soil could collapse, usually killing the tunneler. The weight of the palisades sometimes caused the logs to crash through the tunnel ceilings. Guards sometimes learned of these projects when an unfortunate digger "squalled" for the guards to come to his rescue. A tunnel had to go down at least eight feet and then run horizontally at least thirty feet to clear the camp's palisade and the dead line. Warren Goss helped to dig two tunnels that failed to even cross the dead line. In his second attempt, the tunnel caved in, and he owed his rescue to the guards. If a tunnel extended more than sixty to eighty feet horizontally, ventilation became a problem. Further, John McElroy and his "company" dug a tunnel for forty feet before it collapsed inside the camp. They had lost their direction and had unintentionally dug it in a horseshoe shape that brought the end of the tunnel back to within fifteen feet of where it had begun! Predicting exactly when a tunnel would clear the stockade proved impossible. Reuben Griffitt became a "stockholder" in several of these ventures although he never escaped by tunnel. He found that the final "push out" could take forty-eight hours, forty-eight minutes, or a week.[160]

The guards also created obstacles to defeat the tunnels. Slaves would use crowbars to probe the ground for tunnels. In late July, the guards ringed the prison with a second stockade, two hundred feet outside of the original wall, and began construction on a third wall, in part, to require tunnelers to extend their work even further to reach the outside. The guards detailed prisoners to add a trench inside the dead line to expose any tunnels.[161] By 23 August, a nightly picket line of guards around the camp increased the possibility of detection.

Tunnels did prove to be a source of entertainment for the whole prison. The obvious lack of success of the tunnels suggests that the prisoners worked on them more as an act of defiance and even recreation than from any realistic hope of getting out of the stockade. It became almost the only form of amusement, other than gambling or prayer/patriotic meetings, in the overcrowded prison. The tunnel projects raised morale but also provided false hopes that discouraged the inmates from organizing a mass rush on the poorly armed and badly outnumbered guards. John Northrop of the 76th New York wrote in his diary of one hapless tunneler coming up beneath an armed guard. Another group of diggers reportedly broke into a tent where two of the guards played cards. On another occasion, a tunneler came up underneath a guard sleeping on the ground. One night, a tunnel project ended up on a small hill underneath a campfire where some of the Georgia reserves were sleeping and others warmed themselves. The guards fled in terror. Inmates in Andersonville were "smoked," that is covered in soot from the softwood campfire smoke that drifted across the camp. The superstitious Southerners mistook the first man out of the tunnel for the devil rising from hell! The first tunneler escaped although the guards soon had his partners in custody.[162]

Some men did succeed in getting out. William L. Farmer of the 111th Illinois Volunteers even used the shortcomings of the tunnels to escape. A prisoner at Andersonville for only two weeks after his capture on 8 June 1864, he blackmailed some diggers into allowing him to join them by threatening to report their tunnel to the Confederates. When a man working on the excavation failed to return one night, Farmer drew the lot to crawl in and see if their comrade had escaped or had become trapped in a cave-in. Farmer discovered that the digger had made it out and escaped. Instead of reporting to his partners, he too took the opportunity to flee. He hid in the swamps a quarter of a mile from the prison using the water to shield his scent from the hounds. Slaves concealed and fed him until he could reach the federal lines.[163]

7

Most escapes actually began with the prisoner fleeing from one of the camp's various work details. In his June 1864 returns, for example, Captain Henry Wirz wrote that all of that month's escapees had fled from work details. The volunteers on this duty faced scorn and sometimes physical abuse from men who remained inside the stockade, suffering men who saw them as collaborators and traitors. In addition to the guarded groups of workmen needed to bring in wood and take out the dead, Wirz often had at least three hundred Yankees working outside the walls on parole. He had to continue allowing them to live outside the stockade, even after a group of them assaulted his family and took Wirz's buggy for a joy ride.

Punishments for such transactions and escapes usually only lasted for a few hours. Inmate Herman A. Braun believed that the guards only punished those prisoners of war who had violated oaths by trying to escape while on duty outside of the prison although Pennsylvania cavalryman Aaron Bachman claimed that even under those circumstances the punishments could prove fatal. Bachman heard of a group of prisoners who enlisted in the Confederate Army and, after mutinying, killed two officers and took the rest of the unit as hostages. Supposedly, sick comrades they had to leave behind suffered execution in retaliation for the two dead Confederate soldiers. He also claimed that a dozen well-fed men from the cookhouse work detail obtained pistols and killed the dogs that pursued them in their escape. After their recapture, Bachman claimed that he watched as, starved and chained together day after day, all but three of the men died.[164]

The first officially noted escapes, in April 1864, proved typical of escapes in that the men fled work details. Three men tried to escape on 15 April (names and circumstances unknown), but they had been captured by the next roll call. More than a week later, an inmate fled from the hospital, where he worked as an attendant, but the guards brought him back in less than twenty-four hours. Three men, soon after, jumped a guard while on a wood detail and ran into the woods. The dogs soon tracked them down. A short time later, three more inmates made the same attempt. The guards brought back two men and believed that the third prisoner had drowned. They were mistaken. Tom Williams, the other man, survived to reach the federal lines and then later suffer recapture. In August, eleven men left work gangs after giving oaths that they would not try to escape. Frank Maddox, also known as Mattock, of the 35th United States Colored Troops (formerly the 1st North Carolina Colored Infantry) witnessed a disguised white prisoner named Bardo caught and punished for trying to leave the camp on a work detail of black prisoners. Prisoners Jasper Culver and Lewis Trowbridge made bread at the camp's bakery and loaded the dead/ration wagons, giving them not only access to the outside of the stockade but also rations to take with them during their escape. Private Sidney Moore of the 15th New York Infantry made an escape from the camp bakery and, aided by slaves, traveled north to rescue by McCook's cavalry near Atlanta. Dr. Ashley W. Barrows of the 27th Massachusetts fled the camp's hospital, where he worked as a doctor. The majority members of a burial detail took off on 8 September.[165]

Bribes to guards could facilitate such escapes. Michael Dougherty of the 13th Pennsylvania Cavalry wrote that prisoners used work details as opportunities for illicit trade for food with the guards, thereby creating contacts in the garrison. Captain Wirz claimed that of the thirty men who left in August, of whom the guards caught six, all had bribed guards with federal currency or ran off from work details. William Ray Toney, Roe Asburn, and a third comrade effectively used a twenty-dollar gold piece to persuade a guard to look the other way and to let them flee. Sergeant George H. Fonner of the 101st Pennsylvania made a typical escape. He bribed a guard to allow him to flee from the hospital detail. Fonner reached federal forces near Atlanta under sacks of corn in a slave driven wagon headed to the Confederate army. That the garrison failed to capture such fugitives, Wirz blamed on the guards avoiding the reporting of the men as having escaped. Usually, only during morning roll call were the escapees missed.[166]

Beyond tunnels and escaping from work details, prisoner M. V. B. Phillips remembered that the variety of means of escape attempts were numerous, odd, and "frequently amusing." He wrote of the bean box escape whereby prisoners left the stockade by hiding in the crates on the wagon that had brought in the prisoner's rations. Robert Knox Sneden remembered four or five prisoners escaping by that means on 7 September 1864.[167] John McElroy wrote of a prisoner caught trying to leave the stockade by hanging on to the bottom of the ration wagon. J. N. Hall of the 113th Ohio and a comrade named Williams escaped, in the dark, by passing through where the camp's creek flowed out of the stockade. The dog pack caught Hall but he believed that his friend got away. Frederick Guscetti of the 47th New York attempted to leave by posing as a corpse. As some days more than one hundred men died in the prison, hiding among the bodies did not pose a problem. Several prisoners left by that means until informants exposed this trick to the guards. Stripped almost naked, Guscetti thus rode out of the stockade on the same two mule wagons that brought in rations. Captain Wirz discovered him outside, but pitying the prisoner, ordered clothes for him and he returned to the stockade unpunished. Another soldier trying to leave by this means almost succeeded but his "rising" from the dead frightened and alarmed the black teamster, who then alerted the guard. An Ohio soldier did get out of Andersonville with the daily piles of the dead through the help of his friends. He nearly surrendered when one of his comrades tried to "help" him by suggesting to the guards that they shoot the "corpse" as insurance.[168]

Other prisoners tried to violate the camp's wall directly. Men could still slip undetected through gaps in the wall during autumn fogs. C. A. Smith of the 11th Iowa remembered four men on a dark night, reaching the stockade and simply digging directly under it. They escaped, but, with the help of the dog pack, the guards brought them back the next day. Smith sarcastically wrote that the guards tried to protect the prisoners from becoming lost in the swamps and falling prey to some beast. When rains caused a part of the stockade to fall, the camp authorities had it shored up with cross beams nailed to the interior of the wall. William Burge of the 11th Iowa took advantage of this addition to climb the wall on a dark, stormy night. Despite the rain and having to cross the Flint River, the dogs still tracked him down. The pack handler treated him kindly, and even Captain Wirz only punished him with a large dose of the Captain's famous profanity. John McElroy of the 16th Illinois Cavalry and fifty other prisoners tried to leave the stockade in the dark by climbing over the wall with a rope. The guards, warned by an informant, allowed fifteen men to get over. As each prisoner scaled the wall, the guards silently held a gun to his head and led him away to punishment on the chain gang.[169]

Other prisoners simply walked out of the stockade. George W. Rumble of the 3rd New York Cavalry made up enough of a Confederate uniform to blend in with the guards and then left with a train load of conscripts heading to the front, from where he escaped to the federal lines. Similarly, Henry Clay Damon of the 11th Michigan and William Smith of the 14th Pennsylvania Cavalry traded for gray garments worn by Tennessee federal soldiers. The Confederates who had originally captured them had made them exchange their uniforms for the gray rags their captors wore. When sergeants came in to take roll as usual, the two Yankees slipped out with them, disguised as sergeants. Damon even completed his disguise by carrying what looked like a roll book. They then continued their journey until reaching the Union army in Tennessee. During their twenty-three day journey, they did not encounter any Confederate soldiers.[170]

By means of contrast, Private Lawrence LeBron of the 11th Illinois would claim that he fought his way to freedom, in early September 1864, without anyone's help. He wrote that the Confederates included him in a party of prisoners shipped to another prison camp. He feigned illness and held back until he and his guard were alone. While pretending to need to relieve himself, he and the Confederate soldier stopped. LeBron then allegedly killed the guard; took the Confederate's musket and clothes; and dumped the body over a bridge. Reaching the train at dusk, LeBron rode atop a car, where he pretended to be a guard. Some twenty miles from Andersonville, he jumped from the train. Defying mosquitoes, heat, snakes, alligators, and hostile Southerners of both races, he reached north Georgia and, almost, Sherman's armies. He then avoided Davidson's mistake of trying to pass through the Confederate army. Instead, he used stars to steer him west to Mississippi. After two months of hiding and dodging, he finally returned to federal lines, close to where he had been captured while working as a scout a year earlier.[171]

Several inmates escaped by using ruses to join in prisoner exchanges, what the prisoners referred to as "flanking out." Some men bribed guards for places on these train rides home.[172] The notorious gamblers Charles Ellis and George W. Fechter, as well as J. C. Tarsney (by pretending to be the dead John Fultz) left that way. William Batterton of the 114th Illinois, and others, fell in with men chosen for an exchange and so escaped. Jasper Culver and two comrades did the same but later fell out of the group and hid in the bushes before they could be caught boarding the train without authorization. When the doctors selected sick soldiers for return to the federal lines, the Confederate surgeons passed over Private Passmore W. Hoopes of the 1st Pennsylvania Reserve Infantry. Returning to the stockade, he believed that he would die in the prison. With inspiration born of desperation, he ran to his "shebang" (hovel) and grabbed his haversack. Returning to the gate, he told the guards that the surgeons had selected him for the return to the federal lines and that he had only gone back for his belongings. Always pictured as gullible in these stories, the sentries ordered him to hurry along as the train had started to pull out. Hoopes thus caught his ride to freedom.[173] When sailors received an exchange, Sergeant Hiram Buckingham of the 16th Connecticut Infantry obtained enough of a navy uniform to pass out of the prison by assuming the identity of dead sailor Johnny Sullivan. Prison officials recorded his escape without ever learning how he left.[174]

Federal records credit David Jones, David Hughes, and David Winn [sic? David Weir?], all of Pennsylvania regiments and probably in the same mess, along with scout Thomas Cheshire of Tennessee, in making the greatest of these escapes when figured in miles. The federal Commissary General of Prisoners listed them as traveling more than two thousand miles from Andersonville to Key West, Florida. A newspaper account, however, sets their record straight. The previously mentioned Dr. Barrow in his escape had left Cheshire behind because of his lameness. Angry, Cheshire determined to create his own escape opportunity. He and his comrades bribed a guard to let them escape when they went out one night. Upon leaving Andersonville, they fled through swamps until they found a sympathetic slave. Their new friend carried them in his wagon, under a load of corn, for seventy miles through two towns and across a ferry. Another slave guided them to white Floridians who supported the Union. These allies then gave the fugitives a boat on Ochlockonee Bay, near Tallahassee. The United States mortar schooner *Oliver H. Lee*, en route to Key West, finally rescued the fugitives. These escapees did suffer hardships, including having only raw sweet potatoes to eat, but they had only traveled some two hundred miles while on the run.[175]

8

In any escape attempt, such outside help can prove a most valuable asset. Throughout the South, local people, black and white, aided fugitive federals, sometimes because of the stories of the horrors of Andersonville. This form of resistance likely began when the Confederacy impressed nine hundred slaves to build the prison at Anderson Station. Local whites had opposed the construction of the prison at Anderson, in part, out of fear that the Yankees would organize a slave revolt.[176] Plantation owners helped their workers to evade being taken as workers into the cause of maintaining slavery. Without any connection to the pre-war Underground Railroad, the first work of these African Americans in helping fugitive Yankees likely began out of pity. Tines Kindricks, as an old man, would recall his impressions from helping to build the Camp Sumter prison:

> I tell you, Boss, dat was about de worstest place dat ever I seen. Dat was where day keep all de Yankees dat day capture an' day had so many thare they couldn't nigh take care of them. Dey had them fenced up with a tall wire [sic? wall?] fence an never had enough house room for all dem Yankees. They would just throw de grub to 'em. De mostest dat day had for 'em to eat was peas an' the filth, it was terrible, de sickness, it broke out 'mongst 'em all the while, an all 'de while, an' day just die like rats what had been pizaned.[177]

The Andersonville survivors failed to see the irony of their situation, but Winslow Homer captured it in a painting popularly known as *Near Andersonville* (1865–1866).[178] He painted a slave woman watching federal prisoners escorted back to the prison after a failed escape attempt. She wears a turban, a rite of passage that demonstrated her maturity and ability to handle responsibility; a colored headscarf she wore at home in contrast to the white worn to church. Watching the captured Yankee marked a moment in her own transition from slave to free. When emancipation came, many of her friends and family, perhaps she as well, would wear hats as a symbol of self determination.[179] To black abolitionist Soujouner Truth, this painting showed how the sufferings of the Yankee prisoners at Andersonville became one of the many ways that America would pay for allowing slavery. In another interpretation, the painting represents how white Northerners had helped slaves to escape through the "free states" of the North to Canada, through the "Underground Railroad." Now African Americans helped fugitive white men—white men sent South to end black slavery—escape Southern confinement.

Fear of conspiracies among the enslaved became one of the great common threads of the history of slavery in Georgia and, even as early as 1844, a white Georgian reported of how the state's workers in bondage readily believed that "great men" would soon set them free. Statistics from the slave schedules of the 1850 census, however, show that few black Americans had successfully escaped. The 1860 schedule shows that even fewer of them made that journey successfully following the Fugitive Slave Act of 1850. Anecdotal evidence shows that such fugitives more likely found themselves recaptured, kidnapped, returned to

Winslow Homer, Untitled, ca. 1865–1866, Oil on canvas, The Collection of the Newark Museum

masters, and/or sold to new owners, even when legally free. What few records exist of pre-Civil War escapes omits any mention of Macon and Sumter counties.[180]

To the slave holders and the abolitionists, these escape attempts became so important as to help bring on the Civil War and to turn that conflict into a war of liberation. Except for the rare and isolated slave revolt, the Underground Railroad and escape attempts represented the principal opposition to slavery. Escape, like sabotage and work slow-downs, became part of the popular alternative campaign to bring down the institution of slavery by slaves who chose not to take up the suicidal course of armed confrontation against their masters. This other war depended upon individuals rather than an organized conspiracy. Without membership in organizations, escapees avoided betrayal and the inciting of widespread and violent white retaliation. As their descendents would do in the 1960s by avoiding violence, the runaway slaves also spared their white sympathizers from having to condone threats to life and property for a noble cause. Many more slaves helped others to escape than tried to escape themselves.

Helping prisoners of the Confederacy reach federal lines must have seemed a natural extension of these tactics. Slaves in southwest Georgia, even though far beyond the reach of the famous Underground Railroad and born in bondage, had learned the problems of escaping by the time of the Civil War. By the winter of 1864, patrols for escaped slaves had become so ineffective that the slaves now regarded themselves as all but emancipated. Some of them joined the possibly half-million slaves who escaped to the federal lines, nineteen thousand of whom followed Sherman's nearby march across Georgia. These freedom fighters provided the Union army with information, workers, and distractions for the Confederacy's declining military, and, ultimately, soldiers and sailors.[181]

They also felt that they could help Yankee prisoners despite rumors that the Confederates had spies disguised as escaped soldiers. However, while a great deal has appeared in print about slaves as soldiers, and less about slaves as refugees, little has been written about them as conductors of their own underground railroad for fugitive white men. Some prisoner writers would later emphasize the aid provided by slaves because they wanted to educate the public that emancipation, at the least, had also been an effort by the enslaved to free themselves; it was more than just an abstract Yankee social ideal imposed on all races and classes of the South by federal force and blood. These prisoner narratives omit any portrayal of African Americans as stupid, childish, or naïve—descriptions they often gave of poor Southern whites.[182] Writers of the escape memoirs remembered the slave families as always striving to stay together, even when members lived on different plantations, an important observation often missed by many of the owners.

Unfortunately, the records remain silent on the names of these slaves who dared to help the white fugitives of Andersonville. Almost every credible account of escape from the prison mentions the help of African Americans, however. In 1948, E. Merton Coulter even made the comment, in describing the published memoirs of Henry M. Davidson, that it "is surprisingly free from hackneyed stories of heroic slaves assisting prisoners of war to escape."[183] Coulter's opinion aside, Davidson wrote his book to push for an exchange of prisoners and likely omitted references to the slaves in order to avoid hurting his cause by aggravating already inflamed racial prejudices among his white readers.

The account of Thomas Hinds, native Irishman and teenage member of the 1st Maryland Infantry, best illustrates the help frequently received from blacks during an escape from Andersonville. He had already learned that he could get aid from slaves during a previous unsuccessful attempt to flee near Macon. Hinds left out of Andersonville on the pretense of being part of a detail to gather wood for a shelter on 6 June 1864. To facilitate his escape, he waited until he had a fat, elderly conscript from Mobile of known good nature as his only guard. When the sentry looked in another direction, Hinds quietly slipped into the woods and escaped. The rain from a sudden thunder storm masked his scent from pursuing dogs.

Along his route, slave families often helped him. At different times, they provided him with food, clothes, shoes, money, a gun, a knife, medical attention, and even a map from an atlas. One slave carried the escaped Yankee some distance to conceal Hinds's scent from dogs. His benefactors even tried to fit him in a dress to disguise him as a slave girl. Hinds needed their help, for he had left the prison with no real idea of what to do next. For much of his odyssey, he had a recurring fever and painful, swollen feet.

During his journey, he learned much about slavery in the Old South. On a Dr. Winn's plantation, he discovered that several of the slaves had learned to read, a rarity among slaves. A black blacksmith took him to the plantation prayer meetings. Hinds met a native African, an elderly man who had lived throughout Georgia and had tried to escape several times. The two veteran fugitives likely shared experiences. A black overseer betrayed Hinds near Butler, Georgia, resulting in his capture on 14 June by a posse of old men and boys armed with a motley assortment of weapons. A Confederate officer, home on medical furlough, talked his neighbors out of hanging the Yankee soldier, as a professional courtesy. Instead, they displayed him to the local women before carrying him to jail in Butler. While later in prison in Macon, he overpowered the keeper, who died from a resulting heart attack, and fled in the rain. While still in the yard, Hinds accidentally knocked down a black woman servant and only barely avoided entanglement in a clothes line. Near the jail, he quietly blended into a crowd of fifteen hundred to two thousand people who had gathered around the train depot to welcome Brigadier General John H. Winder as he changed trains en route to his duties at Andersonville.

Slave and free families continued to help Hinds. Near Stone Mountain, a slave took him to a Unionist white overseer who worked for a Mr. Graham of Kentucky, a former schoolmate of Abraham Lincoln. Ironically, Hinds soon after displayed incredible ingratitude when he declined to join forty slaves in trying to reach the federal lines, for fear he would be recaptured and executed for helping them! In July, he finally reached the federal army with the help of a large family of poor white mill workers at Roswell. Unbeknownst to Hinds, General Sherman almost certainly included this family among the civilians he ordered to the North to end their use as skilled workers by the Confederacy. Like almost all of these special prisoners, they likely never acquired the means to return home to Georgia.[184]

Of the one hundred or more African-American soldier inmates at Andersonville, at least one of them, Richard Holmes of Lawrence County, Alabama, a member of the 106th United States Colored Troops, escaped. His records fail to mention how he did it. Holmes had a special disadvantage in that Southern slave patrols had dogs specifically trained to find African Americans. No one offered black soldiers the chance to leave Andersonville by enlisting in the Confederate army.[185]

9

Curiously, a few prisoners benefited from, and some of them even achieved release from Andersonville, for failing in their escape attempts. Jim Mallory supposedly reached the federal lines several times, only to find himself back in Andersonville each time. James R. Compton credited this constant "misfortune" to Mallory being a spy who passed back and forth to the prison with information. Robert H. Kellogg saw four men rewarded with double rations out of admiration for their tunnel after the guards found and stopped their excavation. At Wirz's trial, the prosecution claimed that the camp dogs attacked a Canadian prisoner named "Frado" (popularly known as "Little Frenchy"), who later died in the stocks. Wirz and his witnesses, however, claimed that the dogs did not harm the prisoner and that Frado even laughed at the canines. Little Frenchy, in fact, escaped at least seven times, including once by tunnel and once while on his way to the camp's blacksmith for shackling to the chain gang! On one occasion, even while chained, he escaped. Chains, stocks, and other punishments proved ineffective in containing this man's exceptional case of barbed wire disease. To discourage Frado's escapes, Wirz claimed that he paroled Frado to live and work outside of the stockade, which would have rewarded the prisoner with extra rations. Little Frenchy, however, refused to do physical labor and continued to try to escape. Local people, using dog packs, kept bringing him back, except when he gave up and returned voluntarily. Captain Wirz finally sent him out for exchange but, even on his way home, Frado reportedly escaped again, this time while passing through Macon. He survived to receive exchange in Annapolis, Maryland.[186]

Sergeant Leroy L. Key of the 16th Illinois Cavalry had an equally interesting experience in earning his exchange. After helping to suppress the prison's bandits, he received a job as a cook outside of the stockade, to protect him from the friends of the thieves. When he heard of the pending exchange of his squad, he pleaded to go with them. Captain Wirz, however, refused to allow the kitchen help to leave Andersonville until everyone else had received release. Key and four other men then escaped. The prison's dogs ran past their hiding place without finding them. The fugitives then traveled eight days before civilians apprehended them. Their captors refused to accept bribes to let them go and took them to the jail in Hamilton. The local women did provide them with a fine meal, however. Confederate authorities transferred Key to Macon, where, on five different occasions, Key faked being sick to avoid transfer to a prison camp. He tried unsuccessfully again to escape before he really did become sick and, fortuitously, again missed the train to prison. The Confederate officials finally included him in a special exchange of ill prisoners.[187]

Conversely, some other men did worse than just fail in an attempt to escape from Camp Sumter. Despite their best efforts, they failed repeatedly. Cassius M. Ellis of the 64th New York Infantry became a guest of the Confederate States of America on three separate occasions, in battle at Fair Oaks, Gettysburg, and Petersburg, respectively. He reached freedom once by exchange and twice by escape. While at Andersonville, he witnessed his brother's death. After he escaped from Camp Sumter, Cassius traveled two hundred miles and spent a month in a South Carolina swamp before finding rescue on the coast.[188] John

Burke tried to escape from Andersonville three times, once from a work detail, once in a tunnel, and once while left alone at a burial. In his first escape, his recapture took place in a nearby barn. On his second try, a traitor exposed the tunnel, and the guards captured him and his comrades as they came out. Finally, he suffered arrest by three boys and a disabled soldier. He survived the punishment detail each time. Similarly, William P. Reed, an alumnus of the Cahawba prison, came within forty miles of the safety of Pensacola before dogs tracked him down and their handlers took him back, in chains, to Andersonville. Later, he tried to float to freedom on a log before a slave betrayed him. While on parole in Savannah, he escaped again and lived by begging, before a unionist family took him in. Once again, he suffered recapture. Reed finally jumped from a train and reached safety.[189]

Samuel Griswold, an unarmed Jones County boy, peacefully captured such an Andersonville escapee near his home. The unlucky Yankee had made two other unsuccessful escape attempts. He bitterly complained that the federal government refused to exchange him because his enlistment had run out. The army preferred to exchange Confederates for soldiers with time left on their enlistments rather than for those men who would be released to return home instead of back into the war. The sympathetic Griswolds provided him with a meal, a bath, and a sack of food before sending him back to Andersonville.[190]

Other prisoners had equally unfortunate experiences. Hugh R. Snee and a comrade jumped the boy guarding them on a work detail but succeeded in fleeing only far enough to suffer recapture by the mounted patrol that circled the camp. Shortly afterwards, Snee and other prisoners, while being transferred to another prison, suffered a train wreck. He found himself returned to Andersonville but with severe wounds that went untreated by the prison staff. The unfortunate soldier later tried to leave the camp with the men sent to Sherman's army for exchange by posing as a prisoner from Sherman's command whom he heard had died. The dead man's friends, however, stopped him because they had decided to use this ruse with someone else. Snee later tried to join the men for the exchange anyway. He still took advantage of the confusion in the roll call to act as someone marked for release. From then until Snee slipped out and walked the last few miles to Sherman's lines, he had to hide each time the guards called roll.[191] Hiram S. Daskam of the 3rd Iowa Infantry succeeded in sneaking out of the prison with a group of inmates who believed that they had earned exchange. The camp authorities had lied to them. The train they boarded began their journey to the new prison pen at Florence, South Carolina. He and many other men jumped from the train when they learned the truth. Daskam suffered recapture within a few miles of the federal lines in coastal North Carolina. He only reached safety, near Knoxville, Tennessee, after two more escape attempts.

The last of these particularly cruel twists of fate came at the end of the war. Levi Bizzee escaped from Andersonville only to suffer capture again much later in the war. He died from disease after exchange. Bartholomew O'Connell also freed himself and returned to his unit only to die in battle just before the fighting ended. By 4 April 1865, Captain Wirz learned that federal cavalry had crossed Alabama en route to Georgia. He began organizing transportation and sending his remaining prisoners to the federal lines at a rate of more than one thousand men per day. On 7 April, however, seven men made the last recorded escapes. Gill Sloan likely belonged to that group. Aside from thus missing his chance at almost immediate release, he then traveled the whole length of Florida, suffering recapture and escape twice before staggering into safety at Dry Tortugas. Daniel Bond of the 1st Minnesota left at the same time. He spent more than a month aided by slaves and Confederate deserters before he reached safety at Apalachicola, Florida. On finally reaching safety, however, Bond wrote, "Joy joy forever, my task is done The gates are passed, and heaven is now."[192] By the time he reached that point of safety, however, Wirz had sent his comrades at Andersonville to the federal lines.

Other prisoners also left Andersonville to finally escape only by the war ending. They thus avoided the problem of passing through the Confederate lines. Sergeant John H. White of the 103rd Pennsylvania suffered that fate. He escaped in April 1865 and found himself wandering over much of Georgia in the last days of the war. Disguised as a Confederate soldier, he even traveled as far north as Dalton, Georgia, near the Tennessee state line. A month after his escape, he finally reached federal cavalry commanded by General John Wilson.[193] John Wallace of the 7th Ohio Cavalry escaped that March and had to travel to Nashville, Tennessee, to reach federal lines. Thomas H. Howe and other escaped prisoners of war likewise came out of hiding from caves and forests to join the growing population of refugees caught up in the chaos at the end of the war. E. N. Gilpin of the 3rd Iowa Cavalry, stationed in Macon, wrote about them in his diary on 23 April 1865: "Andersonville is so near that the war is a reality indeed with us. Many of our prisoners who have escaped and have been lying out in swamps for months are coming in almost starved and naked. It is horrible the way they were treated."[194] Presumably, most of these particular escapees had jumped from trains during transfers from the prison. These men at least had the consolation that, unlike hundreds of their comrades released from

Andersonville and other prisons; they avoided dying aboard the civilian troop transport *Sultana* when it exploded on the morning of 27 April 1865.[195]

10

Within all of these stories, some answers emerge on why none of the escapees of Andersonville wrote a book about his adventures. Some of the men who published their memoirs did so, in part, out of the shame of capture and to explain why they failed to escape. Many of these soldiers claimed, probably falsely, to have tried to reach the federal lines numerous times, only to meet defeat from bad luck and circumstances. Prisoners of war commonly share such guilt, all the more so when they feel they have somehow failed in a victorious cause where other men came home as heroes. Men who succeeded in escaping avoided these problems and, thus, lacked that motive to write a book. Other soldiers, such as Hoopes, lacked a book-length story to tell. Some former prisoners, such as Farmer, likely preferred to keep the details of their escapes secret while they lived. The men Agnes Spencer and other Southerners saved surely chose to avoid compromising their benefactors before Southern neighbors by publicizing the names of Southern residents who gave help to fugitive Yankees.

The small number of truly successful escapees, perhaps only two dozen men, also seems to have worked against any of them stopping long enough in their later lives to write a book. Andersonville prisoner Henry M. Davidson all but succeeded in his escape attempt and he did, after his exchange, publish a thick book that covered his flight in detail. He had an exceptional reason, however, to publish his adventures. Davidson, and other former prisoners such as Robert H. Kellogg, quickly put their works out in order to compel the public to lobby the federal government to obtain the exchange of all federal soldiers and sailors held in the South. In this way, he and his fortunate comrades sought to bring about the greatest escape of all, the safe release of all of the imprisoned![196]

Not surprisingly, many of these men who "got out" did so as only one incident in their lives of escape, supporting the theory that they had a form of psychosis. An unknown number of these men avoided returning to the restrictive life of the federal military, leaving them to risk arrest as deserters. Stories of multi-year amnesia victims such as William Newby and John B. Hotchkiss suddenly regaining their identities may actually represent men also escaping from their previous lives.[197] Andersonville escapee Lawrence LeBron, veteran of various adventures as a federal scout, would survive the war and go on to pursue Indians in the West, chase bandits on the Union Pacific Railroad, and deliver mail in Chicago.[198] Private John Bolton of the 17th Indiana Infantry did not stay in Andersonville long. En route to the new Camp Lawton, he escaped while passing through Milledgeville and joined the approaching federal army. Afterwards, while on furlough from his unit, he narrowly missed death when the overcrowded troop car he rode in turned over. He married on 22 August 1868, but left his wife and small children to seek work. Without any further communication, he did not return home until 1919! His wife blamed his decades-long absence on his nature of being "forgetful and careless, and of a wandering disposition." Death caught up with him while he was confined at the soldier's home in Junction City, Kansas, on 25 March 1925. Boston Corbett left Andersonville in time to kill John Wilkes Booth in 1865. He later escaped from a Kansas insane asylum in 1888. Authorities assumed that he died in the hostile weather; however, he actually survived and found refuge with Richard Thatcher, a comrade he had met in Andersonville. Corbett later left for Mexico and points unknown, as well as into Civil War legend.[199]

Former prisoner Robert Knox Sneden made this view of Andersonville as seen from a camp of the guards. It appeared in the 21 October 1865 issue of *Leslie's Illustrated Newspaper.*

THE MEN AT THE GATES[200]

> Planter and stock raisers on the frontiers have similar places for their hogs, horses, mules, horned-cattle, &c., that the Indians, robbers and wolves may be kept at bay. In the East Indies, where the elephant rules ...they are contained and starved into docility—these places are called the 'elephant pounds.' Then, toward the 'yankee pound' we bent our steps...
>
> —*Albany Patriot,* 19 May 1864

> No soldier who served in a rebel prison will ever forget how inhuman human beings make themselves.
>
> —Anonymous writer
> *National Tribune,* June 1881 issue

The guards make up a significant part of the history of any prison. Although the men of the security forces at Andersonville failed to stop some individuals from leaving the prison, they did prevent one of the greatest mass escapes in history, despite having little more than their presence and a log wall to hold back their charges. As months went by, the guards and prisoners, men from very different worlds, came increasingly to merge into one culture, if not one people, all of whose members dreamed of escaping to seemingly anywhere else.

The guards did become a part of the greater legend of Andersonville. Their officers, James H. Fannin and Alexander W. Persons, testified to the service of the garrison at the trial of Captain Henry Wirz. The most often-repeated account of the guards first appeared in 1874, nine years after the prison closed. Its author, Lemuel Madison Park, served at Andersonville in the 1st Georgia Reserves. He made wildly inaccurate (but still often repeated) statements in defense of the Confederate treatment of federal prisoners. Parks, for example, wrongly described his comrades as little better than children and old men who died at the same rate as the prisoners. He claimed to have himself only been a fifteen year old boy when he served at the prison. In fact, he enlisted at age seventeen and turned eighteen as a guard. The problems created by his memoir became worse when later combined with other misinformation published in partisan prisoner memoirs and popular fiction, such as Herbert Collingwood's novel *Andersonville Violets*, wherein the writer described the guards purely from his imagination.

The true history of the guards began with the arrival of the first prisoners. Remains of the battle-experienced 26th Alabama Infantry Regiment, some four hundred men, came with the first prisoners from Richmond. Survivors of the 55th Georgia Infantry from Dalton, less than 270 men, soon joined them. For most of this time, only 250 to 300 men were on duty to watch the original 13,000 Yankee captives.[201] The 57th Georgia infantry regiment from Savannah and Gamble's Florida Light Artillery arrived in late April to prevent a feared mass escape by the growing numbers of Yankees. Lieutenant Colonel D. T. Chandler described the Floridians, commanded by Lieutenant, soon after captain, Charles E. Dyke, as efficient, well-drilled, and disciplined. These gunners brought with them four pieces of artillery, a battery soon supplemented by the heavy guns captured at the Battle of Olustee. Men from other units would also briefly visit Andersonville, usually while escorting new prisoners.

The artillery would remain but, on Sunday, 15 May, all of the regular infantry units except the 55th Georgia returned to the front. The newly arrived 1st Georgia Reserves fired them a salute. Prisoners felt that because of combat experience, the veterans who were now leaving Anderson Station forever had felt sympathy to any fellow soldiers, even from the other side. Testimonials from prisoners about the kindness of the 26th appeared in the Georgia press. The 55th Georgia remained at Andersonville to give the garrison at least some regular soldiers and because they usually failed to muster even one hundred men, even with local recruits who believed that enlisting in the 55th protected them from the draft and meant that they would serve near their Macon County and Sumter County homes.[202]

This 55th had a special and controversial relationship with the prisoners of Andersonville. Except for its original commander, the very troubled Colonel Cyrus Brown Harkie, the 55th reportedly might have been one of the best regiments in the Confederate army. His officers eventually publicly humiliated him by pulling Harkie from a train and making him march up and down a railroad platform. Next, from on top of a stump, he had to go through the manual of arms with a tent poll until he finally signed a letter of resignation. While still under arrest for selling his regiment's mules for his own personal profit (and other charges), Harkie received a transfer to General Winder's staff and eventual posting at Andersonville. Harkie proposed various engineering projects to improve conditions at Camp Sumter but he declined to try to reclaim command of the 55th. He ended the war sick with gonorrhea in a hospital in Macon. After the war, he worked as a railroad surveyor. Whether his death in Randolph County, Georgia, on Christmas Day in 1869 came from accident, suicide, or murder remains unresolved.

On 24 February 1864, the Confederate government formed three ad hoc companies (companies A, B, and C) from the 55th regiment, the usual organization of a battalion, from the some 265 officers and men absent when the federals captured most of the regiment at Cumberland Gap on 9 September 1863. The Confederate government further reduced the regiment's number by detailing several craftsmen, especially cobblers and leather workers, for work in Atlanta. Those men thus avoided service at Andersonville.[203]

Confederate inspectors found what was left of the 55th as unfit even to watch prisoners. Lieutenant Colonel D. T. Chandler, for example, described them as thoroughly demoralized, entirely without discipline, and mutinous. They had little reason to show humanity to Northern soldiers or respect for Confederate regulations. Sickness had decimated the ranks of the 55th; the remains of this unit largely came from men who were away at hospitals during the regiment's disastrous defeat. Five hundred forty-one of their captured comrades were suffering in the federal prisons of Camp Douglas, in Chicago, and Johnson's Island, in Sandusky, Ohio. Captain R. D. Chapman escaped from the latter to report to his regiment on how badly their comrades fared and to serve as adjutant at Andersonville. Prisoner John McElroy remembered the men of the 55th as exceptionally brutal to the Yankees. Other prisoners, however, recalled how these soldiers often violated regulations to trade with the inmates.

Andrew J. Spring testified to this trading and to these soldiers being decent and good Union men. Inmate Henry Clay Damon swore that by the time he escaped from Andersonville in early July 1864 that the camp's administration refused to allow men of the 55th to do sentry duty on the stockade wall because of their strong pro-Union sentiment; that they had told the prisoners that they would themselves flee to federal lines at the first opportunity.[204]

Their commander at Andersonville, Lieutenant Colonel Alexander William Persons of nearby Fort Valley, Houston County, represented the strange complexities of reality, myth, and irony at Andersonville. During his term as overall prison commandant, Persons took many actions to improve conditions for the prisoners and, after being relieved of command of the prison in mid-June 1864, he even began actions in court to have the prison closed as a public nuisance. His Yankee charges blamed his removal upon his humanity. In an attempt to solve the camp's perpetual organizational problems, the government in Richmond officially relieved Persons of command by placing an officer of superior rank to everyone else at Andersonville, Brigadier General John H. Winder. During Persons's term as post "commander," at least three officers present at the prison had out-ranked him. The Yankees falsely remembered Persons as commanding the 26th Alabama, a unit they respected as captors, instead of his 55th Georgia, the regiment so hated in some prisoner legends. The inmates even claimed that he and his regiment later surrendered to the federal army around Atlanta, apparently a corruption of the story of the defeat of the 55th in 1863 at Cumberland Gap, an engagement in which Persons had been absent. He did consider resigning his commission in September 1864, and although a post-war resident of Macon, he died at Americus, near Andersonville, in May 1878.[205]

With the transfer of the other regular infantry to the front, the duty of guarding the thousands of prisoners largely fell to the 1st Georgia Reserves Regiment under Colonel James H. Fannin. They arrived on 9 May. A month later, they received, as reinforcements, the 2nd (Colonel Robert F. Maddox), 3rd (Colonel C. J. Harris), and 4th (Colonel Robert S. Taylor) regiments of Georgia reserves, escorting the prisoners being held in Macon. Together these four units belonged to the 2nd Brigade of the Georgia Reserves. Officially commanded by Brigadier General Lucius J. Gartrell, it often had Colonel Fannin as its ranking officer.[206]

The Confederate government had authorized the creation of five regiments and two battalions of Georgia reserves as volunteers recruited from men exempted from service in the regular army. Under a compromise with the state's rights governor Joseph E. Brown, the Confederate government appointed the jovial and popular Confederate General Howell Cobb of Georgia as overall commander of the reserves while his political enemy Governor Brown chose the other officers of the reserves from men exempted from the national draft. The Reserves included draft evaders and Southern unionists who had lied about their respective ages to avoid conscription. The 1st and 2nd Reserves had formed in Atlanta in late April. The 3rd and 4th came into existence in Macon in early May.[207]

These "soldiers" arrived at Andersonville without training or equipment. They wore what clothes they had brought with them, and some of their number even came without shoes. By January 1865, many of the men wore rags and had to use blankets as substitutes for coats. Their skin darkened in the sun and from exposure to the pine smoke from the stockade. In appearance, they steadily become indistinguishable from their prisoners and the impressed slave workers, especially after the Yankees had become debilitated by the hook worms found so commonly among the native Southerners.[208]

These engravings, from ex-prisoner memoirs. show how the prisoners remembered their guards. (R. S. Davis)

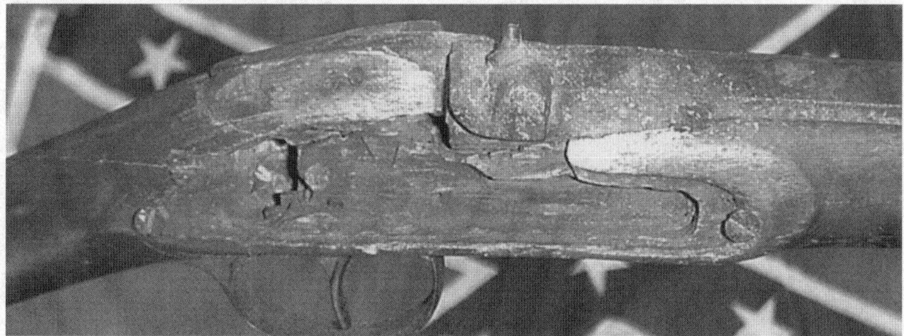

Private Jesse Taliaferro Carter of the 3rd Georgia Reserves carried his own fowling piece when he served as a guard at Andersonville. It is today owned by his descendent Doug Carter.

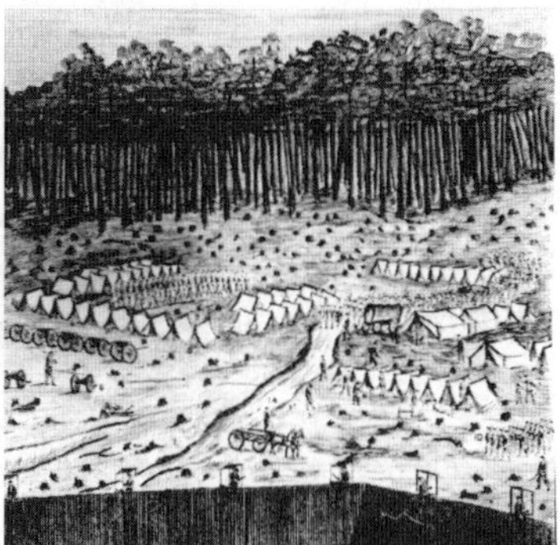

These engravings of the camps of the guards come from a post-war engraving of Andersonville.

These guards also found themselves exposed to a strange new culture. Ezra Ripple remembered that the boys of the reserves had seen hardly anything of the world, or even of the war. Ripple wrote that they found almost everything about their charges of interest to them. The guards had an inordinate desire to own anything of Yankee manufacture. They now met men and boys from cities like Boston, Cincinnati, and New York who were beyond any experiences of the typical Georgian, as well as from such equally distant and exotic locales as the Great Plains, the coast of Maine, and the Great Lakes. Some of the prisoners could also have told, in foreign tongues, of lands beyond the United States. Ripple also described these Reserves as exceptionally trigger-happy.[209]

Certainly the men and boys of the Reserves failed to leave the prisoners with a high regard for Southern intelligence or sophistication. William Burson of the 32nd Ohio Infantry remembered the prison's guards as men of all ages, classes, conditions, and uniforms but the most uncouth group of self-proclaimed soldiers he had ever seen—what B. F. Jones of the 1st West Virginia Cavalry described as the "ragtag" of the "Georgia Crackers." Inmate Charles Richardson described these "soldiers" as "the meanest lot of heathens that ever carried a musket or disgraced the calling of the soldier."[210] Professor Henry C. Cox, once a prisoner at Andersonville, would write, "Of all the men whom God Almighty has allowed to cumber the ground I do not think that any were as mean and cruel as the Georgia Reserves."[211] Inmate W. W. Day similarly wrote of the Georgia reserves as "Old men with long white locks and beards, with palsied, trembling limbs, vied with boys, who could not look into the muzzles of their guns when they stood on the ground, who were just out of the sugar pap and swaddling clothes period of their existence, in [hopes of] killing a Yank."[212]

Lemuel M. Park remembered his comrades the same way. Research by Jane Benson, however, shows that the personal information that survives in the compiled service records of the Georgia Reserves paints a different view of their ages. Almost all of the "soldiers" under age forty-five had seen at least seventeen years, while almost all of the men over age forty-five enlisted while still under age fifty.[213] A few men of other ages received exemptions from regular service because of medical disability but still qualified to volunteer for the reserves. These garrison troops also stood unusually tall for their times; few of their number were under five feet and eight inches.

In the federal censuses of the period, rural Americans, whether living in the North or the South, appeared identical. At Andersonville and up close, however, the Yankees believed that they saw significant differences between themselves and their captors. To inmate Charles Fosdick of the 5th Iowa Infantry, for example, the Georgians represented the great majority of the Southern white population, which he described as desperately impoverished, uneducated, undernourished, and non-slave-holding. He felt that the "Georgia Crackers" had everything to gain by Union victory. They would be almost as emancipated from the political and economic dominance of the planter minority as would the slaves.[214]

Most of the guards did come from poor families in mountain areas of Georgia. Their economy had little dependence upon slavery, and they had more fear of losing the status of their race by emancipation than any ambition of ever being slave owners. These Georgians lived lives of isolation and anonymity, but they now participated in a moment worth remembering and retelling for generations—of being part of a great legend, if not history. For many of these men, they had left their home counties for the only time in their lives. From their new post, they would write home of the gruesome "wonder" of Andersonville. In their surviving memoirs, curiously, they most often denounced the story of the miraculous creation of the Providence Spring inside the stockade by a lightening bolt as an exaggeration or a myth. They also frequently defended the humanity of Henry Wirz, the Andersonville officer hanged by the U.S. government for war crimes.[215]

Augustus C. Hamlin traveled through north Georgia immediately after the war and read letters sympathetic to the prisoners that the guards had sent home. They often wrote of the atrocious conditions at the prison and of their encounters with the Yankees they had heard so much about. Sometimes captors and captives developed relationships that continued for years after the war. During their captivity, a group of the prisoners presented Lieutenant S. F. Mays of the

2nd Georgia Reserves with a gold watch in appreciation for his humanity to them. Prisoner William H. Smith kept the addresses of two guards and the name of a member of the 55th Georgia Infantry held at Camp Douglas to whom he had promised to write, after his exchange, in his diary.[216]

Brigadier General John H. Winder, post commandant at Andersonville, however, came to disapprove of the Reserves and their officers. He even wanted them replaced with militia. Part of his problem may have been that the reserves answered to another officer, Major General Howell Cobb in Macon. Cobb would have liked to remove his reserves from Winder's presence. The Confederate government, however, took away even what militia Winder had, leaving him to depend almost solely on the reserves.[217]

The reserves became the largest part of the some five thousand individual men who served as guards and staff at different times in Andersonville's history. Colonel James H. Fannin, who also served as commandant of the troops, remembered that he seldom had more than a thousand or twelve hundred men fit for duty. Major Timothy M. Furlow of nearby Americus received promotion to lieutenant colonel and command of an ad hoc Georgia militia battalion with which to join the garrison of Andersonville. As only 303 men stood for duty during a day, the ratio of inmates to guards at a particular moment could soar to more than one hundred prisoners per sentry.[218]

Lieutenant Colonel D. T. Chandler's often-cited report on Andersonville of 5 August 1864 illustrated the problems of the camp security at its best. He reported that on paper the various units at Camp Sumter had 3,976 men guarding more than 25,000 Yankees. When teenager B. L. McGough of the 3rd Reserves beat the morning drum, however, only 2,202 of those soldiers actually mustered as present and fit for duty. Even then, they could only arm 966 guards, in even the direst emergency, for use against what later became as many as 33,006 prisoners.[219]

An occasional show of force, such as parading the troops, the calling out of the local militia, or firing a cannon or two reinforced the perceived threat of the garrison's ability to kill at least some rioting inmates during a mass escape. The post commanders, such as Lieutenant Colonel Persons, seemed to understand that they retained power only through the threat of violence. They dared not use it to force the prisoners to make the decision of choosing to join a break out or die quickly. The garrison, for example, would ignore Captain Henry Wirz's pleas to fire on the prisoners, such as when a riot broke out during the hanging of the bandit leaders by the inmates.[220]

Contrary to legend, the sentries shot few men, and the prisoners seem to have carried out few acts of malice against the guards. Even Americans raised with squirreling guns and shotguns needed intense training to use the comparatively complex military weapons of the age efficiently.[221] The guns, provided from the stores of the Macon Arsenal and used to threaten the prisoners, consisted of old flint and steel smooth bore muskets, including some from the Revolutionary War era, refitted for percussion. Some of the Georgia Reserves had knives, guns brought from home, and pikes as armament.

With these antique and inaccurate weapons, the untrained guards, when they shot at prisoners, almost as often accidentally hit men other than their intended targets. Private James E. Anderson of the 1st Georgia Reserves described the guards as "trigger happy," in a letter to President Jefferson Davis, as did his comrade, Charles H. Thiot of Chatham County, in writing home. More often than not, however, the sentries ignored prisoners passing in and out of the dead line area adjoining the walls. Guards would even encourage the Yankees to approach the wall to trade.[222]

The guards, however, took on a terrible responsibility. Added to the myriad problems that the Confederacy inflicted upon the people of the South, it inadvertently created a situation where only a comparatively few men manned a log wall that held back tens of thousands of desperate enemy soldiers. If freed, the starving, sick, and desperate Yankees could spread the horrors of Andersonville to thousands of farms across the state.

As early as 17 April 1864, the disgruntled guards nearly rioted.[223] Often they became sick from exposure to the camp and they reportedly suffered a strange facial malady, likely some form of "camp itch," from exposure to the air of the stockade. Even General Winder came down with what his doctors diagnosed as "gangrene of the face." He was told, as a consequence, to cease entering the stockade. Poor rations and disease decimated their ranks although, contrary to legend, their mortality rate never rose to close to matching that of the prisoners. Sometimes as many as one-third of the men reported sick. A total of 226 guards died at Andersonville, with 117 of that number buried there, including forty-three listed as [name] unknown.[224]

Guard duty also proved almost as monotonous as being a prisoner. Members of the garrison would claim that service at Andersonville became worse than time in the regular army. Each day meant having to face overwhelming numbers of desperate enemy soldiers under abominable conditions that stressed out the relatively few men charged with stopping the world's greatest mass escape. Yankee-born Weld Hamlin provides one example.

Impressment officers found him trying to hide in the Florida swamps in order to avoid serving in the Confederate army against his brothers in the North. Hamlin became a guard at Andersonville as an alternative to imprisonment. Eventually, he deserted, choosing hiding, capture, prison, and a fugitive's life to continuing to serve at Camp Sumter.[225]

Some of these "soldiers" would disappear for days and return with little note made of their absence. As the war crossed north Georgia, many of these troops, fearing for the safety of their families, deserted. Colonel Fannin later testified of liberally granting leaves, so that his men could go home and farm. Likely, this policy discouraged his men from just leaving forever. Members of the reserves also frequently left in details to work as mechanics for the government or to serve as scouts for the Confederate armies in Georgia. The camp adjutant, Lieutenant James Ormond of the 2nd Georgia Reserves, had been a successful Atlanta merchant. When Sherman occupied that city, Ormond passed through the federal lines to learn that while his home was being used as a federal headquarters, the Yankees had treated his family well. He reciprocated by returning to Andersonville with a blanket, shelter tent, and fifty dollars in Confederate money for a prisoner relation of a federal officer.[226]

Desertions thus became a serious threat to the camp's security. In early October, the Macon newspapers published the names of hundreds of the reserves absent without leave. Most of them came from counties occupied or threatened by the federal army although the lists included names of men from counties near Andersonville and from areas in northeast Georgia untouched by the war. During the great transfer of prisoners from Andersonville to other camps, they, along with many of the prisoners, took advantage of the train trip to escape. General Winder wrote in July 1864, that twelve of his men had left without leave and that he feared that all would follow immediately. If inmate Lawrence LeBron did kill a guard and dump the body in a creek during his escape, the missing Confederate soldier likely appeared on the rolls as a deserter. A corporal's guard began searching trains leaving Anderson Station for deserters. The camp's dog packs chased deserters from the garrison as well as the prisoners.

As Camp Sumter lacked a general court martial for much of its history, the guards rarely suffered punishment. The officers likely also took unauthorized absences. In any case, they likely tried to encourage their men to return. Officially, guards could suffer the same disciplines as the inmates except for confinement on the chain gang. In reality, a guard would only stand on a box for a couple of hours, if punished at all. Certainly, the camp lacked professional officers and soldiers to serve as examples for the garrison. D. M. Pass of Gordon

County, formerly of the 4th Reserves, would claim, many years after the war, that he helped a condemned deserter and a friend named Knight to escape. He identifies the prisoners as federals, but he more likely referred to two men from the 55th Georgia. Furthermore, any punishment inflicted on a guard could hardly have been worse than the circumstances of doing service at Anderson Station.[227]

The conditions at Andersonville also proved so bad for the guards that they sometimes joined escaping prisoners. Morgan E. Dowling wrote of a sergeant bribed by prisoners on a work detail to not only allow them to go but to guide them to the federal lines. The deserting Confederate even furnished each Yankee with a gun and ammunition. When other guards set out in pursuit, the fleeing men killed most of the dogs. The pursuers withdrew, also with a number of casualties. This may also have been the escape on 10 June 1864, wherein John Ransom's friend George Hendryx left in a Confederate uniform taking with him a gun and a guide from the garrison. It may also have been the escape where Stephen Payne and thirty comrades bribed a guard. Three nights later, Wirz found seven of the towers empty, the guards having left the stockade with some dozen prisoners who had gone under the wall via a tunnel. Prisoner John Northrop wrote in his diary about nine men leaving by a tunnel and, then, escaping with a guard who joined them. William H. Smith wrote in his diary on 9 October 1864, of a man named Hogan having escaped with four other men, all reportedly armed.[228]

Most of the prisoners and their remaining guards left Andersonville to other prisons in September 1864. This move prevented the rescue of the inmates by Sherman's cavalry. The 5th Georgia Reserves (Lieutenant Colonel Christopher Findlay) arrived from Macon to help with the evacuation. The 1st, 3rd, and 4th Reserves, along with most of the artillery, would help to garrison the new Camp Lawton at Millen, Georgia. At least some of the 1st, 3rd, and 5th would battle Sherman's legions in South Carolina. Members of the 1st and 4th would eventually return to Andersonville, after Millen had to be abandoned, with the prisoners held at Blackshear, Georgia. The Reserves helped in the general exchange and release of prisoners that began in March 1865. The 55th Georgia escorted prisoners to Florence, South Carolina, and would end the war guarding prisoners in North Carolina. A detachment from the regiment under a Captain Chapman defended Savannah and opposed the Yankee march through the Carolinas.[229]

Despite their legendary shortcomings, no other group of men so directly protected the people of Georgia from such a serious menace as did these men of the garrison of Andersonville. It had become as if hell now existed in South Georgia with hardly anyone to guard its gates from the army of demons within. Had the federal prisoners succeeded in making a mass escape, these tens of thousands of desperate men could have inflicted more damage to the civilian population than did Sherman's armies. The effect on Confederate morale would have been devastating. This garrison of largely Georgia soldiers kept that catastrophe from happening.

This vignette of the hanging of the raiders appeared on a post war engraving of Andersonville prison.

THE HANGMAN OF ANDERSONVILLE[230]

> Speaking after mature reflection (33 years) I must say that no braver, truer man ever lived. He had no conception of fear any more than a hungry tiger, and the strange part about him was that no one today seems to tell who or what this enigma Limber Jim was.
>
> —Robert McRay, former Andersonville POW

> To the white men in the waterside business and to the captains of ships he was just Jim—nothing more. He had, of course, another name, but he was anxious that it should not be pronounced.
>
> —Joseph Conrad, from his novel *Lord Jim*

The Civil War came in an era of America history ready for legend, reinvention, and stereotype on a grand scale. Limber Jim of Andersonville could have been a symbol of that era. Some former inmates wrote that Limber Jim had a brother, perhaps in the Confederacy's Cahawba prison but otherwise unidentified, who died at the hands of the prisoner bandits known as the raiders. Most sources agree that such robbers mugged Jim, apparently while he literally had his pants down, resulting in his turning on them. When these gangs of his fellow prisoners robbed other inmates, the legend goes that he led the opposition that put an end to the banditry. The only indisputable fact about him has been that late in the afternoon of 11 July 1864, he personally hanged William "Mosby the Raider" Collins, the man who had robbed him.

The reality of what happened at Andersonville in that summer, however, proved much more complicated than this morality tale and what some writers would want to believe. The truth begins with the identity of the main character in this story. Many men described very different people as this Limber Jim. The inconsistencies about his identity raise many issues about persona in mid-nineteenth-century America. Most of these accounts also include biographical information on adventures before and after Andersonville, so that Limber Jim, even if only as a myth, came to symbolize almost every stereotype of colorful character in his society as reflected in the prison's population.

Dramatic stories, within the even greater legend of Andersonville, could give a heroic character like Limber Jim notoriety far beyond any reality. Telegraphic and railroad communications, starting in the 1840s, quickly spread sensational news to growing numbers of newspapers accessible to a more and more literate America.[231] Cheaply printed books elaborated on these tales and spread them even further. His particular story appeared repeatedly, often with borrowed details, in numerous works of prisoner memoirs, real and fictional, that appeared for decades after the war. In the survivors' memoirs, as represented in John Frankenheimer's 1996 movie *Andersonville,* he symbolized legendary heroic prisoners who overcame the horrors of their environment to save themselves. This story of Limber Jim and his fellow vigilantes countered the image of the captured Yankees as stragglers (coffee "boilers" and "coolers"), cowards, or, at the least, something less than the other soldiers and sailors of the victorious army. Prisoner of war associations included his tale in unsuccessful national campaigns to win special government benefits for former prisoners.[232] From these legends a myth also arose about the situation of civilized men in a savage, disorganized environment imposing the system of laws they brought with them. The story becomes a tale about the enduring power of rule of law and justice rising above barbarism. To many of the soldiers, this situation and the other horrors of Andersonville further represented the moral superiority of the North's free labor society over the slavery- and class-oriented South, even as it ignored that it also perpetuated negative stereotypes of New York's Irish population.[233]

Interest in these tales continues into the present. As a real person, Jim has appeared in the formal histories of Andersonville and the modern movie about the prison although MacKinley Kantor avoided using him as a character in

Andersonville. Kantor likely, in his attempt at fairness to real persons, found this figure too shadowy and controversial for his novel. Far from a hero, Limber Jim has been depicted by some of the prison memoirists as a stereotypical hustler of the era. This problem of finding the breathing person behind these legends continues.

Separating the myth from the reality of Limber Jim may prove impossible for reasons that thwart accurate documentation of many people of his era. The war and Limber Jim came at the beginning of the "golden age" of the use of the *nom de plume.* The term "confidence man" first came into general use in 1849 and rapidly spread after Herman Melville's 1857 novella *The Confidence Man* and as people of unknown background and criminal intent used the expanding steam transportation network to travel far from home to commit fraud under invented identities. Popular pulp fiction that described such characters became manuals for real people, honest and otherwise, seeking new lives. Even persons who remained at home sometimes would adopt a different persona, in various situations and relationships, such as the man who served as the real basis for Robert Louis Stevenson's fictional *The Strange Case of Dr. Jekyll and Mr. Hyde.* Some people assumed middle names and initials, or unofficially took new surnames, even without any intent at fraud. They become new persons and could even adopt the appearance of a different sex. Commonly used but little-understood drugs, such as Laudanum, could also bring about severe personality and identity changes. Making such a change went from a sometimes necessity to becoming almost common. So many people achieved "multiplicity of individual personalities" and identities that public faith in the appearance of middle-class respectability suffered.[234]

Travelers could now leave behind family problems, bankruptcies, and intolerable environments. These growing numbers of strangers overwhelmed the existing community networks of friends and family. Local suspicion of and restrictions against strangers, as a safeguard against dishonest individuals, failed against the explosive growth of urban America. In those years, proof of identification for individuals, when asked for at all, consisted only of personal recommendations that could be fraudulent. Identification through such means as disfigurement and tattooing had ended long before for most peoples. America lacked laws against adding or changing given names, and travelers used passports only on a voluntary basis before the First World War. Finger and ear printing records only began in the 1880s, and then only for known criminals. Even when the extremely limited law enforcement of the age used the telegraph and the wanted poster to seek out fugitives, these efforts most often resulted in the arrest of innocent strangers unable to immediately prove their identity and innocence. The expansion of the R. G. Dun and the John M. Bradstreet companies to nationwide networks for credit reporting in the late 1840s; creation of Allan Pinkerton's national security agency, whose company logo gave rise to the expression "private eye"; and the increased production of city directories reflected the growing problem with people being able to so freely move to new locales and reinvent themselves.[235]

The Civil War further exacerbated this situation. Military establishments of hundreds of thousands of men created huge, mobile communities that provided individuals with work, pay, sustenance, and anonymity while accepting them as whomever they claimed to be. The army and navy acted in ignorance and indifference to past identities used in home towns, other careers, or even previously unfinished enlistments (including due to desertions). Men, and some women disguised as men, disappeared into the war, some of them to forever leave behind their pasts. Some people traded mundane pasts for romantic new lives of high adventure, including as a number of the Civil War's spies. William N. Phelps of the 18th Georgia Confederate Infantry, for example, started the false report of his death at Gettysburg, a battle that took place while he worked in a hospital hundreds of miles away in Richmond. He did this to abandon two wives and to allow him to disappear for decades and live as a soldier of fortune in Central America. Many of these people, when later indigent and elderly, had to go through the ordeal of documenting why they had changed identities in order to prove eligibility to obtain veterans benefits.[236]

As with the Civil War and the mid-nineteenth century as a whole, men used confinement at Andersonville to liberate themselves from their pasts. The search for the real Limber Jim provides examples of the many different facets of this situation. One veteran wrote of Limber Jim as a gigantic Pennsylvanian while Charlie Mosher called him a Kentuckian. The best description of this legendary character comes from *The Smoked Yank*, the often reprinted memoirs of Melvin Grigsby. He described Jim as a "tall, slim, wiry man, good looking, good hearted, full of energy, a lover of fun...."[237] Limber Jim would stand on a box or a barrel to draw a crowd with his jokes, stories, and songs. Observers wrote of him becoming rich from the gambling in his large tent, which held twelve or more men. For protection, he armed his entourage with clubs and knives, while hiring two large men as personal body guards. Ezra Ripple must have described Jim when he remembered a wealthy "merchant prince" who hired Ripple to draw crowds with his violin playing. This patron had a stand on Main Street, opposite the north gate, although he lived in a large board shanty nearby. He loaned Ripple the instrument and paid the musician in doughnuts and sour beer. J. S. Maltman remembered Limber Jim as the "absolute monarch of the entire pen."[238]

Limber Jim would hawk his "root beer" or "sour beer" as a treatment for scurvy, the great fatal scourge of the camp. This drink consisted of corn mush fermented with molasses in a barrel given to him by Captain Henry Wirz, the Confederate officer charged with keeping order inside the camp's open stockade. The drink became bearable when flavored with sassafras roots dug from the prison's swamp and sweetened with molasses. Jim sold this "cure" for five cents per cup, more than his cost for a barrel of the tonic. Prisoner Henry W. Miller saw a sample of this miracle cure: "One day I sold some molasses, when the beer man said it was his treat and handed me a glass. I held it up to the sun, when I discovered it was thick with flies' legs and wings, the other parts of their bodies being dissolved so one could not see through it. Thanking him I said I was not thirsty."[239]

Limber Jim, this king of Andersonville had reasons, some obvious and others now speculative, to want to obscure his real identity, even as he became a larger than life character in his time and place. As with America's growing urban centers, the prison had two different illegal economies, one directly involved and another indirectly involved with crime. Limber Jim likely belonged to both groups. Guards and prisoners allowed to leave the stockade would trade with local farmers for groceries. They would then smuggle the food into the stockade for trading to starving inmates. Prisoner George W. Fechter believed that at least one thousand inmates operated small stores, in addition to the prison's numerous gambling dens.

These sutlers became part of a timely miracle that undoubtedly saved Andersonville from becoming an even worse humanitarian disaster. Soldiers and civilians captured at Plymouth, North Carolina, in April 1864 had a special agreement with their captors whereby these "Plymouth Pilgrims" kept their pay and personal belongings. They thus brought into the Andersonville stockade some one million dollars in cash and goods. The wartime economy in this ad hoc city boomed. Fechter would justify his being one of the largest and most successful merchants and gamblers by claiming that he needed such a business so that he could help less fortunate comrades. With rations so grossly inadequate, the trading of this infusion of wealth with local farmers, through intermediaries like Limber Jim on outside work details, undoubtedly did save the lives of many prisoners, while making some of the prisoner entrepreneurs healthy and wealthy. W. B. Hibbs remembered a prisoner popularly known as "Old Jimmie Bowlegs"

At the center of this post war print of Andersonville, Limber Jim stands at his stall (marked on the engraving as 37), selling his root beer. (R. S. Davis)

starting with only a button but trading so successfully that when he left Andersonville forever in March 1865, accompanied by Limber Jim, he had three thousand dollars in cash.

Controversy still swirls around such men. John Worrell Northrop of New York described men like Fechter and Limber Jim when he wrote of prisoners being gouged by such entrepreneurs while their comrades with nothing left to trade starved, sickened, and died at their feet. Critics described the ad hoc inmate merchants and gamblers like Limber Jim as western "swindlers," men who violated the camp's regulations to smuggle in food for profit to sell to desperate, hungry customers for maximium profits. Defenders of these merchants would claim that the prison's horrible conditions drove these men to do whatever they had to do to survive—the same argument that might also be made for the robberies committed by camp's thieves. Andersonville, therefore, had its version of modern writer Primo Levi's Auschwitz moral "Gray Zone."[240]

The "raiders," men remembered as stereotypical toughs from the gangs of New York City, became the camp's other illicit entrepreneurs. They had first organized at the Belle Island and Cahawba prisons, but they continued their banditry after they transferred to Camp Sumter. For these men, Andersonville must have seemed hardly much different, at least in lifestyle, from their home in the notorious Five Points.[241] They sought profit from the new arrivals, or "fresh fish," through carefully planned individual muggings. Individual or small groups of the raiders would rob single prisoners under the cover of darkness, tents, or crowds. A frequent scam involved arranging for a meeting for a trade for some item like a blanket. When the victim arrived, the thugs would then rob him while screaming that he had tried to steal from them! Leroy L. Key would claim that a camp surgeon reported that some seventy-five men had likely died from being beaten to death by the bandits.

The bandits also extorted money and goods from the camp's merchants while supposedly boasting that they would own everything in the stockade by 4 July. New York prisoner Robert Knox Sneden, however, wrote of the raiders as being so impoverished that they lived in holes in the ground on "Raider's Island," in the camp's swampy middle ground. Their few defenders described them as driven to stealing to survive, but the theft of the money and other belongings could condemn a fellow prisoner to death by starvation.

The general prison population organized to fight back against these most obvious of the camp's predators. As early as 22 May, prisoner James Burton wrote of a raider being captured and having half of his head shaved and otherwise being publicly humiliated, actions that John L. Hoster described as later becoming routine. On the night of 28 June, when a group of raiders attacked a tent near Hoster, the whole "neighborhood" rose up and beat off the bandits. Peter "Big Pete" Aubrey started a defensive force as early as April 1864. Some of the raiders, however, infiltrated his police. Leroy Key formed thirteen police companies, with thirty men and one captain in each.[242] These groups became mutual protection "tribes" that defended themselves from the bandit communities within the greater population of Andersonville. This kind of vigilantism had a history in America, at least going back to the Regulators of South Carolina in the 1760s, but especially in the West; just as street gangs had existed in urban areas long before the creation of the artificial city of Andersonville. Organized crime existed in cooperation between rural and urban America, for just as long.[243]

The classic competitions between the swindler merchants/gamblers and the raiders reached a conclusion in June 1864. Key would remember that the raiders became so bold that they began to rob even the wagons that brought in the rations for the whole population. The camp's authorities finally felt compelled to take action. Burton wrote that a murder and robbery spurred decisive action. Supposedly a raider stabbed to death a sergeant from an Illinois regiment.[244]

The most often published account, however, has prisoner John Urban, alias John G. Dowd, complaining to Confederate Captain Henry Wirz about having a watch stolen.[245] Wirz, from inside the dead line, discussed the situation with the prisoners and chided them for allowing some fifty men to prey upon twenty-six thousand.

Captain Wirz, rather than prisoners, then took the initiative to restore order and end the robberies. Wirz cut off provisions to the prisoners until the inmates stopped the raiding. After two days without food, Aubrey, Key, and probably others went to Wirz and, from him, obtained clubs and a detail of guards for use in arresting the raiders.

As the inmates cheered Wirz, Key and others led the camp's guards to the thieves. The prisoners could only specifically identify a few of the raiders, but they forced more names from the men arrested until eighty-four of the bandits were apprehended. The guards kept the fourteen worst men for confinement. The rest of the bandits received a beating administered as they ran between two rows of the inmates. Three of the raiders died from that punishment.[246]

After Wirz refused to take the responsibility for the punishment of the remaining bandits, Brigadier General John H. Winder, commandant of the prison, at Wiz's suggestion, formally authorized the prisoners to organize trials for the worst of the raiders. A lack of records has left almost no details of the trials. Inmates would write memoirs in which they would claim to have witnessed these events, and even participated in them, along with their close acquaintance Limber Jim. Many accounts thus do exist of the trials, in manuscript form and in print, but these other views have flaws. With the exception of Leroy Key, the authors could hardly have been more than teenage onlookers in a crowd of tens of thousands of prisoners. They only witnessed the major events and seldom even met the leaders in Andersonville, despite how they would often later portray themselves in their writings. Their accounts often appear to confirm the commonly reported details of the trial when, in fact, these works were only dramatically embellished repetitions of the few printed facts. The authors could thus further confuse misinformation from earlier works. Only one of the alleged participants, J. J. Osborne, however, published an account with any detail of the trial.

Contemporary diaries do survive from Andersonville, but as historian William Marvel explained in *Andersonville: The Last Depot*, those diarists seldom provide significant details of the major events that survivors would so spectacularly describe later. This problem more commonly exists in the exaggerated and fictional claims in "autobiographical" works of the Old West, publications by writers who, only incidentally, happened to be in the area of what only later became historical events.

Despite these problems, the basic story of the trial can be assembled. In Leroy Key's account, and other sources, Pete McCullough of the 8th Missouri Infantry served as the judge. According to his eulogist, he even smuggled the wood into the prison for the gallows. A newly discovered record by a man claiming to have survived Andersonville, but who used the post-war name (alias?) of J. J. Osborne, identifies the other officers of the court. Unfortunately, he failed to make any specific mention of Limber Jim or of any of the different men identified as being him.

According to Osborne's account, prisoner Henry C. "Romeo" Higginson had argued for a legalistic solution to the problem of the robbers. Now the raiders called upon him as their defense attorney while Pete Bradley, a raider, tried to find witnesses on their behalf. Higginson's messmate, Sergeant Otis W. Carpenter of the 7th Michigan Cavalry, served as prosecutor. In the lengthy proceedings that followed, the court found few of the defendants guilty. The court sentenced most of the convicted men to beatings and similar punishments.[247]

The six worst offenders, however, were sentenced to die by hanging. Curiously, Higginson also organized the executions of his clients. Wirz arranged for the construction of the gallows and Limber Jim agreed to conduct the hangings, supposedly for a promise from Wirz that he would receive a release to the federal lines. While waiting by the gallows, raider leader Charles Curtis pulled a knife and fought his way through the crowd. Pursuers eventually found him in a hole where he had hidden under a dead prisoner for some two hours. Curtis then received a beating by the mob. Joseph Alvis Jordan, Hiram Grow, and Joseph C. Maxson of Company C of the 85th New York Infantry finally returned him to the gallows.

All of the six condemned men now stood ready for execution. Limber Jim took personal responsibility for William "Mosby" Collins, if not all of the raider leaders. The floor fell from under the men as the crowd roared. Collins fell to the ground when his rope broke or, as one soldier claimed, when Limber Jim cut him free. According to another witness, a man in the crowd asked Jim if that didn't mean that Collins was innocent, to which the hangman replied "not by a d—n sight!" The crowd allowed Collins little reprieve and quickly returned him to the gallows.

Andersonville writers would remember Collins pleading for his life and offering Jim one thousand dollars to set him free. The hangman, however,

Prisoner Robert Knox Sneden drew the sketch of the gallows after the war. (Virginia Historical Society, Richmond VA)

reminded Collins that Collins had mugged him. Supposedly Limber Jim said that "the rope around your neck cost me $176 [the amount Collins had stolen from him], and I will hang you as long as I can tie a knot in it."[248] He then secured the raider to the cross beam while he climbed up on the gallows to pull down enough rope to finish the executions. Without further ado, Limber Jim then sent the raider leader into eternity.

Tens of thousands of prisoners and thousands of guards and visitors watched the execution. Martin S. Harris of the 5th New York Artillery felt that almost ten times more of the raiders should have been hanged. Most of the prisoners likely agreed with Henry E. Olinger of the 20th Indiana Infantry, "it was no doubt, justice, but it was an impressive Sight to me that I never care to witness again."[249] The success of the raiders proved that the prisoners of war in Andersonville had failed to achieve the sort of mutual support that World War II prisoners used to keep up morale and save lives. Key, along with Goody Larkin, Jim Johnson, Ned Carringan, George W. Fechter, and Abel Wadsworth "Wad" Payne did subsequently found a prisoner police force known as the "regulators" that forced sergeants to take care of the sick, keep the camp clean, improve the marsh area, clear the streets, and end thievery.

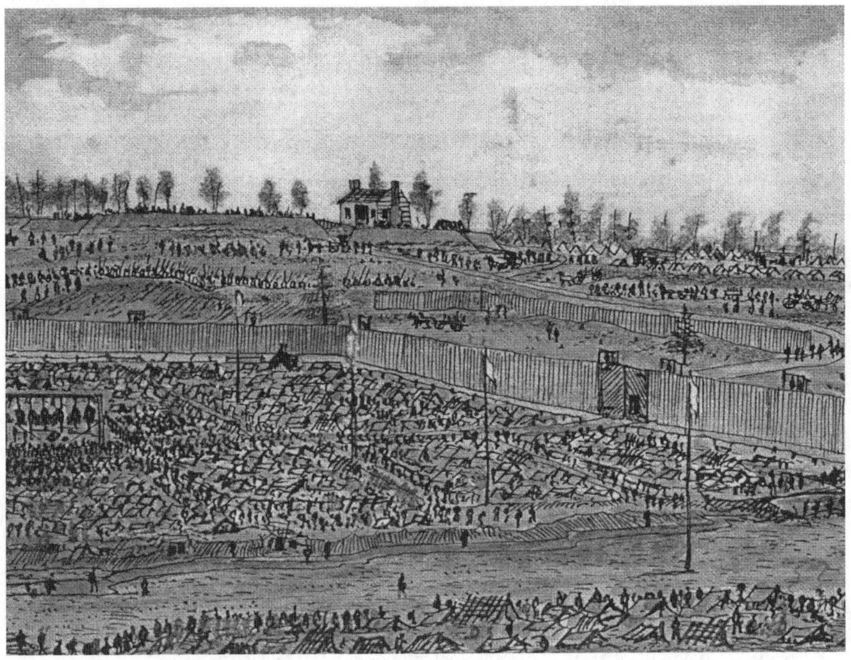

An image of the hanging of the raiders drawn by prisoner Robert Knox Sneden after the war. (Virginia Historical Society, Richmond VA)

A morality lesson does exist in this tale. It has an Orwellian ending, however, that ethics theorists might prefer to avoid exploring. Inmate Robert H. Kellogg would later testify that while the regulators initially performed a valuable service, they soon "deteriorated very much." The members of this new constabulary extracted double rations and taxes as payment for their civil services. They also eventually included former raiders in their ranks. At least once, in October 1864, the general prison population rioted against the regulators.[250]

Limber Jim thus symbolized, to some men, the worst of the worst, a raider, western swindler merchant, gambler, and collaborator, who helped to organize both the execution of the raider leaders and the extortionist police force. In a full accounting, he appears, at best, as a spectacular example of the typical hustler "King Rat" of traditional prison lore. Martin S. Harris of the 5th New York Artillery referred to Limber Jim or a man identical to him when he wrote,

> As an instance of the sympathy existing between the [prisoner] police and prisoners I will state that one of them, formerly their chief, voluntarily went out with the hounds, and aided in the recapture of escaped prisoners. The same man also

> informed the rebels of the existence of several tunnels, which in their attempts to escape our men were cutting under the stockade, without any gain beyond thanks for his treason and scorn for the traitor. The man is now in New York awaiting an "honorable" discharge, which he will probably get, together with all back pay and allowances due, but as others, equally culpable, have been, and will probably escape the punishment so richly deserved.[251]

Other negative memories of Limber Jim also survive. Charles Ferren Hopkins of New Jersey later wrote that "Slim Jim," actually named Ellis, led a gang of thieves before being mugged by a group of his raider colleagues. Hopkins claimed that Jim joined the opposition to keep from being punished himself.[252] George W. Fechter, however, the partner of the aforementioned notorious Andersonville gambler Charles Ellis of the 56th Massachusetts, failed to identify Limber Jim by name although he described Jim as a supplier and a man he knew well.[253]

Michael Regan of the 69th New York also remembered Limber Jim as anything but a hero. He recalled knowing Jim back at Cahawba prison in Alabama. According to Regan, this mystery man had been captured as a civilian sutler. At Cahawba, where he acted as a "black sheep" and as an informant thwarted at least two escape attempts, his fellow inmates beat him nearly to death. Jim later volunteered to execute the Andersonville raiders in exchange for release. Regan, who successfully escaped from Cahawba, later met this man again in Cheyenne, Wyoming. His Limber Jim died there from a gunshot administered over a gambling table in June 1867.[254]

The man Regan described may have been civilian Thomas J. Goodman. James H. Buckley remembered Goodman as Limber Jim and as formerly a lieutenant of the ninety-day enlistment men. The prison's surviving records only describe Goodman as released on 1 April 1865. Problems exist with Goodman as Limber Jim, however. The lists of federal soldiers omit any reference to a man named Goodman as an officer of the ninety-day men. Cheyenne only came into existence in September 1867, and Michael Regan escaped before he had to spend any time at Andersonville and, thus, he had only second-hand knowledge of what happened there. Gambler con men became common characters of this age, and Regan could have mistaken the man he knew at Cahawba with someone he saw later (and briefly) in Wyoming.[255]

Other writers, at the least, suggested different men for identification as Limber Jim. For example, Michigan cavalryman E. W. Nichols's eulogist credited him with being the sole executioner of the raiders although he fails to appear in any record of the raider incident.[256] John McElroy, however, wrote that, in addition to Limber Jim, six other hangmen and two corporals also pulled the props from beneath the scaffold.

Further hindering the understanding of the real man, the memoirists provide conflicting information about the fate of the shadowy figure of Andersonville's most famous inmate. Limber Jim and the other leaders who ended the raider reign took jobs outside of the stockade to protect them from the friends of the bandits.[257] A late arrival to the prison, W. B. Smith, would witness Limber Jim clearing the way for the daily ration wagons using little more than his presence. This man may actually be the inmate remembered by an anonymous Andersonville alumnus in August 1865:

> A brawny prisoner (whose nationality I shall not mention), detailed to supervise the issue of the rations, mounted each wagon as it entered, and indulged to the utmost his proclivities for murder. This he actually effected in one instance at least, besides inflicting innumerable serious injuries upon his fellow-prisoners; but, as he was forwarded for exchange long ago, I suppose ere this he has received an honorable discharge from the United States service in consideration *of his sufferings.* [His emphasis][258]

Robert P. Black, however, claimed that Limber Jim failed to appear inside the stockade again after the executions, that he had heard rumors that the executioner had traveled north or to another prison camp for his own protection. W. B. Hibbs of the 17th Iowa claimed that Jim joined other inmates in bribing guards to let them join in a special prisoner exchange. The executioner reportedly left for Vicksburg, Mississippi, in early March 1865.[259]

Sorting through such records of these individuals to find the true man behind the legendary figure(s) of Limber Jim illustrates a great deal about identity, fame, and reality in Andersonville as well as in the Civil War. This repeating and exaggerating of details suggests that Limber Jim existed only in myth or was actually several men remembered as one person. Some contemporary records, however, do identify one real man as Limber Jim, including William H. Smith's diary entry of 11 December 1864, wherein he recorded visiting Limber Jim in the cook house, and Fechter mentioning Limber Jim in 1865 testimony.[260] George Plumleigh of the 15th Illinois Infantry does not appear in the Andersonville prisoner records, but he left a diary of his time there in the last months of the war. He wrote of meeting the not-yet-legendary Limber Jim during the week of 10 January 1865:

> There is a character here called "Limber Jim" he claims to belong to the 113th Illinois, but wears rebel uniform and goes in and out of prison as he pleases, and I see nothing about him indicating the prisoner of war. He is kind to the prisoners and seems to be well liked. He was at one time chief of police.

Survivor Aaron E. Bachman stated outright, and the often-unreliable memoirist John Ransom implied, that Limber Jim and Sergeant Leroy L. Key, a leader in organizing the suppression of the raiders, were actually the same man. Before the war, Key had built wagons, including the "limber" (tongue), from which he might have been given such a nickname. Key had also worked as a farmer and printer. An Andersonville survivor likely wrote of him when he described a leader in the defeat of the raiders, as a "swarthy, robust man, about thirty years of age, with a heavy black moustache" and commanding a "rude, earnest tone of voice, with a threatening eye and a commanding air."[261]

Key's past encouraged him to hide his background, if not his true name, in the sometimes physically dangerous partisan Civil War era. A member of an old

John McElroy published these engravings of his friend Leroy Key in *Andersonville: a Story of Rebel Prisons* (1879). Unfortunately, he did not include a likeness of Limber Jim, a man he also knew.

Georgia family, this Mississippi-born soldier initially enlisted in the federal army from Bloomington, Illinois. Tuberculosis caused his discharge from the 14th Illinois Infantry, but he then enlisted in the 16th Illinois Cavalry, only to suffer capture.[262] The guards at Andersonville treated Southerners like Key, who were caught in the federal army, with exceptional harshness. To protect such men, some of the prisoners gave them new identities in Northern units.[263]

Leroy Key and Limber Jim must have been different men, however, unless Key's friends described him as two different persons in an elaborate and confused effort to use misidentification to protect Key from vengeful friends of the raiders. Such a scheme seems highly improbable as Leroy Key widely publicized his role in suppressing the raiders as early as 1864 although he failed to mention Limber Jim at all. James Madison Page, Lessel Long, Robert McRay, and other former prisoners also wrote of Key and Limber Jim as different men. John McElroy, whose book served as a collective rather than as an individual prisoner memoir, even went so far as to write that Limber Jim "had all of Key's desperate courage, but not his brains or talent for leadership."[264] As the unofficial federal prisoner historian of the Civil War, McElroy should have known the facts about Leroy Key. He also served in Key's own 16th Illinois Cavalry and resided in Andersonville at the same time. Key escaped from Andersonville and, upon recapture, qualified to participate in an exchange of sick prisoners.

Many of the incidents associated with Leroy Key do appear to come very close to those adventures attributed to Limber Jim. Quite possibly some of the things that happened to Key, including the early encounter with the raiders, through misunderstandings, became part of the stories associated with his more famous hangman comrade. The real Limber Jim's role in putting an end to the raiders could have actually been little more than serving as one of the six executioners on the scaffold. Such a scenario would explain why none of the names of the various persons said to have been this man appear in the records of the trial of the raiders.

Of this Limber Jim, McElroy further wrote that he had been a member of the 67th Illinois Infantry and a man "whose sinewy form, and striking features" reminded him of a Sioux warrior. James Madison Page referred to Limber Jim as "James Laughlin."[265] Critics of these accounts point out that no man by that name served in the 67th, and no member of that unit appears in the surviving Andersonville prisoner lists. As the 67th only existed for ninety days in 1862 as prison guards at Camp Douglas, Ohio, these omissions hardly seem surprising.

A James McLaughlin, however, did serve in the 67th before enlisting in the 1st Illinois Light Artillery.[266] McLaughlin's branch of service matches what John

L. Hoster remembered of Limber Jim: "He is an artillery sergt., wears a fancy red shirt, a sailor cap and has a lurid red stripe on his pants."[267] The nickname Limber Jim might have been derived from the limber on an artillery caisson, as implied by the artillery pants also attributed to this Limber Jim.

The James McLaughlin in question, however, only became a Confederate captive on 27 November 1864, long after the raider executions, and after Andersonville had largely closed as anything but a hospital. McLaughlin's statement in his Civil War pension claim fails to include any mention of Andersonville although it does imply that he spent his entire captivity in Richmond.[268] Limber Jim likely knew McLaughlin and assumed his identity at Andersonville, perhaps only to obtain double rations by answering the roll call at twice, as two different men, one not actually at the prison. Herman J. Peters of the 126th Ohio drew an extra ration by answering as the fictitious John Kate of the 110th Ohio. He knew of other prisoners who did the same.[269] As to Limber Jim wearing an artilleryman's uniform, inmates would strip the dead for any article of clothing. (Henry W. Miller purchased an artillery coat taken by that means.)[270]

Other candidates for the legendary executioner exist, most of whom had reasons for hiding their identity at Andersonville and even for the whole war. Almost everyone who played a major role in the effort to close down the raiders received identification, by someone, as Limber Jim, granting to each of these men, in turn, the most important role in the story. Similarly, each person who claimed, even falsely, the executioner of Andersonville as a personal acquaintance increased the importance and the credibility of his memoirs. References to the artillery uniform, for example, could have also described the previously mentioned Peter Aubrey of the 2nd Massachusetts Heavy Artillery; like Key, identified as the man known as Limber Jim. Curtis H. Terry left such an account. He remembered that "Jim was a great mystery to many of the prisoners and to the rebels."[271] Terry and the men in his Company H of the 27th Massachusetts Infantry, however, knew "Limber Jim" as Jack Williams, a member of their company who became chief gunner on the gunboat *Commodore Perry* before Terry met him again as Limber Jim in Andersonville. Another survivor remembered Limber Jim wearing a sailor's uniform, and John L. Hoster remembered him as wearing an artilleryman's uniform but also a sailor's hat.[272] The clothing would seem right for Williams. Only this circumstantial evidence supports Terry's claims. Federal service records omit any reference to any such Jack Williams.

Similarly, other aspects of the legend of "Limber Jim" imply much but answer little. A James Limber served in the 33rd Illinois Infantry, but he received a medical discharge on 2 February 1864, before Andersonville even opened. The descriptions of Limber Jim's physical features suggest a mixed racial origin and even the possibility that his actual name may have been Limber Jim. The confusion over his identity could come from membership in a marginal part of society that existed outside of the experience of the prisoners who tried to describe him. The now obsolete word "limmer" meant mongrel. "Limber Jim," as a name, also served as a common sobriquet for acrobats, freaks, and long-limbed men in the nineteenth century, as well as for horses. Melvin Grigsby would remember Jim as previously involved with a circus, and other writers described him as a superb athlete. Prisoner Ransom T. "Little Red Cap" Powell, the boy who worked as Wirz's aide and who knew Limber Jim well, remembered a prisoner named Reddy who also operated a successful gaming tent and who performed acrobatics.[273] The term "Limber" also referred to the holes cut in a ship's deck for drainage of the pumps.

Many men at Andersonville used nicknames and aliases. George W. Fechter used the pen name "Charles W. Ross," claiming to fear retribution by Confederates who knew of him as a spy and had hanged one of his comrades.[274] John "Bugler" Ransom wrote that "John Smith" and "numerous" of his family lived in Andersonville. Most often, Ransom knew his fellow inmates only by such nicknames as Minnesota, Big Charlie, Little Jim, Marine Jack, Indiana Feller, Mopey, Skinny, Smarty, Dad, and Doc. Seemingly all ethnic white persons at Andersonville, other than the Germans and the Irish, received the appellate of "Frenchy."[275]

The contemporary records of the prison provide little help with the problem of aliases and even omits the names of many prisoners. For example, the documentation of the presence at Andersonville of Joseph C. Maxson and Otis W. Carpenter, as well as adventurer Lawrence LeBron, appears only in soldier's reminiscences. Harkness N. Lay left a diary of his time at Andersonville, and his time there found a witness in his comrade Henry W. Miller. Lay, however, also fails to appear in the Andersonville records. The story of the previously mentioned Reddy illustrates the problems of the absence of identification. Ransom Powell wrote that after the war Reddy became a famous gambler whom Powell saw in Maryland in 1876, still cheating at cards. Daniel O'Connor also remembered a British soldier, Henry Reddy of the 58th Massachusetts, whom O'Connor claimed Wirz tortured in order to learn of the location of secret documents. The Andersonville records, however, mention only a Peter Reddy of the 8th New York Cavalry, a prisoner who died on 31 October 1864.[276]

Rolls provided the names for the surviving lists, but aside from men who used false identities, other prisoners avoided participating in the roll call as an act of resistance or spite.[277] The record keeping at Andersonville missed many people, some of whom appear in the cemetery records now as unknowns. For example, only some of the men named by the previously mentioned Ezra Ripple appear in the surviving records.

The surviving lists of the prisoners chiefly consist of the names of men who permanently left the stockade by various means, including those men who earned a shallow grave in the camp cemetery. Sometimes special exchanges of selected groups of prisoners, such as sailors, gave certain inmates a way home. Men, otherwise excluded from participating, could assume the names of the dead to achieve freedom, what the inmates referred to as "flanking out." These prisoners might fail to appear in the records as having escaped if other men then assumed their identities at roll call, to obtain extra rations. The guards punished any mess that had men missing, encouraging the recruitment of substitutes for the escapees. John L. Jacobs left in the sailor exchange as the deceased James Matthias of the *Underwriter*. He believed that the final camp records would show Matthias as exchanged and himself as having escaped. In fact, the camp's lists only show Matthias as having died and make no mention of Jacobs at all. Until the records ceased being kept, some prisoner likely continued answering to Jacobs's name to receive an extra ration.[278]

This scam worked well with many of the guards. William D. Hammock, for example, gave up trying to pronounce the names of his Yankees and simply counted heads at roll call. One of the men eventually buried in the prison's cemetery used the identity of Ambrose Spencer of Company D of the 93rd New York Volunteers. A man with exactly that same name and from that unit, however, survived the war. Similarly, W. A. Jamieson, a successful escapee of Andersonville, discovered in 1916 that he had a tombstone in the prison's cemetery, undoubtedly marking the grave of some much less fortunate, now unknown comrade who used his name.[279] Researcher Jack Lundquist has compiled information on almost all of the inmates recorded as being at Andersonville. So far, he has identified 631 men buried in the camp's cemetery for whom no service records exist in their respective units. Lundquist also has the names of 1,205 men reported as having died in the prison but without identified graves. Subtracting the 533 graves marked unknown leaves 672 men unaccounted for, a number almost equal to the previously mentioned number of grave markers of named soldiers without records of service. These statistics imply that almost 650 men were buried under false identities, among the 12,949 prisoner graves at Andersonville.

Prisoners had other reasons for assuming false identities. Conceivably some prisoners used aliases because they wanted their families to assume that they had died in battle rather than as suffering captives whose lives ended in a place with the terrible notoriety of Andersonville.[280] Captain Hiram S. Hanchett of the 16th Illinois Cavalry changed his name and took the appearance of a civilian upon his capture, wrongly assuming that the Confederates would soon release him as a non-combatant. As a consequence, he received the much worse prison confinement for the enlisted men rather than for an officer. Instead of earning early release, he eventually received a death sentence as a spy. (He survived, however.) Some of the raiders assumed aliases to escape discovery, arrest, and prosecution for crimes committed before reaching the prison. Felix DeLabaume of the 39th New York, for example would testify to and provide a drawing of conditions at Andersonville as evidence for Henry Wirz's post-war trial. He would also become active in prisoner of war organizations despite being exposed as Ben Dykes, a deserter from the 7th New York. Similarly, Soren Peterson knew a fellow Dane called "Sandy," a prisoner sutler who, exactly like Limber Jim, made large sums of money from sales to fellow prisoners. Sandy had enlisted and deserted from the federal army twice before collecting still another enlistment bounty. He later paid the Confederates two hundred dollars to arrange his release from the Florence stockade.

Other persons stayed in the shadows of identity for still other reasons. Jim Mallory apparently escaped several times to the federal lines, only to repeatedly find himself back in Andersonville. James R. Compton credited this constant "misfortune" to Mallory being some sort of a spy passing back and forth to the prison. Whatever Mallory's real name or motives, no record of his being at Andersonville exists.[281] Civilian John H. Morris of Herkimer County, New York, also fails to appear in those records although Wirz mentioned him in a letter. He may have been missed deliberately as he profitably collaborated with the Confederacy by buying securities from desperate prisoners at low prices paid in Confederate money. Southern officials allowed Morris to leave the camp and return home with his ill-gotten profits, as they may have done for Mallory and Limber Jim.[282]

Some of the prisoners must have used their arrival at Andersonville to assume new identities that they kept for the rest of their lives. Prisoners and deserters have escaped their pasts by disappearing into war for as long as armies have existed. J. E. Harrison remembered that some of his comrades left the prison in such poor mental condition that they suffered from amnesia. Such men could have even become their Andersonville identities. They would build new lives for themselves. Former prisoners of war such as William "Crazy Jack" Newby of Tennessee and John B. Hotchkiss of New York allegedly regained their memories and returned to their respective homes decades after the war. They may have been suffering from real memory loss or they could have simply used Andersonville to avoid going back, at least for a time, to their former lives. Newby even seems to have been a mental "blank slate" whose condition allowed more than 140 different people to see him, for personal or political reasons, as whomever they individually wanted to believe him to be.[283]

Andersonville's body of tales includes an even greater Civil War epic of identity. Jacques Roellinger deserted from the French army. By 1862, he had come to America and enlisted in the Enfant Perdue ("Lost Children") New York Independent Infantry Battalion. A few days after joining, he deserted, later claiming that he feared that if France became an ally of the Confederacy, and he fell into enemy hands, he would face extradition and execution by his native country. His brother persuaded him to move to Ohio, where he joined the 107th Ohio Infantry Regiment under the name of Jacques Cermann. In the Lost Children, a French foreign legion type of unit of largely French and Italian

Jacques Roellinger from photographs in his pension file. (National Archives and Records Administration)

soldiers that both Union and Confederate soldiers derisively called the "Lost Ducks" (from the sounds of their accents), when one man deserted, another man would informally "enlist" by assuming the identity of the deserter. Someone took the place of Jacques Roellinger and suffered capture at the Battle of Olustee, Florida, on 20 February 1864. This imposter became a prisoner at Andersonville, where he died from scorbutus on 22 August 1864.

Frederick Guscetti now enters the story. He also served in the Lost Children until he became part of the battalion that transferred to the 47th New York Infantry Regiment on 30 January 1864. He suffered near-fatal wounds during his capture at Olustee. Guscetti, however, survived to achieve notoriety at Andersonville as Frado, or "Little Frenchy," likely the man who made numerous inept attempts to escape from the prison and who finally succeeded in March 1865, while on his way to an exchange of prisoners that he mistakenly believed to be a Confederate ruse. After the war, he repaid Confederate Captain Henry Wirz's kindness in trying to exchange him by trying to testify on Wirz's behalf at the captain's war crimes trial. The prosecution barred Guscetti on the grounds that he lost his credibility because he had tried to publicly raise funds for Wirz's defense. Guscetti applied for his own back pay and other compensation but also the same for Jacques Roellinger, whose identity he falsely assumed. Furthermore, in the company of a small boy he claimed as a son, he persuaded the secretary of war that he was Roellinger and that his death had been incorrectly reported at Andersonville. While successfully drawing two pensions, one as Guscetti and another as Roellinger, he also filed for a pension, in which he also acted as a witness, as the father of the deceased Jacques Roellinger, a soldier he represented as shot and killed by the guards at Andersonville in August 1864. (Guscetti apparently confused the Roellinger/Rallinger who died of scorbutus with Jacques Alligier, a member of the 48th New York killed by the guards on 26 October 1864. A woman also falsely filed a pension claim as Roellinger's widow.) He likely would have succeeded in drawing all three pensions except for being exposed by a chance meeting of two of his pension agents who realized they were each filing claims for the same person. On 26 March 1867, a federal court sentenced Guscetti to seven years in prison for pension fraud. He later moved to his native Italy, and from there, he and his wife (later his widow), successfully applied for federal pensions based upon his real identity and service in the Lost Children. These matters became part of the national political debate on the excesses and fraud in the federal pension system when the real Jacques Roellinger, finally and successfully, applied for his own pension, after having to explain his desertion and false identity.[284]

Even visitors to the prison would use aliases while coming to meet prisoners who also used assumed names. In January 1865, Wirz wrote of a suspicious "Mrs. Spaulding" from Americus whose husband, so an informant told him, played a prominent role in a local anti-secession meeting. Wirz may have gotten her name wrong but she also may have used an alias rather than her real name of Agnes Malaput Thuillier Powell (Mrs. Ambrose C. Spencer). Agnes would later hide and provide for at least one prisoner who had escaped from the stockade. On this particular trip, the mystery woman came to visit a federal soldier from nearby Americus who had traveled north at the beginning of the war, married there, and enlisted from Dubuque in an Iowa regiment. He had smuggled a letter to his family by way of a friend among the guards. "Mrs. Spalding" had just returned from the North with the reply, which she now delivered as a family friend. John Northrop remembered a soldier who went by the name of Hirst, a name that Northrup suspected that he used as an alias. He wrote of Hirst being punished after a guard alerted Hirst's wife, who lived nearby, and she came to ask to see her husband. A Mary Rawson of nearby Plains also regularly brought food baskets to a prisoner who used the identity of Peter Kiene of the 16th Iowa. Kiene, a native Iowan, seems like a strong candidate for one of the prisoners using an alias since his pension file omits any mention of his having a wife at that time. This common use of false identities makes finding the real people in these stories nearly impossible.[285]

To further add to the confusion of identity at Andersonville, long after the war, individuals apparently invented persons at Andersonville who never existed. A Warren Lantman, for example, would claim that he had a brother named Vardy who died at Andersonville and whose body was brought home for reburial after the war, while he also had a brother named Benton who died as a Confederate captain in a federal prison; the location of his grave is unknown. Before the war, Benton allegedly had managed a plantation of their father near Albany, Georgia, the largest city to the later site of Andersonville. When his father and brothers returned North at the beginning of the war, Benton supposedly stayed and fought for the South. He refused his father's request to emancipate his slaves. No records have been found that support Warren Lantman's story, however.[286] Similar confusion exists about women prisoners who likely did not exist.

A secret as important as the identity of Limber Jim cries out for a solution, however, even in a bizarre ad hoc city of aliases and in an era where false names were so common. In 1889, Henry Harrison Rood published a history of his unit, company A of the 13th Iowa Infantry Regiment. Eight years later, he gave a paper before the Military Order of the Loyal Legion on this same subject. In both publications, he included a biography of one of his men, Vincent Ferguson "Limber Jim" Stevens of Andersonville. As several members of the company had spent time in that prison, Rood's second-hand account could have been corrected by 1897 if he had published misinformation in 1889.

According to Rood, Stevens had proven himself successful in all games of chance and as a first class scrounger who kept his company well-supplied as a classic soldier hustler. Rood thought that his comrade had acquired the nickname of Limber Jim when he took on a much larger trooper in a fight in Jefferson City, Missouri, and, to everyone's surprise, won. The 13th Iowa served in more than its share of the fighting, and Stevens displayed exceptional courage at the battle of Shiloh. On 9 February 1864, however, his famous luck failed when he fell into the hands of the Confederates during the Meridian Expedition.

Many facts about Stevens support Rood's claims. Vincent Ferguson Stevens, born on 4 May 1842, in Muskingum County, Ohio, to Isaac and Elsie Haines Stevens, did enlist in the 13th Iowa on 27 September 1861, in Davenport, Iowa. He reenlisted on 15 December 1863. His compiled service records described him as five feet, eleven inches tall, with blue eyes, dark hair, and dark complexion, which would seem to agree with accounts of Limber Jim's appear-

Vincent Ferguson Stevens. (Courtesy Randy Stevens)

ance. Goss and Regan wrote that Limber Jim came to Andersonville with the prisoners sent from Cahawba, Alabama, which would agree with the time and place of Stevens's capture, prior to the opening of Andersonville in late February 1864. Stevens later told family members that he worked on the wagon that carried out the dead each day at Andersonville. By that means, he could, as Fechter testified that Limber Jim did, smuggle in food bought from civilians. Plumleigh may have mistaken Stevens's 13th Iowa with the 113th Illinois. According to a deposition by James W. Wickham in Stevens's pension file, upon entering Andersonville he found Vincent suffering terribly from piles and diarrhea, the combination that often proved fatal in Andersonville. Vincent Stevens survived raiders, illness, and the other horrors of Andersonville, however, to see freedom at the end of the war.

Unlike the other possible Limber Jims, we have Vincent Stevens's confession. No one came forward to back up his claim, but no one refuted him by name either. Stevens moved to Linn County, Nebraska, where he married and started a family. In 1897, he gave a talk before a Nebraska convention of the Grand Army of the Republic about his experiences at Andersonville as Limber Jim. Stevens told how he had obtained his nickname because of his acrobatics and how he had helped in suppressing the raiders. When a query as to the identity of Limber Jim appeared in the 4 November 1897 issue of the *National Tribune*, Stevens replied directly to the author. By avoiding making a direct reply in the *Tribune*, however, he saved himself from challenges to his claims by other Andersonville survivors. He may have also been protecting himself from vindictive comrades seeking to learn the whereabouts of "Limber Jim." Stevens died from cancer of the pancreas on 8 May 1911.[287]

Vincent's experience, however, fails to match all of the details of the diverse and sometimes contradictory accounts of Limber Jim. Perhaps the real Stevens failed to measure up to the legend of his other legendary persona and, consequently, the other prisoners mistakenly identified other men they knew as Limber Jim. Contrary to Hibbs's claim, for example, Stevens left Andersonville by traveling through Jacksonville, Florida, at the end of the war, rather than through Vicksburg in March 1865. Hoster described Limber Jim as being an artillery sergeant with a sailor's cap, hardly the uniform of an infantryman although Stevens may have bought or obtained parts of different uniforms from dead prisoners. Also, Stevens did not die in Cheyenne in 1867.

Stevens's claim of being Limber Jim, however, suggests one other lesson in the pitfalls of identification. By his own time, various individuals had identified themselves as such famous characters as Marshal Ney, Theodosia Burr, Davy

Crockett, Sacagawea, Billy the Kid, Jesse James, Butch Cassidy, etc., but lived under aliases after surviving widely reported deaths. Having heard reports that Limber Jim had died, Stevens could avoid confrontation, at least with the real man of legend, when he claimed for himself the identity of Andersonville's most famous legend.

If Stevens made false claims, he assumed the odd position of being the hustler Rood remembered, but also a man who publicly assumed the legendary persona of still another con man, such as Jack Williams, who had worked to keep his real life identity obscure by falsely identifying himself as James McLaughlin. If Stevens and the legendary Limber Jim were one and the same, however, his real name remained hidden, despite his later public confession, by the lack of contemporary and conclusive evidence to substantiate his claim over that of the various other men credited as being the Andersonville hangman. The misidentifications and stories wrongly attributed to Limber Jim thus provided him with social camouflage.

So much confusion and misunderstanding about the identity of Limber Jim would beg the question of whether his true name matters much beyond serving as an illustration of the problem of false identity in nineteenth-century America. He might best remain a legend within an ocean of greater legends about the first of the world's first concentration camps.

His tale does raise important issues. Writers for the respective partisan press of the Civil War, the federal prosecutors of Henry Wirz, the memorialists after the war, and others created false images of Andersonville, making Limber Jim, at times, a myth that existed within a greater fiction. Survivors described the horrors of this prison in lectures, manuscripts, articles, pamphlets, and books. This vast body of information generated legends within the history of Andersonville itself.

The prison's most famous character, Confederate Captain Henry Wirz, for example, has been exposed as having deviated from the facts about the circumstances of his arrival in America, family life, medical training, and permanent injuries. He had the responsibility for the security inside the prison stockade. The prosecutor in the federal military court that had Wirz hanged for war crimes, however, created still another identity for him. The new and largely mythical Wirz served as camp commandant and had life and death control of the guards, supply of rations, tracking dogs, and medicines. This fictional "demon of Andersonville" murdered individual prisoners while the real Wirz, with little real authority, often lay near death or spent time in other parts of Georgia seeking medical attention. While that real man wrote in nearly perfect

English, the fictional war criminal of the prison memoirs cursed Yankees in heavily German-accented, broken English. Wirz would hang as a mythical monster rather than as the (likely equally false) doctor and injured war hero identity he had created for himself.[288] Similarly, the Northern and Southern defenders of Wirz, President Jefferson Davis, and the Confederacy itself, at times created a fictional Andersonville that Confederate General John B. Gordon, who never saw the real prison, described as being no worse than a second-rate hotel.[289]

As Andersonville historian William Marvel wrote, only when we set aside these biases, will the truth about the prison emerge. When studied as a real place, rather than as an agenda, the history of Camp Sumter provides credible answers to such important questions as why confinement in this prison cost so many lives. Limber Jim has a place in all of the very different Andersonvilles. Unraveling the myths around him starts the process of finding the true identity of America's most notorious prison camp.

While Limber Jim played a major role in the history of Andersonville, he and his fame illustrate still more. As shown many times in the Andersonville literary genre, legends of his time had a basis in deliberate falsehood, sometimes for personal profit and protection, but at different times for other partisan purposes. This era of easy new identity and the opportunity for those who wished to "hide" in the Civil War provided the means for creating legends. In this context, the final importance of the story of Limber Jim rests in what came from what later writers wanted to believe.

This illustration of a Father Hamilton, perhaps actually of another priest, appeared in John McElroy, *Andersonville: a Story of Rebel Prisons* (1879).

MISSIONARY TO THE DISTANT REALM

It was one of those sequestered spots outside the gates of the world...where, from time to time, dramas of grandeur and unity truly Sophoclean are enacted in the real, by virtue of the concentrated passions and closely knit interdependence of the lives therein.

—Thomas Hardy, from *The Woodlanders*

Of all of the many personalities to come to this "lonely pine woods," few of them traveled by quite so long and curious a route as did Roman Catholic priest William John Hamilton. As with so many of the other people discussed here, the currents of his time carried him along to many alien lands. He also represented significant social forces in the South that went on almost unnoticed at the time and even since then by historians. Hamilton won a special place in the memories and hearts of the survivors of Andersonville. Like most of them, he had come from outside of the South. He also shared with many of the prisoners a religion and nationality largely alien in the Confederacy. In the terrible isolation of Camp Sumter, this priest and his colleagues bridged the strange land where they found themselves and the reality that the Northern soldiers, sailors, and civilians had known before war and their capture. To many of the inmates, having priests in this bizarre "Golgotha" of the Civil War proved that God could even create a parish in Hell.

Father Hamilton began his trip to Camp Sumter with his birth on 25 March 1832, in Londonderry, Ireland, likely as the son of the Luke and Mary Hamilton who received christening on 15 September 1832, at Lower Chamber in Derry. At an early age, his parents sent him to seminary. In 1851, he entered All Hallows College in Dublin, since 1845 the great Irish missionary college that had been established from St. Columb's in Londonderry. Originally, Hamilton received training for an assignment to St. Helena.[290] A plea for missionaries for the Southern United States by Father John Barry, the administrator for the Southern states, however, resulted in a change in his destination.

On 10 July 1855, in Derry, a Dr. Kelly ordained Hamilton for the priesthood in Savannah, Georgia. The following 27 November, after a stormy voyage, Father Hamilton, with Father Joseph Hasson, arrived in New York, on the U. S. mail steamer *Washington*, out of Southampton. Hamilton received an assignment to the Church of Immaculate Conception in Jacksonville, where he served as one of only two priests in all of Florida. Some letters Hamilton wrote from there survive.

In addition to the growing tensions over slavery that permeated the United States in those years, the new priest wrote of another source of conflict. Irishmen reportedly found themselves, at least initially, on the "lowest rung" of Southern white society. Even in Jacksonville, The American "Know Nothing" Party had reached the height of its considerable political power. This secretive political movement grew up as a national unity alternative to the slavery politics of the period. Hamilton, however, discovered that the anti-foreigner and anti-Roman Catholic prejudices that became the signature of the American Party in the North existed just as strongly in the South. Thousands of his countrymen had come to the South to perform the ditching and engineering tasks for which the local labor force lacked skilled knowledge. The almost exclusively Protestant native Southerners easily added prejudice against Catholic Irishmen to their traditional distain of Northerners, Indians, and African Americans. In the South, rumors even circulated of a "Catholic-Negro alliance" to destroy white Protestants. For reasons unknown, during Hamilton's years in Florida, the number of Irishmen in that then sparsely state drastically declined, while significantly increasing elsewhere in the South.[291]

Unfortunately, we do not have the benefit of Father Hamilton's views about the arrival of the Civil War in 1861. Congressman James G. Blaine would later describe the priest as a Democrat. The war directly affected Hamilton the following year. In May 1862, federal troops entered Jacksonville. They looted and burned his church. Bishop Augustin Verot shortly afterwards transferred Hamilton to Columbus, Georgia, where a convent and Catholic school had been recently established. In the summer of 1864, Hamilton was transferred to the Church of the Assumption in Macon. By that time, he had brought his mother and sister to America to work as his housekeepers.[292]

The priest found plenty to do. Many Irish Catholics had remained in the South after secession and even helped to meet the technical needs, or served in the army, of the new Confederate States of America. Father Hamilton's new position included missionary work. In May 1864, he journeyed to his mission in Americus, Georgia. During this trip, he learned that since the previous February the rebels had established Camp Sumter, a prison stockade at Anderson Station (Andersonville post office) near Americus. He stopped off there for a few hours on his return trip to Macon to see if any of the prisoners needed his services.

Hamilton returned the following week and stayed for three days, with the complete cooperation of Captain Henry Wirz, a Roman Catholic and the staff officer responsible for access to the stockade. After the war, Hamilton described his experience with these words:

> I found the place extremely crowded, with a great deal of sickness and suffering among the men. I was kept so busy administering the sacrament to the dying...I found the stockade extremely filthy; the men all huddled together, and covered with vermin...I went in there with a white linen coat on, and I had not been in there more than ten minutes or a quarter of an hour, when it was covered all over with vermin. When I visited the stockade there was no shelter at all so far as I could see, except that some of the men who had their blankets there had put them up on little bits of roots that they had abstracted from the ground...I saw a great many men perfectly nude; they seemed to have lost all regard for delicacy, shame, morality, or anything else. I would frequently have to creep on my hands and knees into the holes that the men had burrowed in the ground and stretch myself out along side of them to hear their confessions.[293]

Hamilton returned to Andersonville once more, in early in 1865, but he declined to enter the stockade at that time. He would testify on the conditions at the camp at Wirz's war crimes trial in late 1865. He refused to say anything negative about the Confederate captain, however. Hamilton did go to Secretary of War Edwin Stanton with a proposal from Wirz. The rebel captain agreed to confess to his culpability for Andersonville if Stanton would set the date of the execution for two months into the future, which would be after the time that the captain's doctors said Wirz had left to live. Staton declined. Years later, and shortly before his own death, the priest would publicly defend Wirz as a humane man.[294]

Even during the war, word reached the public of Hamilton's connection to Andersonville, starting the misunderstandings about how much time he spent at the prison and obscuring his real services among prisoners of war. The priest did frequently visit the federal officers held in Macon at Camp Oglethorpe and twice smuggled out cash donations from them for the enlisted men held in Andersonville. When the guards caught him sharing news about the latter with these officer prisoners, Hamilton lost his visitor privileges to Camp Oglethorpe.[295] He also collected food and medicine for the prisoners. Even at Camp Oglethorpe, conditions had become bad enough that the priest would have to cleanse himself of vermin in his basement before he could enter his house. Father Hamilton also worked among smallpox victims in the surrounding military camps and hospitals.[296]

Hamilton did write to Bishop Verot about what he found at Andersonville, however. His Grace responded by sending, at different times, fathers Peter Whelan, Henry Peter Clavreul, Peter Dufau, John F. Kirby, and Anselm Usannaz to the prison camp. Bishop Verot twice personally visited the prison to see the conditions there for himself and to minister to the prisoners. Father Whelan borrowed sixteen thousand dollars to purchase flour for the sick inmates, for which the United States government later declined to reimburse him.[297] Andersonville survivors, Protestant and Catholic, would remember the priests aiding the prisoners when so very few representatives of any other faith visited the camp. Martin S. Harris of the 5th New York Artillery, for example, wrote:

> Another noticeable feature, which impressed me, during my long captivity, was the total absence of all clergymen inside the stockade, excepting the Roman Catholic. At all hours while ingress was permitted to visitors, these devoted men were at work. In the drenching rain, in the pitiless sunlight, amid

> everything revolting to soul and sense, they pursued their ministrations—comforting the living, and serving those past all hope.[298]

Whelan did the greatest service of any priest at Andersonville, working among the prisoners every day from 16 June to 1 October 1864. He made such sacrifices despite, or perhaps because, he had been a prisoner of war himself. The federals had held him for several months following his capture with the Confederate garrison at Fort Pulaski on 11 April 1862. He died in 1871 as a result of health problems brought on by his service at Andersonville.[299]

Writer MacKinley Kantor correctly identified Whelan as the principal priest at Andersonville in his novel *Andersonville.* John McElroy, the Protestant author of the greatest memoir of any Andersonville prisoner, however, mistakenly remembered Father Hamilton as the only priest in the prison. McElroy even included an engraving of Hamilton aiding prisoners in his book. His written description of the priest actually matches the elderly, bald Father Whelan. McElroy's statements also led his comrades to misidentifying all of the other priests at Andersonville as William John Hamilton in their published diaries, memoirs, and prints of Andersonville.[300] Hamilton did join Whelan in an unsuccessful effort to obtain General Howell Cobb's help in requesting the release of the prisoners.[301]

Hamilton also continued his work beyond Andersonville. Briefly, he served in Columbus before he returned to his usual position in Macon in 1865. Immediately after the war, the now Very Reverend William J. Hamilton worked for the bishop in Savannah. He helped in the education of the newly freed African Americans, while performing such mundane tasks as marriages and building dedications. Hamilton served as Vicar General in Augusta, Georgia, from 1866 to 1873 before he again served in Columbus. He took charge of church affairs in Florida and Georgia during Bishop Verot's trip to the Vatican Council in Rome in 1870.

In 1873, Hamilton returned to his missionary work. Father J. J. O'Connell referred to him at that time as an "accomplished scholar and devoted clergyman." William John Hamilton served in Mobile, Alabama (1873); Columbus, Georgia (1875); and Appalachicola, Florida (1876–1877). He then confined his activities to Alabama, serving parishioners in Tuscaloosa (1878), Eufaula, Whistler (1879), and Mobile (1880).[302] While in the latter, he resided at the home of Bishop John Quinlan. By 6 February 1883, Father Hamilton suffered from ill health. On that day, the Maine Division of the federal veteran's organization, the Grand Army of the Republic, publicly honored his services to the prisoners at Andersonville. The mortally ill priest personally wrote a letter of thanks from the Church of the Immaculate Conception in Mobile to his former "parishioners." He or an editor, however, erred by referring to the priest's "eleven dreary months" at Andersonville.[303]

Hoping to regain his health, Hamilton transferred to Louisville, Kentucky, on 23 May 1883. He took charge of the cathedral there and resumed as many of his pastoral duties as his health would allow. Hamilton began to recover and believed that he would soon return to Mobile. Instead, he died at the home of Bishop John McCloskey on 1 March 1884. The Andersonville priest received a great funeral mass before his burial in the city cemetery. His obituary appeared in national newspapers.[304]

Many of the survivors of Andersonville belonged to organizations that took note of his passing. The prisoner of war memoir writers would praise Hamilton in their writings, although they often confused him with Whelan and the other priests. In the greater sense, the veterans honored the good that he symbolized as carried out by the entire Roman Catholic clergy that aided the prisoners in the darkest moments of their lives and in one of the worst situations in America's history.

Andrew J. Riddle. (Atlanta History Center)

IMAGES OF A PHOTOGRAPHER[305]

As a former `star-boarder' of Andersonville, I well remember seeing a photographer with his camera in one of the sentinel boxes near the South Gate during July or August (1864), trying to take a picture of the interior of the prison. I have often wondered in later years what success this photographer had and why the public never had an opportunity of seeing a genuine photograph of Andersonville.

—former prisoner John McElroy

Then we listened to their story of their prison life [at Andersonville]....They showed us sketches, of groups, which were taken, there by some artists that were among them. They were very natural. Some then asked how many would believe, that these scenes were real when those sketches were shown in the union lines.

—former prisoner John Squires

In 1865, a writer for the *Richmond Whig* wrote about the already notorious Andersonville, "A photograph of this place, where between thirty and forty thousand Yankees are penned up, ought to be made and preserved. Such a picture was never before seen on earth, and we trust never will be again. Those who visited Andersonville will declare that the spectacle surpasses description."[306]

Unbeknownst to the author of the above claim, a Macon, Georgia, photographer had preserved the reality of the Civil War's most infamous prison camp. Without those photographs, the only visuals from the camp to survive would have been sensationalized drawings made by the prisoners and the post-war government photographs of John F. Engle and James Furlong of Fernandina, Florida.[307]

Andrew J. Riddle, the Macon, Georgia, cameraman, came to Camp Sumter by a typically long and circuitous route for this tragic epic. His journey also tells something of the history of the development of skilled craftsmanship as a business in the American society of his time.[308] His obituary would state that he was born in Baltimore, Maryland, on 28 February 1828, but census records imply that he was actually born in New Castle County, Delaware, as the son of John and Sarah Riddle. (John Riddle did die in Baltimore, where his family resided, in May 1850.) Andrew became involved with photography in 1846, likely by studying under his friend, the famed lithographer Napoleon Sarony of New York. Riddle opened his own photography studio in Baltimore by 1851. Five years later he, with his elderly mother Jane, lived in his studio in Columbus, Georgia. On 6 November 1856, he married Annie Hunley, the daughter of the prominent mill owner Ambrose Hunley, in nearby Harris County. The couple soon had three children. Within a few years, Riddle opened branch studios in Macon and Rome, Georgia.[309]

According to his obituary, when the South seceded, Andrew J. Riddle served in the Confederate army for three years, including, supposedly, three times as a prisoner of war. The only A. J. Riddle who appears in what survives of the Confederate records and meets the criteria of his alleged service spent his time in various Missouri regiments from May 1862 to February 1864.[310] Records of the movements of Andrew J. Riddle of Georgia in 1862–1863, however, make the claims in his obituary of military service suspect. Early in the war, he moved from Georgia and opened a studio at 151 Main Street in Richmond, Virginia.[311] In October 1862, federal authorities arrested him in Charles County, Maryland, when he tried to smuggle a trunkload of photographic supplies from Washington to his new studio in Richmond. The Union Provost Marshal seized

Riddle's goods but allowed him to continue onto Richmond. The following April, he tried to obtain a pass to move through the Confederate lines to Maryland. By 25 September 1863, Riddle had spent four months of what became an eight-month prison term imposed by the federals for trying to smuggle still more photographic supplies, this time from New York through Westmoreland County, Virginia.[312]

In July 1864, he returned to Macon. Confederate officials then conscripted him as a private in the engineers. In addition to reproducing maps for the army, he worked as chief photographer for the western armies under General Joseph E. Johnston. (Johnson also later became a resident of Macon.)[313] During this time, in his capacity as the Confederacy's only verified official photographer, Riddle likely made his photograph of the ironclad *CSS Jackson* and views of the new ordnance buildings in Macon. He mass-produced maps for the army using the photographic method developed by Major Albert H. Campbell in Richmond. The Campbell process used photographs, tracing paper, and sunlight in a crude but effective version of the modern photoduplication process.[314]

On 16 August 1864, Riddle photographed scenes in and around the Andersonville stockade. In one of the endless ironies associated with that place, a man who had himself been a prisoner of war for smuggling photography supplies, now used his camera to record images of his former captor's soldiers and sailors held in the most notorious prison of the world. He photographed the prisoners in such a way that he created a story line of life and burial at Andersonville. During that day, he made seven prints of the interior of the stockade, one of the cemetery, and another of a burial detail in the prison cemetery. For whatever reason, he failed to make a complete series of images by including the removal of the dead and the hospital. Riddle also made at least two portraits during this trip, one of Brigadier General John T. Winder, commandant of the camp and commander of all prisons east of the Mississippi, and another likely of Captain Henry Wirz. Riddle developed and dated the prints of the prison on the next day.

These photographs illustrate the realities of the prison with a credibility beyond anything shown in post war prisoner drawings.[315] He made the only surviving photographs of federal inmates in an operating Confederate prison. (Only after the war did photographers make other pictures of the prison buildings.) At the time Riddle arrived, the Andersonville stockade held more than thirty thousand federal soldiers, sailors, and civilians, black, white, and red, in just over twenty acres. At its maximum occupancy, the camp would hold thousands more men, giving each prisoner barely enough space to lie down. On just the day that Riddle photographed Andersonville, more than one hundred inmates died from starvation, disease, and exposure; six thousand men already lay buried in the cemetery; and twenty-five hundred others waited for what little medical attention the camp's staff could provide. Riddle's camera recorded a sea of tents, some huts, and even the holes in the ground used by the inmates. He made three of the views from where rain had created a large gap in that wall on the east side. The storm that had torn down a section of the wall had been a blessing, breaking a drought, briefly cleansing the prison, and exposing the so called "Providence Spring," a previously unknown, covered source of clean water as an alternative to the marshy creek near the south end of the camp.[316]

The photographs quickly became a part of the larger legend of Andersonville. During the trial of Andersonville officer Henry Wirz, the Judge Advocate announced that he planned to introduce into evidence a group of photographs of the prison. He likely referred to Andrew J. Riddle's work. Ambrose C. Spencer used an engraving from a Riddle photograph in his *A Narrative of Andersonville* (1866). Riddle's photographic process produced only prints. Before the war, however, he had invented a camera that made two photographs at once.[317] One set of his Andersonville prints went to the camp's officials and the other set Riddle retained. In October 1865, Theodore Wiseman moved near Anderson Station and found seven of the Riddle photographs in Captain Wirz's trunk. He would display them at veterans meetings for years afterwards. In 1883, as a resident of Lawrence, Kansas, Wiseman had the photographs copyrighted and published. He then sold complete sets of the prints for two dollars. The War Department acquired a copy of the photographs by 1897.[318]

In the interim, Riddle had the good fortune of being in Macon to photograph one of the symbolic moments of the end of the Civil War. From a window, he made the often reproduced photograph of the arrival of the wagon train carrying Confederate president Jefferson Davis as a prisoner of the federal government. Davis had been arrested by cavalry at Irwinville, Georgia, on 10 May 1865, within a day's journey of the Andersonville prison (by then abandoned). Davis missed seeing it except perhaps through a publication of Riddle's photographs. For the rest of his life, however, the Confederate president would defend his lost nation against charges of cruelty to prisoners at Andersonville.

After the war, Riddle displayed his complete set of Andersonville pictures and eventually sold them to former prisoner of war Daniel S. Camp. Robert H. Kellogg, another Andersonville inmate, had seen Riddle make the photographs on 16 August 1864, and later saw the photographer trying to sell his set of the prints in New York in June 1865. Kellogg acquired the photographs and donated them to the State Library of Connecticut in 1922. He did not donate them to the federal government because he had been warned that souvenir hunters often stole photographs from the War Department. The Kellogg set of prints has been copied and published many times, including for the holdings of the U. S. Army Military History Institute at Carlisle, Pennsylvania.[319]

These photographs of Camp Sumter, the Andersonville prison, represent more than a unique historical record; they also tell much about their creator. Other people of his age changed occupations, as they did addresses, almost at will. He did not achieve any artistic merit with his Civil War photographs, but, significantly, he stayed in the Confederacy and made numerous sacrifices to continue working as a photographer. Riddle might have found another line of work or have returned to the North, even with his family, to continue in his profession. Instead, this professional decided for himself what would be his place and his work.

Andrew J. Riddle would continue his photographic career in Columbus and Macon, sometimes achieving attention for his work in life-size prints, colorization, and studio backgrounds. Riddle displayed his work in his combination "Photographic Temple," candy store, and ice cream saloon in Macon. Later, in Eufaula, Alabama, he opened a combination hotel, photographic studio, and billiard hall. He failed to accumulate capital, however, and later succumbed to the great vices of his era, gambling and alcohol. Andrew J. Riddle died in Columbus on 21 March 1897. He was buried in his family plot in Rose Hill Cemetery in Macon two days later.[320]

The following set of the Riddle photographs of life and death at Andersonville prison is reproduced from Massachusetts Commandery, Military Order of the Loyal Legion, U. S. Army Military History Institute, Carlisle PA.

Vignette of the headquarters at Camp Sumter (Andersonville) drawn after the Civil War. (R. S. Davis)

THE TROJAN WOMEN

If you will promise not to pick the flowers and will keep off the grass, I will take you with me into that Eve-less Eden…

—Charles Richardson, former Andersonville inmate

Andersonville was a city—a market place. All it lacked of being a bazaar was the women.

—George W. Fechter, former Andersonville inmate

The professions that allowed people to travel and reinvent themselves in the nineteenth century largely excluded women. Female con artists, women posing as men, and professional matrons did exist, but they were also more evasive about recording their pasts than their male counterparts. As married women of the time typically had little legal existence and support beyond their husbands, women like the previously mentioned Agnes Malaput Thuillier Powell (Mrs. Ambrose Spencer) and Elizabeth Savells (the widow Walker and later Mrs. Henry Wirz) traveled with their husbands, however reluctantly, even to Andersonville. Women also became prisoners from following husbands into the war. Unlike the male inmates, the women held in Andersonville continued, in their confinement, the legal restraints imposed on all wives of their era.

The stories of the women of Andersonville might end there, but the novelty of their presence among more than thirty thousand men made them a special part of the prison's legends. Their tale would seem to lend itself today to inclusion with such exceptional subjects as cannibalism and sodomy. The vast body of literature about this place lacks even a passing mention of these other subjects.[321]

Perhaps these matters proved too controversial for the nineteenth-century reader, or they would paint such a negative image of the prisoner of war as to hinder the post war efforts to win special pension legislation for former prisoners. A study of the female prisoners, as legend and as reality, does substantiate how far the stories of Andersonville have wandered from the facts. It also added the name of a unique fatality to the Andersonville dead list.

Eleven years after Andersonville terminated operation, former guard B. L. McGough wrote about the prison's women in a brief memoir. Although he claimed to have remembered the women prisoners, he only served there for a few months before his disability discharge on 25 August 1864. He wrote:

> One other incident that took place at Andersonville...and this one was never given to the public in any way. A young couple from Ireland came over to our country during the Civil War, and landed in New York. The young husband was enlisted or drafted in the Northern army. His young wife could not bear the idea of having her young husband leaving her in a strange land among strangers without any kind of protection. They planned a way so that they could be together, the young wife had her hair cut short like a man and clothed herself in her husband's clothes. She enlisted with her husband and they went to the war together. They were sent to Virginia and were taken prisoners by the Confederate army and sent to Andersonville prison. The young wife's sex was discovered in the stockade and was reported to the captain. He had her and her husband brought out of the stockade and placed in a tent in front of his headquarters. A few days later the young wife gave birth to a child, the sex of the child I do not remember. She did well and in a few days was sitting in front of the tent on a camp stool nursing her child. They remained about a month longer and then they disappeared. I was told Captain

> Wirz paroled them out and sent them back to the North. I passed by their tent every day while they were there. I never heard of them after they left. Have often wondered why this incident was never published and given out to the public.[322]

McGough inexplicably merged three women of reality and legend into one person. Other, fragmentary, accounts of the women of Andersonville do appear in print and in the surviving records. As with so much in the traditional telling of the history of Andersonville, however, the reality proves so complicated and confused that the facts become difficult to untangle from the myth.[323]

Edward Wellington Boate testified from personal experience as a prisoner in the 1865 trial of Captain Henry Wirz and tried to set the record straight about the women prisoners. He knew, for example, the "Irish couple" to whom McGough referred.[324] Contemporary records identify them as the Leonards. Twenty-eight year old Irish servant Margaret Larney married Isaac Newton Leonard, a thirty-two year old Massachusetts-born boot maker of Scottish descent, in Springfield, Massachusetts, on 26 August 1862. The following year, when Isaac enlisted for garrison duty in company H of the 2nd Massachusetts Heavy Artillery, she followed him to war, working as a female civilian cook. Veteran Warren Goss remembered that, during the successful rebel attack on Plymouth, North Carolina, she continued making coffee and cooking for the federal soldiers and officers, even while under enemy fire. When the garrison surrendered, she and her husband found themselves among the prisoners sent to Andersonville, where she initially worked in the hospital.[325]

Margaret's name appears in the prison records and in a contemporary newspaper report of the prison. For a time, she lived with Captain Wirz's family but, when she proved too disagreeable, Wirz wrote to his superiors that he had her transferred to Castle Thunder, the prison for civilian prisoners of war in Richmond. While there, she made the acquaintance of the famous Dr. Mary Edwards Walker, the Union army's only female physician and a comrade prisoner of war. Walker would describe Margaret as only "a large stout Irish woman" who remained in the prison only briefly before being sent on to the federal lines. The Confederacy transferred Isaac with other prisoners to Florence, South Carolina. He took an oath to the Confederacy, in February 1865, but he later escaped from "rebeldom" in time to muster out with his unit the following July. He remained in poor health from his treatment in Andersonville and Florence, however, and died in Springfield, Massachusetts, around 1869. Soon after his death, Margaret moved to Kernville, California, with their son George. She died there around 1900, according to records in her efforts to receive a pension as the widow of a federal soldier.[326]

The story of the only person born in Andersonville prison belongs to the one other woman referred to by Boate. She must have often pondered the seemingly unrelated series of events that brought her to the world's largest prison, beginning with her first meeting with Herbert Hunt of Buffalo, New York (born 25 December 1838 in Lubec, Maine). He likely worked on the boats and ships on the Hudson/Erie Canal/Great Lakes/Mississippi River network that made Chicago and New York great cities. While ice skating in Chicago, he met her, Francis Jane "Fannie" "Janie" Scadin (born 1842 Michigan), the daughter of machine part pattern maker Robert Scadin. They married. When the war began, he enlisted in the 61st Illinois Infantry Regiment, where he reached the rank of sergeant before receiving a medical discharge on 22 May 1862.[327]

Their life together must have seemed to have taken a major leap forward when John H. Morris of Herkimer County, New York, employed Hunt to captain his steamship. Had Hunt been aware of Morris's questionable past, however, he likely would have stayed in Chicago. John H. Morris fit the era's stereotype of the entrepreneur of marginal ethics. In complicated law suits, plaintiffs called Morris a swindler as early as the 1840s.[328]

What happened to the Hunts and Morris became widely known through a third-hand account written almost fifty years after the events (in 1915) by Confederate medical officer William Jacob Warren Kerr. In his story, the Hunts married in New York City in the summer of 1865 and took their wedding party on a honeymoon cruise. A federal revenue cutter intercepted Hunt's ship and ordered it to put into North Carolina to pick up a load of corn, during which time Confederates captured the ship. The captors released all of the party except for Captain Hunt. Janie, however, chose to stay with her husband because she presumed that as he was a civilian he too would be released within a few days. Thirteen months later, in July 1864, Dr. Kerr found the Hunts robbed of almost all of their possessions, including five thousand dollars in cash, and being held as prisoners outside of the Andersonville stockade. They had a three day old son he referred to as "Little Harry."[329]

The Kerr account, however, has problems when compared with the fragmentary documentation. No record has been found of the Hunts marrying in New York City, and if they married in Chicago, the civil record would have been lost in the Chicago fire of 1871. Herbert's service record shows him as married by 1862. Kerr mistakenly identified Mrs. Hunt's father as Thomas L. Scadden, which likely contributed to his confessed failure to find the Hunts after the war.

The fragmentary contemporary records of the Hunts prove just as enigmatic. Captain Henry Wirz of Andersonville wrote to the provost marshal in Augusta, Georgia, on 19 May 1864 to request that Herbert Hunt and his wife be transferred to Andersonville. The Hunts had been sent south with seventy federal prisoners captured when Plymouth, North Carolina, fell to the Confederates in April 1864 and had arrived in Augusta on 17 May. The provost paroled them there, likely because of her pregnancy. Wirz, however, needed for the Hunts to testify in an investigation of Morris's situation as a prisoner. He added that Morris had arrived at Andersonville on 18 May and that Herbert Hunt had been the captain of Morris's ship. Andersonville's prisoner registers show that "H. Hunt" had been captured at Fairfield, North Carolina, (no date given) by an otherwise unidentified Captain "Ed. Lurrett."[330] Mrs. Hunt gave birth to a son, Andersonville prison's only native citizen, on 9 July 1864. Prisoner William H. Smith of the 4th Michigan Infantry recorded that birth in his diary. He frequently wrote about Mrs. Hunt and her baby son:

> *July 9, 1864* Mrs. Hunt is blessed with a young son
>
> *November 20, 1864* I have a fine joke played on me by tending Mrs. Hunt's baby
>
> *December 10, 1864* Negro Jack gets 51 lashes for telling lies about Mrs. Hunt
>
> *December 23, 1864* Mrs. Robertson & Hunt have been busy making cake for Christmas
>
> *January 4, 1865* This afternoon Mrs. Hunt and I go over to Mr. Smith's I carry the baby and have a very pleasant visit have an introduction to two young ladies
>
> *January 25, 1865* Mrs. Hunt goes out in the country visiting
>
> *February 1, 1865* I spend this evening with Mrs. Hunt it is a fine moonlit night.331

Kerr claimed that he, then a member of the medical staff, took pity on this family by moving them away from the stockade wall, paroling Herbert to work in the hospital, and obtaining donations of clothes for the child and his mother in Macon. His sympathy likely came in part from memories of the many months that he had spent as a prisoner of war at Camp Douglas and Point

Lookout in 1862. The Hunts thanked him, over his protests, with a gift of almost all they had left, a diamond scarf pin that he still had half a century later.[332]

Even within Andersonville's population of some thirty thousand, the novelty of this birth drew a great deal of attention and received some notice in later memoirs. Ransom Powell, the drummer boy prisoner whom Captain Wirz had made his aide, for example, in 1882 wrote of the Hunts as evidently having been well-off and as appearing as fine looking and accomplished. He added that they had been married for about a year when they arrived at Andersonville and were quite fond of one another. Hospital steward and prisoner Solon Hyde of the 17th Ohio Infantry wrote in 1900 of how Herbert Hunt had been a steamboat captain captured along the coast of North Carolina. Hyde spent evenings with the Hunts and baby Frank when the family took over two abandoned shanties. Mrs. Hunt had freedom to go where she chose and soon had made friends with local women and the wives of Confederate officers.[333]

Hunt family traditions have it that the baby, named Frank Hunt, did not survive Andersonville. Smith made no mention of the baby's death in his diary, but he left Andersonville on 3 February 1865, while the prison records show H. and Janie Hunt did not receive paroles until 15 April 1865. Destitute and trying to obtain government transportation to Chicago, Herbert and Janie found themselves in Cairo, Illinois, on 24 April. Nothing in those records mentions a baby.[334]

The post-war lives of the Hunts also leave a number of questions unanswered. They settled in the Newark-Communipaw area of New Jersey and raised a large brood of children. Herbert continued to work on the sea. Census takers, however, missed them in 1870 and 1880. Herbert Hunt declined to join the seventy percent or more of his comrades upon whose service someone applied for a federal pension (for Hunt's pre-Andersonville tour of duty.) The Hunts made no known effort to publicize or profit from their experience. Their last years were spent in Rocky Hill, Connecticut. Jane passed away in 1894, and Herbert died in 1926.[335]

The Hunts and Morrises also never filed any claim for losses with the United States, and no record of the capture of Morris's ship has been located beyond the Wirz letter.[336] In fact, Andersonville's surviving documents omit any further record of John H. Morris at all.[337] Quite possibly the rebel authorities secretly released him. He more than survived the prison. For the rest of the war, Confederate officials allowed him to pass in and out of their lines, and from prison camp to prison camp, buying securities and checks from desperate federal prisoners for pennies on the dollar paid in Confederate money. After the war, a federal provost marshal tried unsuccessfully to find charges with which to try him. Morris's luck held, however. In 1875, when his wife died, he even succeeded in defeating efforts by creditors who claimed that the allegedly "propertyless" Morris had hidden his assets under his wife's name only to safely receive full and unencumbered control of them again as inheritance when she died. Such a scheme could benefit an unscrupulous husband who took advantage of the growing success of the women's movement in steadily obtaining for married women increasing rights to property under their own names. Morris himself died broke and in obscurity in Herkimer in 1878.[338]

These two real women of Andersonville, Margaret Leonard and Francis Jane Hunt, the only ones prisoner Edward Wellington Boate testified to having seen, consequently became the basis of legends. The Hunts' experience likely inspired a story of a baby being born in Andersonville whose mother died in childbirth. The tale goes on to state that local people raised the child until he disappeared at age two, reportedly reclaimed by his father. Mrs. Leonard likewise may have been the basis of the story of female prisoner Florena Budwin at Florence. In 1889, Andersonville and Florence prison survivor Samuel Creelman told her story and described her grave marker, the only marked grave among the thousands of burials at Florence. Reportedly, doctors discovered "Florena Budwin," a twenty-one-year-old woman born in Philadelphia and disguised as a soldier among the prisoners transferred to Florence. Her husband, "Captain Budwin," had died at Andersonville. The Confederates supposedly failed to learn her alias as a soldier or her real name. Florena worked in the hospital until her death and interment at Florence. Another account of her life had her captured in an attack on Charleston in the autumn of 1864, where her husband died. That version of her life omits any mention of Andersonville.[339]

All stories of Florena Budwin have problems. Creelman made no claim of having actually seen her. No other known memoir or diary by any prisoner mentions her and no records of her or her husband have been found. An anonymous survivor, however, did write of the prisoners at Florence rioting when a civilian woman visited the prison—the only woman that he claimed that they saw in that stockade.[340]

The marker, origin unknown, fails to prove, by itself, that Florena existed. Someone could have erected it as part of a tribute to a legend, a hoax, or a plan to give false credence to some aspiring writer's plans for a novel that would have been passed off to the public as a work of nonfiction. She may have been a woman disguised as a man who allegedly died undetected at Florence. Some friend or family member may have erected the tombstone, even at a random spot, in her memory.[341]

Andersonville also has a story of a marker over the grave of a woman. A visitor to Andersonville after the war saw a plank burial marker to an "unknown lady." Andersonville researcher Kevin Frye has also heard this story as relating to grave 101. Supposedly one of the prisoners on the grave digging detail wrote in his diary about the corpse turning out to be a woman. Clarence Atwater and Clara Barton allegedly marked the grave although Barton failed to mention any such instance in her writings. The story concludes that the park superintendent in 1878 chose to change the marker to simply "unknown."[342] Finally, McGough's account of women disguised as soldiers may refer to yet a fourth couple. Some prisoners remembered two women dressed as soldiers who may have actually have been boys, hermaphrodites, or homosexuals. Whatever these two people may have been, they reportedly left the camp for parts unknown.[343]

The Confederacy did have other women prisoners, although almost all of them were among the inmates of Castle Thunder in Richmond rather than Andersonville. They included women caught as thieves and prostitutes; disguised as men (from both armies); spies; and Union sympathizers. The Confederate States of America refused to afford them the protection and status of prisoners of war but did grant them special considerations, as women, with regard to accommodations.[344]

The surviving records of Camp Sumter provide documentation of the presence of only two women who found themselves there as civilian prisoners of war. They had followed their husbands into this unwanted adventure without some glamorous ploy of disguising themselves as soldiers. They lived, except for these particular circumstances, as married wives of their time did elsewhere.

These two women, like the legendary women captured in the fall of Troy, vanished into their post-war world. As little credible information on their later lives exists as does for their Andersonville experience. Despite their extraordinary experiences, and even though they might have even profited from challenging the growing legends of the women of prisoners, the most extraordinary aspect of the real women of Andersonville is that they were so typical for their times.

William Tecumseh Sherman. (Library of Congress)

BUT UNCLE BILLY DIDN'T COME

> Soldiers that enlisted for their countreys cause. trew noable boys reard & bread in homes of plenty. heare they die of starvation & exposure among the poluted Swamps of georgia. O desptism of the north can you not send a handfull of men to liberate us.
>
> —Sergeant David Kennedy
> 9th Ohio Volunteer Cavalry, 25 June 1864

The famous William Tecumseh Sherman also found himself as a part of the Andersonville story. Did the general "who marched to Hell" do everything he reasonably could have done to rescue the prisoners there, or did he, through some twist of his peculiar legalistic frame of mind, sacrifice them for some imagined higher military purpose? Answers to Sherman's motives, as with so much of his career, seem forever shrouded in myth and psychology.

The truth of Sherman and Andersonville, however, as with so many of these other stories, must be sought, even if it lies more in the realms of psycho-history than in logic. In times where bureaucratic failure could create horrors beyond the control of any individual, men like Sherman became so powerful that the shortcomings and strengths of their personalities could profoundly affect countless people and raise moral issues of the era to a grand scale. As with Andersonville and the Yankee soldiers in Georgia in general, Sherman has become a symbol of unforgivable and inexcusable crimes. The real man's actions thus became issues sometimes without regard for scholarship and reality. His involvement, or lack of it, with the infamous prison camp survives as one of his lesser and least-examined legends.

The losses sustained by the South in Sherman's wake, however, failed to justify the stories.[345] That he ordered the destruction of Columbia, South Carolina, for example, has been refuted by modern scholarship.[346] Similarly, Sherman ordered only Atlanta buildings destroyed that could support the Confederate military efforts at killing his men seldom appears in print. His troops even helped to save from fire the quarter of the city that escaped damage in the fighting between the two armies. When his troops, practically without provisions, walked across Georgia to the sea during a two week period, his "bummers" had only time to forage what they directly encountered. These farms represented only a tiny percentage of the properties in the sixty-mile-wide area around which his fast moving and hungry columns passed. The relatively few families that these blue coats happened upon did have reason to "howl," as Sherman put it, but so did any families, in the North or the South, foraged by any army during the war. Certainly the average Georgia family had more to lose in property to Confederate impressments than to any federal troops.

Sherman did, at least once, answer the charges against him and his army. In early September 1864, Confederate General John Bell Hood wrote directly to Sherman to criticize the orders for the evacuation of civilians from Atlanta as "harsh." The often-heralded pioneer of "total war," William Tecumseh Sherman, used his reply as an opportunity to write a powerful and often published (but seldom read) attack on the broad and comprehensive inhumanity and crimes committed by the Confederate war effort. Sherman wrote, for example, that Confederate armies, including Hood's command, systematically foraged Southern farms to the point of the owners starving. By contrast, the United States daily fed thousands of Southerners from Vicksburg to Virginia, without regard to politics.[347]

Sherman in his very public and effective use of terrorism as a weapon deliberately excluded comprehensive destruction or real war crimes. He even protested the use by anyone of land mines because of possible harm to civilians. The general did feel that, even when real damage proved minimal, the enemy population's fears could prove to be a powerful weapon that Sherman could turn against them. In the South, he hoped to create popular opposition to the war that would for then, and for generations afterwards, successfully counter grassroots support for rebellion. He appreciated the scale of the reputation he acquired for this strategy, writing shortly after his march to the sea of how hundreds of children now cursed his name and thousands of adults daily prayed that he would be speedily sent to Hell.[348]

In the spring of 1864, Sherman did face challenges and opportunities unlike those of any other Civil War federal general. He had orders to pursue and destroy the Army of Tennessee, while ending Georgia's use to the Confederacy. The area of his campaign covered hundreds of thousands of square miles and included the three major enemy ordnance centers of Augusta, Columbus, and Macon, as well as several lesser operations that provided rebel armies with everything from matches to cannons. Only the shortcomings of the South's inadequate railroad network kept this one state, in 1864, from being able to feed, equip, and finance all that remained of the Confederate war effort by itself. The physical labor of thousands of slaves made such supply and provisioning possible, raising modern historian David Carleton's question of if the Old South existed as a slave society or a society with slaves. Emancipation could end that labor source, inspire widespread terror among whites, and prove almost as effective in ending the war as would the destruction of the enemy's armies.

Aside from freeing slaves, Sherman had another special weapon to use against Georgia and the whole of the remaining Confederate States of America—Camp Sumter, the Andersonville prison. By August 1864, the camp's over-crowded and under-fed population had swelled to 33,006, more than six times the stockade's original planned capacity. The guards, nine hundred to twenty-five hundred old men, boys, and green regulars, used the distance to the federal lines, the prospect of exchange, and individual intimidation more than their antique weapons to keep the greatest prison escape of all time from occurring deep within the Confederate States of America. Freeing the union captives in Georgia would unleash the largest, hungriest, and most desperate concentration of troops in the world, far behind the Confederate lines. Even if largely unarmed, these men could still have spread fear throughout what remained of the Confederate States of America. They would have encouraged desertions from the rebel armies while savaging the morale of Southern civilians. The results could have caused more damage to the Confederate cause than Sherman's later march to the sea.

The general had every encouragement to play this "Andersonville card." Escaped prisoners and William Whipple, the conductor of the railroad that served the prison, had made depositions about the horrors there. Sherman

Sherman at Atlanta planning his future campaigns. (Library of Congress)

claimed that he received one hundred letters per day from families of prisoners asking that he arrange for the release of their relatives by any means.[349] From newspaper accounts, the Northern public well knew of the conditions in such prisons. A rescue would achieve a political victory for the Lincoln administration of almost unimaginable value before the critical national elections of November 1864.

Rebel authorities, however, appreciated the threat posed by Andersonville. The camp had been built because of the danger of a mass release of federal prisoners from Belle Island in Richmond. By the spring of 1864, the Confederacy had few troops to spare for guard duty hundreds of miles from the front. It also refused to release to the federal army the Andersonville prisoners while any hope existed of exchanging them for captured Confederates. Rebel leaders believed that Rousseau's federal cavalry raid, in July 1864, had been intended to release the Andersonville captives.

Without transportation in the spring of 1864 to move the prisoners or resources to build new camps, the Confederacy had few means of preventing a mass escape or release of prisoners. Confederate General Joseph E. Johnston urged the transfer of the inmates to more secure areas. The government in Richmond took this to mean that Johnston planned to abandon his defense of Atlanta, the major federal objective and a potential base for a strike towards Andersonville. Shortly afterwards, President Jefferson Davis replaced Johnston with Hood. The latter gave the highest priority to defending Atlanta, but he would also later claim to have been trapped into defending the city to prevent Sherman's army from having the opportunity to release the prisoners at Andersonville.[350]

After Atlanta finally fell to Sherman in early September, he seemed poised to march largely unopposed anywhere he and his "bummers" chose to go. Andersonville's garrison and the local militia had used demonstrations of force and warnings to squelch planned mass escapes by the emaciated prisoners in the isolated prison during the months of May and July. Workmen physically strengthened the stockade to prevent the prisoners from pushing it and the sentinel towers down. On 28 July, the camp gunners fired a cannon shot into the marsh in the southern end of the camp as a warning to the prisoners of what could happen if the desperate men rushed the walls. The next day, additional areas within the stockade were marked with white flags to indicate where large gatherings of prisoners would result in the stockade's being fired upon by the garrison's artillery. The prisoners received encouragement to escape from reports of approaching federal cavalry and the growing expectation that their guards would flee in the face of a stampede by the tens of thousands of inmates. The Yankees had also come to disbelieve the rumors of an imminent general prisoner exchanges. The more than thirty thousand prisoners now grossly outnumbered the guards. They plotted to overwhelm their captors and to hold the local people as hostages.

Sherman's army did make something of an attempt to rescue the men at Andersonville. On 27 July 1864, as his army besieged Atlanta, Sherman dispatched more than five thousand cavalrymen to cut the last rebel railroad to Atlanta and, after achieving that goal, to attempt to rescue the federal prisoners in Macon and Andersonville. These horsemen suffered a major defeat at the hands of General Joseph Wheeler's rebel cavalry in a series of battles that became one of the greatest victories of its kind of the war. Almost one thousand blue-clad troopers thus ended up seeing Andersonville as prisoners rather than as saviors.

Sherman took responsibility for this destruction of his cavalry forces and admitted the mistake of authorizing the rescue of the prisoners of war. His confession appears genuine; not as showing false pity for the Andersonville inmates as a cover for the failure of his men to carry out their primary mission of seriously damaging Atlanta's last railroad in enemy hands.[351] Georgians, however, hardly knew that the primary goal of this raid had been to wreck a railroad. Then, and for generations that followed, they became haunted by the idea of the release of the Andersonville prison population. Inadvertently, Sherman had thus successfully used terror as a weapon.

Could Sherman have accomplished more? Did he want to? Various writers have made exhaustive efforts to try to discern the motivations in the general's complex psyche. One biographer described him as a narcissistic snob with a loathing of the masses, black and white, civilian and military. He did have tremendous contempt for the failings that he saw in other people. Sherman combined a strong legal background with a lifetime of self-imposed personal discipline.[352] He could have concern for the plight of others but only within the narrow confines of the narrow rules he used to govern his world. Sherman set limits, sometimes with dire consequences, in his actions about the prisoners of war, civilian refugees, unionist guerrillas, and slaves who mistakenly looked to him for their salvation.

Did he make his choices to conform to his set rules and disciplined logic; or did he invent reasons to justify decisions? Even if he never admitted it, his ideas did evolve and change over time, but especially how he felt about war against civilians. William Tecumseh Sherman had complex reasons that often appeared as a legalistic singleness of purpose. In Georgia, for example, he determined to use his army efficiently to end the war and restore order. Despite claims by historians of his modern vision of total war, he avoided both pursuing to destruction his opponent's army and devastating Georgia. Although, his dispatches reveal his initial indecision on how to proceed after literally chasing the Confederate military from Georgia, Sherman ultimately decided to turn his army South for the now famous march to the sea and beyond. The result proved more devastating for Southern morale than to personal property. He helped to end the Confederate States of America with minimum loss to his troops and to the Southerners, in such a way as to maintain the traditional local social order and to avoid the anarchy that he found so reprehensible. To achieve that end, the fiery general excluded emancipation, total war, national politics, or revenge from his plans. Reportedly, when he learned that some of his prisoners were given starvation "retaliation rations," the same as given to the federals held at

Andersonville, the general ordered full meals restored to all of the rebels in his custody.

Sherman and Andersonville thus represented the differences between the myths and the reality of his campaign. "Campfire tales" about the prison received wide-spread retelling that combined the notoriety of Andersonville with the negative reputation of Sherman, while concealing far more important realities. One account, for example, tells of an exchange of prisoners near Atlanta when the general turned down a trade of sick Andersonville prisoners for healthy Confederates. Supposedly, in despair, 150 disabled federals found enough strength to then flee their captors for the safety of the nearby federal lines in the greatest single escape of the war.[353]

Sherman, however, actually only declined to accept soldiers from other commands, men who were of more service to him as continuing as prisoners and as a liability to the Confederates. These men came from forces in Mississippi and, if released, would have been returned there to be of no use to Sherman. Most of the disappointed 137 federals were returned to Andersonville without incident although some of them did escape from the train during the return trip to the prison and reached the federal lines, despite a posse and dogs pursing them. No one fired on the fleeing men, but Yankee soldier J. B. Ritner wrote that the federal pickets shot the pursuing canines. Sherman might have, for humanitarian reasons, exchanged more men, but to do so he would have uncharacteristically violated his hard and fast rules to focus only on what advanced his campaign goals. Confederate authorities turned down Sherman's offer to trade some one thousand civilian workers he found in Atlanta for any federal soldiers.

In another story circulated by veterans after the war, foragers brought in a group of emaciated escapees from Andersonville after Sherman's men had captured the Georgia capitol of Milledgeville. The fugitives pleaded for an immediate rescue of the thousands of their sick comrades still at Camp Sumter. The general, however, continued his march to he east, abandoning the men left at Andersonville to their fate. Colonel Charles D. Kerr told this story long after the war, although he had neglected to mention any such incident in his diary. Over time, this tale has expanded to having the escaped men, all but skeletons, appearing in Milledgeville during a Thanksgiving dinner being held by Sherman's troops. Any contemporary account of these events has disappeared, along with any record that the few federal troops still in the town on that date (and who were preparing to leave) even observed Thanksgiving! Corydon E.

Foote repeated the same tale, but he reported it happening on the march near Sandersville, Georgia, and days later.[354]

This story likely has a basis in Sherman's interview with escapees who reached the general around Atlanta or stories reported by the men he had received by exchange. Possibly the tale originated with a riot that happened during an unsuccessful attempt by the soldiers at Andersonville to join their comrades in the previously mentioned exchange. Dr. R. J. Massey, however, wrote that Sherman did abandon twenty-eight of his sick soldiers in Milledgeville. Massey claimed that Sherman told him to bury them if they died and to send them to Andersonville if they lived.[355] The general seemingly placed his greater objective above slowing his march with sick and wounded men, escaped prisoners, and freed slaves.

Sherman did concern himself with the men at Andersonville—in his own unique way and within the confines of what his biographers described as his legalistic logic. The editors of the first publications of his letters omitted what he wrote on Andersonville. Likely, they sought to protect for posterity the irascible general's reputation. For example, in one letter, Sherman wrote to the men he abandoned at Andersonville to "be of good cheer" for, he erroneously assured them, their release and revenge would "soon" come. Sherman also promised that he would ask the Confederates to improve their circumstances. Upon hearing of the horrible prison conditions from the escapees, he arranged for private sources to send the starving and sick prisoners a supply of combs, barber shears, and underwear. Even this aid failed to reach the inmates until the end of the war. Upon capturing Savannah, Sherman did send his cavalry to try to find the prisoners transferred to Blackshear, Georgia. By that time, however, those men had been sent back to Andersonville.[356]

On 26 April 1865, in North Carolina, General Joseph E. Johnston surrendered the remnants of several forces, including the Army of Tennessee, to Sherman. For many Americans, the Civil War ended on that day as the Confederate States of America spun off into chaos, then oblivion, and, finally, romantic memory. In far-off Georgia, however, the last remnants of the Southern nation held on a while longer. The Confederate flag rose again over the ruins of Atlanta. In Macon, railroad officials met in a convention with the rebel government to plan for rebuilding the tracks torn up during Sherman's march. At Andersonville, barracks had been built and conditions had been improved, no thanks to General Sherman, although the men returned there appeared in even worse shape than when they had left. These last prisoners were evacuated to federal lines under the direction of Captain Henry Wirz, the officer in charge of the prisoners. Before the year ended, the United States government tried Wirz for war crimes and hanged him. General Sherman, more responsible than Wirz for prisoners remaining at Andersonville, however, received a hero's welcome in Washington and a full military review.

Over the decades that followed, the survivors of Camp Sumter would write books, give interviews, conduct lecture tours, contribute to panoramic prints of the prison, and form prisoner of war associations. Overwhelmingly, they would paint Wirz, the prison, and the people of the South in the worst possible light. In the glow of Sherman's success and popularity, however, they failed to boast that they contributed to his glory when he abandoned them to their terrible fate.

This engraving of Andersonville, based upon an Andrew J. Riddle photograph (see chapter six), appeared in Ambrose Spencer's *A Narrative of Andersonville* (1866).

WHAT THE WITNESS NEVER TOLD[357]

> It is a Revered thing to see an ancient Castle not in decay, But how much more it is to behold an ancient family Which has stood against the waves And weathers of time.
>
> —Francis Bacon from *The Wisdom of Our Ancestors*

Norton P. Chipman, judge advocate and prosecutor in the military commission trial of Captain Henry Wirz of Andersonville, seldom missed an opportunity to question the loyalty and credibility of the defense's witnesses. Wirz's attorneys lacked both the government's financial resources and the time to do the same to the persons that the prosecution called upon to testify. They, however, did successfully raise questions about the suspect background of the prosecution's most often quoted witness, Ambrose Spencer.

Not every aspect of this colorful character's background received attention at the trial, however. His incredible genealogy, for example, played a role in his lack of credibility but also serves as the basis for a strange judicial history of the American individual, general public, and courts. Families of prominence have fallen very publicly for as long as they have been achieving notoriety, and the Spencers of New York State also became one of the first dynasties of the United States to collapse. It did so in spectacular fashion as part of the history of a new nation, a country that had hardly existed long enough to develop its own peculiar type of generational family scandal.

In the nineteenth century, such events became more than local affairs. Beginning in the 1840s, telegraphic communication and railroads spread news nationwide almost as quickly as it happened. Advances in printing technology provided forums whereby memories, combined with current events, could create sensational sagas for sale to a growing and increasingly literate America.[358] Moralists used these personal failures to point out the false value of social prominence. Critics cited such family history to bemoan the perceived loss of social stability, brought about by the economic ruin of the Panic of 1837 (1837–1845). They saw in such tales—and in the parallel rise of confidence men and women—proof that the stable, moral middle class was being lost to the increasingly widespread temptations of the age, including the popular reading of sensational books about generational family scandal!

At the same time, the early nation fostered the somewhat contradictory ideal of each generation proving the worth of its blood by succeeding on its own merit, even if those people came from families of prominence and advantage. Consequently, having an important ancestry proved as much a burden as an advantage. A young man, entering the world with a respected name but without a practical purpose for his life, sometimes destroyed himself very publicly in struggles to match earlier family notoriety.[359]

The death of Ambrose C. Spencer on 12 April 1876, illustrates these points. Newspapers across the nation, in connection to his last great scandal, mentioned his illustrious grandfather and namesake, New York Supreme Court Chief Judge Ambrose Spencer, and his father John C. Spencer, former secretary of war and of the treasury. Press accounts also reminded the public that in 1842 Ambrose's brother achieved the distinction of being the only officer of the United States Navy hanged for mutiny. The Spencer family history, in this way, thus served as background for telling the titillating and bizarre tale of how Ambrose C. met his own end. Individual papers added details of related sensational events connected with this family, and each article encouraged further investigation for an interested audience.

This Ambrose C. Spencer, who rose to such prominence in the wake of the nationwide sensationalism about the Andersonville prison, still draws that kind of attention. He achieved notoriety as a "Southern planter" whose testimony helped to justify the federal prosecution and execution of Captain Henry Wirz, one of the officers of the prison. A widely circulated print of the prison after the war even included a vignette of "Ambrose Spencer, a philanthropic Southern planter, and Samaritan to prisoners."[360] MacKinley Kantor knew nothing of Spencer's family and background but undoubtedly used him as a model for Ira Claffey, the major fictional character in his Pulitzer Prize-winning novel *Andersonville.* Saul Levitt would include Ambrose in his Emmy Award-winning play *Andersonville Trial.*

Ambrose C. Spencer began his colorful journey from truth to lies to legend around 1814 in Canandaigua, Ontario County, New York, as the son of John Canfield Spencer (1788–1855) and Eliza Scott Smith (1789–1869), the daughter of J. Scott Smith. John had left Albany for rural Canandaigua, where he subsequently earned his own considerable success without the assistance of his father Ambrose (1765–1848), a party boss, congressman, mayor of Albany, and New York State Supreme Court chief justice. This Ambrose, twice, had the famous DeWitt Clinton, famed promoter of the Erie Canal and governor of New York, as a brother-in-law. The two men, however, were as often at odds as they were allies; the Clintons and the Spencers also owned lots in what became New York City's Hell's Kitchen. Friends would remember the elder Ambrose as one of the first men to foresee the coming slavery crisis. As historian Henry Adams wrote, his greatest achievement, however, may have been that his public career thrived despite personal politics—inconsistent enough to destroy any good man in New England. The Spencers certainly had their critics. One enemy, for example, would describe Ambrose as a "minus quality" and his son John C. as "the political millstone of the West."[361]

Ambrose C. Spencer, Jr. in his youth. (Courtesy Eric Montgomery)

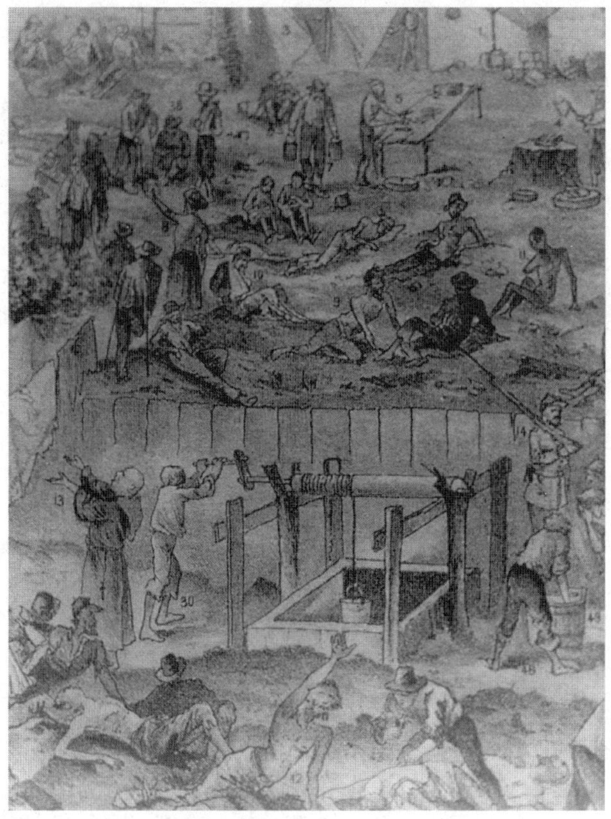

This vignette from a post-war print of Andersonville shows (bent over, lower left corner): "Ambrose Spencer, a philanthropic southern planter, and Samaritan to prisoners." (R. S. Davis)

This Ambrose Sr., however, had first earned national notoriety in court case as complicated and bizarre as anything that his controversial descendants experienced. That case had particular irony for the Spencers on several levels, including that it pioneered the issues of newspaper coverage of scandal. In 1803, President Thomas Jefferson used the Sedition Act, the same law that he had so often and so savagely attacked, to have newspaper publishers sued for slander. He specifically launched a vendetta against the people who published the story that Jefferson had, previously, secretly hired newspaper publisher James Callender to attack the administrations of Presidents George Washington and John Adams, in part over their support of the Sedition Act. Jefferson also anonymously sponsored the booklet, *The Prospect Before Us*, in which Callender called Washington a traitor, thief, and perjurer.

Callender, however, later turned on Jefferson. Aside from reporting the dark history of his past services to the now new president, he also reported on Jefferson's sexual relationship with the slave Sally Hemmings. Callender, soon after, mysteriously fell from a ferry and drowned. His critics felt it appropriate that he died face-down in a mud puddle.

For reprinting reports of Jefferson and Callender, Harry Croswell, publisher of the small New York county newspapers the *Wasp* and the *Balance*, found himself a victim of one of Jefferson's libel suits under the Sedition Act. The president's supporters picked him because of his obscurity and, presumably, his lack of influential friends and his inability to afford top notch attorneys. (Ironically, decades later, that same issue of qualified legal counsel would arise in the trial of Henry Wirz by military commission.) Croswell lost in the local court and then appealed to the New York Supreme Court, using the famous Alexander Hamilton and a top team of anti-Jefferson (Federalist) lawyers to argue his case.

Ambrose Spencer, Sr., at that time, a member of the Federalist Party and the attorney general for the State of New York, represented the State and argued, based on English law, that truth by itself fails to serve as a defense against slander. Hamilton made a precedent-setting argument for freedom of the press, despite the fact that he and his fellow Federalists now found themselves fighting a law and arguments that they had previously supported. Spencer countered that society needed protection from potential civil strife by protecting its officials from intrusions into their private lives. Ironically, he was now prosecuting Croswell for reporting that Jefferson paid persons to make such intrusions into private lives and to publish accusations against public figures while Croswell, a clergyman, had actually declined to print information about Jefferson's private life.

A hostile court divided two to two, which should have meant that Croswell failed to earn a new trial. The state, however, permitted Croswell a new trial that this time he won (although by then, Hamilton had died in his famous duel with Aaron Burr). The State of New York also passed a law and a constitutional amendment reversing—and denying—Spencer's arguments. Ambrose Spencer Sr., who had only carried out his responsibilities as a public official, earned criticism from inside and outside of his party.[362] After the War of 1812, he radically changed his allegiance and eventually became the head of the pro-Jefferson-Republican party in New York.

Ambrose Spencer Sr. achieved further notoriety, in part, as a result of another court case that echoed of his family's later legal adventures, the trial of Irishman James Graham for the murder of Hugh Cameron and Alexander

McGillavrae in Delaware County, New York, in 1813. Graham, after arguing with the victims at a logging bee, allegedly succeeded in ambushing them in a woods and beating them to death with a handspike. This circumstantial case became a "whodunnit" that drew national attention, complete with a sensational escape and a well-attended hanging. Ambrose received fame as the judge of this trial without any of the controversy of Graham's guilt being attached to him.[363]

A politician, lawyer, and compiler of the codification of New York law, John C. Spencer, son of this Ambrose, also had a notable but strange career. John would first come to public notice when Martin Van Buren, the New York governor and later president of the United States, appointed him to prosecute Masons accused of murdering their neighbor and former lodge brother William Morgan in 1826. The latter had announced plans to publish the secret rites of the order before he mysteriously disappeared. Without a corpse or adequate public funds, Spencer failed to pursue the prosecution to success.[364] This bizarre case drew public attention at a time when different forms of apocalyptic fervor was sweeping upstate New York. These movements created, among other faiths and ideals, the Spiritualists, the Primitive Baptists, the Women's Movement, and the Church of Jesus Christ of Latter-day Saints. Public suspicion of the Masons and their secret rites now became, to many believers, still another sign of the "End of Time" as foretold in the Book of Revelation. John Spencer paid for his notoriety with assassination attempts, presumably by persons sympathetic to the Masons, who had until that time been a cherished American institution. Spencer did seek to benefit from the resulting national backlash against the Masons in the Morgan case. This group did lose prestige, and Spencer's strange career took a quirky path upward.

That journey next took him to Washington. As a member of congress, John drew attention for compiling a confused report that denounced the national bank and for authoring the strongest attack in print made against fellow Whig and president of the United States John Tyler. After everyone in Tyler's cabinet but Daniel Webster had resigned, however, John C. Spencer become the president's new secretary of the treasury,

Spencer fit in well with the bizarre environment of John Tyler, the head of a family that would have its own major scandals. In 1843, Spencer led a purge of Tyler's enemies from the federal government. During an accidental cannon blast that killed several people, two of the cabinet members lost their lives. These deaths, coupled with the resignation of Daniel Webster as secretary of war, created the need for a new cabinet. In the subsequent reorganization, Spencer became the new secretary of war.

In 1844, however, Spencer too resigned after refusing to deposit secret service funds in a clandestine account to finance a private invasion of Mexico. His leaving likely also had to do with the national scandals involving his sons and the refusal of the president to have the acquitted captain of the *Somers* retried for hanging Spencer's son Philip. Tyler did, however, unsuccessfully nominate Spencer as a justice of the U. S. Supreme Court and, later, as a district judge for the federal court of New York. Alexis de Tocqueville interviewed him for Tocqueville's classic *Democracy in America*; the American edition of which John would edit.[365]

One writer would sum up John C. Spencer as a political opportunist of national notoriety, "alternately a Jackson man, a Clay man, an Adams man, an anti-Mason, a Scott man, a Whig, and is now a Tyler foco."[366] Another political enemy wrote:

> Up to the period when the active intrigues of Mr. Secretary Spencer commenced, I had hopes that with prudence he might win the favorable opinion of the Democratic party; but when I found that the reigns of power had been placed in Spencer's hands, I gave up all as lost. A man who in thirty years of active political toil is owned by no political party, confided in by no party, riding only on the created waves of every faction, always operating for himself, and relying on the rotten crutch of abolition and anti-masonry for support, I foresaw the overthrow of the president's hopes.[367]

During these years, Ambrose C. Spencer, Jr., like his two brothers, grew up in their father John's absence. Ambrose attended the Canandaigua Academy with Stephen A. Douglas, of the later Lincoln-Douglas debates fame, before going on to Middlebury College in Vermont, where his classmates included the later famous Reverend Doctor Byron Sunderland.[368]

Young Spencer failed to graduate, but he did marry a local woman in January 1838. A classicist and intellectual, Ambrose probably saw a true soul mate in his bride, Agnes Malaput Thuillier Powell (born in Sussex, England in 1811), who would achieve some notoriety as a capable artist. Agnes's father, Peter Malaput Thuillier Powell, former banker, librarian, and concert hall owner of Hastings, England, had brought his family to Vermont, where he became a farmer of modest means.[369]

Ambrose and his wife settled almost immediately in the new city of Cleveland, Ohio. He likely sought a state that had much lower standards for appearing before the bar than New York's requirement of seven years of classical education and/or legal training. Stephen A. Douglas had left New York State for the same reason. In Ohio, Ambrose became a partner in a law firm, local commissioner for the State of New York, nurseryman, and city alderman, while his wife worked as a teacher. As a member of the national Whig party, Ambrose earned public notice in the party's local Vigilance Committee and the Young Men's State Convention. The couple had a daughter Laura Isabella, born on 25 September 1838, and, by 1842, had completed their family with two sons, DeWitt Clinton "Morris" and John Clayton Spencer. Despite having made his own life and family, Ambrose continued to use the title of "junior" until the death of his prominent grandfather and namesake in 1848.[370]

Ambrose Jr. and his brothers, however, already had serious problems that attracted more than local interest. Philip, John's alcoholic son, spent three years as a freshman at Union College before taking a commission in the Navy. A career at sea had become a common option for aimless male members of prominent families of the period. On 21 December 1842, the captain of the U. S. warship *Somers*, Alexander Slidell Mackenzie, fearing that some members of his crew had plotted to mutiny and to become pirates, tried and hanged their alleged leader, Philip Spencer. Pundits would blame Philip's demise on his choice of pirate adventure novels as reading material and also reported that Philip's brother Ambrose suffered from "alienation" of the mind and had committed "scores" of forgeries in Ohio, as he had previously done in New York State. Newspaper accounts also described him and his surviving brother, John Jr., as "desolate." The latter, accused of having previously forged his father's name, found a position at sea as a purser on the U.S.S. *Columbus*, through the influence of an uncle.[371] John Jr., in that position, died of disease off the coast of Africa on 29 December 1845.[372]

Secretary John C. Spencer's enemies seized upon this scandal to attack father and sons, as shown in the *Louisville Journal*:

> Mr. Spencer, the Secretary of War, is most unfortunate in his sons. One [sic, two] of them committed forgery in New York a couple of years ago, fled from justice, and has been wandering up and down in the country, a swindler by trade; and another, it appears, has just been hanged for mutiny and contemplated piracy. Evidently there's scoundrel blood in the

> veins of the family. We think, however, that is has only been modified in its transmission from the parent fountain. The father is politically what the boys are morally—a swindler and a pirate. If the father is unfortunate in his sons, the sons are equally unfortunate in their father.[373]

Unfortunately for his family, Ambrose C. Spencer still lived. This last male child would later testify that he first came to the South on 8 October 1840.[374] During the controversy following his brother Philip's death, the press described him as a pirate "in the Gulf of Mexico." In fact, he had moved to the then independent Republic of Texas where he joined Jacob Snively's mercenaries on a Texas government-sanctioned raid. The national press network reported Secretary John C. Spencer's son, Ambrose, as working as the expedition's judge advocate.

In this action, Ambrose continued a family tradition. The early Spencers had served as soldiers in America's "defensive" wars with Great Britain that involved invading Canada, even when doing so proved politically unpopular in upstate New York. Ambrose's grandfather had served in the American Revolution and his father had fought in the War of 1812. Ambrose's uncle, Captain Ambrose Spencer, died during the War of 1812 campaigns in upstate New York when he rode into a British regiment of soldiers to enquire as to who they were. Now the younger Ambrose joined an offensive campaign to continue fulfilling the "Manifest Destiny" of the United States to conquer all of North America. These "filibusters," from the Dutch word for pirates, later sought tremendous gain from foes less formidable than Great Britain. Their greatest filibuster success, the Republic of Texas, had been conquered from Mexico. Snively's men raided Mexican merchants on the Santa Fe Trail before being arrested and largely disarmed by a superior force of United States troops. On the way back to Texas, despite having only five guns, Snively's men fought off attacks by superior numbers of Comanche Indians.[375]

Upon returning to Agnes and his children, Ambrose began a curious, and not completely understood, odyssey across the South. White native Southerners had largely divided between the wealthy cotton planters and a much larger class of small farmers. This society often lacked professional and technological training. Northern and foreign-born persons like the Spencers helped fill this gap as teachers, merchants, and technicians. These Yankees sometimes drew criticism in the South as the failed "refuse" of the North and were suspected of being abolitionists set upon ending slavery by encouraging bloody slave revolts.

The fact that some of these new arrivals, such as Ambrose C. Spencer, had unsavory pasts, darkened the image of their whole class.[376]

The Spencers, in the South, began as educators. They served as principals at the Lawrenceville Female Academy in Gwinnett County, Georgia, by 1845.[377] A few years later, Ambrose become principal and Agnes vice principal of St. John's Academy in Darlington, South Carolina. He gave a speech to the St. David's Masonic Lodge there, where he served as its secretary despite his father's earlier role as the prosecutor in the Masonic murder. Students would remember him as a brilliant teacher and excellent disciplinarian, dark and tall, with scars on his neck, from "a wild life on the frontier." He falsely claimed to have attended the United States Military Academy. His pupils, however, also described him as "high tempered and unpopular in the village," having had a shooting scrape with one man and challenging another to a duel.[378]

Ambrose likely had other problems as well. The couple ceased having children by the time he returned from Texas. In 1850, Agnes and their children resided in Vermont while Ambrose stayed in the South. When John C. Spencer, Sr., died on 14 February 1854, he left one-third of his estate to Agnes and the children in a will that he had carefully worded in such a way so as to keep his estate from ever benefiting Ambrose. For reasons not now known, he contemptuously referred to his son in the will only as "A. Spencer."[379] With married women having few property rights at that time, however, this complicated effort eventually failed.

Ambrose would later testify to moving to Sumter County, Georgia, by 1854. Agnes opened a select school for young women in Americus in 1856. Through the guardian of the inheritance from her father-in-law, she bought a house and lot in Americus the following year. Agnes and Ambrose remained there as late as 1858, when their son DeWitt, an Americus merchant, briefly attended Union College in Schenectady, New York, on a special scholarship in honor of his great grandfather, Ambrose Sr.[380]

The Spencers new home had a conflicted reputation. A writer from nearby Plains described the people of Sumter County in a positive way in 1859:

> The population of this primitive, rural district is of very simple character and is wholly agricultural. With very few exceptions there is a near equality of wealth and social position. None very rich, and none poor, they live in great friendship. They exercise themselves much in offices of kindness and good neighborship. Neighbors speak of each other

> with great respect and proper appreciation of merit and character. There has been no neighborhood quarrel for more than twenty years, that is to say, not since the settlement of this county by the white man.... What makes this the more noticeable is that there is an unusual admixture of religious orders. Here as elsewhere in Georgia the Methodists and the Baptists, old school new, are intermingled with a sprinkling of Presbyterians, &c. In addition to this there is here a considerable church of Universalists.... What is however very commendable and Christianly they never allow their zeal to descend to personal bickering or [to] interrupt kind and neighborly feeling.[381]

Other sources told a different story. When students in Americus became dissatisfied with their education, they burned down their log school house. Teachers, as part of their jobs, had to also act as notaries. Local Whigs and Democrats would sometimes riot. Sheriffs would face organized violence when they tried to sell property at public outcry.[382]

By the time of the 1860 federal census, Ambrose C., Agnes, Laura, and DeWitt had moved to Savannah, Georgia, where Ambrose worked as a lawyer and owner/editor of the *Savannah Evening Express.* In those years, Savannah had one of the most prominent Northern communities of any Southern city. At that time, Ambrose's and Agnes's other son, John, worked in Albany, Georgia, as a clerk. Their daughter Laura married Leonard Edward Welch in Savannah on 14 July 1860. This new branch of the Spencer family would, alternatively, live in Albany and Savannah. Ambrose gave up his newspaper on 17 March in exchange for two thousand dollars worth of his debts. By the following year, the Spencers must have been back in Sumter County. At that time, for reasons unknown, Ambrose accused local newspaperman Charles W. Hancock of slander and asked for the official filing of a related deposition of his son DeWitt C. Spencer.[383]

The coming of the Civil War gave Ambrose even more opportunities for complicating his life. While many Yankees returned home rather than aid the new Confederate States of America, he enlisted as a private in an Albany company of the 4th Georgia Confederate Infantry. He received a special leave, likely for recruiting purposes, and he eventually hired a substitute as his replacement in the 4th Georgia. At the same time, Ambrose also unsuccessfully campaigned for commissions for himself and his son John, even falsely claiming

John as a native Georgian and himself as a veteran of the Mexican War. He also recruited 165 south Georgians to serve in the "Alexander Stephens Artillery," a unit he proposed to create if the Confederacy would only give him a commission and cannons. The new government, however, ignored Ambrose's efforts. In July 1863, students of the public school in Talladega, Alabama, unsuccessfully petitioned to have their principal "A. Spencer" released from service in Marx's [Goldthwait's] battery. This A. Spencer, quite likely Ambrose Spencer of Sumter County, eventually rose to the rank of corporal and seems to have continued to serve into 1863. That year, however, as an "assistant surgeon," Ambrose granted a medical discharge to a Confederate soldier, despite holding no such position or even being a doctor or nurse. Spencer's wife received salt in 1864 as the wife of a Confederate soldier in service. Many Northern-born Americans in the Confederacy took active roles in the Confederate government but would claim, at the end of the war, the status of "secret Yankees" who had actively supported the federal cause throughout the conflict. They now appear as opportunists who supported making a profit more than any political cause.[384] Ambrose Spencer belonged to that class of "Unionist."

In any event, he determined, as he wrote, "to show the world that myself, my family, and my fortunes are embarked in the grievous enterprise" of the war for Southern secession.[385] His two sons did serve the Southern cause. DeWitt enlisted briefly in the 1st Georgia Infantry and later became a militia captain. John served as a sergeant in the cavalry, where he distinguished himself for gallantry in action. In the last days of the war, he offered to raise a company of African Americans for the Confederacy.[386] At the same time, however, a George Eliphaz Spencer served as a scout for federal General Grenville Dodge and later as a colonel of the 1st Alabama Cavalry of the United States Army. He claimed to be a descendent of Ambrose's distinguished father and grandfather (and therefore Ambrose's brother or nephew) when in fact George was only a distant cousin. A writer, in refuting the traditional view of carpetbaggers as corrupt and immoral, would still describe George Spencer as the exception that proved the stereotype.[387]

Back in Sumter County, in 1864, Agnes bought two two-hundred-acre lots near Americus, some nine miles from the newly opened Camp Sumter (Andersonville) Confederate prison. She and other ladies tried to aid the federal prisoners. On a return from a trip to the North, Agnes apparently tried to bring a letter to a prisoner who had been a Sumter County neighbor before the war. The letter came from his wife. On one freezing night, slaves directed an escapee from the prison to the Spencer home. Ambrose and Agnes helped the fugitive reach the federal lines. Reports also reached Andersonville that Ambrose had held a Unionist meeting in nearby Americus.[388]

At the same time, Ambrose became the only person to apply for the job of Confederate claims agent for his congressional district. He impressed Confederate officials with the prominence of his father and grandfather. Confederate Congressman Mark A. Blansford, however, later criticized the appointment, describing Spencer as being of bad character and disloyal to the Southern cause. Ambrose kept the job because of the high quality of his work. He would eventually file vouchers for traveling 2,288 miles, between 7 August and 31 December 1864, during investigations of hundreds of claims for property seized by the Confederate government. A competent bureaucrat, Spencer became of greater value to the agricultural Confederacy than as a soldier. The end of the war found him in Florida surrendering as a sutler and as a private in the 4th Georgia Infantry. He received a formal parole in Albany, Georgia.[389]

In the last months of 1865, Ambrose C. Spencer achieved fame beyond—but without attention called to—his earlier notoriety and his distinguished ancestry. In the *New York Times*, he published an anonymous attack on Confederate Captain Henrich "Henry" Wirz, the Confederate officer in charge of security inside of the prison stockade at Andersonville. On 17 August 1865, federal prosecutor Colonel Norton P. Chipman hired Spencer as a special bailiff to serve warrants to potential witnesses for Wirz's war crimes trial.[390] At the end of that month, Ambrose C. Spencer also traveled to the capitol to testify as "Colonel Spencer" in the Wirz trial. There he weaved tales of incriminating conversations held in his presence, of civilians bringing wagon loads of food to the camp that verbally abusive prison officials (other than Wirz) turned back, and of abundant crops in the vicinity of the Andersonville that could have fed the starving prisoners.

Wirz's attorney, former New York City lawyer Orrin Smith Baker, successfully discredited Ambrose. He proved that "the colonel," far from being an authority on events at Andersonville and the local agriculture, had spent the war away from the prison working for the Confederate government. Wirz himself would denounce Spencer's testimony of hearing incriminating conversations as an outright falsehood. Aside from Ambrose contradicting himself in almost every line of his own testimony, any federal civilian court in 1865 would have disqualified him on the grounds of being a former Confederate official without a pardon and because his work as an employee of the prosecutor had compromised him as a witness. The military tribunal eventually, despite Spencer's "help," found Captain Wirz guilty. Wirz was hanged on the future site of the United States Supreme Court building.[391]

Ambrose Spencer's involvement in this celebrated case became a triumph, despite the fact that he likely had only saw Andersonville as a Confederate guard, if at all.[392] He had now earned his own notoriety. Through nationwide newspaper coverage of the trial, his testimony received vast circulation. He wrote a best seller, *A Narrative of Andersonville* (1866), largely from a copy of the trial transcript provided to him by Chipman. It drew such criticism, however, that even two former prisoners wrote separate volumes to defend Wirz and condemn Spencer's book. Other former inmates also joined Southerners in attacking *A Narrative*. Modern writers have been equally negative. Historian Ovid L. Futch, for example, described it as "ridiculously fallacious."[393] Curiously, Spencer's critics failed to mention the dark past of Ambrose and his family. Ambrose's father had won fame trying Masons and his grandfather had achieved notoriety arguing against truth as evidence. Ambrose now found his moment in legal history as a star witness in the world's first great war crimes trial.

Spencer's cooperation in the trial against Wirz, however, failed to win him a federal job. Despite letters of endorsement from his mother and Secretary of State William Seward, the government passed over Ambrose for the position of federal district attorney for Georgia. Perhaps he failed because he reneged on his promises to provide evidence against Captain R. B. Winder of Andersonville prison. The *Augusta Chronicle* reminded the public of Spencer's Confederate past when it announced that he had been chosen as a delegate to the National Union Convention in 1866. Had he gone, he would have been in the company of many of Georgia's greatest leaders. Spencer, however, appears in none of the convention's records.

Ambrose C. Spencer did find life dangerous in Sumter County. Groups of African Americans and local whites, respectively, organized armed self-defense groups, even before the war ended. Ambrose would claim that he fled for his life in 1867. In DeKalb County, Illinois, he used his family connections to find employment as a clerk for a railroad. His attempt to obtain a job in the United States Foreign Service failed, despite his claim of being able to speak French and Spanish, and to read German. He soon gave up his clerk's job to practice law. By 1870, Agnes, Ambrose, and John C. Spencer lived in Chicago, where Ambrose operated Ambrose Spencer & Company, auctioneers. DeWitt C. Spencer and his sister, Laura, continued to live in Albany, Georgia.[394]

Agnes probably moved in with Laura and her growing family by 1872. Ambrose then went on to Marion, Illinois, where he worked as a federal district attorney. When the Ku Klux Klan murdered Isaac Vancil, Williamson County's first native white person, because of his alleged sexual excesses, Ambrose tried to prosecute the alleged killers of Vancil under the Ku Klux Klan Act. After he failed to win a conviction, one of the defendants successfully sued him for false imprisonment. As a result, Ambrose was arrested on 6 January 1873 and spent a brief time in prison. He never paid a fine of four thousand dollars for defamation of character.[395] Ironically, Spencer had fled the South to escape racial vigilantes, only to suffer defeat at the hands of the Klan in a northern state.

About this time, Ambrose began living in Cape Girardeau, Missouri, where,while still married to Agnes, he married Laura Alice Murphy, a widow formerly of Memphis, Tennessee. Ms. Murphy had earlier married Wilson John Jeffers of Marshall, Texas, and had a child by him. The Jefferses had split up when she learned that Jeffers already had a spouse. Jeffers, an Irishman, then moved to Kansas. Even though Ambrose took her money and left her alone and destitute, when Jeffers returned, she refused to go back to him. The Klan had lynched Vancil for this same type of the immorality for which the era became famous.

The characters for Ambrose's dramatic end had assembled; only they now lacked a stage. In 1873, Ambrose sold insurance in Columbia, Missouri, and gave one or two lectures at the university there, while accompanied by a woman identified as his wife. The following year, according to St. Louis city directories, he worked there as a newspaper editor and, in 1875, as an attorney.[396] On 12 April 1876, Ambrose C. Spencer, by now almost entirely deaf, worked in Linn, Missouri, as an insurance agent and lawyer. Laura Alice still lived with him. Wilson Jeffers entered the town on that day and sought out the couple. He eventually found Ambrose, whom he shouted at and then chased down the street, before finally shooting him dead as the last act in this multi-dimensional lover's triangle.

Ambrose's demise brought him and his family one final great moment of celebrity in the American press. Newspapers recycled his past and the circumstances of his brother Philip's execution, along with most of the details of the various cases of bigamy that brought about his own bloody end. (No one, however, mentioned his marriage to Agnes.) The first trial of Jeffers ended with a hung jury, but a retrial earned him a twelve-year prison sentence.[397]

In "Scraps of History," one of the stories about Ambrose's family that circulated following his murder, an acquaintance described him as "a somewhat dissolute man, a man of unusual talent and ability as a lawyer."[398] The article then recorded the history of the Spencer family with special emphasis on the hanging of Philip. It described as strange that a bloody murder in an obscure village should draw attention to a tragedy at sea decades earlier. The author had just missed the point. The first fall of a purely United States dynasty had been covered in the national media. The writer only noted that, "We are a believer in Fate…some men, and some families, are the victims of Destiny."[399]

The Spencer family had made a final contribution to the United States. Its members had created a colorful history as notable for its decline and end as its record of public service. In another strange way, America had come of age. With Ambrose's death, except for the occasional study of the hanging of Philip and the Wirz trial, his family's colorful past quietly disappeared into obscurity, however, Ambrose's immediate family almost faded out of existence. Agnes lived in Albany, Georgia, with her daughter's family. Her son DeWitt moved to Colorado where he became so impoverished by 1879 that he was arrested in Denver as a thief. He died as a merchant in Conejos, Colorado, in 1880 and her son John passed away similarly in Anniston, Alabama, in 1891, both apparently without issue. Agnes died in Albany, Georgia, on 22 November 1889, remembered in her funeral notice as the daughter-in-law of John C. Spencer, secretary of war and the treasury. Her daughter Laura died in 1913.[400]

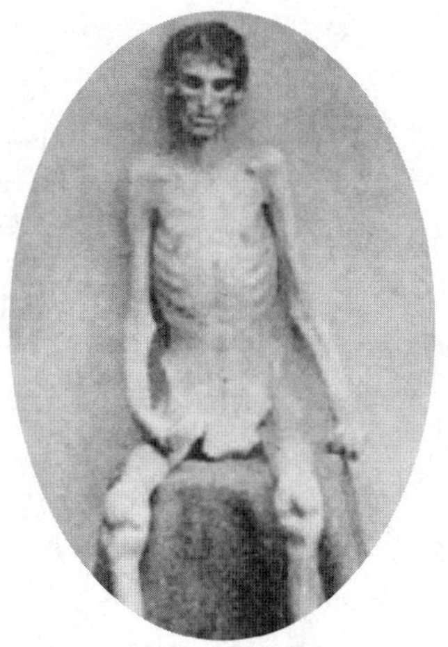

Henry Wirz (left) as drawn by former prisoner Robert Knox Sneden for the cover of the booklet *The Demon of Andersonville* and (right) a widely published photograph of an Andersonville survivor.

THE DEVIL'S ADVOCATE[401]

No person shall be held to answer for a capital, or otherwise infamous crime, unless on a presentment or indictment of a Grand Jury...nor be deprived of life, liberty, or property, without due process.... In all criminal prosecutions, the accused shall enjoy the right to a speedy and public trial, by an impartial jury of the State and district wherein the crime shall have been committed...to have compulsory process for obtaining witnesses in his favor, and to have the assistance of counsel for his defense.

—Fifth and Sixth Amendments (Bill of Rights),
Constitution of the United States of America

Forbearance toward a conquered foe having ever been the attribute of the truly great, I cannot conceive how justice will be vindicated, or the character of the country elevated, by the trial and execution of this man [Henry Wirz].

—anonymous survivor of Andersonville

O. S. Baker had no connection to Andersonville beyond serving as the primary defense attorney for Captain Henry Wirz, an officer of that Confederate prison, in the world's first great war crimes trial. For the battle he waged for his client he should stand in renown with such other defense attorneys as John Adams and Clarence Darrow. Despite the nationwide attention that the trial brought him, however, contemporary and later sources omit any biographical information on Baker. He disappeared so thoroughly after the trial that even his correct name became lost to historians.[402] O. S. Baker serves as a good example of a person in a world where fate gave otherwise insignificant people like Baker and Wirz roles in major events. As pointed out in the largely fictional, award-winning play *Andersonville Trial*, even beyond any practical considerations of the situation at the prison, commitment to principles also became the great issue at Wirz's trial and in many different ways. Such personal commitment may have played a larger role in one's life in the Civil War era than in any other period of American history.

The outcome of the trial would have been the same for the hapless Confederate captain without Baker, but otherwise the man assigned to the prosecution would also have had to conduct the defense. In so publicly battling against a blatantly partisan tribunal that both prosecuted and judged, Baker made a protest for the traditional United States legal system, even during extraordinary times of perceived threats to and by the national government. The Supreme Court, even in the case *Ex parte Milligen*, refused to explore the constitutionality of such military tribunals except in one very narrow and specific set of circumstances. The high court has left the arguments of the otherwise obscure Baker as the principle defense of impartial due process of law.

This defense counsel, as with so many people connected with Andersonville's story, became a part of its history through a long and convoluted route. The past events in Baker's life inspired him to step forward to rescue a helpless, impoverished client in order to defend the profession and legal system he served. This same life experience also encouraged him to almost completely disappear into the national landscape when everyone else connected with the trial received notoriety. If O. S. Baker viewed what he did as heroic, he seemingly avoided accolades for his efforts and returned to the same obscurity from which he had emerged. Almost all of the credible information that researchers have had about Baker begins with 24 August 1865, when he volunteered to serve as Wirz's attorney. The trial and what the general public ever knew about him ended two months later, when his fight for his client ended with Wirz's death.

Orrin Smith Baker. (R. S. Davis)

This silence that surrounds the real Baker raises its own questions. Judge advocate and prosecutor Norton Parker Chipman believed that Wirz acted as part of a giant Confederate conspiracy that continued to try to protect the captain even after the war. Contrary to a scene in the play *Andersonville Trial*, however, Chipman declined to openly ask any questions about Baker's past or present, perhaps out of fear that he would lose Baker as the defense attorney and he would have to take over that task for himself. A trial with the prosecution also conducting the defense would have destroyed the last shred of credibility that public passions gave this trial. Investigators for the federal army compiled files on hundreds of suspicious persons in Washington, Virginia, and Maryland. They compiled no information in regards to Wirz's principal attorney, however.[403] The widely published court record only referred to him both as O. S. and O. L. Baker.[404]

O. S. Baker did worse, however, than fail to win personal fame from his great courtroom battle. Playwright Saul Levitt solved the problem of the absence of information on this lawyer's background in *Andersonville Trial* by creating the fictional Otis H. Baker, a mercenary Baltimore resident who was opposed to slavery and the war, recruited and paid by a committee that, like Otis Baker, existed in Levitt's gifted imagination.[405] Scholars, lacking any better information, used this imaginary Baker and his motive for serving as Wirz's attorney.[406]

Baker's fame does rest solely in his defense of Hartmann Heinrich "Henry" Wirz, a captain and mid-level manager in an internment camp where almost thirteen thousand inmates died of starvation, disease, and exposure. Wirz's duties principally consisted of keeping the prison rolls, allowing prisoners to leave the stockade on work detail, and arranging services within the walls (such as wells and sanitation). Wirz could decide when and if the prisoners received whatever rations that had arrived. Guards, while on duty on the stockade wall, could take orders from him. Nevertheless, like the quantity and quality of the rations, medicine, and guards, desperately needed camp improvements proved beyond anything he had any authority to do, as attested to by witnesses at his trial.

Andersonville's chief administrative officer, commandant and Brigadier General John H. Winder spent much of his time away from the camp and apparently avoided even entering the stockade.[407] Quite likely, Winder gave Wirz, his long time subordinate, what was initially a non-critical position out of pity for the crippled officer. The Confederate captain spent much of his time away from the prison trying to obtain treatment for his perpetually festering arm. Prisoners frequently heard rumors that he had died.[408] Confederate inspectors described him as an exceptionally competent man, however, in stark contrast to the bureaucratic bungling and pettiness of many other officers at Andersonville. Some prisoners also held him in high regard. His daughter would remember prisoners giving him gifts, some of them handmade.[409]

Of the camp's officers, most of the inmates had contact only with Wirz, or the "Old Dutchman," as the prisoners called him. The Confederate captain gave the bizarre appearance, to some of the soldiers, of the jailer of Hell. Alexander McLean came to know Wirz well during his many months at Andersonville. In 1866, he wrote of his introduction to the prison and Wirz on 30 May 1864:

> He [Wirz] then mounted his white horse and led the way into the prison, with revolver in hand, cursing the "Yanks," now and then pointing his revolver at some poor boy who was too sick to keep up, swearing he would blow their brains out unless they got to their places. The gates were swung open and we were marched in. What a sight met our view! It beggers

> description! There were men with nothing to cover their bodies but poor remnants of drawers. Many were destitute of hats, shoes, coats and pants, and black as Ethiopians. Some had ragged old blankets for tents, some had holes dug in the ground, in which they vainly sought shelter, others had nothing but the burning sun by day and the cold blue heavens by night; the latter class was by far the largest; there they were wallowing in their own filth. The ground was literally alive with maggots. Near the gate was a long row of dead, lying with their ghastly faces upturned to the glaring sun; many of the bodies were entirely uncovered except by the patches of revenous flies.[410]

Wirz would write to his superiors about prisoners exaggerating about the prison's conditions, but the deaths of one-third of the men who entered his stockade spoke far louder to the post-war Northern public than his protests and excuses. The camp had become so infamous that even the prison slang developed by its inmates would eventually become standard Americanisms.[411]

Many prisoners believed that Wirz ignored their suffering while he obsessed upon thwarting a mass escape. His sentries would sometimes fire their ancient and inaccurate weapons upon prisoners who entered a picket line area within the interior, the infamous "dead line" of Andersonville, to keep prisoners from approaching the wall to escape.[412] Survivors of the prison described him in the national press as a monster who yelled obscenities while inflicting vicious dogs, trigger-happy guards, and brutal punishments upon hapless prisoners. Former inmate Prescott Tracy made a deposition, as early as 19 August 1864, wherein he called Wirz a "brutal monster" who ordered men all but randomly shot. Tracy, however, claimed that the Swiss-born Wirz did give humane treatment to prisoners who, "like him," were "Germans."[413]

These prisoners, and some historians since, erroneously identified Wirz as the commandant and top officer in the camp administration, with powers and authority beyond anything actually held by the real, largely powerless, clerical functionary. This misunderstanding came from the fact that his superiors spent as little time at the prison as possible and often Wirz found himself left in charge by default. He performed efficiently the responsibilities he should not have had but would pay dearly for by being the right man in the wrong place. His trial failed to produce any credible account of his acting with personal cruelty or evidence of his role in any conspiracy. Even some prisoners, despite their prejudice against Wirz, would later write of incidents of his kindness to them. Several Andersonville alumni even dared to come forward to defend him at his trial and in print.[414]

Wartime passions proved enough to bring Wirz to trial, but he had other associations that the prosecution could hold against him. His Swiss birth, German accent, and Roman Catholicism added to his negative image in an Anglo-Saxon American Protestant culture already prejudiced against immigrants, Roman Catholics, and Germans. The latter made up the largest immigrant group and the second largest population of Roman Catholics in the largely native and Protestant United States of that time. Many Americans readily believed such bizarre rumors that the Pope had ordered Abraham Lincoln assassinated and that federal defeats in battle came from cowardly German soldiers. Bigots ascribed Wirz's alleged actions to some "natural" inhuman "Teutonic" regimentation. That he was actually Swiss would hardly have helped him as the famous "Swiss Guards" of history and legend had a widespread reputation as brutal mercenaries. As Wirz lay in the Old Capitol Prison in Washington, entrepreneurs outside his cell sold photographs of a hunch-backed dwarf whom they falsely identified as this "Demon of Andersonville."[415]

Winder died before the war ended. He could have been the center for the rage about Andersonville although he could also have proven that he frequently complained about the conditions at the prison to the Confederate government. Wirz had no one of influence to save or stand for him. Federal prosecutors chose to ignore the native-born American officers, politicians, and civilians who actually had held the official authority for the food, guards, tracking dogs, materials for shelter, medicine, transportation, and other major aspects of the camp. Without fear of arrest or prosecution, some of these former Confederate officers even appeared as prosecution witnesses at the Wirz trial.

Tribunals, by their nature, are not fair trials but a means of suppressing or oppressing opposing public opinions. The victors of the Civil War used the trial of Wirz as a condemnation of the sufferings of all prisoners held by the Confederacy and even of all of the losses in a war in which many Northerners felt that the privileged classes of the South had brought about. Preserving the Union and ending slavery seemed insufficient, by themselves, to justify the 620,000 war dead and, in fact, created the post war national pragmatism movement that rejected blind adherence to idealistic causes, including civil rights, patriotism, and anti-imperialism. Specifically, the Wirz trial became a battlefield between the Democrat press that blamed Lincoln's administration for the failure to reopen the prisoner exchange and the Republican newspapers that wanted to credit potential Democrat voters in the South as responsible for the Civil War and the horrors of Andersonville. Henry Wirz's mortal peril, thus, almost became incidental in the national spectacle unfolding in Washington.[416]

Two very different countries had come to exist within the same nation, as illustrated by this controversy over Wirz. The war and Andersonville came from their incompatibility. In the North, the resulting struggle created a stronger, more progressive nation that ended the conflict better able to win this war after four years of fighting than at the beginning of the great conflict. By contrast, the plantation/colonial economy of the Civil War South needed, among many other resources, a unified modern transportation system, experienced administrators, and facilities for tens of thousands of prisoners. Lacking the resources to change, the South failed to meet the needs of its soldiers, civilians, and prisoners. The Confederate States of America consequently lost its bid for independence, and thousands of captured federals lost their lives.

The horrors of Andersonville, this "Golgotha" of the American Civil War, thus came to exist without the efforts of individuals or conspirators.[417] Many of Wirz's defenders failed to understand this last fact and have tried to find callous Northern leaders and Northern policies to blame. That bureaucratic incompetence, economics, geography, and technology, without any deliberate plan, could produce such an unimaginable Hell on Earth proves beyond the understanding of most people even today.

The Andersonville trial of Henry Wirz thus had all of the elements that historian Gary Bass identified as the five propositions of the war crimes trial: the pretense of legalization, protecting soldiers, placing citizens before foreigners, mass outrage, and non-state actors. This concept of crimes against humanity that served as the basis for these proceedings existed long before Wirz and Andersonville, going back to at least the ancient Greeks. Victorious nations, however, considered trials as unnecessary as late as Napoleon's exile to St. Helena in 1815. The European powers openly accepted the determination of guilt and punishments as the prerogatives of the winners over the defeated. Formalizing such ideas into a legal tradition began in the liberal nations following atrocity reports during the Crimean War (1854–1856) by the first modern war correspondents.

The United States has officially held itself to a higher standard, however, such as in its unique, formal refusal to recognize the right of conquest. In that same light, through its famous General Orders No. 100, the federal army adopted German-American Francis Lieber's *Instructions for the Government of the Armies of the United States* (1863). When Chipman accused Wirz of violating "the rules of war," he must have referred to the Leiber work, although the trial failed to meet Lieber's criteria for military justice. The Lieber standards actually only allowed for the trial of someone like Wirz either for treason or as a civilian. To have done the latter would have then discredited the government's case that Wirz acted with the responsibilities of a member of the military. The Confederate government, however, had rejected General Orders No. 100 on the grounds that it essentially allowed for unrestricted guerrilla warfare and retribution. After Andersonville opened, twelve European nations accepted similar standards at Geneva in 1864.[418]

Wirz served at Andersonville in ignorance of these rules. He certainly had no idea that one day he could face prosecution under anything like them. Union soldiers arrested Wirz in front of his wife and children, at the abandoned Andersonville prison on 7 May 1865, as he prepared to leave, he mistakenly believed, to start a new life. The former Confederate captain had presumed that the general amnesty granted at the end of the war would extend to him.[419]

Not everything, however, appeared to be working against Wirz, at least initially. To save himself from being held legally responsible for Andersonville, he initially had the services of the partnership of James William Denver, James Hughes, and Charles F. Peck, one of the most prestigious law firms in Washington. The government's initial effort to prosecute Jefferson Davis had just ended in failure and in the humiliation of Joseph Holt, the federal army's judge advocate general. Holt also faced widespread criticism for trying the Lincoln conspirators by military commission, thereby ignoring the jurisdiction of Washington's operational civilian courts. Justification for the use of military commissions and the possible future prosecutions of Davis and other high Confederate officials now seemed dependent upon the outcome of the Wirz trial.

Secretary of War Edwin Stanton personally read the charges prepared by Judge Advocate Chipman, before the court, on 21 August 1865, the first day of the trial. The United States accused Wirz of conspiring, with the highest Confederate officials, to cause the deaths of Americans held as prisoners by the Confederate States of America. Specifically, the government accused them of operating Andersonville as a savage extermination facility.

Such extreme claims, however, challenged the moral right of the Union cause and threatened to mire the federal victory with accusations of vindictiveness. Stanton arranged to have the commission dissolved and a new court of the same members convened the next day to hear a revised list of charges. He had Davis, Confederate Secretary of War James A. Seddon, and Robert E. Lee removed from the list of conspirators. Although Chipman would later restore all of the names deleted from the charges, when the trial finally began only the name of Henry Wirz remained as the sole conspirator. The Judge Advocate charged Wirz with culpability for the murder of more than ten thousand men, a record for an American citizen that still stands. Wirz also faced charges of having personally committed specific acts of murder of individual soldiers. His lawyers countered with claims of double jeopardy and lack of jurisdiction. The commission, consisting of nine federal officers, could and did ignore these and almost all other defense objections.

Defense counsel James Hughes then asked for three days to review the situation as, he claimed, the government had neglected to send him the revised charges until the day before and that, in fact, he only learned of the trial beginning that morning from reading an announcement in the newspaper. Judge Advocate Norton Chipman argued for the trial to continue. The court ignored Hughes's pleas.

Hughes likely assumed that he would defend Wirz before a civilian trial or military court-martial where he could successfully argue that Wirz fell under the general amnesty granted to all other Confederate soldiers at the end of the war. The concept of a military commission that investigated, prosecuted, judged, and even defended, if necessary, the defendant by whatever rules and standards the court arbitrarily chose was beyond his experience or, likely, his imagination. This board of federal officers had unfettered reign to limit or to take the proceedings wherever they chose. In this environment, the trial evolved into an investigation of Andersonville itself.

James Hughes declined to even try to represent a client under such conditions. In a huff, he picked up his hat and law books to leave the defendant and the courtroom. He publicly called the trial a mockery of justice, especially as the court and the judge advocate so openly worked together without even a pretense of impartiality. Except for the then-absent German immigrant Louis Frederick Schade, Hughes's partners followed him out the door, as Wirz cried and begged for them to stay.[420]

The actions of Denver, Hughes & Peck raise a number of questions, the answers to which even Wirz likely never knew. The list begins with why the firm even took on the penniless Henry Wirz as a client. Other questions would include why the partners did not do more to prepare a defense of the captain and why they then abandoned him when he needed their services the most. They risked much by defending Wirz. The Wirz file, in their otherwise extensive legal case papers, contains only a copy of a letter to him that excused their abandoning him by arguing that if they continued to provide him with counsel, they inadvertently "would further encourage the prosecution in persisting in arbetiary [*sic*, arbitrary] and disgraceful acts of power, without regard to law, justice or fairness."[421] The lawyers wrote that if forced to act both as defense and as prosecution, the court would surely allow Wirz a fair trial. Denver, however, wrote to his wife that he found it curious that Wirz would be tried, first, before the many more prominent men who had been accused. Denver believed that the federal government would make every effort to hang the captain from Andersonville.[422]

On 24 August, the third day of the Wirz trial, Louis Schade, the last of Wirz's attorneys, announced that he agreed with his partner's reasons for leaving but, as a matter of conscience, he would remain. Baker then stepped forward from the audience and offered his "assistance" to Schade. The *New York Times* referred to him, in different articles, as O. H. Baker and O. S. Baker, Esq., of the Washington bar. Reporters for the Washington press identified him as O. S. Baker, attorney of Washington, as did Norton Chipman in his later book on the trial. The city directories, local court records, and Martindale directory of attorneys refer to only one Washington area lawyer of that time named Baker, the then newly arrived attorney Orrin S. Baker.

Had Saul Levitt known Baker's real background, he would have had a far more interesting character for his play. Levitt would, however, have had a hard time summarizing that life in just a couple of lines of dialogue. Born in Orleans, Massachusetts, on 23 September 1827, the confusion over the name of the seventh of the nine children of Obadiah and Polly Higgins Baker began with his birth. The future defender of Henry Wirz started life as Obadiah Baker, Jr., the second son of that name, his older brother apparently having died as a child; this second Obadiah thus became what has been termed "a replacement child." He had deep roots in New England. One of his grandfathers, Benoni Baker, had served his country on land and sea during the American Revolution. Benoni, reportedly, became a Quaker and a sea captain after the war. Benoni's wife, Abigail Snow, descended from Stephen Hopkins of the *Mayflower*.

Benoni and Abigail had moved by 1814 from coastal Orleans to Stirling in central Massachusetts.[423] By mid-century, their son Obadiah Sr. had moved his family to the same area. His son, future lawyer Obadiah Jr., afterwards declined to join his father and brothers in the family boot-making business. In 1849, physician A. M. Peterson in Westborough wrote to Obadiah Jr., offering money, books, and a suit of clothes to prepare him for September examinations. Baker, then living at nearby Upton, would keep the letter until his death forty years later, as one of his few remaining possessions. In 1850, a census taker found Obadiah as "O. Smith Baker" living in a boarding house in Millbury, Massachusetts. He attended the Millbury Academy that year, perhaps through the efforts of Peterson.[424]

The whereabouts of Obadiah Smith Baker for the next few years remains a mystery but on 9 May 1853, while living in Belvidere, New Jersey, he married Sarah Matlock Van Voy, a young woman of nearby Johnsonburg who had a modest inheritance. As he referred to himself as "Esq." by then, he likely had already begun, at least as an apprentice attorney, to do legal work. The couple almost immediately moved to New York City, where, on 15 May 1854, Obadiah received his formal admission to the bar.[425]

Obadiah Baker's reasons for choosing a career in law and the circumstances of his training remain unknown. Like Abraham Lincoln, he had struggled to find a place in one of the Northern society's most highly regarded professions. His idealism and respect for rule of law likely originated in his sacrifices to become an attorney. Only a few years earlier, Baker's struggle would have been even harder. In 1846, New York's new state constitution reduced the requirements to practice before the bar from among the most stringent in the United States to (as some critics charged) practically no requirements at all. At almost the time that he chose law as his profession, however, the newspapers covered in great detail, the famous legal battle over the murder of Dr. George Parkman of Harvard in Baker's native state. For whatever reason, Baker now joined New York's glut of attorneys, what Walt Whitman called the "Tomb Shysters of Gotham."

Obadiah took his profession seriously, however. Two decades later and one thousand miles to the West, almost the only property he still possessed consisted of four hundred to six hundred law books. In 1858, Baker earned some local notoriety in New York for representing creditors against George P. Edgar. The latter, a jeweler, had grossly misrepresented his assets and subscriptions to obtain large loans to pay for the publication of his newspaper *The Way of Life.*[426] Obadiah also found himself charged, at least from 1857 to 1860, with debts he had failed to pay.[427]

In those first ten years that the Bakers lived in New York, Obadiah experienced the last stable family life he would have. They also made several trips to visit his family in Massachusetts. The couple produced four children, Eugene (b. 1855), Charles (b. 1858), Sarah (b. 1860, dead by 1862), and Lesbia (b. ca. 1861). A census taker in 1860 reported that Obadiah possessed personal property valued at fourteen thousand dollars and thirty-five hundred dollars worth of real estate. The family also had four servants. A credit reporter for R. G. Dun & Company, later that same year, described Baker as being responsible, upright, refined, and of quiet tastes and moderate means. The reporter, however, failed to find the family as having any bankable assets beyond eight hundred dollars worth of furniture. He wrote "as evidence of their condition," that the Bakers had taken in boarders "of high respectability and quiet habits."[428]

With the coming of the Civil War, the Bakers very publicly supported the cause of the Union. Obadiah would one day claim that no one held the memory of Abraham Lincoln in higher regard. He wrote to Andrew Johnson, a Tennessee unionist leader and later president of the United States, to ask what aid he and his friends could give to the war effort. Sarah wrote an article for *The Continental Monthly* about the Ladies' Loyal League, of which she and feminist pioneer Susan B. Anthony became members. Obadiah would write to his wife that he hoped that when their son Eugene became twelve that the boy would enlist in the army and see Richmond fall as a drummer.[429]

The war also offered Obadiah, as it did so many other Americans, a chance at a new life. In 1862, he took the name of Orrin Smith Baker and moved his family just across the East River to Brooklyn. He then traveled to federally occupied Norfolk, Virginia. Leaving the practice of law behind, Orrin opened a grocery and a shoe store, while also starting the *Norfolk Union* newspaper in partnership with W. W. Shore. Initially, he wrote home to Sarah about his great success. He became a very vocal leader among the unionist minority in federally occupied Virginia and strove to keep Confederate sympathizers from stealing or disrupting President Lincoln's efforts at new elections.[430]

While in this position, Baker accepted a commission of second lieutenant to recruit Virginians to serve in the 16th Virginia Infantry Regiment, a unit created to protect the Washington area. In Baker's brief military career, however, he succeeded simultaneously in resigning his commission, being placed under arrest for desertion, and receiving a medical discharge. (A boyhood injury had left him with a "compressed" chest that interfered with his breathing.) The federal adjutant general reviewed these options and then decided to accept Baker's resignation on 7 May 1863. The 16th Virginia hardly lasted much longer, being abolished on 10 June 1863. It had suffered defeat in trying to protect local bridges from raiders. Baker's financial ventures also failed at this time, likely suffering from the local business closings imposed by the army in retaliation for Confederate guerrilla activity. Leaders in the military and the Lincoln administration had debated whether to treat Norfolk as a port open to business or a hostile occupied military town. Businesses like Baker's lost out. The local quartermaster also fell behind in making payments to Baker, making it difficult for him to provide Sarah with even the ten dollars per week that he tried to send to her. By the summer of 1863, he had not seen his family in months and, because of wartime communications problems, he had not heard from Sarah in three months. Federal authorities closed down his newspaper in August 1862 for having reprinted an article that ridiculed the competence of Admiral Louis Malesherbes Goldsborough.[431]

His Virginia efforts in ruins, Baker returned to the practice of law. He moved to Alexandria, Virginia, where a federal court had opened for hearing claims cases. He received admission to the Virginia bar on 3 October 1864. The next day, he also obtained an appointment as a commissioner of chancery. Baker opened an office on Prince Street and later on Cameron Street.[432] In 1865, he moved his business across the river to the District of Columbia, where he received admission to the bar on 26 April 1865 and took on a new lawyer, Philip H. Reinhard, as a partner. The firm handled pension and claim cases.[433] In pursuit of this business, Baker found himself in the Court of Claims rooms of the Capital Building on 24 August 1865, where he discovered the claims court temporarily replaced by the Wirz trial.

At that moment, Orrin Smith Baker came forward to volunteer to help Lewis Schade in defending Henry Wirz. One newspaper reported that he had consulted with James Hughes, Wirz's former principal attorney, before making this offer.[434] For Baker to take on such an unpopular client for free would seem very unlikely since Baker had so long supported the Union and had even briefly served as an officer in the federal army. His brother-in-law, William Van Voy, had died as a lieutenant in the Spottsylvania Campaign, and his elderly mother-in-law now wore black continuously for all of the young men she had known who were now numbered among the war dead. Perhaps he felt that he needed the publicity of a high profile trial that he believed would be brief. Baker's past, however, showed that he fought passionately for his causes. He now set out to do battle for Wirz's right to a fair trial.

Schade and Baker initially assured Henry Wirz that with just the evidence and witnesses at hand, the court had to acquit the Confederate captain.[435] Had Baker known just how truly a lost cause he faced, however, he might have remained seated, silent, and anonymous. The charges of injustice made by Wirz's former attorneys had merit. The United States had used such military tribunals to try enemy combatants of sovereign nations since at least the Mexican War of 1846–1848 although the United States did not officially recognize the Confederate States of America as any sort of a nation which could produce enemy combatants. Such a commission ignores the rules of either an American civilian criminal trial or a court martial, both of which have a basis in the American and Anglo-Saxon legal traditions. Except for the use of extreme torture, a military commission, as it evolved by the time of the Civil War, bore a striking resemblance to the infamous practices and procedures of the Roman Inquisition that had executed Bruno and punished Galileo in the 1600s. Military tribunals and the Inquisition were built on precedents in the same Roman military law that had developed in the Latin nations of Europe, including in France, long the model for the world's armies. Such trials also worked from the position that the court existed beyond any determination of guilt or innocence. It established the crime and then assigned punishment to the persons in command. These defendants were the commissioned officers who, by right of position more than what they actually did, were considered to have been responsible for any actions taken under their command of the army for whom they served. By that standard, Wirz became guilty by simply serving as an officer at Andersonville. The court convened only to document the issues before it and to assign the appropriate punishment.

For Stanton, Holt, Chipman, and other federal officers, such tribunals served as well-scripted morality plays that would conclude with preplanned public object lessons in the government dispatching well-deserved justice.[436] This special military court had almost unlimited powers of the combined investigation and prosecution of individuals because it dealt with special circumstances determined to be outside of the authority and beyond the rules of regular courts. Its officers served as both as judge and jury. The court made its own rules of evidence and procedure, in theory, in order to facilitate the discovery of criminal conspiracies that might otherwise use the regular rule of law to thwart exposure and prosecution. A judge advocate prosecuted the case and, at the discretion of the court, he would also simultaneously represent the defense. The defendant did not speak, and the court had the right to keep any defense counsel silent while the judge advocate conducted the "trial."

United States Judge Advocate General Joseph Holt defended these commissions as being "unencumbered by the technicalities and inevitable embarrassments attending the administration of justice before civilian tribunals" in order to bring to justice persons otherwise beyond the law.[437] Throughout history, criminals have used perjured witnesses, intimidated judges, and corrupt juries to defeat justice. These methods, to some sociologists, define true organized crime, as practiced by McGirth's gang, John A. Murrell's "Murrellites," and the Pony Club, bandit groups that, coincidentally, achieved legendary status in early Georgia. Military tribunals prosecuted, without any overriding means of impartial review, those publicly unpopular personifications they perceived as enemies of the state. Such courts, under these circumstances, easily fall victim to partisanship, public passion, political pressure, and personal prejudice.

In his later defense of the court's jurisdiction, Norton P. Chipman, the judge advocate for the Wirz trial, outlined the reasons for trying the Confederate captain by such a tribunal. He described Wirz's crimes as being against the rules of war, violations of which went beyond any other court then in existence. Chipman further argued that the civil rights, and other articles in the United States Constitution that guaranteed due process in a civilian court, failed to apply when used to protect persons bent on using the Constitution in the destruction of the Constitution, such in dealing with the members of the conspiracy called the Confederate States of America. Chipman thus made the classic argument that the protections and ideals of the United States Constitution could be too dangerous and too potentially self-destructive to be practiced.[438]

The Wirz trial took on particularly odd turns. Just as the Inquisition tried its victims, in part, for being a part of cults that the Church refused to recognize, the United States now planned to try Wirz for conspiring with the Confederate States of America, a government that it officially refused to recognize. While the American press condemned Wirz for coming from a European society that failed to appreciate American justice, now Americans prepared to try him outside of the traditions of an American style impartial trial in proceedings based in the most extreme of the European militarism that Americans claimed to find so repugnant in the actions of men like Wirz.

Saul Levitt would write his largely fictional drama on the Wirz trial around the issue of moral responsibility for committing crimes while acting under military orders from superiors. In the real trial, the case became a battle over the issue of subordinating an individual's (Wirz's) civil rights by a military tribunal. The United States military had instituted a policy of treating the men of the officially non-existent Confederate army as soldiers to save the men of both armies from being treated as criminals. This policy had protected everyone from the lowliest private to General Robert E. Lee from prosecution.

Holt had decided to move the court away from any consideration of the civil rights of the defendant and towards a review of the tragedy of Andersonville. He stacked the commission with men who would find no pity for Wirz. All but one of the nine members of the ruling commission had served on the war's battlefields and one had lost a son in the fighting. Each of these officers also awaited a promotion. In addition, the majority of the board had political ambitions in states with widespread hatred of the Confederacy. The president of the court, General Lewis "Lew" Wallace had served on the military commission that tried and convicted the Lincoln assassins. He had voted them guilty, thus proving that he accepted the validity of military commissions. Wallace privately expressed his conviction of Wirz's guilt, as well as that he wanted the trial over so that he could join a financially lucrative private military campaign in Mexico. Other members of the commission also seemed distracted and, as the trial stretched out over two months, increasingly acted as if wanting to finish this ordeal as quickly as possible for themselves. The effects of the brutal summer heat in the courtroom hardly improved anyone's patience.[439]

The defense of Wirz fell almost solely on Baker. Louis Frederick Schade, who pleaded that his now-absent partners had handled any trial preparation of the case, hardly participated. On the one occasion when, Baker being "severely indisposed," Schade had the defense by himself, he proved unable to proceed. Chipman used the opportunity to raise questions about Schade giving Wirz money and passing letters from him. The prosecution even raised questions about Schade's loyalty, as the lawyer had supported slavery and opposed the Republican Party. The court, angry at Schade's lack of preparedness, postponed the proceedings until Baker could arrive. When Baker eventually did appear, he used his apology for his absence to slip in an explanation of the struggle he went through to mount a defense: "I am now doing every day two men's work. I am examining witnesses from 7 o'clock in the morning until 11 o'clock, when it is time to come here. Again at half past 3 I am in my office, where I work until dark. I do in one day's work in court and another day's work in my office. How can any man work more?"[440] The court reporter offered him the services of a shorthand clerk.

Wirz, in declining health and suffering severe stress, proved too mentally unbalanced to help his advocates in the defense. Four marines carried him into and from the courtroom each day.[441] Wirz recovered enough to keep a diary. It appeared in print, giving the public his impressions of the conduct of the trial:

> What a mockery this trial is, they say they are anxious that I should have justice done to me, and then when a witness is put on the stand to give testimony they try every thing to break him down, if they cannot do it they try to assail his private character, when they had their witnesses up, they not only were allowed to state everything I said, everything I done,

> but even what they heard others say that I had said so and so, done such and such things, and now where I wish to prove by my witnesses what I also said and done, it is said inadmissible.[442]

Early in the trial, Baker realized that the court essentially overruled any objection that he made and sometimes blunted the value of his arguments by silencing him before he could finish raising issues or asking questions. They only allowed him to cross-examine the prosecution's witnesses as a courtesy and, even then, only within narrow limits. It would decide even to accept blatant hearsay on the validity of individual testimony. The court also banned Baker from chal-

O. S. Baker, standing center, defends Henry Wirz as Wirz lies on a couch beside him in this engraving that appeared in *Harper's Weekly,* 21 October 1865.

lenging the credibility of any witness or asking questions on matters other than those raised by the judge advocate's questions.[443] The prosecution used 160 well-paid witnesses. Baker saw no use in trying to cross-examine most of them. Usually, he could do little beyond listening, day in and day out, as they told horror stories, frequently from hearsay, about conditions and events at Andersonville. Of the rest, he unsuccessfully objected to their testimony. Chipman used the witnesses to try to link to people like Jefferson Davis who were still omitted from the official charges against Wirz. The testimony only rarely related to Wirz and, at times, came from obvious perjurers. Some of the prosecution "witnesses," critics would charge, even lied about being at Andersonville.

The German-American press called Baker's defense weak, but he had to act tactfully and to carefully choose his moments to fight. Those writers failed to appreciate that the court could have had him silenced or even punished for delaying the proceedings, in the court's opinion, unnecessarily. Historian Gayle M. Koerting concluded, "Yet a distinguishing character trait emerged concerning Baker throughout the course of the trial. He would stubbornly defend Wirz to the best of his ability despite the dictates of military law."[444] The court could, and did, prevent prosecution witnesses from testifying on behalf of the defendant. It could veto any questions proposed by Baker. For example, when Baker asked prosecution witness and former Andersonville quartermaster Captain J. H. Wright if Wirz had authority over the prison's rations, Chipman objected to the question as irrelevant and the court sustained the objection.

The judge advocate also had the sole right to question any witness before any appearance in court. In one exceptionally heated exchange, Baker charged that Chipman used this privilege as a means to influence the witnesses' testimony. The judge advocate had defense witnesses, even former prisoners, questioned as to loyalty and honesty. Frederick Guscetti, for example, had his integrity challenged just for having solicited donations for Wirz's defense. In another typical incident, Martin S. Harris earned Chipman's disdain for having written articles for a New York newspaper that defended Wirz. The zealous judge advocate called his writings, by defending Wirz, as too disloyal to the United States to consider him as a credible witness.[445]

Repeatedly Baker complimented the judge advocate on his fairness but, at one point, the verbally battling attorneys talked of settling an issue outside of the court, presumably with their fists. Baker, however, also urged that the court avoid allowing the trial to sink to the level of animosity sometimes found in the informality of a justice of the peace court. At other times, he would lecture or lower himself to petty arguments with the court and Chipman. Sometimes Baker pushed only to get in the last word, straining what little credibility he had with this board.[446]

Orrin Baker did manage to raise many questions about the conduct of the trial, including the failure of Chipman to provide him with all of his requested witnesses and Chipman's use of leading questions. Even the commission would raise doubts about the prosecution's tactics and, on such occasions, Baker would then jump in to try to widen any breach between Chipman and the court. He would also tactfully use ridicule and humor to win points—at least with the audience. When Thomas C. Alcock testified that Wirz had taken gold from him, for example, Baker invoked laughter from the onlookers when he forced Alcock to admit that he had himself first stolen the gold from someone else in Jackson, Mississippi! In another instance, Baker offered to have himself physically thrown out of the court if he meant any offense to the integrity of any federal soldier.

Frequently the court did threaten to have Baker removed for good. He and Schade themselves offered to resign several times and did quit on 28 August. Even then, when Baker tried to give his reasons for resigning, the court ordered him silenced. A desperate Wirz cried out to him, "you might stay to help me, and you should not mind even if the Court does sometimes overrule you."[447] When the tribunal continued the next day, the court read a letter from Wirz explaining that he had persuaded Baker and Schade to remain and asking the court to reinstate them. The board agreed, and Baker continued to work night and day in a hopeless defense of a nationally reviled, penniless client near idiocy, in a seemingly endless trial where the prosecution had every advantage. Baker's efforts seemed as only a formality for a defendant facing the gallows at the hands of a prejudiced court. As tactfully as he could, Baker pleaded for the subpoenaing of more defense witnesses, including Robert E. Lee, to deny the conspiracy charge. He used that opportunity to slip in a summary of his dying client's problems that the court likely failed to appreciate: "Here, then is sickness and misery struggling against opulence and power. Here is abject poverty grappling with untold millions; here is a poor destitute, distracted, and shut-up prisoner, with powerless and inefficient counsel, endeavoring to compete with all the ability and power and means that the most powerful Government can bestow to crush him."[448]

The military commission allowed Baker to present 32 of the 106 witnesses Chipman subpoenaed for him. Thirty-six other defense witnesses still waited to appear when the court arbitrarily ended the trial after sixty-three almost insufferably hot days.[449]

Baker now demanded two weeks to prepare a closing argument. The court eventually allowed him twelve days. The judge advocate also insisted upon reviewing the defense's closing argument to insure that it excluded any mention of Chipman's failure to provide Baker with all of the witnesses he had requested. Baker finally declined to make a closing argument. Instead of accepting Chipman's offer to present both sides of the case in his conclusion, the court allowed the clerk to read a defense that the clerk had helped Wirz to write. Some scholars have misread the court record and assumed that Baker had finally withdrawn from the case for good. In fact, he stayed with his client to the end. Wirz mentioned in that paper that his counsel had helped him in preparing the legal arguments, implying that Baker wrote almost "Wirz's" entire often-published complex, legalistic summation.[450]

That paper illustrated how Baker had achieved a victory over his otherwise nemesis Norton Chipman. Throughout the trial, with the court's cooperation, Chipman had tried to link Wirz to a giant conspiracy involving the leaders of the Confederate government, and specifically Jefferson Davis. Had Wirz/Baker claimed that the captain had only followed orders, that confession would have condemned the leaders of the Confederate government. Baker instead argued that the prosecutor, lead by his heart rather than his head, had built a case without any legally credible evidence that any crime had been committed by Henry Wirz or any other individual in command at Andersonville.[451] Overall, by arguing his case within generally recognized rules of evidence, Baker made an implied defense of civilian courts as a just alternative to an unrestrained military tribunal influenced by popular partisan demands for revenge. While Chipman and Holt claimed that such a tribunal found the truth by ignoring those rules, Baker made a case that the evidence actually proved his client innocent. More importantly, he demonstrated that, without an impartial legal structure, the results of the trial gave the public appearance of the government figuratively conducting a lynching.

The court, however, finally found Henry Wirz guilty of conspiracy and murder. On the day of the execution, Schade brought Wirz the news that President Andrew Johnson would not grant a stay of execution. A subsequent interview with the condemned man seemed to quote Wirz as blaming Baker for the outcome of the trial, pointing out that Wirz had never chosen Baker as his attorney. In what almost became his last words, Henry Wirz wrote a public letter to Baker to set his views on record for all time:

> My Dear Sir: I am truly sorry to see that the New York Herald has spoken of you in the article headed "Wirz" in such a manner as to reflect upon you. I have not said a word that could be construed into such a thing. I merely stated that I had not selected you as my counsel, but accepted of your services cheerfully. I will say again, as I said before, I believe you done all you could for me, and therefore accept my thanks, the thanks of a dying man. H. Wirz 10th November, 1865[452]

A writer has quoted Baker as calling Wirz the bravest man he had ever seen. To the end, Henry Wirz refused to confess to any crime but stated that he hoped that his ghost would return to haunt the men who had lied at his trial. Later that day, at his bungled public execution, the rope failed to break his neck, and he instead strangled to death. Wirz died on a gallows on the future site of the United States Supreme Court building, as onlookers called for him to remember Andersonville.[453]

As his last actions in this Andersonville affair, Orrin Baker made pleas to the Secretary of War on behalf of Private James W. Duncan of the 5th Louisiana Infantry, the prison's baker. Duncan had defected to the federal forces in February 1865 and had come to Washington to testify for Wirz.[454] Upon Duncan entering the courtroom, Chipman had him arrested for war crimes. Duncan eventually faced a military tribunal in Savannah, Georgia, far beyond any help from Orrin S. Baker. Despite the efforts of a prestigious team of local

The execution of Henry Wirz on the future site of the United States Supreme Court Building. (National Archives and Records Administration)

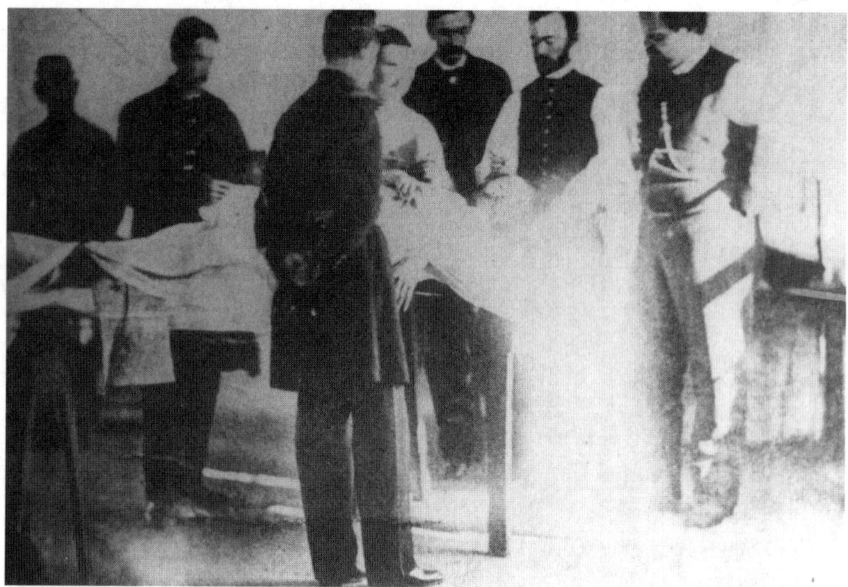

For no known reason, Wirz's corpse was subjected to an autopsy. Parts of his body, including his skull, were taken as souvenirs. (Western Reserve Collection)

defense attorneys, Duncan received a sentence of fifteen years in prison. Petitions from his wife, his jailers, and former Andersonville prisoners failed to win him a pardon. He either escaped from, or the officials allowed him to leave, Fort Pulaski, Georgia on 11 July 1867, without any discernible effort being made to recapture him.[455]

Judge Advocate General Holt boasted that by successfully using the power of the military tribunal to prove to the public and to history that a vast Confederate conspiracy had existed, the trials of the Lincoln conspirators and of Wirz proved the value of such commissions. Norton Chipman would make the same claims about the Wirz trial in a book decades later. In both trials, however, the prosecution actually failed to produce any evidence of any plot. Furthermore, of all of the men, except Wirz, whom Chipman claimed participated in the Andersonville conspiracy, only Private Duncan ever faced trial and the court actually found him guilty only of kicking unidentified prisoners on undetermined dates. Baker had very publicly exposed the injustice of the military commissions to the nation. Jefferson Davis and the other Confederate leaders were saved from having to face trial before such courts.[456]

A phalanx of reporters gave this trial a national stage before an interested audience. More than three hundred thousand federal soldiers had died in ending the South's "rebellion," and one in ten of those men had succumbed while prisoners of the Confederate States of America. On both sides, more men suffered in captivity than died in battle. The Northern public who wanted to know that they won a victory against evil by means of virtue, and prosecution of someone for the horrors of Andersonville seemed both a perfect and comprehensible tool to obtain that vindication. A few newspapers, however, exposed the injustice of the trial.

Anyone who missed the initial press coverage of Baker's ordeal in the Wirz trial could read about it elsewhere. Within a year of the execution of Henry Wirz, the *New-York Times* articles on the trial appeared in a booklet as *The Demon of Andersonville* and prosecution witness Ambrose Spencer also published abstracts of the court transcript as a book. The official government publication of the minutes of the proceedings came two years later.

The Supreme Court eventually ruled such military commissions as unconstitutional because they lacked the approval of Congress. This decision in *Ex parte Milligen*, however, came only in the framework of where and when fully operational civilian courts existed. The decision failed to address such issues as the means of trial for violation of the rules of war.[457] In 1918, the *New-York Times* joined French legal expert Leon Bourgeois in calling for using the legal precedent of the Wirz trial to prosecute the Kaiser after World War I. The *Times* identified Henry Wirz, incorrectly, as another "German" and argued for the use of his case as a model for British and American courts in prosecuting Germans for cruelty to prisoners of war. A relative of some of the men held at Andersonville, however, responded with a denouncement of the Wirz trial as "unjust in the extreme."[458] Franklin Roosevelt would use the precedent of the Civil War trials, including that of Wirz, to guarantee that normal court procedure would not save World War II German saboteurs from harsh punishments. Such prosecutions by the military commissions that Baker tried so hard to expose as unjust continue as topics of controversy even today.[459]

All but one of the stars of the trial of Henry Wirz benefited from this notoriety. Books and articles, some exonerating (even some by former Andersonville prisoners) and others condemning the Confederate captain, appeared in print for decades. In 1909, the United Daughters of the Confederacy (UDC) erected a monument to him in the town of Andersonville. The UDC and some writers since 1865 have honored Louis Schade for his efforts on the captain's behalf, as if he alone had defended Wirz. Schade actually championed Wirz's cause better in the press after the captain's conviction than he did in person during the trial. This lawyer remained in Washington until his death in 1903. Over the years, he

This battery of reporters made the Wirz trial one of the most extensively covered court proceedings in American history. (National Archives and Records Administration)

remained an idealist in an increasingly negative and pragmatic world, waging the "good fight" for a number of lost causes, including against American imperialism. Schade has a lengthy sketch in *The National Cyclopedia of American Biography*.

Norton Chipman also has a biographical article in that same work. Several major political appointments came to him in the decades after the trial, as well as a term as one of the few congressmen to represent the District of Columbia. In 1876, he began a successful public career in California, where he died in 1924. For the rest of his life, he would defend and greatly distort both the conduct and results of the Wirz trial. He even re-fought the trial in a book in 1911 to deny the unfairness of the prosecution of Wirz. Chipman, however, chose to avoid making Baker and Schade, whom he described only as "well-known" Washington attorneys, an issue.

Other participants in the Wirz trial also achieved fame. Lew Wallace received his share of political patronage, while achieving a notable literary career for writing *Ben-Hur*, a novel about prejudice and gross injustice in the time of the Jesus. He died in 1905.[460] Denver, Hughes & Peck prospered despite the firm's brief involvement with and abandonment of Captain Wirz. A few months after the trial, the firm successfully represented the federal government's claim to the gold of the Richmond banks that had been in possession of the Confederate government.[461]

Baker's fame would come from historical studies of the trial long after his death rather than from anything he did in the rest of his life. In the years immediately after Wirz's execution, Orrin S. Baker disappeared from public notice. He remained in Washington for some years although his partnership with Reinhard had likely ended even before the Wirz trial.[462] If he had hoped that a grateful Denver, Hughes & Peck would award him with a partnership for saving the firm from the Wirz trial, he received another disappointment. In 1866, however, O. S. Baker registered for the right to appear before the Supreme Court, and he became a justice of the peace in Washington. The following year, he declined to contest a lawsuit that he had mishandled a client's funds. In 1867, Baker served as a Washington delegate to the Border States Convention in Baltimore that sought to obtain full voting rights for black as well as white men, and, in early 1869, as a delegate to the Washington convention of the Universal Franchise Association, an organization promoting the right of women to vote.[463]

On 13 December 1869, however, the court of the city of St. Louis admitted him to the bar. Baker had apparently made this move to try to escape from his debts, but he found more trouble in his new locale. In 1874, seamstress Annie L.

McCarron sued him for one thousand dollars that she said that she gave him during their phony marriage. She claimed to have met him on 20 April 1870, and that he represented himself "as a stranger in a strange city, sick and pining for the sympathetic love of a heart that would beat in union with his own, and fill the 'aching void' created by the loss of his former wife."[464] At his insistence, she married him in his office on 23 June 1870, in a ceremony performed by a man he claimed had the authority to perform the ceremony. The couple boarded at various places about the city, while living on her earnings. Orrin S. Baker, according to McCarron, "looked old and seedy and feeble" when they married, but after she provided him with "money to get on in the world," funds that bought him new clothes and dinners in the finest hotels, Baker became "fat and sleek and saucy."[465] On 1 June 1873, when his now-pregnant new wife learned that he had decided to return east to visit his original wife and children, he told her that he did not give a damn what she thought about it. Annie gave birth on 3 December 1873, and one year later, sued Baker for the one thousand dollars. Too late, she had "discovered to her sorrow that, instead of the upright, pious Christian gentleman she was led to believe him to be, he is an overbearing, fretful, profane, unprincipled man—a base fraud and deceit."[466]

Baker denied all of her claims but her story has more than a ring of truth. He did have clients but, overall, he knew failure more than success. In 1872, he wrote a brief memoir on the back of a canceled check that he received for legal work for Turkish bath operator Dr. George F. Adams:

> This is the first Thousand dollar fee I ever received. I was admitted to practice law on the 15th of May 1854 in the city of New York and from that time to this over Eighteen years I have worked through many adventures, losses, discouragements, and heart rendering sufferings for this fee and yet when the blessing came I had earned it in two months and fourteen days and took a thanksgiving dinner with the giver of it yesterday. nov.29.1872 O. S. Baker[467]

The court ruled in favor of Annie and had Baker's property seized to satisfy her judgment. All that the sheriff could find of value amongst his belongings consisted of two desks, a carpet, four bookcases, and some four hundred books on law. He had already sold hundreds of his other volumes on law, scholarship, and science to settle debts left over from his time in Washington. Before the

McCarron suit, he likely had planned to settle his debts there and return to the District of Columbia.[468]

During those troubled years, he must have seen little of his original family. In 1866, Sarah and the children left Brooklyn and moved to Willbraham, Massachusetts, presumably near his relatives. When Orrin moved to St. Louis, they joined her relatives in Rockford, Illinois. Leaving his latest problems, and some of his clients behind in St. Louis, by 1876, Orrin began practicing law in the Oakland-San Francisco area.[469] San Francisco, in those years, became home to some of the West's most successful businessmen, many of whom had complex legal dealings in areas like silver mining that involved equally sophisticated litigation. The fire resulting from the San Francisco Earthquake of 1906 destroyed any records of how well Baker did in his new environment.

In 1887, he made one last great effort to pull his family together by going to work in Los Angeles as the sales representative for the City of Paris, San Francisco's and the West's greatest dry goods store. Sarah and their grown children joined him there in the frontier "City of Angels." Orrin had enrolled their son Eugene in Yale's law school, where the younger Baker made his own history. He captained his school to victory in the first intercollegiate game of American football, a sport he helped to invent. Eugene went on to work as a bookkeeper for the San Gabriel Valley Land & Water Company, the beginning of a long career in real estate that would lead him to a role in the founding of several California towns, including Burbank.[470]

By the following year, however, Orin had returned to San Francisco, with Sarah and the younger two children. O. S. Baker then made one last move. Sarah had him committed to the Napa Hospital for the insane on 2 April 1889. He suffered from delusions of having been to Hell, and of having money in the Palace, San Francisco's most expensive hotel. He finally became incoherent. His actions at the Wirz trial in 1865 suggest that he had the beginnings of his final illness even then. Napa, a state institute for the indigent, had a notorious reputation for the extremely poor treatment of its inmates. Ironically, Baker had fought his greatest case defending the mentally incompetent Henry Wirz, an officer of a nightmarish prison camp; now Baker spent the last three months of life as a hopeless, mentally deranged, prisoner in a similarly notorious institution. He died from exhaustion on 12 July. Sarah and the younger children rejoined Eugene in Los Angeles. Despite her husband's brief and conflicted career as a lieutenant in the army, Sarah received a federal Civil War pension for his service. In death, Orrin thus did a better job of providing for her than he did in life.[471] Despite his major participation in an historical event, even in death,

Orrin Baker failed to draw serious public attention. He most likely lies in an unmarked grave under the Lincoln Hills Golf Course, the site of the former Golden Gate Cemetery in San Francisco.

This complete silence on his life must come, at least in part, from a deliberate effort on his part. In defending Wirz, he risked the animosity of many people. Additionally, Baker had so adamantly supported the Union that he likely had personal problems with having aided anyone who had served the Confederacy, all the more so because his dogged defense of Wirz quite likely helped to save Jefferson Davis and other Confederate officials from prosecution and the gallows.

In some ways, his obscurity seems appropriate. Baker's very public work in the Wirz trial occurred as an incident in a long career notable for a lack of important cases. The lawyer Baker of the real and fictional Andersonville trial existed only in the proceedings of that courtroom. For Orrin Smith Baker, born Obadiah Baker, his life was a journey from coast to coast during which, success and permanence, like notoriety, eluded him. He finally serves as an example of one of unknown thousands of Americans affected by, and who affected, even in death, the great events of the Civil War by acting upon their convictions. This new age allowed him to play a major role in one of the Civil War's most important trials but then returned him to the obscurity he otherwise knew.

This engraving, made after the Civil War, shows the interior of Camp Lawton at Millen, Georgia. D. W. Vowles is likely the officer with the sword in the center of the illustration. (Hargrett Rare Book and manuscripts Library, University of Georgia Libraries)

THE LAST MAN TO GET AWAY [472]

Where such people first came from, no one knows; where they are to go at last, nobody cares.

—W. H. Burton, from *The History of Norfolk*

For years the Northern press carried stories and illustrations of the horrors of such infamous prisons as Andersonville. Some eleven percent of the total federal military's wartime mortality came from the captives of the Confederates. The Northern public expected prosecution of any Confederates responsible for the mistreatment of prisoners of war. Immediately following the Civil War, federal judge advocate general Joseph Holt urged secretary of war Edwin Stanton to order the arrests and trials of the Confederate officials responsible for the "alleged cruel treatment" of federals held as prisoners by the "so-called" Confederate States of America. Of the men specifically listed by Holt, Captain Henry Wirz eventually hanged and three other men served at least brief prison terms.

Captain D. W. Vowles, an officer at Andersonville and still later the commandant of the Confederate prison Camp Lawton in Millen, Georgia, made Holt's list but escaped arrest and prosecution.[473] Although Vowles, of the men sought, had the best chance of avoiding punishment, he successfully evaded any accounting for his actions.

In the early 1970s, I first read the story of Vowles and attempted to learn what became of him after Camp Lawton. Secondary sources omitted any mention of his post war fate and even his exact name remained a mystery. Standard sources such as *The War of the Rebellion*, *Confederate Military History*, *Southern Bivouac*, *Southern Historical Society Papers*, and *Confederate Veteran* had few references to him at all. What I found on Vowles, after several years, consisted only of very brief information on his life before the Civil War.

Like his captives, before the war Vowles had little reason to imagine he would find himself in a prison camp. Born on 13 August 1831, in Warrenton, Fauquier County, Virginia, to Newton and Lucy Sisson Vowles, he appears in the 1850 census as Washington [the "W" in D. W.] Vowles and living with his brother, Dr. Newton Elwyn Vowles, in Cooper County, Missouri. At that time, he worked as a clerk.[474] D. W. also studied law for a time. Eight years later, the local credit reporter for the R. G. Dun & Company (today's Dun & Bradstreet) found him back in Fauquier County and described him as an adventurous young man who had recently served with William Walker's "filibusters" in Walker's bizarre private conquest of Nicaragua. Wounded four times in that adventure, Vowles rose to the rank of brevet major in Walker's mercenary army. Walker had conducted one of the most successful and colorful of the several campaigns by American mercenaries during those years. Beyond what he later claimed, however, Vowles's involvement in that project remains one of his many mysteries.[475]

Returning to the United States, D. W. Vowles hoped to obtain a commission with the regular United States army. He wrote to Secretary of War John B. Floyd with an offer to raise a company of volunteers to serve in the "Mormon War" then starting in Utah between the United States and the settlers there. Secretary Floyd declined Vowles's offer, pointing out that the recently enacted enlistment law only allowed the army to accept whole regiments of volunteers.[476]

By 1860, Vowles again lived with his brother Newton, now in Marion County, Missouri. D. W. studied allopathic medicine and, in 1861, graduated from Missouri Medical College (also known as McDowell Medical College, in St. Louis, today part of the Washington University School of Medicine). The new doctor moved across the Missouri River to Fowler, Illinois. The secret of his later disappearance rests in that move.[477]

Understanding that secret begins by exploring his background role in the little known complexities of the Civil War in the midwest. As a native Virginian from Missouri, both slave states, D. W. Vowles almost naturally embraced the cause of Southern independence. At one point in the early days of the war, he physically counted as one-third of General Sterling Price's whole command in Missouri.[478] His greatest service came in his new home of Illinois, however, where he became one of the first men north of the Missouri River to join the Southern cause and from where he raised a company. As reflected in the federal census records, even before the arrival of war refugees to resettle north of the Ohio River, southern Illinois had a large population from the Southern states. Some of the men of Illinois traveled south to join the Confederate cause. As could be shown by many other examples, support for the Confederate States of America existed beyond the secessionist and even the slave states.

Vowles next served at Price's great victory at the Battle of Lexington, Missouri, on 18–29 September 1861. Among others, he claimed credit for the idea of having slaves roll bales of water-soaked hemp forward as mobile shields for the soldiers during the battle. By that time, Vowles held the rank of lieutenant colonel and served as aide-de-camp and inspector general of the 2nd Division of the Missouri State Guard, in the state of Missouri's own and separate defensive war against the United States military.

The State Guard later disbanded, and most of its members joined the Confederate army. Vowles eventually saw service in six battles in four states and received a commendation for his actions at Lexington. During the late spring and summer of 1862, he worked in Mississippi to integrate the former Missouri state forces into the regular army. On 16 August 1862, as the war in Missouri degenerated into bushwhacking and the federal army seized his brother Newton, D. W. received orders to report to Richmond. The Confederate army commissioned him as a captain on 16 August 1862.

His career in the Confederate capitol proved as enigmatical as the rest of his life. Sometimes he served in the Nitre and Mining Bureau, but he also took assignments from Adjutant General Samuel Cooper as an assistant adjutant general. On 11 December 1862, Vowles received orders to join the staff of Brigadier General John Winder, provost marshal general for Richmond and commissary general of prisons east of the Mississippi River. While under Winder, Vowles served as a commissioner to judge military offenses in Richmond. His unsuccessful effort to receive a promotion to major and a transfer to the Marine battalion serving on the Virginia ironclads did produce letters of recommendation carrying high praise from his superiors.[479] Vowles did organize three hundred Confederate deserters being held at Castle Thunder into two companies. As "Winder's Legion," these men helped in the defense of Richmond.[480] In 1864, General Winder requested that Vowles come to Georgia to investigate reports that the federal prisoners at Camp Sumter, the notorious Andersonville prison, included spies sent by General Sherman to work in conjunction with local people in overthrowing the guards at the prison camp. Vowles went but over the protest of Richmond officials who did not wish to lose his service in judging military cases.[481]

Vowles probably came to wish that he had stayed in the Confederate capital. Winder and his staff could do little beyond trying to keep more than thirty thousand prisoners, many of them from Illinois, from overwhelming the some one thousand poorly equipped and inadequately trained guards. Vowles had the task of uncovering any plot to make that disaster happen. Federal survivors of Andersonville remembered him as Captain "Bowers" and as working in the camp bakery with Private James W. Duncan of the 5th Louisiana Infantry, likely as a cover. Prisoners and camp officials alike also suspected Duncan of stealing camp supplies.[482] To Winder's regret, Vowles had to leave before he could conclude his inquiries.

The general had found a new way to prevent a mass escape. On 28 July, Captain Vowles received orders to find a location for a new stockade to contain most of the prisoners at Andersonville. He and the general's son, Captain William S. Winder, selected a site five miles from the Augusta-Savannah railroad, near Millen, Georgia.[483] Despite hearing protests about the local water quality and the insecurity of Georgia to federal raiding parties, General Winder then ordered the construction of Camp Lawton, named for Confederate quartermaster general A. R. Lawton, to proceed. In late September, prisoners from Andersonville arrived at this forty-two acre stockade that General Winder assumed stood as the largest prison in the world. He claimed that it had a capacity for thirty-two thousand to forty thousand inmates, the maximum number held at Andersonville but now in twice the space. By November, the camp held almost eleven thousand prisoners, and at least 488 federals eventually died there.

Confederate officials had learned a great deal about building such camps by the autumn of 1864, and what they did at Millen makes a compelling argument that the earlier horrors of Andersonville came about from mistakes and poor planning that had terrible consequences rather than from some conspiracy to maliciously murder prisoners of war. The new camp had the free-flowing water supply that Andersonville lacked. The prisoners divided the resulting stream into drinking water and, below a dam, water for sanitation. Camp Lawton also had its own supply depot for gathering and stockpiling provisions. The interior of the stockade had ample space, trees, and even brick baking ovens for the prisoners. One inmate remembered that the inmates received twice the daily rations issued at Andersonville.

Captain D. W. Vowles oversaw all of these operations as the new prison's commandant. Former prisoner John McElroy of the 16th Illinois Cavalry Regiment remembered him as the best of the Confederate prison commanders, a decent man but also a good disciplinarian and an efficient, careful, tactful administrator. One prisoner wrote of the commandant, "he is inclined to be hasty and quick-tempered, but does everything in his power to alleviate our misery."[484] When an attempt at a mass enlistment of prisoners into the Confederate army almost turned into a riot, Vowles ordered his guards out of the stockade and allowed this potentially dangerous situation to evaporate without anyone getting hurt. He also refused to tolerate "raiders," prisoners who robbed other inmates. After Vowles had such men punished, many of the raiders enlisted in the Confederate army. While shootings of prisoners seemed to occur regularly at other prison camps, North and South, apparently Vowles's guards shot no one.

He did have critics. Some of the prisoners reported that General Winder found evidence to support charges that Vowles took bribes to place healthy men on the list of sick inmates offered for exchange. If General Winder believed these accusations, he still recommended Vowles for promotion on 22 October. A witness at the post-war trial of Andersonville's Henry Wirz claimed that Vowles refused to place prisoner Major Archibald Boyle's name on Camp Lawton's roster. He omitted Boyle's name from the records to keep him out of any prisoner exchange. Because Boyle had led black troops, the Confederacy refused to recognize him as an officer and confined him as long as possible and as if he was an enlisted man at Andersonville and Millen.

By 25 November, the approach of General Sherman's army forced the permanent evacuation of Camp Lawton. Vowles remained behind to settle accounts and then traveled to Augusta to await further orders. From that point, he vanished from the Confederate records.[485] In fact, Vowles had apparently disappeared. Certainly, he had reason to hide. In 1865, Captain Henry Wirz of Andersonville, a middle management functionary at the prison, went to the gallows for war crimes. Private James W. Duncan, with whom Vowles had served at that same prison, received a fifteen-year sentence from a federal military court the following year.[486]

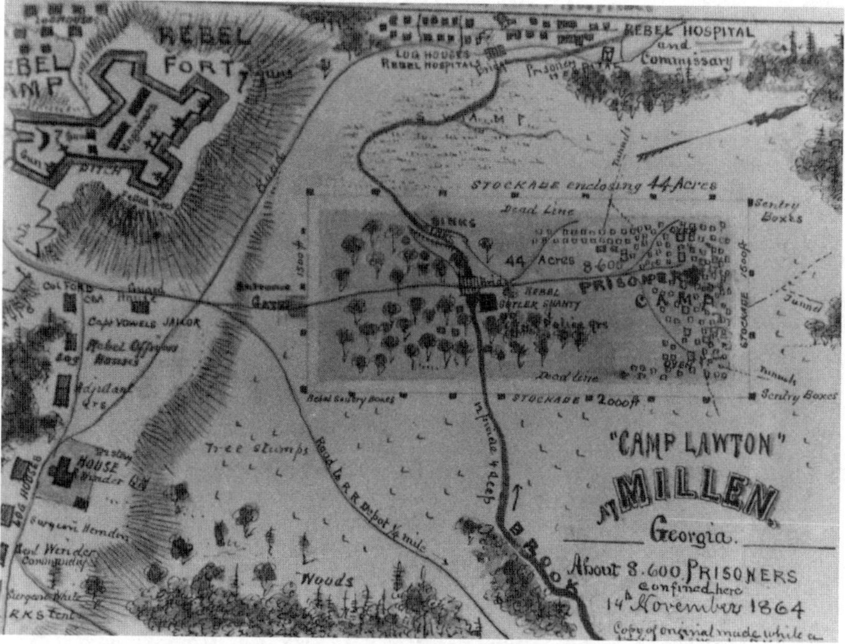

Former prisoner Robert Knox Sneden drew these sketches of Camp Lawton from memory. (Virginia Historical Society, Richmond VA)

Over the years, I searched for Vowles in books on Civil War prisons and on Confederate exiles to Brazil and Mexico, but without success. My search of sources at the Society of Genealogists in London also proved unsuccessful. Visits and requests made of archives and libraries in Georgia, Missouri, Texas, and Virginia, including in state pension files, failed to locate more information on him. My search of the manuscript and microfilm resources of the National Archives of the United States also proved unsuccessful. Examination of the multi-million name international databases assembled by the Genealogical Society of Utah for use in its family history centers, and later on the Internet, also drew a blank. I even, unsuccessfully, contacted the television show *Unsolved Mysteries* about doing a Vowles segment.

Just as he seemed beyond locating, information on Daniel Washington Vowles surfaced and almost by accident. While unsuccessfully searching for information on John M. Stewart, a Confederate engineer from Missouri, I looked again at microfilm of a card catalog of Civil War service records available at the Missouri Department of Archives and History. I had previously checked the catalog for Vowles but, in doing so again, I found him mistakenly listed as a Union veteran applying for admission to the Missouri Soldiers Home in 1907.

The archives subsequently provided me with a copy of the brief application of Daniel Washington Vowles. Missouri officials had rejected his request because he resided across the state line in Quincy, Illinois. A witness in his claim wrote of having known Vowles for thirty years.

Newspaper articles graciously provided by the Quincy-Adams County Historical Society from the *Quincy Whig* around the time of Vowles's death provided me with information on his later years. The first piece appeared in the evening following the celebration of his "ninety-fifth" (*sic*, eighty-eighth) birthday, on 14 August 1919. In an interview earlier that day, Vowles had told of his adventures in Nicaragua with William Walker, his service under Sterling Price in Missouri, and his duties in Richmond. His eulogist, in the obituary that followed on the next day, claimed that, despite his adventures, he had outlived his seven siblings and survived as the last of Walker's filibusters. The reporter wrote that Vowles had moved to Washington, DC, after the war, where he practiced medicine and held a government position. Because of failing health, he later moved to Quincy. Vowles had recruited a company of Southern sympathizers for the Confederacy in that area during the war, and he likely felt safe there. He married Mrs. Tamantha E. Inghram at nearby Fowler on 8 May 1884.

In death he still left unanswered questions. His obituary mentioned his efforts in a failed effort to relieve Vicksburg in 1863 although his service records lack any reference to his serving in that campaign. Similarly, both the interview and the obituary omitted any mention of his duty at Andersonville and Camp Lawton, as if he feared some sort of reprisals for his actions at those camps—even to the day he died more than fifty years after the war. He also made no mention of his whereabouts from 1864 to 1874. From 1874 to 1878, he lived in Washington, DC, where he worked as a physician and as a messenger for the doorkeeper of the United States House of Representatives. The latter job paid the then extensive annual salary of twelve hundred dollars and must have come to him through strong political connections. He held this government position without having received the required pardon for his service as a Confederate officer and for serving in Confederate prisons. Census takers in 1870 and 1880 missed him although an enumerator did find him and his wife in Chapin, Morgan County, Illinois, in 1900. The year before, however, he appeared as a "venerable Illinois physician of Fowler, Adams County," in a nation-wide advertisement for a medical book.[487]

Without knowing about his career at Andersonville and as commandant of Camp Lawton, the Quincy newspaper and the *New York Times*,[488] which reprinted his obituary, failed to mention his one great notoriety, that one of the last survivors of those prisons had finally escaped from his past, from the United States government, and (almost) from history.

The Last Of Walker's Filibusters Is Dead

These photographs of D. W. Vowles appeared in print on the day that he died.

Georgia's Andersonville monument dedicated to all American prisoners of war. (National Park Service)

SELECTED BIBLIOGRAPHY

Aside from the sources listed below and those cited in the standard histories of Andersonville, researchers should also consult Ronald J. Caldwell, "Andersonville: A Bibliography," a resource that the James Earl Carter Library of Georgia Southwestern State University has posted on its website.

Prisoner Accounts, Interviews, and Memoirs

Of all that is written, I love only what a person hath written with his blood.

—Friedrich Nietzsche

ARTICLES AND INTERVIEWS

Cox, Henry C. "Six Months in Andersonville Prison." *Educational Bi-Monthly* 8 (April–June 1914): 293–94.

Drake, J. Madison. "Fast and Loose in Georgia." In Patrick Allen, ed., *Literary Savannah*. Athens GA: Hill Street Press, 1998.

Hopkins, Charles F. "Hell and the Survivor." *American Heritage* 33 (October–November 1982): 84.

Key, Leroy L. "Raiding in the Andersonville Prison." *New-York Times*, 11 December 1864.

"Lawrence LeBron, Grant's Trusted Scout, a Chicago Letter Carrier." *Sunday Record-Herald* (Chicago), 19 May 1901.

Maltman, J. S. "Andersonville Prison." *Michigan University Magazine* 2, no. 8 (1867):347.

Mann, T. H. "A Yankee in Andersonville." *Century Magazine* 40 (July–August 1890): 447–61, 606–23.

McLean, Alexander. Appendix in James A. Mowris, *A History of the 117th Regiment, NY Volunteers* (Hartford CT: Case, Lockwood and Company, 1866).

Miller, Henry W. Found in Basil Meek, *Twentieth Century History of Sandusky County* (Chicago: Richmond-Arnold, 1909) 918–21.

Smith, Charles H. "Escape From Andersonville Prison in 1864." *Potter County Historical Society Quarterly Bulletin* 47 (January 1978).

Smith, Charles M. "From Andersonville to Freedom." In *Military Order of the Loyal Legion of the United States*. 57 vols. Wilmington NC: Broadfoot, 1991. vol. 8:87–156.

"Story of the First Federal Prisoner to Enter Andersonville." *Augusta* (GA) *Chronicle*, 5 June 1909.

BOOKS

Boggs, S. S. *Eighteen Months a Prisoner Under the Rebel Flag*. Lovington IL: self-published, 1889.

Braun, Herman A. *Andersonville: An Object Lesson on Protection*. Milwaukee WI: C. D. Fahsel, 1892.

Burge, William. *Through the Civil War and Western Adventures*. n. p., n. d.

Burson, William. *A Race for Liberty*. Wellsville OH: G. W. Foster, 1867.

Creelman, Samuel. *Collections of a Coffee Cooler*. Pittsburgh: Pittsburg Photo Engraving, 1890.

Daskam, Hiram S. *The Adventures of an Escaped Andersonville Prisoner*. Hammond IN: C. B. Harrold, n. d.

Davidson, H. M. *Fourteen Months in Southern Prisons*. Milwaukee: Daily Wisconsin Printing House, 1865.

Day, W. W. *Fifteen Months in Dixie*. Owatonna MN: The People's Press, 1889.

Dougherty, Michael. *Prison Diary of Michael Dougherty*. Bristol PA: Charles A. Dougherty, 1908.

Dowling, Morgan E. *Southern Prisons: Or Josie the Heroine of Florence*. Detroit: William Graham, 1870.

Dufur, Simon Miltimore. *Over the Dead Line; or, Tracked by Blood Hounds*. Burlington VT: Free Press, 1902.

Ellis, E. R. *Biographical Sketches of Richard Ellis*. Detroit: W. Graham Print Co., 1888.

Faller, Leo W. and John L. Faller. *Dear Folks at Home*. ed. Milton E. Flower. Carlisle PA: Cumberland County Historical Society, 1963.

Ferguson, Joseph. *Life Struggles in Rebel Prisons*. Philadelphia: James M. Ferguson, 1865.

Forbes, Eugene. *Diary of a Soldier, and Prisoner of War in the Rebel Prisons*. Trenton NJ: Murphy & Bechel, 1865.

Fosdick, Charles. *Five Hundred Days in Rebel Prisons*. Blythe Dale MO: self-published, 1887.

Genoways, Ted and Hugh H. Genoways, eds., *A Perfect Picture of Hell: Eyewitness Accounts by Civil War Prisoners From the 12th Iowa*. Iowa City: University of Iowa Press, 2001.

Goss, Warren L. *The Soldier's Story of His Captivity at Andersonville*. Boston: Lee and Shepard, 1867.

Griffitt, Reuben C. *Six Months in Rebel Prisons*. Martinsville IN: Martinsville Republican, 1909.

Grigsby, Melvin. *The Smoked Yank*. n. p., 1912.

Hamlin, Augustus C. *Martyria—or, Andersonville Prison*. Boston: Lee & Shephard, 1866.

Harrold, John. *Libby, Andersonville, Florence*. Philadelphia: Wm. B. Selheimer, 1870.

Hinds, Thomas. *Tales of War Times*. Watertown: Herald, 1904.

Hitchcock, George A. *From Ashby to Andersonville*. Edited by Ronald G. Watson. Campbell CA: Savas Publishing, 1997.

Hyde, Solon. *A Captive of War*. New York: McClure, Phillips, & Co., 1900.

Keen, Joseph S. *Experiences in Rebel Prisons*. Detroit: Detroit Free Press, 1890.

Kelley, Daniel G. *What I Saw and Suffered in Rebel Prisons*. Buffalo NY: Mathews and Warren, 1866.

Kellogg, Robert H. *Life and Death in Rebel Prisons*. Hartford CT: L. Stebbins, 1865.

Le Bron, Lawrence. *Adventures of Buckskin the Scout*. Omaha: Rural Weekly, n. d.

Long, Lessel. *Twelve Months in Andersonville*. Huntington IN: self-published, 1886.

Lopez, Joseph E. *Capture, Escape and Re-capture of Joseph E. Lopez*. n. p., n. d.

Lyon, W. F. *In and Out of Andersonville Prison*. Detroit: George Harland, 1907.

Maile, John L. *Prison Life in Andersonville*. Los Angeles: Grafton, 1912.

McElroy, John. *Andersonville: A Story of Rebel Military Prisons*. Toledo: D. R. Locke, 1879.

Northrop, John Worrell. *Chronicles from the Diary of a War Prisoner*. Wichita: self-published, 1904.

Page, James Madison. *The True Story of Andersonville Prison: A Defense of Henry Wirz*. New York: Neale Publishing, 1908.

Phillips, M. V. B. *Life and Death in Andersonville*. Chicago: T. B. Arnold, 1887.

Ransom, John L. *Andersonville Diary, Escape, and List of Dead*. Auburn NY: self-published, 1881.

Richardson, Charles. *Story of a Private*. Milwaukee: George Richardson, 1897.

Ripple, Ezra Hoyt. *Dancing Along the Deadline*. Edited by Mark A. Snell. Novato CA: Presidio Press, 1996.

Sabre, G. E. *Nineteen Months A Prisoner of War*. New York: American News Company, 1865.

Smith, C. A. *Recollections of Prison Life*. Muscatine IA: R. A. Holmes, 1875.

Smith, Frank W. *Smith's "Knapsack" of Facts and Figures, '61 to '65*. Toledo: Spear, Johnson, & Co., 1884.

Smith, W. B. *On Wheels and How I Came There*. New York: Hunt & Eaton, 1893.

Sneden, Robert Knox. *Eye of the Storm: A Civil War Odyssey*. New York: Free Press, 2000.

———. *Images From the Storm*. New York: Free Press, 2001.

Stearns, Amos E. *Narrative of Amos E. Stearns*. Worchester MA: Franklin P. Rice, 1887.

Tait, Magnus. *My Rebel Prison Life*. n. p., 1888.

Tyler, William N. *The Dispatch Carrier*. Port Byron IL: Globe, 1892.

Urban, John W. *Battle Field and Prison*. Edgewood NJ: Edgewood Publishing, 1882.

MANUSCRIPTS

Alabama Department of Archives and History: R. T. Powell to Governor of Alabama, 30 September 1894. 24th Alabama file (Regimental Files).

Andersonville National Historic Site: Hugh R. Snee memoirs.

Dallas Public Library: "Experiences of Thomas Cheshire During the Civil War."

Emory University, Woodruff Library, Special Collections: John Burton diary.

John L. Hoster diary.

Illinois State Historical Library: James H. Buckley diary.

James Jennings memoir.

Stephen E. Payne memoir.

Indiana Historical Society: George Mussen memoirs.

Henry B. Sparks diary.

Kansas State Historical Society: Boston Corbett Collection

Manuscript Society Information Exchange Database: Memoir of J. G. Sidery (Accession #90A-48).

Newberry Library: Daniel Bond memoirs.

Richmond National Battlefield Park: Aaron Bachman memoirs.

Southern Historical Collection, University of North Carolina at Chapel Hill: Louis Manigault Scrapbook.

State Historical Society of Wisconsin: John Squires memoirs.

"War Story of Soren Peterson."

Wisconsin newspaper clipping scrapbooks.

State Library of New York: Samuel E. Preston memoirs.

Jan Botkin Therkilden: Jasper Culver memoir.

University of Notre Dame, Rare Books and Special Collections: Andersonville/Wirz Collection.

University of Virginia, Special Collections: James Langstaff Dunn Collection.

William E. Smith Collection.

Virginia Historical Society: Robert Knox Sneden memoirs.

Western Reserve Historical Society: William P. Palmer memoirs.

Primary Sources (other than by prisoners)

History is never really about resting places, about arrivals—conclusions— it's a long journey through memory, stopping off here and there to break bread with the dead.

—Simon Sharma

ARTICLES

Boate, Edward W. "Edward W. Boate: a Federal Report." *Journal of Confederate History* 13 (1995): 73–74.

Gordon-Burr, Lesley Jill. "Storms of Indignation: The Art of Andersonville as Post War Propaganda." *Georgia Historical Quarterly* 75, no. 3 (1991): 587–600.

Kerr, Charles D. "Address by Colonel Charles D. Kerr." *Military Order of the Loyal Legion of the United States.* 257 volumes, 26:213–14. 1887. Reprint, Wilmington NC: Broadfoot Co., 1992.

Kerr, W. J. W. "Sad Ending of a Wedding Trip." *Confederate Veteran* 23, no. 7 (July 1915): 318.

"Rev. George W. Nelson's Narrative." *Southern Historical Society Papers* 1, no. 4 (April 1876): 243–58.

"Sketches of Life of B. L. McGough." *The Jackson Progress-Argus* (Jefferson GA) 1 July 1876.

Webster, Albert Jr. "A Jaunt in the South." *Appleton's Journal* (13 September 1873): 323–25.

BOOKS

Andrews, Eliza Frances. *The War-Time Journal of a Georgia Girl, 1864–1865*. New York: D. Appleton, 1908.

Austin, Jeannette Holland, comp. *Georgia Obituaries, 1740–1935*. n. p., 1993.

Bethel, Elizabeth. *Preliminary Inventory of the War Department Collection of Confederate Records, Record Group 109*. Athens GA: Iberian Press, 1994.

Brandenburg, John David and Worthy, Rita Brinkley, comps. *Index to Georgia's 1867–1868 Returns of Qualified Voters and Registration Oath Books (White)*. Atlanta: self-published, 1995.

Chapman, Robert Duncan. *A Georgia Soldier*. Houston TX: Robert L. Sonfield, Jr., 1994.

Chipman, Norton P. *The Tragedy of Andersonville*. San Francisco: self-published, 1911.

Confederate Reminiscences and Letters. 20 vols. to date. Atlanta: Georgia Division, United Daughters of the Confederacy, 1997– .

The Correspondence of Robert Toombs, Alexander H. Stephens, and Howell Cobb. Edited by Ulrich B. Phillips. Washington: American Historical Association, 1970.

Felton, Rebecca Latimer. *Country Life in Georgia*. Atlanta: Index Printing Company, 1919.

Evans, Tad. *Milledgeville, Georgia, Newspaper Clippings (Southern Recorder)*. 12 vols. Savannah: self-published, 1995–1997.

Foote, Corydon E. *With Sherman to the Sea: A Drummer's Story of the Civil War*. New York: John Day, 1960.

Grant, Ulysses S. *The Papers of Ulysses S. Grant*. Edited by John Y. Simon. 15 vols. to date. Carbondale: Southern Illinois Press, 1981– .

Hafner, Arthur W. *Directory of Deceased American Physicians 1804–1929*. 2 vols. Chicago: American Medical Association, 1989.

Henderson, Lillian. *Roster of the Confederate Soldiers of Georgia, 1861–1865*. 6 vols. Hapeville: Longino & Porter, 1960.

Hood, John Bell. *Advance and Retreat*. New Orleans: Hood Orphan Memorial Fund, 1880.

Kean, Robert G. H. *Inside the Confederate Government: The Diary of Robert Garlick Hill Kean*. Edited by Edward Younger. New York: Oxford University Press, 1957.

Martin, George A. and Metcalf, Frank J. *Marriage and Death Notices From the National Intelligencer, 1800–1850*. Microfilm edition. Washington: National Genealogical Society, 1976.

Military Order of the Loyal Legion of the United States. 100 vols. Wilmington NC: Broadfoot, 1997.

O'Keeffe, B. Elmer, ed. *The Search for Missing Friends*. 8 vols. Boston: New England Historical Society, 1996.

Pierson, Hamilton W. *Letter to Hon. Charles Sumner with "Statements" of Outrages Upon Freedmen in Georgia, and an Account of my Expulsion from Andersonville, Ga., by the Ku Klux Klan*. Washington DC: Chronicle Print, 1870.

Rawick, George P. , ed. *The American Slave: A Composite Biography*. 41 vols. Westport CT: Greenwood Press, 1972–1979.

Ritner, Jacob. *Love and Valor: Intimate Civil War Letters of Captain Jacob and Emeline Ritner*. Edited by Charles P. Larimer. n. p., 2000.

Rowe, Carolyn M. *Index to Individual Pardon Applications From the South, 1865–1898*. Pensacola: self-published, 1996.

Sherman, William T. *Memoirs of General William T. Sherman*. 2 vols. New York: Appleton, 1875.

———. *Sherman's Selected Correspondence*. Edited by Books B. Simpson and Jean V. Berlin. Chapel Hill: University of North Carolina Press, 1999.

The Union Army. 8 vols. Washington: Federal Publishing Company, 1908.

GOVERNMENT PUBLICATIONS (OTHER THAN OF THE NATIONAL ARCHIVES)

Joint Committee on the Conduct of the War. *Returned Prisoners*. Washington: Government Printing Office, 1864. A copy is found in Records of the United States Senate, Record Group 46, National Archives and Records Administration.

Report on the Treatment of Prisoners of War by the Rebel Authorities. Washington: Government Printing Office, 1869.

Roster Commission. *Official Roster of the Soldiers of the State of Ohio*. 12 vols. Cincinnati: Ohio Valley Press, 1888.

Trial of Henry Wirz. Washington DC: Government Printing Office, 1868.

United States Court of Claims No. 10703 *Benjamin B. Dykes v. The United States*. no date. Entry 576, Records of the Quartermaster General, RG 92.

U.S. War Department. *The War of the Rebellion: A Compilation of the Official Records of the Union and Confederate Armies*. 128 vols. Washington: Government Printing Office, 1880–1897.

MANUSCRIPTS

Georgia Archives: Civil War Miscellany Collection.

D. C. Smith Papers (AC 76–323).

Ambrose Spencer Papers (microfilm roll 199/25).

Sumter County deedbook N (1859–1863) and deedbook O (1863–1869).

Baker Library, Harvard Business School: R. G. Dun & Company Collection.

Bancroft Library, Indiana University: James Hughes Collection.

Connecticut Historical Society: Robert H. Kellogg Collection.

Daughters of the American Revolution Library: Laura Spencer Welch membership application (7075).

Hargrett Rare Books and Manuscripts Library, University of Georgia Libraries: Robert Williams Collection (MS 12).

Henry E. Huntington Library: Charles Deal Kerr diary.

Library of Congress: E. N. Gilpin diary.

Papers of Andrew Johnson.

Papers of Elizabeth Cady Stanton and Susan B. Anthony.

South Carolina Historical Society: Louis Manigault Collection

Bancroft Library, Yale University: Journal of Ambrose Spencer (Elias Viles Collection of Diaries of Indian Campaigns).

MANUSCRIPTS AND MICROFILM, NATIONAL ARCHIVES AND RECORDS ADMINISTRATION, NARA, WASHINGTON DC.

Andersonville Cemetery file. Series S. Military Fortifications and National Cemeteries. War Department General and Special Staffs. Record Group 165.

Applications for Commissions. Entry 261. Records of the Secretary of War. Record Group 107.

Appointment Papers. Records Relating to the Appointment of Federal Judges, Marshals, & Attorneys. Records of the Department of Justice, Record Group 60.

Area File of the Naval Records Collection, 1775–1910 (National Archives microfilm M625). Records of the Secretary of the Navy. Record Group 45.

Case Files of Investigations by Levi C. Turner and Lafayette C. Baker, 1861–1866 (National Archives microfilm M797). Records of the Adjutant General. Record Group 94.

Commutations of rations claims. Entry 139B. Records of the Commissary of Prisoners. Record Group 249.

Compiled Service Records of Confederate Soldiers Who Served in Organizations From the State of Georgia (National Archives microfilm M266). War Department Collection of Confederate Records. Record Group 109.

Compiled Service Records of Confederate Generals and StaffOfficers, and Non-Regimental Enlisted Men (National Archives microfilm M331). War Department Collection of Confederate Records. Record Group 109.

Confederate Papers Relating to Citizens or Business Firms (National Archives Microfilm Publication M346). War Department Collection of Confederate Records. Record Group 109.

Eighth Census of the United States (1860) (National Archives Microfilm Publication M653). Records of the Bureau of the Census. Record Group 29.

General Index to Pension Files, 1861–1934 (National Archives microfilm T287). Records of the Veterans Administration. Record Group 15.

Internal Revenue Assessment List for the District of Columbia, 1862–1866 (National Archives microfilm M760). Records of the Internal Revenue Service. Record Group 58.

Internal Revenue Assessment List for Virginia, 1862–1866 (National Archives microfilm M793). Records of the Internal Revenue Service. Record Group 58.

Letters of Application and Recommendation, Grant Administration (National Archives microfilm M968). General Records of the Department of State. Record Group 59.

Letters Received by the Confederate Adjutant and Inspector Generals, 1861–1865 (National Archives microfilm M474). War Department Collection of Confederate Records. Record Group 109.

Letters Received by the Confederate Secretary of War (National Archives microfilm M437). War Department Collection of Confederate Records. Record Group 109.

Letters Received by the Secretary of the Navy From Commanding Officers of Squadrons ("Squadron Letters") (National Archives microfilm M89). Records of the Secretary of the Navy. Record Group 45.

Letters Received by the Secretary of War: Registered Series, 1801–1870 (National Archives microfilm M221). Records of the Secretary of War. Record Group 107.

Lists of Union Prisoners Escaped From Confederate Prisons, 1864–1865. Entry 4318. United States Army Continental Commands. Record Group 249, pt. 1.

Naval Records Collection of the Office of Naval Records and Library. Records of the Secretary of the Navy. Record Group 45.

Pardon Petitions and Related Papers Submitted in Response to President Andrew Johnson's Amnesty Proclamation of May 29, 1865 "Amnesty Papers" (National Archives microfilm M1003). Records of the Adjutant General. Record Group 94.

Passenger Lists of Vessels Arriving in New York 1820–1897 (National Archives microfilm M237). Records of the United States Custom Service. Record Group 36.

Pension claim files. Records of the Veterans Administration. Record Group 15.

Prisoners held in the CSA (slips). Entry 108. Records of the Commissary of Prisoners. Record Group 249.

Records and Pensions (R & P) Manuscripts. Records of the Adjutant General. Record Group 94.

Register of Letters to the Secretary of War, 1861–1870 (National Archives microfilm M22). Records of the Secretary of War. Record Group 107.

Scouts, deserters, and prisoners of war (depositions of). Entry 874. Pt. 4. Records of Continental Commands. Record Group 393.

Selected Records of the War Department Commissary General of Prisoners of War Confined at Andersonville, Georgia, 1864–65. National Archives Microfilm Publication M1303. Records of the Commissary of Prisoners. Record Group 249.

Statements of Escaped Union Prisoners, Refugees, and Confederate Deserters. Entry 4294. Records of Continental Commands, Record Group 393, pt. 1.

Subject File of the Confederate States Navy. National Archives microfilm M1091. War Department Collection of Confederate Records, Record Group 109.

General George H. Thomas (papers of). General's Papers. Records of the Adjutant General. Record Group 94.

U. S. Military Academy Cadet Application Papers, 1805–1866 (National Archives microfilm M688). Records of the Adjutant General. Record Group 94.

Unfiled Papers and Slips Belonging to Confederate Compiled Service Records (National Archives microfilm M347). War Department Collection of Confederate Records. Record Group 109.

Union Provost Marshal's File of Papers Relating to Individual Civilians (National Archives microfilm M345). War Department Collection of Confederate Records. Record Group 109.

Wirz correspondence, 18 May 1864 to 19 March 1865. Entry 10 (ch. 9, vol. 227). War Department Collection of Confederate Records. Record Group 109.

Wirz trial (file MM2975). Records of the Judge Advocate General. Record Group 153.

NEWSPAPERS

Advertiser and Register. Mobile AL. (Only known copy of this newspaper is found at the Alabama Department of Archives and History. It has not been microfilmed.)

Atlanta Constitution. Atlanta GA.

Atlanta Journal. Atlanta GA.

Cullman Progress. Cullman AL. (The only copies of this newspaper are found in the Alabama Department of Archives and History and have not been microfilmed.)

Daily Columbus Enquirer. Columbus GA.

Evening Sentinel. Centralia IL.

Macon Daily Telegraph. Macon GA.

Nashville True Union. Nashville TN.

National Republican. Washington DC

National Tribune. Washington DC

New York Times. New York NY

Sumter Republican. Americus GA.

Washington Chronicle. Washington DC

Secondary Sources

The greatest part of a writer's time is spent in reading in order to write: a man will turn over half a library to make one book.

—Samuel Johnson

ARTICLES

"A Gold Watch Presented to an Officer at Andersonville." *Athens* (GA) *Banner*, 26 April 1912.

Cross, David F. "Why did the Yankees Die at Andersonville?" *North & South* 6 (September 2003): 26–31.

"Controversy—Partisan Comments on Andersonville." *Blue & Gray Magazine* 3 (December–January 1985–1986): 22–37.

"Curious War Stories." *Atlanta Constitution*, 28 April 1888.

Davis, Robert S. "A Soldier's Story: The Records of Hubbard Pryor, 44th United States Colored Troops." *Prologue: The Quarterly of the National Archives* 31, no. 4 (Winter 1999): 268–72.

Dobson, Wayne. "All Were Prisoners There," in *Andersonville: The Southern Perspective*. Edited by J. H. Segars. Atlanta: Southern Heritage Press, 1995.

Fonner, D. Kent. "Villian or Victim? Henry Wirz was the Last Casualty of the Civil War." *America's Civil War* 1, no. 8 (November 1988): 138.

Futch, Ovid. "Andersonville Raiders." *Civil War History* 2, no. 4 (1956): 47–60.

Gillispie, James M. "Guests of the Yankees: A Reevaluation of Union Treatment of Confederate Prisoners." *North & South: The Official Magazine of the Civil War Society* 5, no. 5 (July 2002): 40–49.

Hall, James O. "Major Henry Wirz Again." *Surrat Courier* (newsletter) (January 1991).

Healey, David Healey. "Back Roads: Few Escaped From Fort Delaware." *Blue & Gray* 19 (April 2002): 28–29.

Hesseltine, William B. "*Andersonville* Revisited." *Georgia Review* 10, no. 1 (Spring 1956): 92–110.

Holley, Peggy Scott. "The Seventh Tennessee Volunteer Cavalry: West Tennessee Unionists in Andersonville Prison." *West Tennessee Historical Society Papers* 42 (1998): 39–58.

Inscoe, John C. "'Escaping Through Deserter Country': Fugitive Accounts of the Inner Civil War in Southern Appalachia." In Kenneth W. Noe and Shannon H. Wilson, eds. *The Civil War in Appalachia: Collected Essays*. Knoxville: University of Tennessee Press, 1997.

Johnson, Ludwell H., III. "Blockade or Trade Monopoly?: John A. Dix and the Union Occupation of Norfolk." *Virginia Magazine of History* 93, no. 1 (1985): 54–78.

Lathrop, George Parsons. "The Bailing of Jefferson Davis." *The Century* 33 (February 1887): 636.

Lovett, Howard Meriwether. "Macon in the War Between the States." *Confederate Veteran* 32, no. 1 (1924): 52.

Madison, James H. "The Evolution of Commercial Credit Reporting Agencies in Nineteenth-century America." *Business History Review* 48, no. 2 (Spring 1994): 164–86.

Marvel, William. "The Andersonville Artist: The A. J. Riddle Photographs of August 1864." *Blue & Gray Magazine* (August 1993): 18–23.

McConnell, Stuart. "The William Newby Case and the Legacy of the Civil War." *Prologue: The Quarterly of the National Archives* 30, no. 4 (Winter 1998): 247–56.

Meaney, Peter J. "The Prison Ministry of Father Peter Whelan, Georgia Priest and Confederate Chaplain." *Georgia Historical Quarterly* 71, no. 1 (1987): 1–24.

Morsberger, Robert E. and Katherine M. "After Andersonville: The First War Crimes Trial." *Civil War Times Illustrated* 13, no.4 (July 1974): 30–41.

Newman, John Q. and Trent Sands, eds. *The Encyclopedia of Altered and False Identity*. San Diego: Index Publishing Group, 1996.

"Rev. William J. Hamilton sketch." *The Record: Official Organ of the Diocese of Louisville* (8 March 1884): 81.

Rogers, George A. and Saunders, R. Frank, Jr. "Camp Lawton Stockade, Millen, Georgia, CSA." *Atlanta Historical Journal* 25 (Winter 1981): 80–94.

Sallee, Scott E. "'Big Pete' McCullough: The Hanging Judge of Andersonville." *Blue & Gray* 22 (Summer 2003): 22–25.

Tindle, Lela. "Whatever Became of Boston Corbett?" *Civil War Times Illustrated* 30 (May–June 1991): 48–57.

"Tunnels and Traitors." *Blue & Gray Magazine* 3 (December–January 1985–1986): 53.

Williams, David. "'The Faithful Slave is About Played Out': Civil War Slave Resistance in the Lower Chattahoochee Valley." *Alabama Review* 52, no. 2 (April 1999): 83–104.

Woolfolk, Sarah Van V. "George E. Spencer: A Carpetbagger in Alabama." *Alabama Review* 19, no. 1 (January 1966): 41–52.

BOOKS

Asbury, Herbert. *The Gangs of New York*. New York: Alfred A. Knopf, 1927.

Bailey, Anne J. and Fraser, Walter J. Jr. *Portraits of Conflict: A Photographic History of Georgia in the Civil War*. Fayetteville: University of Arkansas, 1996.

Barfield, Louise C. *History of Harris County Georgia*. Columbus GA: self-published, 1961.

Barker, A. J. *Prisoners of War*. New York: Universe Books, 1975.

Bates, Ralph O. *Billy and Dick From Andersonville Prison to the White House*. Santa Cruz CA: Press Sentinel Publishing, 1910.

Beers, Henry Putney. *The Confederacy*. Washington DC: National Archives Trust, 1986.

Blakeslee, Bernard F. *History of the 16th Connecticut Volunteers*. Hartford CT: Case, Lockwood & Brainard, 1875.

Blakey, Arch Frederic. *General John H. Winder, CSA*. Gainesville: University of Florida Press, 1990.

Blanton, DeAnne and Cook, Lauren M. *They Fought Like Demons: Women Soldiers in the American Civil War*. Baton Rouge: Louisiana State University Press, 2002.

Bonner, James C. *Milledgeville: Georgia's Antebellum Capital*. Athens: University of Georgia Press, 1978.

Bordewich, Fergus M. *Bound for Canaan: The Underground Railroad and the War for the Soul of America*. New York: Armistad, 2005.

Brockett, L. P. *Woman's Work in the Civil War: A Record of Heroism, Patriotism and Patience*. Philadelphia: Zeigler, McCurdy & Co., 1867.

Brown, Daniel P. *The Tragedy of Libby and Andersonville Prison Camps: a Study of Mismanagement and Inept Logistical Policies*. Ventura CA: Golden West Historical Publications, 1980.

Brown, Louis A. *The Salisbury Prison: A Case Study of Confederate Military Prisons, 1861–1865*. Wendell NC: Avera Press, 1980.

Bryant, T. Conn. *Confederate Georgia*. Athens: University of Georgia Press, 1953.

Bryant, William O. *Cahaba Prison and the Sultana Disaster*. Tuscaloosa: University of Alabama Press, 1990.

Burrows, Edwin G. and Mike Wallace. *Gotham: A History of New York to 1898*. New York: Oxford University Press, 1999.

Cangemi, Joseph P. and Casimir J. Kowalski, eds. *Andersonville Prison: Lessons in Organizational Failure*. Lanham MD: University Press of America, 1992.

Capers, Gerald M. *Stephen A. Douglas: Defender of the Union*. Boston: Little, Brown, & Company, 1959.

Casstevens, Frances H. *George W. Alexander and Castle Thunder: A Confederate Prison and Its Commandant*. Jefferson NC: McFarland & Company, 2004.

———. *"Out of the Mouth of Hell": Civil War Prisons and Escapes*. Jefferson NC: McFarland & Co., 2005.

Castel, Albert. *General Sterling Price and the Civil War in the West*. Baton Rouge: Louisiana State University Press, 1968.

Chitwood, Oliver P. *John Tyler Champion of the Old South*. New York: D. Appleton-Century, 1939.

Coleman, Kenneth and Charles Stephen Gurr, eds. *Dictionary of Georgia Biography*. 2 vols. Athens: University of Georgia Press, 1983.

Connelley, William Elsey, *A Standard History of Kansas and Kansans*. 5 vols. Chicago: Lewis, 1918.

Coulter, E. Merton. *Travels in the Confederate States: A Bibliography*. Baton Rouge: Louisiana State University Press, 1994.

Coyle, William. *Ohio Authors and Their Books*. Cleveland OH: World Publishing, 1962.

Craig, John C. *Craig's Daguerreian Registry*. 3 vols. Torrington CT: self-published, 1996.

Current, Richard Nelson. *Lincoln's Loyalists: Union Soldiers From the Confederacy*. Boston: Northeastern University, 1992.

Czitrom, Daniel J. *Media and the American Mind*. Chapel Hill: University of North Carolina Press, 1982.

Davis, Burke. *Sherman's March*. New York: Random House, 1980.

Davis, Robert S. *Cotton, Fire, & Dreams: The Robert Findlay Iron Works and Heavy Industry in Macon, Georgia, 1839–1912*. Macon: Mercer University Press, 1998.

Denny, Robert E. *The Civil War Years*. New York: Sterling, 1992.

———. *Civil War Prisons & Escapes: a Day by Day Chronicle*. New York: Sterling Publishing, 1993.

Dickey, Luther S. *History of the 103d Regiment, Pennsylvania Veteran Volunteer Infantry*. Chicago: L. S. Dickey, 1910.

Doyle, Robert C. *A Prisoner's Duty: Great Escapes in U. S. Military History*. Annapolis: Naval Institute Press, 1997.

———. *Voices From Captivity: Interpreting the American POW Narrative*. Lawrence: University of Kansas Press, 1994.

Dyer, Frederick H. *A Compendium of the War of the Rebellion*. Des Moines: self-published, 1908.

Dyer, Thomas G. *Secret Yankees: The Secret Circle in Confederate Atlanta*. Baltimore: John Hopkins University Press, 1999.

Elliott, James W. *Transport to Disaster*. New York: Holt, Rinehart, and Winston, 1962.

Ervin, Eliza C. and Horace F. Rudisill. *Darlingtoniana: A History of People, Places and Events in Darlington County, South Carolina*. Columbia SC: R. L. Bryan, 1964.

Erwin, Milo. *The History of Williamson County, Illinois*. Marion IL: n. p., 1876.

Evans, David. *Sherman's Horsemen*. Bloomington: Indiana University Press, 1996.

Facts and Figures vs. Myths and Misrepresentations Henry Wirz and Andersonville. Atlanta: Georgia Division UDC, 1921.

Feis, William B. *Grant's Secret Service: The Intelligence War from Belmont to Appomattox*. Lincoln: University of Nebraska Press, 2002.

Flanigan, James C. *History of Gwinnett County Georgia*. 2 vols. Hapeville GA: self-published, 1959.

Futch, Ovid L. *History of Andersonville Prison*. Gainesville: University of Florida Press, 1968.

Gannon, Michael V. *Rebel Bishop: The Life and Era of Augustin Verot*. Milwaukee: Bruce Publishing, 1964.

Geier, Clarence R. and Stephen R. Potter, eds. *Archaeological Perspectives on the American Civil War*. Gainesville: University Press of Florida, 2000.

Gleeson, David T. *The Irish in the South, 1815–1877*. Chapel Hill NC: University of North Carolina Press, 2001.

Gleeson, Ed. *Rebel Sons of Erin: a Civil War Unit History of the Tenth Tennessee Infantry Regiment*. Indianapolis: Guild Press, 1994.

Gleeson, Janet. *Millionaire: The Philanderer, Gambler, and Duelist who Invented Modern France*. New York: Simon & Schuster, 1999.

Grant, Donald L. *The Way It Was in the South: The Black Experience in Georgia*. Secaucus NJ: Carol Publishing Group, 1993.

Hall, James O., William A. Tidwell, and David W. Gaddy. *Come Retribution: The Confederate Secret Service and the Assassination of Lincoln*. Jackson: University Press of Mississippi, 1988.

Halttunen, Karen. *Confidence Men and Painted Women: A Study of the Middle-class Culture in America, 1830–1870*. New Haven: Yale University Press, 1982.

Hayford, Harrison. *The Somers Mutiny Affair*. Englewood Cliffs NJ: 1959.

Hays, Louise F. *History of Macon County, Georgia*. Atlanta: Burke, 1933.

Hesseltine, William B. *Civil War Prisons: A Study in War Psychology*. New York: Frederick Ungar, 1964.

Hitt, Michael D. *Charged with Treason: The Ordeal of 400 Mill Workers During Military Operations in Roswell, Georgia 1864–1865*. Monroe NY: Library Research Associates, 1992.

Holcombe, R. I. *History of Marion County Missouri*. 1884; repr., Hannibal: Marion County Historical Society, 1979.

Joslyn, Mauriel P. *Immortal Captives*. Shippensburg PA: White Mane, 1996.

Kasson, John F. *Rudeness & Civility: Manners in Nineteenth-Century Urban America*. New York: Noonday Press, 1991.

Kelbaugh, Ross J. *Directory of Maryland Photographers 1839–1900*. Baltimore: Historic Graphics, 1988.

Kennett, Lee. *Marching Through Georgia*. New York: HarperCollins, 1995.

———. *Sherman: a Soldier's Life*. New York: HarperCollins, 2001.

Kraynek, Sharon L. D. *Medina County, Ohio Recollections of Medina Characters (1874–1908)*. Apollo PA: Closson Press, 1998.

Laffin, John. *The Anatomy of Captivity*. New York: Abelard-Schuman, 1968.

Lawrence, Alexander A. *A Present for Mr. Lincoln: The Story of Savannah from Secession to Sherman*. Macon: Ardivan Press, 1961.

Lawson, John D. *American State Trials*. 17 vols. St. Louis: F. H. Thomas Law Book Company, 1917.

Leonard, Elizabeth D. *All the Daring of the Soldier: Women of the Civil War Armies*. New York: W. W. Norton, 1999.

Levitt, Saul. *The Andersonville Trial*. New York: Dramatists Play Service, n. d.

Love, William D. *Wisconsin in the War of the Rebellion*. Chicago: Church & Goodman, 1866.

Lovett, Rose Gibbons. *The Catholic Church in the Deep South: The Diocese of Birmingham in Alabama, 1540–1976*. Birmingham: n. p., 1980.

Lynn, John W. *800 Paces to Hell: Andersonville*. Fredericksburg VA: Sergeant Kirkland's Museum, 1999.

Mackay, James Mackay. *Allan Pinkerton: The First Private Eye*. New York: John Wiley & Sons, 1996.

Marvel, William. *Andersonville: The Last Depot*. Chapel Hill: University of North Carolina Press, 1994.

McAdams, F. M. *Every-day Soldier Life or a History of the 113th Ohio Volunteer Infantry*. Columbus OH: Charles M. Cott, 1884.

McElroy, John. *Si Klegg*. Washington: National Tribune, 1916.

McFarland, Philip J. *Sea Dangers: The Affair of the Somers*. New York: Schocken Books, 1985.

McMurry, Richard M. *Atlanta: Last Chance for the Confederacy*. Lincoln: University of Nebraska, 2000.

McPherson, James. *Battle Cry of Freedom: The Civil War Era*. New York: Oxford University Press, 1988.

Miller, John C. *Alexander Hamilton: Portrait in Paradox*. New York: Harper Brothers, 1959.

Monroe County Historical Society. *Monroe County, Georgia: A History*. Forsyth: self-published, 1979.

Morsberger, Robert E. and Katherine M. Morsberger. *Lew Wallace: Militant Romantic*. New York: McGraw-Hill, 1986.

Munden, Kenneth W. and Henry Putney Beers. *The Union: A Guide to Federal Archives Relating to the Civil War*. Washington: National Archives, 1989.

The National Cyclopedia of American Biography. 63 vols. New York: James T. White, 1896.

Nevins, Allen, James I. Robertson, Jr., and Bell I. Wiley, eds. *Civil War Books: A Critical Bibliography*. 2 vols. Baton Rouge: Louisiana State University Press, 1967.

Nichols, James L. *Confederate Engineers*. Tuscaloosa: Confederate Publishing Company, 1957.

O'Connell, J. J. *Catholicity in the Carolinas and Georgia*. New York: D. & J. Sadlier, 1878.

Parrish, T. Michael, and Willingham, Robert M. Jr. *Confederate Imprints*. Austin TX: Jenkins Publishing, 1987.

Pasley, Jeffrey L. *"The Tyranny of Printers": Newspaper Politics in the Early American Republic*. Charlottesville: University Press of Virginia, 2001.

Perry, Albert J. *History of Knox County, Illinois: Its Cities, Towns and People*. Chicago: S. J. Clarke, 1912.

Potter, Jerry O. *The Sultana Tragedy: America's Greatest Maritime Disaster*. Gretna LA: Pelican Publishing Company, 1992.

Power, John C. *History of the Early Settlers of Sangamon County, Illinois*. Sangamon County IL: Edwin A. Wilson, 1876.

Pryor, Dayton. *The Beginning and the End: The Civil War Story of Federal Surrenders Before Fort Sumter and Confederate Surrenders After Appomattox*. Bowie MD: Heritage Books, 2001.

Rachels, David and Robert Baird. Introduction to Herbert W. Collingwood, *Andersonville Violets: A Story of Northern and Southern Life*. Tuscaloosa: University of Alabama Press, 2000. Reprint of 1889 edition.

Roberts, Edward F. *Andersonville Journey*. Shippensburg VA: Burd Street Press, 1998.

Roberts, Nancy. *Civil War Ghosts and Legends*. Columbia: University of South Carolina Press, 1992.

Robinson, H. L. *Pittsfield, N. H. in the Great Rebellion*. Concord NH: Republican Press Association, 1893.

Rood, Henry H. *History of Company "A" 13th Iowa Veteran Infantry*. Cedar Rapids IA: Daily Republican, 1889.

Savas, Theodore P. and David A. Woodbury. *The Campaign for Atlanta and Sherman's March to the Sea*. Campbell CA: Savas Woodbury, 1994.

Seager, Robert. *and Tyler too: A Biography of John & Julia Gardiner Tyler*. New York: McGraw-Hill, 1963.

Sensing, Thurman, *Champ Ferguson: Confederate Guerilla*. Nashville: Vanderbilt University Press, 1942.

Shankle, George E. *American Nicknames: Their Origin and Significance*. New York: H. W. Wilson, 1955.

Sheldon, Addison Erwin. *Nebraska: The Land and the People*. 3 vols. Chicago: The Lewis Publishing Co., 1931.

Sheppard, Peggy. *Andersonville Georgia USA*. Leslie GA: Sheppard Publications, 1973.

Shreeve, Lyman S. *The Hamlin Family*. Exira IA: self-published, 1902.

Sifakis, Stewart. *Compendium of the Confederate Armies: Kentucky, Maryland, Missouri, the Confederate Units and the Indiana Units*. New York: Facts On File, 1995.

Singer, Jane. *The Confederate Dirty War: Arson, Bombings, Assassination and Plots for Chemical and Germ Attacks on the Union*. Jefferson NC: McFarland, 2005.

Smith, Gordon B. *History of the Georgia Militia*. 4 vols. Milledgeville GA: Boyd Publishing, 2000.

Speer, Lonnie R. *Portals to Hell: Military Prisons of the Civil War*. Mechanicsburg PA: Stackpole Books, 1997.

———. *War of Vengeance: Acts of Retaliation Against Civil War POWs*. Mechanicsburg PA: Stackpole Books, 2002.

Stevenson, R. Randolph. *The Southern Side; Or, Andersonville Prison*. Baltimore: Turnball Brothers, 1876.

Surdam, David G. *Northern Naval Superiority and the Economics of the American Civil War*. Columbia: University of South Carolina Press, 2001.

Townsend, Billy. *Camp Lawton: Magnolia Springs State Park*. Atlanta: Georgia Department of Natural Resources, 1975.

Tzabar, Shimon. *The White Flag Principal: How to Lose a War and Why*. London: The Penguin Press, 1972.

United States Sanitary Commission. *Narrative of Privations and Sufferings of the United States Officers and Soldiers While Prisoners of War in the Hands of the Rebel Authorities*. Philadelphia: King and Baird, 1864.

Vischer, A. L. *Barbed Wire Disease: A Psychological Study of the Prisoner of War*. London: Bale & Danielsson, 1919.

Wagner, Margaret E., Gary W. Gallagher, and Paul Finelman. *The Library of Congress Civil War Desk Reference*. New York: Simon & Schuster, 2002.

Walker, Anne K. *Backtracking in Barbour County: A Narrative of the Last Alabama Frontier*. Richmond VA: Dietz Press, 1941.

Werner, Emmy E. *Reluctant Witnesses: Children's Voices from the Civil War*. Boulder CO: Westview Press, 1998.

Wiley, Bell Irvin. *The Life of Johnny Reb: The Common Soldier of the Confederacy*. Baton Rouge: Louisiana State University Press, 1978.

Williams, David *Rich Man's War*. Athens: University of Georgia Press, 1998.

Williford, William B. *Americus Through the Years*. Atlanta: Cherokee Publishing Company, 1975.

Wilson, Carol. *Freedom at Risk: The Kidnapping of Free Blacks in America, 1780–1865*. Lexington: University Press of Kentucky, 1994.

THESIS AND DISSERTATIONS

Boyd, Harry G. "Civil War Prisoners of War: A Study of the Changes in Disposition of Federal and Confederate Prisoners of War, Between the Shelling of Fort Sumter and the Surrender at Appomattox Courthouse." Ph.D diss., California State University, 1992.

Gardner, Douglas Gibson. "Andersonville and American Memory: Civil War Prisoners and Narratives of Suffering and Redemption." Ph.D diss., Miami (OH) University, 1998.

Koerting, Gayla M. "The Trial of Henry Wirz and Nineteenth Century Military Law." Ph.D diss., Kent State University, 1995.

Meekins, Alex Christopher. "Caught Between Scylla and Charybdis: The Civil War in Northeastern North Carolina." Master's thesis. North Carolina State University, 2001.

Wilson, Spencer. "Experiment in Reunion: The Union Army in Civil War Norfolk and Portsmouth, Virginia." Ph.D diss., University of Maryland, 1973.

MANUSCRIPTS

Georgia Archives: Alphabetical Card File [of Confederate Records].

Georgia Historical Society: James Duncan file (folder 13). O'Bryne Family Papers.

Hargrett Rare Books and Manuscripts Library, University of Georgia Libraries: Andersonville vertical files.

Library of Congress: Works Projects Administration. "Annals of Cleveland, 1818–1935." 200 vols. Unpublished typescripts, 1938–1940. Newspaper division.

INTERNET RESEARCH WEB SITES

The sites below do not include the sites to the libraries and archives listed above.

Alabama Virtual Library (First Search, OCLC): http://www.avl.lib.al.us/

American Civil War Homepage: http://sunsite.utk.edu/civil-war/

American Civil War Home Page: http://www.civilwarhome.com/

Ancestry: http://www.ancestry.com/

Andersonville Prisoner Lookup: http://www.montezuma-ga.org/chamber/plookup.htm

Augusta Chronicle Online Archives: http://augustaarchives.com/

Brooklyn Daily Eagle Online (1841–1902): http://www.brooklynpubliclibrary.org/eagle/

Civil War Home Page: http://www.civil-war.net/

Civil War Maps (Library of Congress): http://memory.loc.gov/ammem/collections/ civil_war_maps/

Colorado Digitization Program: http://www.cdpheritage.org/newspapers/index.html

Genforum (Civil War): http://genforum.genealogy.com/

HeritageQuest Online: http://www.heritagequestonline.com/

Making of America (MOA), Cornell University: http://cdl.library.cornell.edu/moa/

Making of America (MOA), University of Michigan: http://www.hti.umich.edu/m/moagrp/

Mystic Seaport: Ship and Yacht Register List: http://www.mysticseaport.org/library/initiative/ShipRegisterList.cfm

Navy Historical Center: http://www.history.navy.mil/

NewspaperArchive.Com: http://newspaperarchive.com/DesktopDefault.aspx

Questia Online Library: http://www.questia.com/

Rootsweb: http://www.rootsweb.com/

The Civil War: http://www.civilwar.com/

United States Army Military History Institute: http://carlisle-www.army.mil/usamhi/

USGenWeb: http://www.usgenweb.com/

Wisconsin Local History and Biography articles: http://www.wisconsinhistory.org/wlhba/

Appendix A

THE TRIAL OF THE RAIDERS

> Not long ago a friend wrote me from Savannah that Wirz's admirers in Georgia intended to erect a monument in his honor. Now, I think the poor man is no more worthy of a monument now than he was at the time deserving of being hanged. His name should be forgotten.
>
> —Father Henry D. Clavreul, quoted in Norton B. Chipman, *The Tragedy of Andersonville* (1911)

The following two seldom-used documents relate to the role of Captain Henry Wirz of Andersonville in the trial and punishments of Andersonville's bandits. They appear here to give as close an account of that controversial aspect of the prison's history as possible.

From *New-York Times*, December 11, 1864, p. 1, c. 4.

"RAIDING" IN THE ANDERSONVILLE PRISON.
AN EXTRAORDINARY STORY OF OUTRAGE AND
ITS PUNISHMENT—SIX MEN HUNG.

From the *Boston Journal*

We have received from Rev. J. M. CLARK, one of the delegates of the Christian Commission, the following particulars of the execution of the prisoners at Sumter Prison who were tried and condemned by their fellow prisoners for robbery and murder. The statement is made by Leroy L. KEY, who acted as Chief of Police, and under whose direction the execution took place. He says:

When I arrived there were some 4,000 prisoners, but the number increased till in September there were from 32,000 to 35,000. In August and September the deaths were from 75 to 125 per day. For a time the prisoners treated each other decently, but there were some bad fellows among them. These bad men increased in number, and began a series of atrocious wrongs against their fellow-prisoners.

1. They would decoy men from their tents with the promise of a blanket or an extra ration, or something desirable, and then rob and plunder them, and all resistance was in vain, as they had the victim fully to their power, in their own tent.

2. They would go out in a body, and meeting a man in the street, would demand of him his money, or whatever he had. If he resisted, they beat him so that he would die of the injuries. The Surgeon declared that not less than 75 men died from this cause alone.

3. Spotting a tent in the daytime, they would go out at night, five or six in number, enter the tent, and with a knife or razor threaten the victim till he "shelled out." Some men were thus severely wounded before they would "shell out."

4. Many men traded to make a little money to get an extra ration. These "raiders," going to these petty traders, inquired of them how they got along in their business, and then demanded of them a tax, saying "in two hours you must pay us $100, or more." If the man refused, they beat him.

These things run on and became worse and worse until we could bear it no more. "Raiders" numbered, about the 20th of June, 150 or 200, and it became absolutely necessary for the other prisoners to take some measures for the other prisoners' defense; for the "raiders" swore that by the 4th of July they would have every cent in camp or kill the resisters.

Up to this time the Confederate authorities kept no order or discipline within the lines. I spoke to a few of my friends to organize a band of protectors against these raiders. We began to organize, and had proceeded in the formation of thirteen companies, with thirty men and a captain in each. Before the organization was complete, I was one day walking on the north side of the camp, when I saw ahead of me the chief of the raiders, and in pursuit of me five men on the "double quick," with knives in their hands. The chief slapped me on the shoulder and turned me round, saying to me, "I understand that you are getting up a band to clear out the Irish," I replied, "The report is false and you are mistaken." "Well, you are getting up a band to some purpose; what is it for; if not to clean out the Irish?" Meanwhile the five men closed around us, forming a ring around CURTIS and myself.

He again demanded to know the object of the band. Said I to him, boldly, "we are organizing a band to clean out the 'raiders,' and if you are one of them we intend to clean you out." They did not proceed to violence, but the leader put his knife into his left hand and with his right hand offered to shake hands with me. They then let me go. That night much raiding was done in the camp and we heard in various quarters the cries of men, "help! murder!" The cook-house was on the outside of the camp, on the stream above, and men were detailed from the prisoners on parole of honor to do the cooking. All rations were drawn into the lines of the stockade in wagons—rations of cornbread, a small piece of pork or beef; sometimes a pint of cooked beans to a man, not amounting in all to enough for a meal for one day. Soup was probably allowed once a week, but we did not get it oftener than once in three weeks, and then it was nothing but a little grease on a chip.

The condition of the prisoners was somewhat relieved by the arrival of some men captured at Plymouth, who had just been paid off and who brought into camp thousands of dollars. By trading and bartering around, most of the men got some of this money. I regard it as an act of merciful Providence that those men were captured and sent to Sumter Prison, for otherwise many more men must have died from starvation.

The day after CURTIS stopped me in the street word came that no more rations would be sent into camp until we delivered up the raiders into the hands of the rebel authorities; for they had raided upon the wagons, and had stolen the rations belonging to a detachment on the south side of the camp. We then perfected the organization of our band, and commenced seeking for and arresting the raiders. We laid hold of 150 or 200 men, who were known to be engaged in raiding, and turned them over. Out of the number, the worst cases, twenty in all, were retained outside the camp under guard, and the rest returned within the stockade. The arrests within were continued, until the number of bad cases sent out was about 100. Capt. WIRZ selected twenty-four Sergeants from those that knew most of the matters in dispute, and out of this number appointed twelve jury men and a Judge-Advocate, whose name was PETER McCOLLAR, of the 8th Missouri.

The accused had a fair and just trial, and eleven men were proved guilty, but the chief criminality laid upon six men, of whom CURTIS was the leader. These men were sentenced to be hung, and Gen. WINDER approved of the sentence, and ordered me to erect a scaffold and superintend the execution. I procured the timber where I was directed, and with a detail of men erected the scaffold and made all ready. The time fixed for the execution was Monday, 4 o'clock P.M., July 11, 1864. When the men were brought in and turned over to us. Capt. WIRZ took his guards outside and left the prisoners, the convicted criminals, in our charge. My guards were armed with a stout club, fastened to the right wrist by a cord. Six men were appointed executioners, and each took his stand upon the stage behind the criminal.

Most of the criminals were Roman Catholics and a Priest [sic] came in to attend them. He requested us to have mercy upon the men, and earnestly plead for them; and after he had got through CURTIS asked me to spare him as he had never done me any harm. I told him it was not for me to pardon him. I was appointed to see that the men were hung; but if he had anything to say, I would hear his confession on the scaffold. Then he said he would not stand it, and made a break for the lines, and ran about the camp until he was recaptured. He was brought back perfectly exhausted.

While CURTIS was absent, the other criminals were taken on to the scaffold, and the ropes placed around their necks, the executioners standing behind them. Immediately after CURTIS was brought back, he was delivered to the executioner, and taken on to the scaffold likewise. No confessions were made, but the men disposed of their property, and CURTIS gave his watch to the priest, Father WHALEN.

A vast number of the 33,000 prisoners of war were assembled around the scaffold. At length the order was given to pull the trigger, when five of them swung off and met their death. One rope broke and the prisoner was injured by the fall. He was brought up again, the rope adjusted, and as the drop was disarranged he was pushed off and met his death.

This terrible example put an end to raiding, and the prisoners were no more troubled with the assaults and depredations of the high-handed scoundrels. There was, however, a large number of men who disapproved of the trial and execution, from whom trouble was anticipated and it was feared that at the executions a crowd would arise and attempt to rescue the criminals. A stillness as of death pervaded and it seemed as if the influence of a breath of wind would have let loose the sympathizers with the raiders, and prevented the execution. But the deed of terrible justice was triumphantly completed. The Chief of Police and executioners were immediately removed beyond the lines, and a new Chief of Police appointed.

2

The following newspaper clipping details many of the proceedings of the trials of the raiders. O. S. Baker unsuccessfully tried to enter an "imperfect" account of the raider trial into evidence in the trial of Andersonville captain Henry Wirz. Quite likely he referred to this article. It originally appeared in the *New York Mercury* of 20 August 1865. No run of the newspaper survives. The clipping used here comes from file Apz (EB) 1865, Entry 409, Records of the Adjutant General, Record Group 94, National Archives and Records Administration.

ANDERSONVILLE PRISON
Was Captain Wirz Guilty of the Enormities Charged to Him?

THRILLING EPISODE OF PRISON LIFE
How an Organized Gang of Ruffians Preyed upon Their Fellow-Prisoners

SIX OF THEM SENTENCED TO BE HANGED
Detailed Statement of the Whole Proceeding by the Official Reporter of the Court &c. &c. &c.

The treatment said to have been received by Union prisoners at the hands of the Confederate authorities at Andersonville, seems to be among the bitterest subjects now connected with the late war. Various accounts have been published representing the nature and causes of treatment—some describing Captain Wirz, the Commandant of the prison, as a monster, in comparison with whom Nero would not be a circumstance, others—and those the most intelligent and trustworthy, and who had superior opportunities of knowing the facts, both from natural confinement for months in the Andersonville stockade, and subsequently by intimate intercourse with Capt. Wirz for months—have boldly come forward and defended him from the charge of cruelty to his prisoners; and while admitting the fearful suffering—which, indeed, it would be hard to overdraw—endured by the unhappy men in that wretched "d—d bullpen," to use Wirz's own words, maintain that such sufferings were solely the result of the poverty and want of resources in the Confederacy.

Before coming to our present purpose of giving the particulars of a thrilling episode of prison life, which hitherto has been but briefly alluded to by the press, we may be permitted to refer to some of the statements made against Captain Wirz, especially to one which bears upon the very subject of this trial. A person in the Washington *Chronicle*, who appears to have been a prisoner at Andersonville, but whose statements are as consistent with the facts as that [of] a horse chestnut and a chestnut horse mean the same thing, makes several charges against Captain Wirz. Next to malignity, stupidity is the most intolerable thing to deal patiently with. This person, who signs himself "S. H., Co. C, 8th Pennsylvania Cavalry",[489] says that the "raiders at Andersonville were deserters from the United States Army, that they were known to be so by Captain Wirz", and that "they received favors from the Rebel authorities not accorded to the loyal Union prisoners"—such as permission to go outside of the stockade to work, to obtain better rations than other prisoners, and even permitted to bring plenty of wood on returning every evening.

The writer of the article happening to know all the facts in connection with the modus operandi of the machinery in Andersonville, brands every one of the foregoing statements as shameful, ignorant falsehoods. Again, "Wirz was aware of the existence of this gang and their depredations, and although their poor victims time and again complained of them to him, the hardened villain took no notice of their complaints, encouraging their oppressors in their inhuman barbarities." The truth is that Wirz, whenever he heard of an act of oppression by one man—any man—toward another, would be down upon him like a thunderbolt. Wirz had his failings; but his worst fault was impulsiveness. And to charge him with conniving at raiders, is a piece of donkeyism that his most inveterate enemies at Washington, when his trial comes on, will not be guilty of.

A long paragraph in the same article headed, "An Outbreak", describes the attacks of the raiders which brought on the trials and execution which it is our object to describe. There was no "outbreak." It was the mere culmination of a system carried on in the camp by a set of scoundrels and thieves. If the founders of the prosecution against Wirz have no better grounds to go upon than such statements as we have referred to, the sooner they abandon their case the better.

Captain Wirz or the authorities at Andersonville never gave the slightest encouragement to desertion. We happen to know, having seen some fifty letters per day from prisoners at Andersonville, addressed to Captain Wirz, offering to take the oath of allegiance to the Confederacy. The letters were handed by

Captain Wirz to the writer of this article, and were by his orders destroyed, and never attended to.

"Think," said Wirz, "only think of a United States soldier in prison deserting to the Confederacy! The fellows only want to get away. Damn your deserters! I don't like them, North or South!"

One charge against Wirz is that the stockade was only 200 yards wide by the same number of yards long. Another, when the smallpox broke out, Wirz had the men inoculated from the filthiest matter he could find.

The stockade by measurement was twenty-nine acres in extent. When the smallpox broke out at Andersonville, the most salulatious spot outside the stockade was selected, to which the patients were removed, and the most experienced physicians appointed to attend them. The result was that there were less than forty deaths from smallpox at Andersonville.

As to inoculation, it can be affirmed that not a single person was isolated at Andersonville, unless perhaps by his own desire, but the person who makes the statement we refer to must have had Belle Island, or some other Confederate prison in his imagination.

On this subject we will merely say, that as Captain Wirz's trial will, in all likelihood, take place in a few days, and that witnesses are summoned from all quarters against him, it would show a higher sense of fair play and self respect, on the part of the high-toned and honorably conducted press to abstain from publishing such stupid lies about the helpless prisoner who cannot defend himself until he appears before the bar or public justice.

If Captain Wirz is condemned after a fair trial, and after his witnesses get a fair opportunity of telling all they know about him, let him be dealt with as his conduct deserves.[490] But if the newspapers, now so clamorous to condemn Wirz had been only one-tenth as zealous in trying to urge the Executive to exchange the Andersonville prisoners, the Federal Government would not have to answer before their God for at least 11,000 lives ruthlessly thrown away.

The Raiders—Their Trial

Toward the close of the month of June, 1864, when there were some 35,000 Union prisoners at Andersonville, some four or five hundred gougers, robbers, muggers, garrotters, and (if, in the execution of their infamous proceedings became necessary), murderers, banded themselves into a regular organization. Men were beaten and robbed and knocked down in broad daylight. At night, when a man retired to his poor quarters, he was awoke by finding a ruffian's knee on his stomach, brandishing a knife over him, another ruffian holding him down by the throat, and threatening that if the poor wretch made any resistance his "bloody heart would be cut out." A reign of terror spread itself over the prison. Men lay down in their miserable tents at night in terror; and they woke in the morning unrefreshed, the terrors of the banditti still haunting them. It was a terrible time. But what appeared to be every man's business was nobody's business, and no man dared grapple with this infamous organization. Just as a compact band of guerrillas may at any moment descend from a mountain upon an unsuspecting and unarmed village. At length a man named Dowd was attacked before his own tent by a dozen of the band, and all but murdered; he was robbed of money, watch, etc. He was brought next morning by the Rebel squad before Captain Wirz, and having stated his case, his appearance, broken face, eyes swollen, head strapped up, and his shins all kicked and bruised, all seconding his appeal to the captain.[491]

Capt. Wirz— "By God, until every scoundrel of that gang is brought out of the stockade, I swear I shall not permit a single ration to be sent into the stockade. Until you hear from me send not a ration into the stockade. The d—d cowards! Thirty five thousand soldiers, and yet [they do] not have the pluck to defend themselves against the damned scoundrels, the bloody Yankee thieves, that are preying on their poor prisoners, Bush give me my pistols!"

Bush gave Wirz his pistols, and he proceeded to the stockade; and the gang, under the pressure of hunger, began to be brought out. Some three thousand men formed themselves, after a long dead silence of hunger and thought, into a vigilance committee, and some one hundred and twenty villains were taken out, and the triumphant shouts of the poor fellows in the stockade, and placed in ball and chain.

On the representation of the facts at headquarters, the following order was issued:

Order Authorizing the Formation of a Court to Try the Ruffians

Camp Sumter Andersonville, Ga. June 30, 1864.
General Order No. 57

I. A gang of evil disposed persons among the prisoners of war at this post, having banded themselves together for the purposes of assaulting, murdering, and robbing their fellow prisoners, and having committed these offenses, it becomes necessity to adopt measures to protect the lives and property of the prisoners against the acts of these men; and in order that this may be accomplished, the well-disposed prisoners may, and are hereby authorized to establish a court among themselves for the trial and punishment of all offenders.

II. On such trials the charges will be distinctly made, with specifications, setting forth time and place, a copy of which will be furnished the accused.

III. The whole proceedings will be properly kept in writing, the testimony fairly written out as nearly in the words of the witnesses as possible.

IV. The proceedings, findings, and sentence in each case will be sent to the commanding officer for record, and, if found in order, and proper, the sentence will be ordered for execution. By order of

John H. Winder, Brig.-Gen

W. S. Winder, A. A. G.

To Capt. Henry Wirz, commanding, etc.

The morning on which the order was issued, about three hundred sergeants, the head of every ninety men in prison, were summoned to Captain Wirz's headquarters, when the order was read to them.[492] Every man of the three hundred approved of the formation of the court for the trial of the raiders and gougers, and garrotters. Twenty-four were selected from the number, from which twelve were balloted for a jury, as follows.

Members of the Jury

The sergeants George W. Merwin, 5th Michigan Cavalry, Company B, Foreman; Benjamin Bartell, 67th Pennsylvania, Company K; Thos. C. Hurlbert, First Connecticut Cavalry, Company B; J. Western Dana, 56th Massachusetts, Company K; J. S. Banks, 3rd Ohio Cavalry, Company I; Thomas J. Sheppard, 97th Ohio, Company E; John S. Benjamin, 64th New York, Company E; Egbert Webb, 5th Michigan Cavalry, Company C; Wm. C. Measick, 7th Michigan Cavalry, Company H; Stephen T. Brown, 7th New York, Company C; Henry Miller, 1st Michigan Sharpshooters, Company I; Samuel West, 7th New York Heavy Artillery, Company H.

Edward Wellington Boate, 42nd New York, was unanimously appointed official reporter of the Court.

Sergeant O. W. Carpenter, 7th Michigan Cavalry, was appointed to prosecute; and private (since Major) H. C. Higginson, 19th Illinois, Company K, was assigned as counsel to defend the prisoners.

The best and most convenient arrangement that could be made at the time, was to try the prisoners before the jury, who after the verdict constituted themselves a court of twelve, and then after due deliberation decided upon the punishment to which each convicted person was sentenced.

First Day's Prosecution

William Collins, alias Mosby, 88th Pennsylvania, Company D, was the first of the prisoners tried; but as it was understood that more evidence could be had than what was brought against him the first day, his case was postponed. [Mosby was subsequently tried, found guilty, and hanged.]

Patrick Murphy, 52nd NY, Company B, and John Sarsfield, 140th NY, Company C, were charged with assaulting with intent to murder (if necessary) and highway robbery. They pleaded not guilty.

John G. Dowd, 97th NY, Company D, was the first witness. The appearance of this man excited the horror and pity of everyone present. His head and face, arms, legs, and body generally bore marks of the most brutal violence. He testified as follows:—On the 28th of June, about one o'clock, I was sitting in my tent, when Sarsfield came along, crying out "Who wants to buy a watch?" (Sarsfield's object was to find out who had money.) I asked him what his watch was worth, and he replied twenty dollars. Sarsfield left, and soon after returned with the prisoner Murphy. Sarsfield renewed the offer to sell the watch, and while doing so, the other prisoner grabbed at my pantaloons, which I had in my hand, cleaning. In the scuffle I was struck with "brass knuckles" in the face, by Sarsfield as I believe. I then took my knife out of my pocket to defend myself. Several others then attacked me and one of them snatched the knife out of my hand, and, in doing so, cut me across the hand. Sarsfield had a dagger in his hand, and threatened if I resisted he would cut my heart out and throw it in my face. I was frequently struck with the "brass knuckles." I saw one of the men (not on trial) take hold of the chain of my watch and draw it out. I was then knocked down and turned over. They took hold of my watch pocket and turned it out. It contained a pocketbook containing $136, which the raiders carried off.[493]

Sergeant Joseph Rivers, 22nd NY, Co. M, swore that on the 26th inst., while looking for some of his boys, he was met by a man who brought him to his tent to sell him a blanket. Outside the tent they met Sarsfield, opposite his tent, who said he had a better blanket to sell; called witness a s-n of a b—h, and dragged him back into the tent and assaulted witness with a screw. Sarsfield took witness by the pocket, and took of it, $50.04, together with some small articles, a spoon, a comb, etc. He also took his haversack and blouse, in which there was tobacco. They then tried to knock him down; tried to pull him down by the hair. He made a struggle and got away.

R. C. Spicer, 76th New York, Company E, swore that he was present at the attack on Dowd. Murphy was not there, but he recognized Sarsfield as one of the men who attacked Dowd with a knife, with which he struck him on the head. Sarsfield's character is that of a thief and a robber; he goes about choking and robbing men and threatening to cut their throats if they say a word or make any resistance.

N. Baldwin, 76th New York, Company C, while proving that Murphy did not take part in the riot, swore that Sarsfield was one of the men who attacked Dowd; witness stated that he knew Sarsfield to be a robber; the day before he decoyed five men into his tent, and, with others swore he would kill those five men if they made any noise, and then robbed them.

Joseph Terril, 101st Ohio, Company E, swore that he knew Sarsfield, who was generally seen in company with two men, one of them named Delaney; witness saw as many as twenty or thirty men a day come out of Sarsfield's tent, their pants nearly torn off; the first that would be heard, after these men entered the tent, would be the man gasping for breath; Sarsfield and his gang raided on witness one night.

The result of the examination into this case was the acquittal of Murphy, and the conviction of Sarsfield, who was sentenced to be hanged.

Second Day's Proceedings

William John Kennedy, 52nd New York, Company C; Patrick Delaney, 83rd Pennsylvania, Company E; John Sullivan, 76th New York, Company F; Peter Gilmore, 145th Pennsylvania, Company J; Owen Farley, news agent of the Cavalry Corps, Army of the Potomac; William Hollings, 145th Pennsylvania, Company G; John Connolly, 52nd New York, Company C; Andrew Muir, United States steamer *Waterwitch*, were next put on trial.

The charges were similar to those in the previous case.

The prisoners pleaded not guilty.

Newton Baldwin, of the 76th New York, Company C, swore that Sullivan's business was that of robbing the prisoners and that he was one of those who attacked Dowd. He struck Dowd, who had his pant's off, and his tent torn down. Dowd was imploring Sullivan to let him put on his pants. Witnesses saw Sullivan rob an orderly-sergeant who had come in that evening, and was induced to go to Sullivan's tent. Witness tented within a dozen yards of Sullivan. Next day five men were taken at different times to Sullivan's tent, when they were robbed by Sullivan, Delany, and Sarsfield. Those men (so robbed) had only just come into the camp. Witness saw one man stretched in the tent. Sullivan and another of the prisoners were holding him down, and they threatened to cut his throat unless he lay still. This was of daily occurrence. Delany was generally present at these robberies. Sarsfield generally did the cutting out business, while the others held down their victims.

Sergeant Carpenter—Why did not the men in that neighborhood clear out that gang?

A. Well, there were so many of them there, and they were all so armed with clubs, that people were afraid of them. Sullivan carries a club with an iron nut at the end of it. Saw Delany rob a watch from a man on the street a few days ago. He came up to the man, who had a stick of wood on his back, and said, "This is a very good hat you have on." The man clung to the hat. Delany then grabbed the watch and carried it off. The prisoner, Mullings, acted as a runner for the gang. He went out, picked up, and brought to the tent the men intended to be robbed. Mullings picked up two of the five men robbed in Sullivan's tent. Whenever a lot of prisoners came into the prison Mullings would go among them, asking if they wanted to buy blankets or rations. By this means he decoyed them to Sullivan's tent, where they would be robbed. (The newcomers were those among whom the robbers plied their infamous trade, as they were ignorant of the robberies carried on by a band of scoundrels.) The general conversation of these men was about robbing, and how much they took from such and such a man. Heard one fellow say, "I got $20 out of that fellow; I got nothing out of that other son of a b—h." Saw Muir engaged in robbing Dowd. Saw him on top of Dowd, trying to cut out his pocket and fumbling in it. The first time he saw Muir engaged in robbing was when he and the others attacked the orderly-sergeant. Muir had not the same appearance when he attacked Dowd as he had at present. Then he wore whiskers and mustache; at present they were shaved off. Never saw Farley do anything, although he was frequently present among the gang when the robberies were going on.

R. E. Spicer recalled: saw Sullivan, Delaney, and Gilmore rob a man the day before; he resisted, when Sarsfield came up and brandished knife at him; Sullivan was also engaged in the attack on Dowd; saw Delaney in Sullivan's tent take hold of men, gag them; and take their money away. By "gagging," he meant putting something in their mouth, so that they could not cry out. While robbing on those occasions, heard them threaten men that if they made any noise they would cut their throat; one day last week while they were robbing a man in Sullivan's tent, witness heard one of the gang say two or three times; "Here is a razor, cut his throat," Sullivan, Delaney, and Gilmore were present at the time; Sullivan carried a club with a knob of iron at the end; a few nights previously, went to rob a man who had a watch; some of the persons in the next tent made a noise, and his purpose was defeated. Next night, between 11 and 12 o'clock. Delaney came to that tent, told one of the men in it to "come here;" the man hesitated, "Are you not coming?" said Delaney; the man was lying down in his tent at the time, he rose, when Delaney struck him in the head with a club having an iron knob in the end; he then struck another of the men in the same tent; Delaney then came to a boy fifteen years of age who was lying outside the same tent and beat him with the wooden end of the stick; saying that if he heard any more noise he would knock their brains out and, "let every man mind his own business;" knew Delaney to shove men into the tent, and rob them; knew him to draw men into the tent by telling them he had something to sell them.

Joseph Farrel, 101st Ohio, Co. B, swore that some night ago a gang came to mug him; but could not identify any of them among the prisoners. A few days ago he saw a man go into Sullivan's tent with a watch in his pocket, and saw him leave without the watch. While the man was in the tent he heard a scuffle, and soon after he saw the man's feet sticking out from under the tent, and heard him gasping for breath.

This closed the prosecution.

Mr. Higginson called several witnesses for the defense, the effect of whose evidence, while it left the case against the other prisoners untouched, was to clear Connolly and Mullings from the most heinous crimes of assault with intent to murder. There was no evidence against Kennedy and Farley.

The jury, after an hour's deliberation, returned the following verdict: Kennedy and Farley, not guilty; Connolly and Mullings, guilty of robbery; sentenced each to wear a ball and chain 25 lbs. weight, for four months; Gilmore's case suspended; Sullivan, Delaney, and Muir guilty of all the charges, sentenced to be hanged by the neck until dead.

Third Day's Proceedings

Richard Allen, 83rd Pennsylvania, Company E, William Wrixon, alias Curtis, United States steamship Powhatttan; Thomas F. O'Connell, 9th Maryland, Company D, were put on their trial charged with the same offense as against those previously tried.

Daniel Hayes, United States, Company L, swore that one day last week, Allen and his party, including Curtis, came to his tent. He then forced a man named Prentis out of the tent, threw him down on the ground and, threatened his life unless he would tell where the other watch was—in the custody of a friend. Prentiss got the watch from the friend, came out and handed it to Allen and Curtis.

On cross-examination, it appeared that this witness was not inside his tent when this robbery was committed. He was some twenty yards from it. But he saw the watch taken.

Mr. Higginson.—Is it not singular that you and your party did not make some resistance to save your watch? A. There were upward of twenty men in the gang that came to the tent, and they were all dangerous men, armed with weapons.

William Prentiss, 16th Illinois Cavalry, Company I, the man referred to in the evidence of the last witness, confirmed the statement of Hays; adding at when Allen & Curtis demanded the second watch he tried to escape from the tent, but was taken hold of, jerked down, four or five of the gang having hold of him and threatening that if he did not give information where the other watch was they would cut his throat. Curtis alias Wrixon, said he would cut out his (Prentiss's) heart. They had their knives out ready to do so, and he expected to be murdered every moment. They had him by the throat and their hands on his mouth. While accompanying them to where the second watch was deposited, they said if witness "went down there and got them into a muss, they would not give two cents for his life."

James M. Friend, of the 16th Illinois Cavalry, Company I, stated that, last Saturday night, while he was lying in his tent, Curtis and a man named Delany came and woke him up. They asked him who was lying in the back of his tent? Witness replied "No person." Curtis then charged the witness with having been down to their quarters and robbed them of a blanket. Having denied this, Curtis struck him on the face with a razor and cut him. The wound was a ghastly one, across the side of the cheek. Witness put up his hand, and received a gash between the thumb and the first finger. They then made several passes of the razor at him, but he succeeded in creeping away from them on his all fours, and tried to throw his pocketbook into the "dead-line", but did not succeed in throwing it far enough, and he picked it up again, when one of them grasped it from him, saying, as he did so, "God d—n you, that is all we wanted." There were four hundred and forty nine dollars in the pocketbook. He had been trading a little.

J. P. Erwin, 103rd Pennsylvania Regiment, Company B, swore that Wrixon, alias Curtis, had some weeks previously choked him down, and somebody else came up and robbed him.

Other witnesses testified to other charges against Curtis, Allen, and O'Connell.

This closed the prosecution.

Witnesses were called for the defense, but the testimony was vague, and only went to prove that they never saw the prisoners guilty of any crime.

The jury returned a verdict finding Richard Allen and Thomas F. O'Connell guilty of robbery and assault; and they were sentenced to be handcuffed and shackled during their imprisonment. Wrixson, alias Curtis, they found guilty of all of the charges preferred against him, and he was sentenced to be hanged.

Wrixon denied that he was guilty, adding:—"I am not a citizen of the United States. I am a deserter from the United States Army, and took the oath of allegiance, and demanded to be tried by a court of Confederate officers.["]

Upon this statement, the Court ordered the official reporter to make a note of the prisoner's objection to his trial and conviction.

This was made out, and prisoner was brought to headquarters under the escort of Confederate soldiers.

On coming before Captain Wirz:

Wirz—"Well, my man, what is the matter?"

Curtis—"I am a deserter. I wish to be tried by Confederate officers."

Captain Wirz—"Take this man before General Winder, and take the official reporter's note concerning Curtis's objection."

Brought before General Winder:

Winder—"Well, what do you want! Have you been tried?"

A. "Yes, sir but I am a deserter from the United States service, and I deny that they have any power to try me down there."

General Winder.: "Let us see. What have they [done] to you down below."

Curtis.—"They have sentenced me to death."

General Winder.—"Well, what do you want me to do?"

Curtis.—"I want to be tried by Confederate officers."

General Winder.—"Very well; I cannot get Confederate officers to try you, but I shall try you myself, and from all that I have heard of your case, I shall order you to be shot. The Yankees have sentenced you to be hanged. Which do you choose?"

Curtis hung his head, and he was brought down to the stocks.

William Curtis, alias Mosby, of the 88th Penn., Company D, was again put on trial on charge of robbing, assaulting, and with being the leader of a gang of thieves.

Charles W. Ross,[494] of the 5th Ohio Cavalry, identified the prisoner, who went by the name of Mosby, called after the celebrated Confederate raider of that name. Saw him engaged in several raids in the prison. Saw him take biscuits from a man who was peddling them in the street. Had seen him decoy men into his tent who had only come into the camp the same day. This man complained of having his watch and ten dollars taken from him. Saw Mosby instigate other men to rob the prisoners—little boys. Saw him point out where to go and rob persons. Saw one of those men strike a little boy who had a box of peanuts to sell, and then rob the little boy of his box of peanuts, and tell the boy, who had began to cry, to dry up, or he would whip him.

Cross-examined.—Why did you not go and raise a crowd to try to put down those men?

A. I did not do so, as I was too much interested in keeping quiet. He had too strong a gang for me. I often heard Mosby called the head of a gang. I swear he was the head of a gang of thieves.

George Ogleby, of the 4th Kentucky Cavalry, Company A.—I know the prisoner at the bar as "Mosby." Saw Mosby come up to a German who was buying some onions, asking the person from whom he sought them could change the bill. He said no; but said that this man (pointing to Mosby) could, the onion seller passing the bill at the same time to Mosby, who carried it off, and lay down in his tent. The German demanded his change. The onion seller said he knew nothing about it. Mosby came back from his tent, and the German asked him for his bill. "Get along," Mosby said, "I know nothing of your bill." A crowd gathered around them. Mosby told the German to clear out, or he would give him a thrashing. The German went away and did not get the bill. It appeared to me that the onion seller and Mosby were acting in concert. Both their tents adjoined on another.

Joseph Ackers, of the 14th Connecticut, Company I, testified that he knew the prisoner. Knew a man to be robbed one night in his tent. It was midnight. Heard the man cry in his tent. Just before the cry he saw Mosby creep along the tent and then go inside. I know Mosby not to take much part in the robberies himself, but I know him to be a planner of robberies for others. I know it because I heard him lay the plans to rob persons. When any person came along who had things for sale, Mosby's gang would go along, he leading the way, and take the articles from the owners by force and violence sometimes. Saw the gang attack parties selling articles, when a fight ensued, Mosby taking part in the fight. Heard Mosby tell his men to be ready to go round at night, and take boots or shoes or any other articles they could find.

James Keating, of the 42nd New York, Company [?], was called for the defense. Said: I heard Mosby say he would not go hungry, while he could steal anything. He was called a raider, a name which he deserved.

Mr. Higginson said that after he had heard of Mosby's character, he declined to address the jury in his defense.

The jury found Mosby guilty of robbing and assaulting his fellow prisoners, and with being the leader of an organized band of thieves, robbers, and garrotters, and he was sentenced to be hanged.

There were several others tried, and found guilty, and sentenced to wear ball and chain for terms varying from ten days to the remainder of their imprisonment, but the six convicted and sentenced to death were regarded as the ringleaders of the organization.

There were about ninety others remaining untried, all well known thieves; but it was considered that the execution of half a dozen would be sufficient to strike terror into the hearts of the other evil-doers; and the smaller fry were, after a warning, turned into the camp.

In the meantime, the report of the proceedings was prepared, amply setting forth the pros and cons—the evidence for the prosecution and that for the defense. When prepared, it was sent forward to General Winder.

In the meantime, the convicts were placed in the stocks, awaiting the decision at Headquarters.

It would be impossible to describe the feeling which pervaded the camp at this moment. Wagers were offered by every man who had a dollar, whether or not the convicts would be ordered for execution. It was evident that the culprits themselves did not believe they were to die; although a worthy priest named Father [Peter] Whelan, from Florida, who had been attending the prisoners for several months before was unceasing in his labors in trying to impress upon them the real nature of their position.[495]

Approval of the Sentence of the Court General Orders No. 61

The Court authorized by General Order, No. 57, June 30, 1864, having tried and sentenced the following named men to the punishment attached and set opposite their respective names, the Court is authorized to execute the sentence in the above case.

Patrick Sarsfield to be hanged; John Sullivan, to be hanged; Patrick Delany, to be hanged; William Wixon, alias Curtis, to be hanged; William Collins, alias Mosby, to be hanged. By order of Brig.-Gen. John H. Winder.

Robt. W. Brown, Lt. Col. and Adj.

The Execution

Capt. Wirz had the convicts brought to his headquarters, and informed them of their doom, telling them that before sunset next day they would be in eternity. He told them therefore to prepare themselves for their fate, and said he would attend to any request of theirs; and he would send for whatever clergy man they might desire should be with them at their last moments.

Next morning, a scaffold was commenced to be erected in the prison on a spot where every prisoner in the camp could have a sight of the execution, which was ordered to take place at 4 o'clock on Monday, July 11.

A detachment of Confederate soldiers, with Captain Wirz at their head, rode toward the stocks where the six unhappy men were held. The stocks were unlocked, and the six convicts led back into the prison, preceded by Father Whelan (the only clergyman who could be had to attend them), who offered up fervent prayers as the cortege moved in. Having arrived at the foot of the scaffold, Curtis made a bolt through the cordon of Union prisoners several ranks deep with staves in their hands, being a portion of the vigilance committee detailed for the duty to keep order during the execution. Curtis was soon brought back and pinioned. The convicts having ascended the scaffold, Father Whelan begged of the crowd to forego the execution—to have mercy on them. But not a single voice of the thousands were raised on their behalf. The prisoners then begged for mercy; but the cry was "The mercy you showed your fellow-prisoners." After half an hour's delay, meal bags were drawn over their heads and faces, and they were launched into eternity, amid the stillness of death which reigned over the awe struck camp, with its thirty-eight thousand spectators of the terrible act of retributive justice which had fallen over the miserable criminals.

The rope on which Mosby hung broke when he was swung off, and he fell heavily to the ground. Some voices said, "Don't hang him,"; but they were unheeded, and he was soon again on the scaffold, and he shared the fate of his companions. After the execution, a man could take a dollar on the tip of his finger, and no one would dare touch it. No more beating, gauging garroting, or mugging was experienced, and every man slept at night without apprehension.

It was a terrible but a needed and proved to be a salutary lesson.

Appendix B

RESEARCHING ANDERSONVILLE PRISONERS, GUARDS, AND OTHERS

Encased and lettered as a tomb,
And scored with prints of perished hands,
And chronicled with dates of doom...
I trace the lives such scenes enshrine,
Give past exemplars present room,
And their experience count as mine.

—Thomas Hardy, from
"On An Invitation to the United States"

The real world always trumped the virtual and it always would.

—Dean Koontz, from *One Door Away From Heaven*

In finding the often illusive people involved in the history of Andersonville, the Internet has proven to be an important tool. Every chapter in this book uses some important information; located through queries posted on or searches made of the World Wide Web. Internet web sites used here include Familysearch.com, Genforum, Genweb, HeritageQuest, Rootsweb, Ancestry.com, and Genealogylibrary.com. Most of these sites can also allow searches by keyword, such as "Andersonville" and "Limber Jim," even by using the subject word as a surname.

Other sites, for historical research, allow for searches by surname or keyword. First Search (OCLC) and Research Libraries Information Network (RLIN) accesses information on millions of volumes and manuscript collections. Questia, Making of America (Cornell University), and Making of American (University of Michigan) allow word searches of millions of printed pages. Search engines on other web sites, such as Newspaperarchive.com, Augustaarchive.com, and Ancestry.com now scan images of newspapers such as the *New York Times* and *Augusta Chronicle*, reading decades of newsprint at the speed of light. The future appears bright for finding even more historical gems buried in such resources.

In addition to these sources and other resources cited below, Andersonville researchers seek answers and exchange information on a number of Internet Civil War web sites, such as the Civil War Home Page and the Andersonville chat room on rootsweb.com.

Background

Confederate Camp Sumter, Andersonville Post Office, Anderson Station, on the Sumter-Macon County line, served a prison camp from late February 1864 to early May 1865. Today, Andersonville National Historic Site, 496 Cemetery Road, Andersonville GA 31711 (www.nps.gov/ande) Tel: (912) 924–0343, operated by the National Park Service, still serves as an active national cemetery and as a memorial to all American prisoners of war.

Many family stories mistakenly place relatives at Camp Sumter. The Civil War and the Confederate States of America had other prisons. Andersonville's inmates almost exclusively consisted of federal sailors, privates, civilians, corporals, and sergeants. The only officers held there had commanded African-American soldiers. Officer's prisons included Libby Prison in Richmond VA, and Camp Oglethorpe in Macon GA.

Andersonville did hold the greatest number and concentration of inmates to its time, or for generations afterwards. Almost 40,000 prisoners entered the camp of which 12,949 died there. Built to accommodate only 9,000 men, at its height, it held 33,006 men. Inmates lived in filth and sickness, while subsisting on starvation rations. The breakdown in the prisoner exchange agreements between the warring sides and the type of administrative incompetence and fraud common to both sides created this humanitarian disaster. The most notable historical works on the prison include Ovid Futch, *History of Andersonville Prison* (1968); William Marvel, *Andersonville: The Last Depot* (1994); Edward F. Roberts, *Andersonville Journey* (1998); and John W. Lynn, *800 Paces to Hell: Andersonville* (1999).

Prisoners

Many of the records of Camp Sumter survive because they were seized as evidence for use in the trial of the prison's Captain Henry Wirz. Among these documents can be found the most complete original roster of Andersonville prisoners, "Original Register of Federal Prisoners of War Confined at Andersonville, Ga. 1864–5," microfilm roll 1 of *Andersonville Confederate Prison Records, 1864–1865* (National Archives Microfilm Publication M1303), Record Group 249. This microfilm also includes hospital and dead lists. These records omit some soldiers, especially from the early days of the camp. Misspelled names and even some aliases appear in this record.

The Andersonville National Historic Site originally had a computer database built around an incomplete and otherwise faulty copy of the above register. This compilation has been copied at least twice onto the Internet. The database does indicate if additional information for a prisoner can be found in the library of Andersonville National Historic Site. The library gladly accepts donations of material relating to the history of the prison and any people connected with it. Lists of the prison's known dead have been published many times, most notably in *The Roll of Honor* series.

The National Archives and Records Administration, 700 Pennsylvania Ave. NW, Washington DC 20408–0001, has extensive records on prisoners of war, including claims for money due for commutation of rations, in Records of the Commissary of Prisoners of War, Record Group 249. The latter documents show money paid to men for rations they failed to receive because of their confinement as prisoners of war. Few of the records in RG 249 have been microfilmed, including the alphabetically arranged slips of paper that summarize the prisoner records in Entry 108.

The National Archives also has military service records. When a soldier has a captivity record, it appears on a thin sheet of paper in an envelope in the soldier's National Archives compiled service record. The Broadfoot Company has published lists of the service records by state or unit type as Janet B. Hewett, comp., *The Roster of Union Soldiers 1861–1865* (33 vols., 1998). The federal pension records, also at the National Archives, frequently contain information on captivity. For more information on related records see Kenneth W. Munden and Henry Putney Beers, *The Union: A Guide to Federal Archives Relating to the Civil War* (Washington, 1986).

Jack Lundquist has prepared the most extensive list of prisoners at Andersonville, Cahaba, and many other Confederate prisons. Aside from standard sources, he has added extensive information found in state adjutant general lists. Jack has donated a copy of his work to the Andersonville National Historic Site.

Dozens of Andersonville prisoners published accounts of their experiences. Unpublished writings exist in manuscript repositories across the country. No complete bibliography of this material exists. Some of the online catalogs reference these materials, such as the Online Catalog Library Corporation (OCLC or "First Search" available at major university libraries), Research Libraries Information Network (RLIN), and the book catalog of the Library of Congress.

Guards and Camp Personnel

Jack Lundquist (see above) has also compiled a database on the Andersonville guards. The Andersonville National Historic site has files on guards, camp personnel, and other persons associated with the prison. Many of the camp personnel also have files in *Compiled Service Records of Confederate Generals and Staff Officers and Non-Regimental Enlisted Men* (National Archives microfilm M331), Record Group 109.

For most of Andersonville's history the guards consisted of the 2nd Brigade of the Georgia Reserves (1st through 4th regiments) and the members of the 55th Georgia Volunteer Infantry Regiment absent when most of the regiment suffered capture at Cumberland Gap. Other units that served at the prison, at different times, included the 57th Georgia Confederate Infantry, local Georgia militia units, the 26th Alabama Confederate Infantry Regiment, Gamble's/Dyke's Florida Artillery, and Furlow's Militia Battalion.

The National Archives has compiled service records of most of the Confederate soldiers. These files have a comprehensive index by the Broadfoot Company: Janet B. Hewett, *The Roster of Confederate Soldiers 1861–1865* (16 vols., 1996). The individual service records for Georgia troops have been microfilmed in *Compiled Service Records of Confederate Soldiers Who Served in Organizations From the State of Georgia* (National Archives microfilm M266), Record Group 109. Individual service records of the 55th and 56th/57th regiments also appear in volume five of Lillian Henderson, *Roster of the Confederate*

Soldiers of Georgia (1960). Lengthy lists of deserters from the Georgia Reserves appeared in the *Macon Daily Telegraph* for October 1864. For other Georgia records see the Alphabetical Card Catalog [of Confederate service] on microfilm at the Georgia Archives in Morrow GA.

Reminiscences by Georgia guards and civilians of Andersonville survive in many places including in *Confederate Reminiscences and Letters* (20 vols. to date, 1995–) and the Civil War Miscellany Collection, Georgia Archives. Records of the Florida soldiers appear in David W. Hartman, *Biographical Rosters of Florida's Confederate and Union Soldiers* (1995) and *Compiled Service Records of Confederate Soldiers Who Served in Organizations From the State of Florida* (National Archives microfilm M251), RG 109. The Alabama Department of Archives and History has a file of material on the 26th Infantry. The service records for Alabama soldiers appear in *Compiled Service Records of Confederate Soldiers Who Served in Organizations From the State of Alabama* (National Archives microfilm M311), RG 109.

Other

The greatest record of Andersonville, although filled with prejudiced and perjured testimony, survives as the trial testimony of Captain Heinrich "Henry" Wirz, a Confederate officer of the prison. Witnesses included civilians, guards, and inmates; the complete transcript of the trial is file MM2975, RG 153 Records of the Bureau of Military Justice, in the National Archives and Records Administration. The best of the many publications on the testimony from the trial in print is the *Trial of Henry Wirz* (Washington, 1868). For names of some of the witnesses from that work see "Andersonville Testimony," *Georgia Genealogical Society Quarterly* 31 (1995): 163. The Brooklyn Historical Society of New York has, for Andersonville, a day book (1864), hospital records (1864), and a register of deaths.

NOTES

INTRODUCTION

1 Ovid L. Futch, *History of Andersonville Prison* (Gainesville: University of Florida Press, 1968); William Marvel, *Andersonville: The Last Depot* (Chapel Hill: University of North Carolina Press, 1994); John W. Lynn, *800 Paces to Hell: Andersonville* (Fredericksburg VA: Sergeant Kirkland's Museum, 1999); and Edward F. Roberts, *Andersonville Journey* (Shippensburg VA: Burd Street Press, 1998).

2 See my articles "Some Soldiers from Andersonville and Other Civil War Records," *Heritage Quest Magazine* 65/3 (September/October 1996): 90–91; and "Escape from Andersonville: A Study in Isolation and Imprisonment," *Journal of Military History* 67/4 (October 2003): 1065–82.

3 See chapter 2.

4 I first read this work in a seventh grade Georgia history class upon the recommendation of my teacher, Ted Key. Mr. Key later became a Georgia teacher of the year. As a history professor, I often hear the complaints about history teachers who failed their students. I was blessed that when I needed a good history teacher, I had among the best including Mr. Key, Ms. Martha Senkbeil, and the late Dr. Paul Dobson.

5 Peter J. Meaney, "The Prison Ministry of Father Peter Whelan, Georgia Priest and Confederate Chaplain," *Georgia Historical Quarterly* 71/1 (Spring 1987): 1–24; Marvel, *Andersonville*, 35–38, 259 n. 13.

6 See chapter nine.

7 See chapter ten.

8 See Sharon L. D. Kraynek, *Medina County, Ohio Recollections of Medina Characters (1874–1908)* (Apollo PA: Closson Press, 1998).

9 See chapter three.

10 For the long-term effects of the darker side of the new America, see R. Gregory Lande, *Madness, Malingering, and Malfeasance: The Transformation of Psychiatry and the Law of the Civil War* (Washington DC: Brassey's, 2003).

11 Lonnie R. Speer, *War of Vengeance: Acts of Retaliation Against Civil War POWs* (Mechanicsville PA: Stackpole Books, 2002) 130.

12 David Rachels and Robert Baird, introduction to *Andersonville Violets: A Story of Northern and Southern Life* by Herbert H. Collingwood (1889; repr., Tuscaloosa: University of Alabama Press, 2000) xx; Lesley Jill Gordon-Burr, "Storms of Indignation: The Art of Andersonville as Post War Propaganda," *Georgia Historical Quarterly* 75/3 (Fall 1991): 587–600. For the history of this genre see Douglas Gibson Gardner, "Andersonville and American Memory: Civil War Prisoners and Narratives of Suffering and Redemption," (Ph.D. diss., Miami University, 1998).

13 See, for example, Morgan E. Dowling, *Southern Prisons: Or Josie the Heroine of Florence* (Detroit: William Graham, 1870); Ralph O. Bates, *Billy and Dick From Andersonville Prison to the White House* (Santa Cruz CA: Press Sentinel Publishing, 1910) 1, 97–99; William Coyle, *Ohio Authors and Their Books* (Cleveland: World Publishing, 1962) 38–39; Allen Nevins, James I. Robertson, Jr., and Bell I. Wiley, eds., *Civil War Books: A Critical Bibliography*, 2 vols. (Baton Rouge: Louisiana State University Press, 1967) 1:186, 190.

14 For criticism of the prejudices reflected in Kantor's novel see William B. Hesseltine, "*Andersonville* Revisited," *Georgia Review* 10/1 (Spring 1956): 92–110.

15 See chapter eleven.

16 John Elwood Clark, *Railroads in the Civil War* (Baton Rouge: Louisiana State University Press, 2001) 31.

17 James Gillispie, "Guests of the Yankees: A Reevaluation of Union Treatment of Confederate Prisoners," *North & South: The Official Magazine of the Civil War Society* 5 (July 2002): 40–49; Dayton Pryor, *The Beginning and the End: The Civil War Story of Federal Surrenders Before Fort Sumter and Confederate Surrenders After Appomattox* (Bowie MD: Heritage Books, 2001) 381. Capt. Henry Wirz would face charges of cruelty from the federal government because the Confederacy had the prisoners at Andersonville inoculated to protect them from small pox.

CHAPTER ONE

18 John Elwood Clark, *Railroads in the Civil War* (Baton Rouge: Louisiana State University Press, 2001) 31.

19 In addition to what appeared in the contemporary Southern newspapers, pamphlets containing accounts by escaped and exchanged Confederates received distribution across the South. For these works see T. Michael Parrish and Robert M. Willingham, Jr., *Confederate Imprints* (Austin TX: Jenkins Publishing, 1987).

20 Except where noted, the information in this chapter comes from the general histories of Andersonville: William Marvel, *Andersonville: The Last Depot* (Chapel Hill: University of North Carolina Press, 1994); Ovid L. Futch, *History of Andersonville Prison* (Gainesville: University of Florida Press, 1968); John W. Lynn, *800 Paces to Hell: Andersonville* (Fredericksburg VA: Sergeant Kirkland's Museum, 1999); and Edward F. Roberts, *Andersonville Journey* (Shippensburg VA: Burd Street Press, 1998). Until almost the end of the war, the only officers held at what became Camp Sumter commanded black troops.

21 Deposition of Michael P. Suber, 10 December 1875, petition of Benjamin B. Dykes, 29 September 1875, and miscellaneous receipts, *Benjamin B. Dykes v. United States*, general jurisdiction #10703, United States Court of Claims, RG 123, National Archives and Records Administration (NARA), College Park MD. Dykes and his family had owned land in the area since the 1840s, but he acquired his land around Anderson Station in 1857. Henry K. Dykes to B. B. Dykes, 11 July 1842, Sumter County deed book G (1845–1847), 149, microfilm roll 132/2; Senus H. Clark, James Stewart, and Virgil Powers to B. B. Dykes, 23 March to 2 July 1857, deeds, Sumter County deed book M (1857–1859), 84, 95, 149, 300, microfilm roll 132/5, Georgia Archives, Morrow GA; Lynn, *800 Paces*, 115.

22 *Benjamin B. Dykes v. United States*, deposition of Major James M. Moore (11–12 December 1876), United States Court of Claims, general jurisdiction #10703, RG 123, NARA. For the confusion over the name of the community of Anderson see "Anderson or Andersonville," *Macon* (GA) *Daily Telegraph*, 2 July 1864; Marvel, *Andersonville*, 253–54; Ambrose Spencer, *A Narrative of Andersonville* (New York: Harper & Brothers, 1866) 16. Also see the correspondence of Henry Wirz, Anderson GA, entry 188 (ch. 7, vol. 24), War Department Collection of Confederate Records, Record Group (RG) 109, NARA; and G. E. Saber, *Nineteen Months A Prisoner of War* (New York: American News Company, 1865) 80–81. It is traditional (and required by law in many states) to refer to a community by the name of its post office. The print *Map of Andersonville*, now in the Library of Congress, includes a drawing of the village of Anderson Station. Margaret E. Wagner,

Gary W. Gallagher, and Paul Pinkelman, *The Library of Congress Civil War Desk Reference* (New York: Simon & Schuster, 2002) 608.

23 "Plains of Dura," *Daily Intelligencer* (Atlanta GA), 24 June 1859, 2.

24 *Benjamin B. Dykes v. United States*, deposition of Maj. James M. Moore (11–12 December 1876), United States Court of Claims, general jurisdiction #10703, RG 123, NARA; Futch, *History of Andersonville Prison*, 2–4; Roberts, *Andersonville Journey*, 20–23; Marvel, *Andersonville*, 17–19; Peggy Sheppard, *Andersonville Georgia USA* (Leslie GA: Sheppard Publications, 1973) 79; "Andersonville," *Indiana Weekly Messenger* (Indiana PA), 15 September 1880, 1.

25 Jack F. Cox, *History of Sumter County, Georgia* (Roswell GA: W. H. Wolfe, 1983) 408–10; Samuel Heys File, *Confederate Papers Relating to Citizens or Business Firms* (National Archives microfilm M346, roll 440), War Department Collection of Confederate Records, RG 109, NARA; Albert Webster, Jr., "A Jaunt in the South," *Appleton's Journal* (13 September 1873): 323; Donald L. Grant, *The Way It Was in the South: The Black Experience in Georgia* (New York: Birch Lane, 1993) 84.

26 "Story of the First Federal Prisoner to Enter Andersonville," *Augusta* (GA) *Chronicle*, 6 June 1909, 6.

27 Anonymous, "Fourteen Months in Prison," MSS 5:1 Un3:8, Virginia Historical Society, Richmond VA; "The Yankee Prisoners" and "Camp Anderson" in *Sumter* (Americus GA) *Republican*, 1 April 1864, 3, and 6 May 1864, 2; Marvel, *Andersonville*, 14–29; Nelson Tift, "Doughterty County," *Journal of Southwest Georgia History* 7 (Fall 1986): 16.

28 B. H. Baldwin, "Reminiscences of Andersonville in War Days," Wisconsin scrapbooks, State Historical Society of Wisconsin, Madison WI.

29 Futch, *History of Andersonville Prison*, 100, 102, 106, 109, 111; Marvel, *Andersonville*, 28, 67–68, 168–70, 196, 216–17; Lynn, *800 Paces*, 103–36.

30 Roberts, *Andersonville Journey*, 43.

31 "Story of the First Federal Prisoner to Enter Andersonville," *Augusta* (GA) *Chronicle*, 5 June 1909, 6; "As to the Dead-line," *National Tribune* (Washington DC), hereafter *NT*, 27 September 1883, 4; T. H. Mann, "A Yankee in Andersonville," *Century Magazine* 40 (July–August 1890): 457.

32 Frank W. Smith, "After Many Years," *NT*, 20 September 1883, 2; A. C. Brown, "Andersonville, Ga.," *NT*, 14 February 1889, 3.

33 Lynn, *800 Paces*, 200–2, 213–14.

34 Marvel, *Andersonville*, 174–79.

35 William H. Smith diaries, vol. 1, 7 July 1864, MSS 13164, Special Collections, University of Virginia Libraries, Charlottesville VA; "Capt. Wirz was a Martyr," *Augusta* (GA) *Chronicle*, 30 May 1909, 4; Theodore P. Savas and David A. Woodbury, *The Campaign for Atlanta and Sherman's March to the Sea* (Campbell CA: Savas Woodbury, 1994) 36, 63–64, 246, 396; Arch Frederic Blakey, *General John H. Winder, CSA* (Gainesville: University of Florida Press, 1990) 187–90; David Evans, *Sherman's Horsemen* (Bloomington: Indiana University Press, 1996) 144–45, 161, 376.

36 Morton R. McInvale, "'That Thing of Infamy': Macon's Camp Oglethorpe During the Civil War," *Georgia Historical Quarterly* 63/2 (Summer 1979): 287–88. Among the federal prisoners, the officers held at Camp Oglethorpe became renowned for their tunneling schemes.

37 Basil Meek, *Twentieth Century History of Sandusky County* (Chicago: Richmond-Arnold, 1909) 920; Futch, *History of Andersonville Prison*, 51; Marvel, *Andersonville*, 111.

38 Solon Hyde, *A Captive of War* (New York: McClure, Philips, & Co., 1900) 226, 248–49; Lynn, *800 Paces*, 166–67. For the ethnic nature of the federal army see William L. Burton, *Melting Pot Soldiers: The Union's Ethnic Regiments* (Ames: Iowa State University Press, 1988).

39 "Unofficial Poet Laureate of the Rockies," *Brooklyn Daily Eagle*, 5 October 1902, 42.

40 "Statements of Escaped Union Prisoners, Refugees, and Rebel Deserters," p. 45, entry 4294, Records of Continental Commands, RG 393, pt. 1, NARA.

41 James A. Mowris, *A History of the 117th Regiment, NY Volunteers* (Hartford CT: Case, Lockwood and Company, 1866) 298.

42 James Burton diary (MSS 120), entries of 30 April, 5 May, 14 June, and 23 June 1864, Special Collections, Woodruff Library, Emory University, Atlanta GA.

43 Burton diary, 30 April 1864; Spencer, *A Narrative of Andersonville*, 97–98, 109.

44 Futch, *History of Andersonville Prison*, 109.

45 Roberts, *Andersonville Journey*, xviii-xxiii, 41–42; Blakey, *General John H. Winder, CSA*, 175. For works on Andersonville as an example of administrative failure, see Joseph P. Cangemi and Casimir J. Kowalski, eds., *Andersonville Prison: Lessons in Organizational Failure* (Lanham MD: University Press of America, 1992); Daniel P. Brown, *The Tragedy of Libby and Andersonville Prison Camps: a Study of Mismanagement and Inept Logistical Policies* (Ventura CA: Golden West Historical Publications, 1980); and David F. Cross, "Why did the Yankees die at Andersonville?," *North & South* 6 (September 2003): 26–27. Ovid L. Futch, in his generally balanced history of Andersonville, titled the second chapter "Gross Mismanagement." Futch, *History of Andersonville Prison*, 11.

46 Roberts, *Andersonville Journey*, 41–42.

47 Robert A. Taylor, *Rebel Storehouse: Florida in the Confederate Economy* (Tuscaloosa: University of Alabama Press, 1995) 117–19.

48 Blakey, *General John H. Winder CSA*, 189; Lynn, *800 Paces*, 183–84, 214, 216, 293; Free Lance, "Southern Prison Life," *NT*, 5 August 1882, 2; Ransom T. Powell, "Brave Little Red Cap," *NT*, 5 August 1882, 2; *NT*, 12 October 1882, 1; *NT*, 30 November 1882, 3; Magnus Tait, *My Rebel Prison Life* (n. p., 1888) 9, 21.

49 Lonnie R. Speer, *War of Vengeance: Acts of Retaliation Against Civil War POWs* (Mechanicsville PA: Stackpole Books, 2002) 123. For the history of the supply problems of Confederate States of America, see David G. Surdam, *Northern Naval Superiority and the Economics of the American Civil War* (Columbia: University of South Carolina Press, 2001).

50 Lynn, *800 Paces*, 64. Powell has what is probably the unique distinction of being the hero of a novel before the discovery and publication of his memoirs; see Ransom J. Powell, *The Civil War Memoirs of Little Red Cap*, ed. H. L. Scott (Cumberland MD: H. L. Scott, 1997) and G. Clifton Wisler, *Red Cap* (New York: Lodestar Books, 1991). Henry Wirz's daughter Cora fondly remembered Powell as devoted to her father and family. "Major Wirz at Andersonville," *Confederate Veteran* 28/7 (July 1920): 276.

51 Burton diary, 5 May and 17 July 1864.

52 Mowris, *A History of the 117th Regiment, NY Volunteers*, 300–302

53 Notebook, Louis Manigault Collection, South Carolina Historical Society, Charleston SC; "Andersonville," *Hillsdale* (MI) *Standard*, 12 May 1868, 1.

54 Richard Thatcher, "Boston Corbett's Prison Life," Boston Corbett Collection, Kansas State Historical Society, Topeka KS; Futch, *History of Andersonville Prison*, 61–62; John W. Urban, *Battle Field and Prison Pen* (Edgewood NJ: Edgewood Publishing, 1888) 342–43.

55 William H. Smith diaries, vol. 2, MSS 13164, Special Collections, University of Virginia Libraries, Charlottesville VA; James W. Elliott, *Transport to Disaster* (New York: Holt, Rinehart, and Winston, 1962) 127–29. Lugenbeal had a genuine talent for survival. On his return home, he traveled on the ill-fated transport *Sultana*. When the ship exploded, he escaped by breaking open a crate that contained a live alligator. Lugenbeal killed the reptile with a bayonet and then used the crate as a makeshift lifeboat.

56 Marvel, *Andersonville*, 223, 231, 234; Ed Gleeson, *Rebel Sons of Erin: A Civil War Unit History of the 10th Tennessee Infantry (Irish) Confederate States Volunteers* (Indianapolis IN: Guild Press, 1999) 309–10; Futch, *History of Andersonville Prison*, 115. The men of the 19th Massachusetts/10th Tennessee/United States Volunteers qualified for pensions from both the State of Tennessee and the United States. The other defectors likely were the Irishmen, Englishmen, Germans, and Spaniards of [John Hampton] Brooks's foreign battalion and not the men who formed the Confederacy's 1st (Tucker's) Foreign Battalion/Regiment. The latter did likely include some survivors of Andersonville but from men who had transferred to other prisons. The men of Brooks's battalion were sent back to the Confederate prisons after trying to mutiny. Stewart Sifakis, *Compendium of the Confederate Armies: Kentucky, Maryland, Missouri, the Confederate Units and the Indian Units* (New York: Facts On File, 1995) 181, 187; Alexander A. Lawrence, *A Present for Mr. Lincoln: The Story of Savannah from Secession to Sherman* (Macon GA: Ardivan Press, 1961) 173–74.

57 Robert K. Sneden, *Eye of the Storm: A Civil War Odyssey*, ed. Charles F. Bryan, Jr., and Nelson D. Lankford (New York: Free Press, 2000) 210–13; Lynn, *800 Paces*, 74–75, 78. The two wagons were rented from W. N. Pickett. Marvel, *Andersonville*, 28. The prisoners named their new streets Broadway (also Main), Market, South, and Wall.

58 Marvel, *Andersonville*, 21.

59 Joseph Ferguson, *Life Struggles in Rebel Prisons* (Philadelphia: James M. Ferguson, 1865) 80.

60 "War Story of Soren Peterson," manuscript, State Historical Society of Wisconsin, Madison WI; "What a U. S. Officer says of Andersonville prison," *Advertiser and Register* (Mobile AL), 23 August 1865, 1; Wirz to L. B. Thomas, 21 January 1865, Wirz correspondence, entry 10 (ch. 9, vol. 227), War Department Collection of Confederate Records, RG 109, NARA; Lynn, *800 Paces*, 196; "The Eagle and the Wirz Trial," *Brooklyn Daily Eagle*, 9 October 1865, 2. The only known copy of the *Advertiser and Register* is manuscript 49–5017, Alabama Department of Archives and History, Montgomery AL.

61 Louis A. Brown, *The Salisbury Prison: A Case Study of Confederate Military Prisons, 1861–1865* (Wendell NC: Avera Press, 1980) 165–66; James McPherson, *Battle Cry of Freedom: The Civil War Era* (New York: Oxford University Press, 1988) 796–97, 802; Marvel, *Andersonville*, 92, 238–39.

62 H. L. Robinson, *Pittsfield, N. H. in the Great Rebellion* (Concord NH: Republican Press Association, 1893) 66; Emmy E. Werner, *Reluctant Witnesses: Children's Voices from the Civil War* (Boulder CO: Westview Press, 1998) 104; *Report on the Treatment of Prisoners of War by the Rebel Authorities* (Washington: Government Printing Office, 1869) 1096, 1124; Addison Erwin Sheldon, *Nebraska: The Land and the People*, 3 vols. (Chicago: The Lewis Publishing, 1931) 3: 357; John Worrell Northrop, *Chronicles From the Diary of a War Prisoner* (Wichita KS: Wining Printing, 1904) 67.

63 Evans, *Sherman's Horsemen*, 268–69; Northrop, *Chronicles*, 63, 109–10; Peggy Scott Holley, "The 7th Tennessee Volunteer Cavalry: West Tennessee Unionists in Andersonville Prison," *West Tennessee Historical Society Papers* 42 (December 1998): 39–58. The treatment of Tennessee Unionists at Andersonville may have influenced Andrew Johnson, as president of the United States, to deny Capt. Henry Wirz of Andersonville a pardon. Johnson had been the military governor of federally occupied Tennessee, and many of the Tennessee prisoners came from his East Tennessee.

64 Robert H. Kellogg, *Life and Death in Rebel Prisons* (Hartford CT: L. Stebbins, 1865) 243–44; *Macon* (GA) *Daily Telegraph*, 30 May 1864, 2; H. A. M. Anderson to Wirz, 13 May 1864, Wirz correspondence; R. T. Powell to governor of Alabama, 30 September 1894, 24th Alabama file, regimental files, Alabama Department of Archives and History, Montgomery AL; Richard Nelson Current, *Lincoln's Loyalists: Union Soldiers From the Confederacy* (Boston: Northeastern University, 1992) 215–17; Frederick H. Dyer, *A Compendium of the War of the Rebellion* (Des Moines: self-published, 1908) 11. Wiley C. Andrews, the one member of the 1st Georgia Battalion (USA) known to have been at Andersonville, survived. Daniel Cox of the same unit may have also survived Andersonville. A [James] Marion and William Weaver of the 1st Georgia State Troops Volunteers Cavalry Battalion (USA) also supposedly went to Andersonville and survived, but no records of their imprisonment have survived. Robert S. Davis, "White and Black in Blue: The Recruitment of Federal Units in Civil War North Georgia," *Georgia Historical Quarterly* 85/3 (Fall 2001): 362–64, 370; Ernest Parker, *Days Gone By: Gilmer County, Georgia* (Ellijay: Gilmer County Genealogical Society, 1999) 18–19, 217. For the soldiers of the 1st Alabama at Andersonville, see Glenda M. Todd, *First Alabama Cavalry, USA* (Bowie MD: Heritage Books, 1999).

65 Reuben C. Griffitt, *Six Months in Rebel Prisons* (Martinsville IN: Martinsville Republican, 1909) 26–27; S. S. Boggs, *Eighteen Months a Prisoner* (Lovington IL: self-published, 1889) 72; Marvel, *Andersonville*, 41–43, 155–56, 175; Robert E. Denny, *The Civil War Years* (New York: Sterling, 1992) 319; John David Smith, "Let Us All Be Grateful That We Have Colored Troops That Will Fight," in Smith, *Black Soldiers in Blue: African American Troops in the Civil War Era* (Chapel Hill: University of North Carolina Press, 1993) 49, 145. DNA tests strongly suggest that Thomas Easton Hemings, one of the African-American soldiers who died at Andersonville, had President Thomas Jefferson as a biological grandfather. Lynn, *800 Paces*, 172. As a consequence, the slave owner who wrote a declaration that all men had basic human rights had a grandson, through a slave woman, who died at "Andersonville in the war to make that declaration apply to all men." For the controversy around the Hemings children, see Jan Ellen Lewis and Peter S. Onuf, *Sally Hemings and Thomas Jefferson* (Charlottesville: University of Virginia Press, 1999) and Cynthia H. Burton, *Jefferson Vindicated: Fallacies, Omissions, and Contradictions in the Hemings Genealogical Record* (Keswick VA: self-published, 2005).

66 "Statements of Escaped Union Prisoners, Refugees, and Confederate Deserters," p. 47, Records of Continental Commands, RG 393, pt. 1, NARA. For a very different experience by African-American soldiers captured by the Confederacy see Robert S. Davis, "A Soldier's Story: The Records of Hubbard Pryor, 44th United States Colored Troops," *Prologue: The Quarterly of the National Archives* 31/4 (Winter 1999): 269–70.

67 Sneden, *Eye of the Storm*, 213.

68 "Statements of Escaped Union Prisoners, Refugees, and Confederate Deserters," p. 47, Records of Continental Commands, RG 393, pt. 1, NARA.

69 Ironically, John Wilkes Booth originally plotted to kidnap Abraham Lincoln in order to exchange him for an agreement that the United States government would resume the prisoner exchange. William A. Tidwell, James O. Hall, and David W. Gaddy, *Come Retribution: The Confederate Secret Service and the Assassination of Lincoln* (Jackson: University Press of Mississippi, 1988) 264.

70 Rebecca Latimer Felton, *Country Life in Georgia* (Atlanta: Index Printing Company, 1919) 85. In 1922, Felton became the first woman to serve in the United States Senate.

71 Consolidated report, 24 July 1864, in U.S. War Department, *The War of the Rebellion: A Compendium of the Official Records Union and Confederate Armies*, 128 vols. (Washington DC: Government Printing Office, 1898–1911) ser. 2, vol. 7, p. 493; Lynn, *800 Paces*, 253, 293–94, 298; William B. Hesseltine, *Civil War Prisons: A Study in War Psychology* (New York: Frederick Ungar, 1964) 133–58; Futch, *History of Andersonville Prison*, 11–29; James O. Hall, "Major Henry Wirz Again," *Surrat Courier* (January 1991), 6; Gordon B. Smith to author, 8 December 2003, in author's possession, Hanceville AL.

72 Dayton Pryor, *The Beginning and the End: The Civil War Story of Federal Surrenders Before Fort Sumter and Confederate Surrenders After Appomattox* (Bowie MD: Heritage Books, 2001) 379–80; Marvel, *Andersonville*, 233, 234.

73 Roberts, *Andersonville Journey*, 86; J. S. Lemmon, "The Last to Leave Andersonville," *NT*, 7 August 1884, 7; Lee Camp, "The Last of Andersonville," in vol. 15 of *Confederate Reminiscences and Letters, 1861–1865* (Atlanta: Georgia Division, United Daughters of the Confederacy, 1995) 55; Elliott, *Transport to Disaster*, 44–45; Futch, *History of Andersonville Prison*, 115–16; Ted and Hugh H. Genoways, eds., *A Perfect Picture of Hell: Eyewitness Accounts by Civil War Prisoners From the 12th Iowa* (Iowa City: University of Iowa Press, 2001) 252–53; Pryor, *The Beginning and the End*, 383; Marvel, *Andersonville*, 240. Robert S. Merrill reported seeing federal medical staff still unloading supplies at Andersonville on 5 May 1865. Robert S. Merrill diary, SPR471, Alabama Department of Archives and History, Montgomery AL.

74 L. P. Brockett, *Woman's Work in the Civil War: A Record of Heroism, Patriotism and Patience* (Philadelphia: Zeigler, McCurdy & Co., 1867) 372; "Returned Prisoners at Annapolis," *Burlington* (VT) *Hawk-Eye*, 24 December 1864, 1.

75 For the history of the Freedman's school at Andersonville see the issues of *The American Missionary* reproduced at Cornell University's "Making of America" Web site, http://cdl.library.cornell.edu/moa; Sheppard, *Andersonville Georgia USA*, 66–67; Grant, *The Way It Was*, 222, 226; and Hamilton W. Pierson, *A Letter to Hon. Charles Sumner with "Statements" of Outrages Upon Freedmen in Georgia, and an Account of my Expulsion from Andersonville, Ga., by the Ku Klux Klan* (Washington DC: Chronicle Print, 1870). Dykes reportedly sold the site of the prison cemetery, if he owned it, to a Mr. Gilbert in the North. Gilbert allegedly intended to sell the property for a profit to the government or otherwise exploit it. Dykes also unsuccessfully sued the United States government for wood taken by federal soldiers from the cemetery property after the war. Federal investigators, in responding to Dyke's claim, wrote "the Army at the capture of the prison, were not in a mood to ask anyone permission to occupy grounds made sacred by the sacrifice in cold blood of over 13,000 Union men.... Their humor would have been better suited by hanging claimant, who they might well have believed to have been an aide and abettor in those inhuman wrongs." *Benjamin B. Dykes v. United States*, "Brief for Defendants" and deposition of Capt. S. C. Greene, 13 July 1866; deposition of Maj. James M. Moore (11–12 December 1876), United States Court of Claims, general jurisdiction #10703, RG 123, NARA.

76 Marvel, *Andersonville*, 241, 248; Marvel, *Andersonville*, 241, 248; Capt. S. C. Greene to Capt. [?], 13 July 1866, Capt. H. R. Crossman to Maj. Gen. D. H. Rucker, 7 March 1868, deposition of Capt. A.W. Corliss, 15 January 1877, and deposition of Maj. James M. Moore, 11–12 December 1876, *Benjamin B. Dykes v. United States*, general jurisdiction #10703, United States Court of Claims, RG 123, and United States Court of Claims, #10703 (n.d.), entry 576; Records of the Quartermaster General, RG 92, NARA; Hamilton Pierson, *A Letter to Hon. Charles Sumner with "Statements" of Outrages upon Freedmen in Georgia, and an Account of my Expulsion from Andersonville, Ga., by the Ku Klux Klan* (Washington DC: Chronicle Print, 1870) 26–27. Among the bodies returned home for reburial was prisoner Vardy Lantman, according to his brother Warren, *Atlanta Constitution*, 29 June 1905, p. 11, c. 2-3. No records have been found that support Warren Lantman's story.

77 "Excerpt From a Letter Written by J. A. Tigner Regarding Andersonville Prison," in vol. 9 of *Confederate Reminiscences*, 243; "Andersonville," *NT*, June 1881, 43; "Twenty Years After," *NT*, 29 May 1883, 2; W. O. Johnston, "Andersonville," *NT*, 27 March 1890, 3, Brown, "Andersonville, Ga.," *NT*, 14 February 1889, 3; "Andersonville," *Hillsdale* (MI) *Standard*, 12 May 1868, 1; Webster, "A Jaunt in the South," 324–25; B. B. and Elizabeth Dykes to United States of America, 9 February 1875, Sumter County deed book Q (1873–1876), 293–94, microfilm roll 132/19, Georgia Archives, Morrow GA.

78 [no title], *Atlanta Constitution*, 27 September 1886, 2; Samuel Creelman, *Collections of a Coffee Cooler* (Pittsburgh: Pittsburgh Photo Engraving, 1890) 37; H. S. Beaman, "Another Comrade's Visit to Andersonville," *NT*, 10 May 1883, 7, "Twenty Years After," *NT*, 29 May 1883, 2; Brown, "Andersonville, Ga.," *NT*, 14 February 1889, 3; H. H. Lyman, "Andersonville," *NT*, 12 April 1888, 5; "Memorial Day at Andersonville," *NT*, 13 June 1889, 8; Mary A. Hovey, "A Recent Visit to Andersonville," *NT*, 25 October 1888, 3; "Andersonville Prison Purchased," *NT*, 5 June 1890, 2; "A Genuine Relic of Andersonville Prison," Boston Corbett Collection, Kansas State Historical Society, Topeka KS; Webster, "A Jaunt in the South," 324–25. Broadsides and pamphlets from such organizations as the Union Ex-Prisoners of War Association, Illinois Prisoner of War Association, Andersonville Survivors' Association, and Western Andersonville Survivors Association, can be found in the Boston Corbett Collection, Kansas State Historical Society, Topeka KS. Kinny G. "Jerry" Kennedy and George Washington "Wash" Kennedy were likely the same man. Sumter County (GA), pp. 379B-380, *Ninth Census of the United States (1870)* (National Archives microfilm M593, roll 174), Macon County (GA) Enumeration District 38, p. 579A, *Tenth Census of the United States (1880)* (National Archives microfilm T9, roll 156), Macon County (GA) Enumeration District 30, pp. 211A, *Twelfth Census of the United States (1900)* (National Archives microfilm T623, roll 210), Records of the Bureau of the Census, RG 28, NARA; G. W. Kennedy to J. W. Stone, 15 May 1890, deed, Sumter County (GA) deed book W (1890–1892), 673, microfilm roll 132/15, Georgia Archives, Morrow GA. For ghost stories about Andersonville see Nancy Roberts, *Civil War Ghosts and Legends* (Columbia: University of South Carolina Press, 1992) 10–23.

79 *Proceedings of the Department Encampment of Georgia GAR.* (Savannah: Times, 1891) 21–25, *Journal of the Sixth Annual Session of the Department Encampment of Georgia*… (Savannah: Braid & Sutton, 1894) 19–23, copies in the Minnesota Historical Society, Minneapolis MN; *Andersonville Prison Park—National Cemetery*, undated pamphlet in the Sumter County file, File 2 Counties, Georgia Archives, Morrow GA.

80 "Bullock at Andersonville," *Atlanta Constitution*, 4 June 1870, 1.

81 *Journal of the Tenth Annual Encampment of the Department of Georgia* (Atlanta: Eclipse Print, 1898) 14, copy at the Minnesota Historical Society Minneapolis MN; *Andersonville Prison Park—National Cemetery*, undated pamphlet in the Sumter County file, File II Counties, Georgia Archives, Morrow GA; Roberts, *Andersonville Journey*, 236–40; Louise F. Hays, *History of Macon County, Georgia* (Atlanta: Burke, 1933) 341; "In Vindication of Wirz," *Confederate Veteran* 17/4 (April 1909): 200; Celestine Sibley, "Lancaster's Appeal Defeats Wirz's Statute," *Atlanta Constitution*, 20 February 1958, 9; Lucian Lamar Knight scrapbooks, vol. 7, p. 153, Georgia Archives, Morrow GA; Sheppard, *Andersonville Georgia USA*, 58–65; [no title], *Durango* (CO) *Democrat*, 15 May 1909, 2. The UDC even failed to obtain an appropriation from the Georgia legislature in 1958 to have the monument repaired. In 1939, efforts to build a "peace monument" in the national cemetery that would unite North and South by presenting Southern excuses for Andersonville went nowhere. Lucian Lamar Knight scrapbooks, vol. 33, pp. 143–46.

82 "Capt. Wirz was a Martyr," *Augusta Chronicle*, 30 May 1909, 4. The text of these signs appeared in the *Atlanta Constitution*, 13 May 1906, 3. The sign on the hotel at the park gave statistics of deaths at different Civil War prisons.

83 *Andersonville Prison Park—National Cemetery*, undated pamphlet in the Sumter County file, File II Counties, Georgia Archives, Morrow GA; Guy Prentice and Marie C. Prentice, "Far from the Battlefield: Archaeology at Andersonville Prison," in Clarence R. Greier and Stephen R. Potter, eds., *Archaeological Perspectives on the American Civil War* (Gainesville: University Press of Florida, 2000) 176. The history of Andersonville since the Civil War has extensive additional documentation in the vertical files of the Hargrett Rare Books and Manuscripts Library of the University of Georgia Libraries, Athens GA.

84 Sheppard, *Andersonville Georgia USA*, 79–80; Andrew S. Chancey, "Race, Religion, and Agricultural Reform: The Communal Vision of Koinonia Farm," in John C. Inscoe, ed., *Georgians in Black and White: Explorations in the Race Relations of a Southern State, 1865–1950* (Athens: University of Georgia Press, 1994) 246–65.

CHAPTER TWO

85 An earlier version of this essay appeared as "Escape From Andersonville: A Study in Isolation and Imprisonment" in *Journal of Military History* 67/4 (October 2003): 1065–82.

86 Deposition of Henry Clay Damon, 25 July 1864, Henry Clay file, 11th Michigan Infantry compiled service records, and headquarters' diary, pp. 205–6, papers of Gen. George H. Thomas, General's Papers, Records of the Adjutant General, Record Group (RG) 94, National Archives and Records Administration (NARA), College Park MD. Robert K. Sneden claimed that the prisoners actually had only three pistols, two of which belonged to the camp's bandits. Robert Knox Sneden memoirs, vol. 5, p. 632, Virginia Historical Society, Richmond VA.

87 Pension claim of Henry C. Damon, application 299,113, certificate 259,832, Records of the Veterans Administration, RG 15, NARA.

88 William T. Sherman, *Memoirs of General William T. Sherman*, 2 vols. (New York: Appleton, 1875) 2: 112.

89 "Rev. George W. Nelson's Narrative," *Southern Historical Society Papers* 1/4 (April 1876): 253. The publications based upon escapee information included the United States Sanitary Commission, *Narrative of Privations and Sufferings of the United States Officers and Soldiers While Prisoners of War in the Hands of the Rebel Authorities* (Philadelphia: King and Baird, 1864); and Records of the United States Senate, Joint Committee on the Conduct of the War, *Returned Prisoners* (Washington DC: Government Printing Office, 1864), RG 46, NARA. For the story of the "Immortal 600" Confederate prisoners see Mauriel P. Joslyn, *Immortal Captives* (Shippensburg PA: White Mane, 1996); and James Robert McMichael file, Civil War Miscellany Collection, Georgia Archives, Morrow GA.

90 William D. Love, *Wisconsin in the War of the Rebellion* (Chicago: Church & Goodman, 1866) 1039; *Trial of Henry Wirz* (Washington: Government Printing Office, 1868) 301–6; Jasper Culver memoirs in the possession of Jan Botkin Thorkidsen of Arvada CO. Culver continues to testify against Wirz as a major character in the award-winning play *Andersonville Trial* by Saul Levitt.

91 Douglas Gibson Gardner, "Andersonville and American Memory: Civil War Prisoners and Narratives of Suffering and Redemption," (Ph.D. diss., Miami University, 1998) 234; John C. Inscoe, "'Escaping Through Deserter Country': Fugitive Account of the Inner Civil War in Southern Appalachia," in Kenneth W. Noe and Shannon H. Wilson, eds., *The Civil War in Appalachia: Collected Essays* (Knoxville: University of Tennessee Press) 159; Love, *Wisconsin in the War of the Rebellion*, 1039; *Trial of Henry Wirz*, 301–6. For more on Civil War escapes in general see Frances Harding Casstevens, *"Out of the Mouth of Hell": Civil War Prisons and Escapes* (Jefferson NC: McFarland & Co., 2005) and Robert E. Denny, *Civil War Prisons & Escapes: a Day by Day Chronicle* (New York: Sterling Publishing, 1993).

92 Ted and Hugh H. Genoways, eds., *A Perfect Picture of Hell: Eyewitness Accounts by Civil War Prisoners From the 12th Iowa* (Iowa City: University of Iowa Press, 2001) 6–8.

93 Gardner, "Andersonville and American Memory," 233–34.

94 Charles M. Smith, "From Andersonville to Freedom," (1894) in vol. 8 of *Military Order of the Loyal Legion of the United States* (Wilmington NC: Broadfoot, 1991–) 87–156; Charles M. Smith, "Escape From Andersonville Prison in 1864," *Potter County Historical Society Quarterly Bulletin* 47 (January 1978): n. p.; "Personal and Social," *Atlanta Journal*, 29 March 1889, 4.

95 William B. Hesseltine, *Civil War Prisons: A Study in War Psychology* (New York: Frederick Ungar, 1964) 249–50; Gardner, "Andersonville and American Memory," 104, 238–39; William N. Tyler, *The Dispatch Carrier* (Port Byron IL: Globe, 1892) 1; Morgan E. Dowling, *Southern Prisons: Or Josie the Heroine of Florence* (Detroit: William Graham, 1870); Ralph O. Bates, *Billy and Dick From Andersonville Prison to the White House* (Santa Cruz CA: Press Sentinel Publishing, 1910) 1, 97–99; William Coyle, *Ohio Authors and Their Books* (Cleveland: World Publishing, 1962) 38–39; Allen Nevins, James I. Robertson, Jr., and Bell I. Wiley, eds., *Civil War Books: A Critical Bibliography*, 2 vols. (Baton Rouge: Louisiana State University Press, 1967) 1:186, 190. The Dowling book may have been based in part upon the real experience of Mary Rawson and soldier Peter Kiene. Testimony of Mary Rawson, *United States v. Henry Wirz*, file MM2975, p. 1695, Records of the Judge Advocate General, RG 153, NARA. Escapes from Andersonville remains a popular subject for fiction, as shown in MacKinley Kantor's Pulitzer Prize-winning novel *Andersonville*; the motion picture *Andersonville*; and the book *Journey to Freedom* by William Dennis Sheehan. For failed plans on a movie on that theme in 1973 see "*Escape From Andersonville* filming slated in 2 Weeks," newspaper clipping in Andersonville vertical file, Hargrett Rare Books and Manuscripts Library, University of Georgia Libraries.

96 Robert C. Doyle, *A Prisoner's Duty: Great Escapes in U. S. Military History* (Annapolis: Naval Institute Press, 1997) 6, 8–9.

97 C. A. Frazer, "Marion County Prisoner of Rebels Kept Diary in Andersonville Prison," newspaper clipping from the *Evening Sentinel* (Centralia IL) in the possession of Bob and Margie Goldsby, available on the Jesse Altom Web site, http://www.stkusers.com/lindas/jesse.html; J. Madison Drake, "Fast and Loose in Georgia," in Patrick Allen, ed., *Literary Savannah* (Athens GA: Hill Street Press, 1998) 63–65; Warren L. Goss, *The Soldier's Story of His Captivity at Andersonville* (Boston: Lee and Shepard, 1867) 162, 173, 177–78.

98 Amos E. Stearns, *Narrative of Amos E. Stearns* (Worcester MA: Franklin P. Rice, 1887) 38; William Marvel, *Andersonville: The Last Depot* (Chapel Hill: University of North Carolina Press, 1994) 203; John Worrell Northrop, *Chronicles From the Diary of a War Prisoner* (Wichita KS: Wining Printing, 1904) 67.

99 T. C. Jackson to Josie Jackson, 30 May 1864, William P. Palmer Collection, Western Reserve Historical Society, Cleveland OH.

100 John W. Urban, *Battle Field and Prison Pen* (Edgewood NJ: Edgewood Publishing, 1882) 338; Lessel Long, *Twelve Months in Andersonville* (Huntington IN: self-published) 69; John L. Ransom, *Andersonville Diary, Escape, and List of Dead* (New York: n. p., 1881) 68–69. For accounts of prisoners faking the wearing of the ball and chains see "Edward W. Boate: a Federal Report," *Journal of Confederate History* 13 (1995): 73–74.

101 Stephen E. Payne memoir, Illinois State Historical Library, Springfield IL; H. C. Brown, "At Andersonville Prison," *National Tribune* (Washington DC) hereafter *NT*, 31 August 1922, 2; Henry B. Sparks diary, Indiana Historical Society, Indianapolis IN; Herman A. Braun, *Andersonville: An Object Lesson on Protection* (Milwaukee WI: C. D. Fahsel, 1892) 21; *Sumter Republican* (Americus GA), 22 April 1864, 3; Samuel Gfruerer, "Union Soldier Defends Memory of Wirz," 1905 article in Andersonville vertical file, Hargrett Rare Books and Manuscripts Library, University of Georgia Libraries, Athens GA; Lonnie R. Speer, *Portals to Hell: Military Prisons of the Civil War* (Mechanicsburg PA: Stackpole Books, 1997) 261; Free Lance, "Southern Prison Life," *NT*, 5 August 1882, 2. The prison eventually had sixteen cannons although no more than eight were permanently positioned on the stockade. Marvel, *Andersonville*, 263, n. 46, 283, n. 27; *Trial of Henry Wirz*, 331.

102 Harry G. Boyd, "Civil War Prisoners of War: A Study of the Changes in Disposition of Federal and Confederate Prisoners of War, Between the Shelling of Fort Sumter and the Surrender at Appomattox Courthouse," (Ph.D. diss., California State University, Fullerton, 1992) 181–82; Marvel, *Andersonville*, 38.

103 Quoted in Bernard F. Blakeslee, *History of the 16th Connecticut Volunteers* (Hartford CT: Case, Lockwood & Brainard, 1875) 49.

104 H. Clay Hartwell, "As to the Dead-Line," *NT*, 27 September 1883, 5.

105 Henry E. Olinger diary, 29 June 1864 and William H. Smith diaries, vol. 2, MSS 13164, Special Collections, University of Virginia Libraries, Charlottesville VA.

106 James Jennings memoir, Illinois State Historical Library, Springfield IL.

107 Reuben C. Griffitt, *Six Months in Rebel Prisons* (Martinsville IN: Martinsville Republican, 1909) 10–12. Amos Stearns also remembered that the drummer boys wore tin stars on their caps to indicate their status as prisoners on parole. Stearns, *Narrative of Amos E. Stearns*, 23.

108 Northrop, *Chronicles*, 173; Ransom, *Andersonville Diary, Escape, and List of Dead*, 68–69; Robert K. Sneden, *Eye of the Storm: A Civil War Odyssey*, ed. Charles F. Bryan, Jr., and Nelson D. Lankford (New York: Free Press, 2000) 219.

109 Bernard F. Blakeslee, *History of the 16th Connecticut Volunteers* (Hartford CT: Case, Lockwood & Brainard, 1875) 99; Joseph S. Keen, *Experiences in Rebel Prisons* (Detroit: Detroit Free Press, 1890) 24, 42; Northrop, *Chronicles*, 173; Griffitt, *Six Months in Rebel Prisons*, 76; Memoirs of Samuel E. Preston, State Library of New York, Albany NY; Jasper Culver memoir in the possession of Jan Botkin Thorkidsen of Arvada CO. Culver's group crossed paths with Spring and his comrades. Spring, like Culver, testified at the trial of Confederate Capt. Henry Wirz.

110 Joseph P. Cangemi and Casimir J. Kowalski, eds., *Andersonville Prison: Lessons in Organizational Failure* (Lanham MD: University Press of America, 1992) 14–15; Richard F. Hemmerlein, *Prisons and Prisoners of the Civil War* (Boston: Christopher, 1934) 92–93; Griffitt, *Six Months in Rebel Prisons*, 43; John L. Maile, *Prison Life in Andersonville* (Los Angeles: Grafton, 1912) 32; Sergeant Oats [John B. Vaughter], *Prison Life In Dixie* (Chicago: Central Book Concern, 1880) 101–2; Marvel, *Andersonville*, 64, 89–91, 153; Norton P. Chipman, *The Tragedy of Andersonville*, 2nd ed. (San Francisco: self-published, 1911) 247–48, 262. For the use of dogs in hunting slaves see Frederick Law Olmstead, *The Cotton Kingdom*, ed. Arthur M. Schlesinger (New York: Alfred A. Knopf, 1953) 386–87.

111 Free Lance, "Southern Prison Life," *NT*, 9 September 1882, 2.

112 John McElroy, *Andersonville: A Story of Rebel Military Prisons* (Toledo: D. R. Locke, 1879) 181–83; Maile, *Prison Life in Andersonville*, 33–34; Joseph E. Lopez, *Capture, Escape and Re-capture of Joseph E. Lopez* (n. p., n. d) 15. A copy of the Lopez memoir can be found in the US Army Military History Collection, Carlisle PA.

113 H. M. Davidson, *Fourteen Months in Southern Prisons* (Milwaukee: Daily Wisconsin Printing House, 1865) 242–305.

114 Hugh R. Snee memoirs, Andersonville National Historic Site, Andersonville GA.

115 Daniel G. Kelley, *What I Saw and Suffered in Rebel Prisons* (Buffalo: Mathews and Warren, 1866) 60; Melvin Grigsby, *The Smoked Yank* (1881; n. p., 1912) 126–28; Ovid L. Futch, *History of Andersonville Prison* (Gainesville: University of Florida Press, 1968) 53–54; Griffitt, *Six Months in Rebel Prisons*, 73–74; George A. Hitchcock, *From Ashby to Andersonville*, ed. Ronald G. Watson (Campbell CA: Savas Publishing, 1997) 245; Anonymous, "Fourteen Months in Prison," MSS 5:1 Un3:8, Virginia Historical Society, Richmond VA.

116 Futch, *The History of Andersonville Prison*, 77, 81, 120; *The Daily Mississippian* (Selma AL), 3 August 1864, 1; Winder to Samuel Cooper, 24 June 1864, U.S. War Department, *The War of the Rebellion: A Compilation of the Official Records of the Union and Confederate Armies*, 128 vols. (Washington DC: Government Printing Office 1880–1901) ser. 2, vol. 7, pp. 410–11; Blakey, *General John H. Winder, CSA*, 187. The only known issue of the *Daily Mississippian* is at Petersburg National Battlefield Park, Petersburg VA.

117 Marvel, *Andersonville*, 193–94; Wirz to R. B. Thomas, 17 January 1865, entry 11, RG 109, NARA; L. P. Brockett, *Woman's Work in the Civil War: A Record of Heroism, Patriotism and Patience* (Philadelphia: Zeigler, McCurdy & Co., 1867) 96, 105.

118 Ambrose Spencer, *A Narrative of Andersonville* (New York: Harper & Brothers, 1866) 34–35, 97–98, 109; "Reminiscences," in vol. 1 of *Confederate Reminiscences and Letters, 1861–1865* (Atlanta: Georgia Division, United Daughters of the Confederacy, 1995) 99.

119 Monroe County Historical Society, *Monroe County, Georgia: A History* (Forsyth GA: self-published, 1979) 155; "Escaped Prisoners Recaptured," *Daily Columbus* (GA) *Enquirer*, 1 September 1864, 2.

120 John W. Lynn, *800 Paces to Hell: Andersonville* (Fredericksburg VA: Sergeant Kirkland's Museum, 1999) 77; John R. Tate, "Rebels Could Not Keep Him," *NT*, 22 July 1897, 2; memoirs of Aaron Bachman, Richmond National Battlefield Park, Richmond VA. The "Z. T. Walker" may have been George Thomas Walker, the ten-year-old son of William and Dorenda Walker of Macon County, who frequently visited Andersonville and who fed escaped prisoners for months. He had three older sisters. Alice Walker Lovelace, "Reminiscences," in vol. 2 of *Confederate Reminiscences*, 57; Macon County GA, p. 53, *Eighth Census of the United States (1860)* (National Archives microfilm M653, roll 130), RG 29, NARA.

121 Northrop, *Chronicles*, 173. Brumer and Hoyt were captured by the Confederates near New Bern NC and returned to Andersonville.

122 Keen, *Experiences in Rebel Prisons*, 49–50; Lopez, *Capture, Escape and Re-capture*, 4–5, 10–15.

123 Martha Shepherd Hill, "Lucy Lewis Herrington, a Patriotic Confederate Woman" in vol. 8 of *Confederate Reminiscences*, 79.

124 Marvel, *Andersonville*, 73, 139, 145–46, 158–61, 172, 219, 229–30, 302–3; Wirz to R. B. Thomas, 9 January 1865, Henry Wirz letter book, 18 May 1864 to 19 March 1865, pt. 1, entry 10 (chapter 11, vol. 227), War Department collection of Confederate Records, RG 109, NARA; Free Lance, "Southern Prison Life," *NT*, 5 August 1882, 2. A Mary Rawson of Atlanta resettled in Iowa during the Summer of 1864. Excerpts from her diary at the Atlanta History Center, however, do not mention Andersonville. Micki Waldrop, Atlanta History Center, to author, 27 April 2001, in the possession of the author, Hanceville AL.

125 Claim of Adam R. Head, commutations of rations claims, entry 139B, Records of the Commissary General of Prisoners, RG 249, NARA; "Statement of an Escaped Union Prisoner," *Nashville* (TN) *True Union*, 25 August 1865, 2; Chipman, *The Tragedy of Andersonville*, 151–52; *Trial of Henry Wirz*, 357; McElroy, *Andersonville*, 139–41; Marvel, *Andersonville*, 7, 194–96, 243–44.

126 Smith, "From Andersonville to Freedom," 8:87–156; *Trial of Henry Wirz*, 43–66; Smith, "Escape From Andersonville Prison"; Walton County (FL), pp. 944, 951, 966, 991, *Eighth Census of the United States (1860)* (National Archives microfilm M653, roll 109), RG 28, NARA.

127 Each of these compilations contain names not found on other lists. Most of these records are in Records of the Commissary General of Prisoners, RG 249, NARA, which also has the claims the soldiers filed for lost rations and related correspondence. For other lists see Union Prisoners Escaped From the CSA in Records of Continental Commands, RG 363, pt. 1, NARA. Contemporary newspaper accounts and other credible sources include names of escapees not found on any of these lists.

128 "Original Register of Federal Prisoners of War Confined at Andersonville, Ga. 1864–5," *Selected Records of the War Department Commissary General of Prisoners of War Confined at Andersonville, Georgia, 1864–65* (National Archives microfilm M1303 roll 1), RG 249, NARA. Jack Lundquist has recently replaced the old Andersonville database with more accurate lists of the names. An official accounting of the number of individual prisoners placed the total at 44,882. Historian William Marvel, however, points out that this number counts some prisoners transferred from and back to Andersonville two and even three times, inflating the total by more than 3,000 men. Marvel, *Andersonville*, 305, n. 72. Lowering the total number of individual prisoners raises the mortality rate from the official percentage of 28.12 percent to over 31.58 percent and even 35 percent, depending on which number of dead is used in the calculation. The claim that Andersonville held 60,000 individual prisoners has no support in the records.

129 Including at the Macon County GA Chamber of Commerce Web site: http://www.montezuma-ga.org/chamber/plookup.htm.

130 For accounts of escaping from the trains, see "Statements of Escaped Union Prisoners, Refugees, and Confederate Deserters," entry 4294, Records of Continental Commands, RG 393, pt 1, NARA. The fictional film rendering of an 1863 Mississippi raid, *The Horse Soldiers*, presents the classic example of the notoriety of Andersonville. The characters have serious discussions of their fate if captured and sent to that infamous prison, even though the prison and its Andersonville name would not exist until several months later!

131 Consolidated return, August 1864, *OR*, ser. 2, vol. 7, p. 70; morning reports, 1 April 1864, (National Archives microfilm M1303, roll 6), RG 249, NARA; "The Prison Camp of Southwestern Georgia," *Macon* (GA) *Daily Telegraph*, 30 April 1864, 2.

132 See for example Charles Fosdick, *Five Hundred Days in Rebel Prisons* (Blythe Dale MO: self-published, 1887) 40; deposition of Prescott Tracy, H. C. Higginson, and Silvester Noirot in S. S. Boggs, *Eighteen Months a Prisoner under the Rebel Flag* (Lovington IL: self-published, 1889) 68 ; Thomas Hinds, *Tales of War Times* (Watertown NY: Herald, 1904) 80.

133 McElroy, *Andersonville*, 292; George W. Rumble, "Escaped From Andersonville," *NT*, 27 December 1923, 7; W. F. Lyon, *In and Out of Andersonville Prison* (Detroit: George Harland, 1907) 50.

134 Register of prisoner escapes, vol. 1, RG 249, NARA; Fiosdick, *Five Hundred Days*, 32; Boggs, *Eighteen Months a Prisoner*, 68.

135 Spencer, *A Narrative of Andersonville*, 271; morning reports (National Archives microfilm M1303, roll 6), RG 249, NARA. This chart apparently gave historian Ovid L. Futch the number of escapes as 329. Futch, *History of Andersonville Prison*, 49, 115. Former inmate Frank W. Smith claimed that Confederate sources placed the number of men who escaped at 340. Smith, *Smith's "Knapsack" of Facts and Figures, '61 to '65* (Toledo: Spear, Johnson, & Co., 1884) 34.

136 Consolidated report, July 1864, *OR*, ser. 2, vol. 7, pp. 517–18; Hemmerlein, *Prisons and Prisoners of the Civil War*, 15; morning reports (National Archives microfilm M1303, roll 6), RG 249, NARA; William H. Smith diaries, vol. 1, 18 October 1864, MSS 13164, Special Collections, University of Virginia Libraries, Charlottesville VA.

137 Marvel, *Andersonville*, 203.

138 Lopez, *Capture, Escape and Re-capture*, 13; Marvel, *Andersonville*, 203.

139 "Captive's Tales Handed Down," *Los Angeles Times*, 16 October 1955, H6; Richard Thatcher, "Boston Corbett's Prison Life," Boston Corbett Collection, Kansas State Historical Society, Topeka KS; pension claim of Adam Fornof, application 443,916, certificate 317, 763, RG 15, NARA. J. K. P. Ferrell was "recaptured" at a veterans' meeting in 1912 by former Andersonville officer Alfred Judson. "Is a Prisoner in Fraternity," *Los Angeles Times*, 8 September 1912, 16.

140 Diary of William Morgan Davies, in the possession of Barbara J. Carter, Poughkeepsie NY.

141 Hinds, *Tales of War Times*, 90–143.

142 "The Situation," *New York Herald*, 12 October 1864; Hiram S. Daskam, *The Adventures of an Escaped Andersonville Prisoner* (Hammond IN: C. B. Harrold, n. d.) 13–16.

143 Note in the diary of Harkness N. Lay in the possession of Richard D. Goff, Corpus Christi TX.

144 Michael Heiman, "Fighting Them Over," *NT*, 3 September 1896, 3 and 10 September 1896, 3; Frazer, "Marion County Prisoner of Rebels Kept Diary in Andersonville Prison"; Marvel, *Andersonville*, 237–38.

145 Griffitt, *Six Months in Rebel Prisons*, 16; Hinds, *Tales of War Times*, 83; Long, *Twelve Months in Andersonville*, 58–59; Boyd, "Civil War Prisoners of War," 87; Speer, *Portals to Hell*, 338; George Mussen memoirs, p. 20, Indiana Historical Society, Indianapolis IN; morning reports (National Archives microfilm M1303, roll 6), RG 249, NARA.

146 Pension of Lawrence LeBron, application 589,066, certificate 611,608, RG 15, NARA.

147 "The Prisoners in Georgia," *New York Herald*, 18 September 1864, 4.

148 A. J. Barker, *Prisoners of War* (New York: Universe Books, 1975) 147; Shimon Tzabar, *The White Flag Principal: How to Lose a War and Why* (London: The Penguin Press, 1972) 128–30; John Hope Franklin and Loren Schweninger, *Runaway Slaves: Rebels on the Plantation* (New York: Oxford University Press, 1999) 274–75.

149 David Healey, "Back Roads: Few Escaped From Fort Delaware," *Blue & Gray* 19 (April 2002): 28–29; "The Need of Troops," *Janesville* (WI) *Weekly Gazette*, 29 July 1864, 2; "Statements of Escaped Union Prisoners, Refugees, and Confederate Deserters," entry 4294, RG 393, pt. 1, NARA.

150 Simon Miltimore Dufur, *Over the Dead Line; or, Tracked by Blood-Hounds* (Burlington VT: Free Press, 1902) 109.

151 "Kansas Vet Escaped From Andersonville," *NT*, 18 December 1930, 6; H. C. Brown, "At Andersonville Prison," *NT*, 31 August 1922, 2; Ransom T. Powell, "Brave Little Red Cap," *NT*, 12 October 1882, 1; pension application of DeLayvan R. Streeter, certificate 966221, RG 15, and service record of the same, 100th Ohio Infantry, RG 94, NARA; Roster Commission, in vol. 7 of *Official Roster of the Soldiers of the State of Ohio* (Cincinnati: Ohio Valley Press, 1888) 426; Lynn, *800 Paces*, 19; *Trial of Henry Wirz*, 505.

152 John R. Tate, "Rebels Could Not Keep Him," *NT*, 22 July 1897, 3.

153 Deposition of John R. Porter, depositions of scouts, deserters, and prisoners of war, entry 874, pt. 4, RG 393 Records of Continental Commands, NARA; William Elsey Connelley, vol. 3 of *A Standard History of Kansas and Kansans* (Chicago: Lewis, 1918) 1263.

154 Mussen memoirs, pp. 21–33.

155 Register of prisoner escapes, volume 1, RG 249, NARA; claim of Josiah Dye, commutation of rations claims. For the difficulties of reaching the federal fleet off the Georgia coast, see Thomas G. Dyer, *Secret Yankees: The Secret Circle in Confederate Atlanta* (Baltimore: John Hopkins University Press, 1999) 138.

156 Morning reports (National Archives microfilm M1303, roll 6), RG 249, NARA.

157 "From Camp Sumter," *Macon* (GA) *Daily Telegraph*, 7 May 1864, 2; "Tunnels and Traitors," *Blue & Gray Magazine* 3 (December–January 1985–1986): 53; Joseph Williams to Robert Williams, 16 July 1864, Robert Williams Collection, MS 12, Hargrett Rare Books and Manuscripts Library, University of Georgia Libraries, Athens GA.

158 Consolidated return, June 1864, *OR*, ser. 2, vol. 7, p. 438; "Escaped Prisoners Recaptured," *Daily Columbus* (GA) *Enquirer*, 1 September 1864, 2; Smith, *Smith's "Knapsack,"* 32–33; John Harrold, *Libby, Andersonville, Florence* (Philadelphia: Wm. B. Selheimer, 1870) 57; Mussen memoirs, p. 18; James Madison Page, *The True Story of Andersonville Prison* (New York: Neale Publishing, 1908) 143–46. The *Kendell County (IL) Record*, 24 September 1864, 2 includes a description of Andersonville from an anonymous soldier of the 4th Illinois Cavalry who tunneled out.

159 "Our Trip to Andersonville," *Albany* (GA) *Patriot*, 19 May 1864, 2.

160 Frank Daniel, "The Mention of Andersonville Ignites Miss Pepper's Temper," *Atlanta Journal*, 15 December 1959, 27; Griffitt, *Six Months in Rebel Prisons*, 72–73; Robert H. Kellogg, *Life and Death in Rebel Prisons* (Hartford CT: L. Stebbins, 1865) 98; Hinds, *Tales of War Times*, 81–82, 87–88; Dufur, *Over the Dead Line*, 133–34; Cangemi and Kowalski, *Andersonville Prison*, 14–15; Charles Richardson, *Story of a Private* (Milwaukee: George Richardson, 1897) 58; Sergeant Oats [John B. Vaughter], *Prison Life In Dixie* (Chicago: Central Book Concern, 1880)_103.

161 Goss, *The Soldier's Story*, 162, 173, 177–78; McElroy, *Andersonville*, 411; Lynn, *800 Paces*, 200–2. For the psychological benefits of building tunnels see Barker, *Prisoners of War*, 151–52.

162 Northrop, *Chronicles*, 107–8; H. C. Saint-Pierre, "Appearance of the Devil," *NT*, 26 February 1902, 2.

163 "Tamaroa, Ill., Holds One of Two Men Who Escaped War Prison," unidentified newspaper clipping in William L. Farmer file, Southern Illinois University Museum, Carbondale IL.

164 Braun, *Andersonville*, 50; Aaron Bachman memoir, Richmond National Battlefield Park.

165 "The Prison Camp of Southwestern Georgia," *Macon* (GA) *Daily Telegraph*, 30 April 1864, 2; morning reports (National Archives microfilm M1303, roll 6), RG 249, NARA; "Letter From Surgeon Van Aernam," *Cattaraugus Freeman* (Ellicottville NY), 18 August 1864, 2; Henry B. Sparks diary; in vol. 9 of *Confederate Reminiscences*, 244; Marvel, *Andersonville*, 203; Chipman, *The Tragedy of Andersonville*, 266; consolidated return, June and August 1864, *OR*, ser. 2, vol. 7, pp. 438, 708; Jasper Culver memoir, Jan Botkin Thorkidsen, Arvada CO.

166 Michael Dougherty, *Prison Diary of Michael Dougherty* (Bristol PA: Charles A. Dougherty, 1908) 45; George H. Fonner data, Civil War Plymouth Pilgrims Descendants Society, http://home.att.net/~ewppds/homepage.htm; "The Prisoners in Georgia," *New York Herald*, 18 September 1864, 4; consolidated return, August 1864, *OR*, ser. 2, vol. 7, p. 708.

167 M. V. B. Phillips, *Life and Death in Andersonville* (Chicago: T. B. Arnold, 1887) 44–45; Robert Knox Sneden memoirs, p.44. One of these escapees was likely later prominent Colorado newspaperman David F. Day. George Vest Day, "Memoirs of the Dave Day Family," in Donald L. Griswold, ed., *The 1961 Brand BookP* (Denver: Denver Westerners, 1962) 146.

168 McAdams, *Every-day Soldier Life*, 322–23; McElroy, *Andersonville*, 411; Marvel, *Andersonville*, 191; "Original Register of Federal Prisoners," (National Archives microfilm M1303 roll 1), RG 249, NARA; John C. Power, *History of the Early Settlers of Sangamon County, Illinois* (Sangamon County IL: Edwin A. Wilson, 1876) 96; G. E. Sabre, *Nineteen Months A Prisoner of War* (New York: American News Company, 1865) 105; Chipman, *The Tragedy of Andersonville*, 233; Dufur, *Over the Dead Line*, 130–32.

169 C. A. Smith, *Recollections of Prison Life* (Muscatine IA: R. A. Holmes, 1875) 30; William Burge, *Through the Civil War and Western Adventures* (n. p., n. d.) 41–44; McElroy, *Andersonville*, 139–41; Ransom T. Powell, "Brave Little Red Cap," *NT*, 19 October 1882, 7.

170 "Return," *Rochester* (NY) *Daily Democrat*, 17 October 1864, in the G. W. Rumble file, Andersonville National Historic Site; deposition of Henry Clay Damon, 25 July 1864, Henry Clay Damon compiled service records; Lynn, *800 Paces*, 203. Englishman James Gillespie escaped by the same means but he suffered recapture near the federal lines. Frances H. Casstevens, *"Out of the Mouth of Hell": Civil War Prisons and Escapes* (Jefferson NC: McFarland & Company, 2005) 185.

171 "Lawrence LeBron, Grant's Trusted Scout, a Chicago Letter Carrier," *Sunday Record-Herald* (Chicago), 19 May 1901, n. p. LeBron anonymously published his adventures in a booklet for young people as *Adventures of Buckskin the Scout* (Omaha: Rural Weekly, n. d.). He claimed to have been well-known to General Grant as a scout, but he appears nowhere in William B. Feis, *Grant's Secret Service: The Intelligence War from Belmont to Appomattox* (Lincoln: University of Nebraska Press, 2002). LeBron also does not appear in the Andersonville prison records although he is mentioned in a copy of the memoirs of prisoner James Jennings in the Illinois State Historical Library, Springfield IL.

172 Peter Liberty, "How They Got Out," *NT*, 14 February 1895, 3.

173 Jasper Culver memoir, Jan Botkin Thorkidsen, Arvada CO; *Delaware County* (PA) *American*, 21 December 1864; McAdams, *Every-day Soldier Life*, 322–23; Marvel, *Andersonville*, 191; "Personating the Dead," *Washington Post*, 9 June 1890, 4.

174 Blakeslee, *History of the 16th Connecticut Volunteers*, 99; "Original Register of Federal Prisoners," (National Archives microfilm M1303 roll 1), RG 249, NARA.

175 Register of prisoner escapes, vol. 1, RG 249, NARA; "News From the Gulf," *New York Herald*, 24 November 1864, 4; "Experiences of Thomas Cheshire During the Civil War," typescript, Dallas Public Library, Dallas TX.

176 Edward F. Roberts, *Andersonville Journey* (Shippensburg VA: Burd Street Press, 1998) 21. The slave workers at Andersonville suffered special punishments from the guards although to what extent remains unknown. On 10 December 1864, "Negro Jack" received fifty-one lashes "for telling lies about Mrs. Hunt," a white female prisoner. Rebecca Latimer Felton saw where a guard had shot a slave for saying something offensive. William H. Smith diary, Special Collections, University of Virginia, Charlottesville VA; Rebecca Latimer Felton, *Country Life in Georgia* (Atlanta: Index Printing Company, 1919) 85.

177 George P. Rawick, ed., vol. 9 of *The American Slave: A Composite Autobiography* (Westport CT: Greenwood Publishing, 1972) 182; Futch, *History of Andersonville Prison*, 77.

178 For the background of this painting, see Marc Simpson, *Winslow Homer: Paintings of the Civil War* (San Francisco: Bedford Arts, 1988) 241–45; and Gardner, "Andersonville and American Memory," 61–83.

179 Sallie Clayton, *Requiem for a Lost City: a Memoir of Civil War Atlanta and the Old South*, ed. Robert S. Davis (Macon: Mercer University Press, 1999) 85.

180 Larry Gara, *The Liberty Line: The Legend of the Underground Railroad* (Lexington: University of Kentucky Press, 1961) 7, 37; Wilbur H. Siebert, *The Underground Railroad From Slavery to Freedom* (1898, repr., New York: Arno Press, 1968) 378. Also see Carol Wilson, *Freedom at Risk: The Kidnapping of Free Blacks in America, 1780–1865* (Lexington: University Press of Kentucky, 1994).

181 William W. Freehling, *The South vs. The South: How Anti-Confederate Southerners Shaped the Course of the Civil War* (Oxford: University Press, 2000) 26–27, 85; Fergus M. Bordewich, *Bound for Canaan: The Underground Railroad and the War for the Soul of America* (New York: Amistad, 2005) 5; Hesseltine, *Civil War Prisons*, 249; David Williams, "'The Faithful Slave is About Played Out': Civil War Slave Resistance in the Lower Chattahoochee Valley," *Alabama Review* 52/2 (April 1999): 98–100; Edmund L. Drago, "How Sherman's March Through Georgia Affected the Slaves," *Georgia Historical Quarterly* 57/3 (Fall 1973): 361–75; James M. McPherson, *The Negro's Civil War* (New York: Ballantine Books, 1991) 56; Lynn, *800 Paces*, 205. For self emancipation during the Civil War also see Armistead L. Robinson, *Bitter Fruits of Bondage: The Demise of Slavery and the Collapse of the Confederacy, 1861–1865* (Charlottesville: University of Virginia Press, 2005).

182 Walter L. Williams, "The 'Sambo' Deception: The Experience of John McElroy in Andersonville Prison," *Phylon* 39/3 (Fall 1978): 261–63. Medal of Honor winner and Andersonville survivor David F. Day would provide free advertising for his local African Methodist church, which responded by making him its one white member. He also provided Thanksgiving dinner each year for his African-American acquaintances because of the aid given to him by slaves when he escaped from Andersonville and Florence prisons. "Thanksgiving," *Durango* (CO) *Democrat*, 26 November 1908, 4, and "This is Gratitude," *Durango* (CO) *Democrat*, 13 November 1909, 3. He claimed to have been well known to Gen. Grant, but he appears nowhere in Feis, *Grant's Secret Service: The Intelligence War from Belmont to Appomattox* (Lincoln: University of Nebraska Press, 2002).

183 E. Merton Coulter, *Travels in the Confederate States: A Bibliography* (Baton Rouge: Louisiana State University Press, 1994) 66.

184 Hinds, *Tales of War Times*, 90–143; "Homicide," *Macon* (GA) *Daily Telegraph*, 21 June 1864, 2. For the story of the mill workers sent to the North, see Michael D. Hitt, *Charged with Treason: Ordeal of 400 Mill Workers During Military Operations in Roswell, Georgia 1864–1865* (Monroe NY: Library Research Associates, 1992). "Mr. Graham" may have been Josiah Graham. Dekalb County (GA), p. 336, *Eighth Census of the United States (1860)* (National Archives microfilm M653, roll 119), Records of the Bureau of the Census, RG 28, NARA. He was likely related to the notorious blind slave trader William H. Graham of Stone Mountain who died at the hands of one of his abused servants in 1853. The slave hanged. Franklin M. Garrett, *Atlanta and Its Environs*, 2 vols. (Boston: Lewis Publishing, 1954) 1:358.

185 Register of Prisoners, vol. 1, RG 249, NARA; Pension of Richard Holmes, widow's application 536,561, certificate 375,735, RG 15, NARA.

186 Lynn, *800 Paces*, 210–11; Kellogg, *Life and Death in Rebel Prisons*, 185; *Trial of Henry Wirz*, 121, 125–27, 130–31, 146, 520–21, 543, 557, 673, 679, 715–16. "Frado" may have been the Vincenzo Bardo who later testified for Capt. Wirz's defense. Seemingly everyone at Andersonville not a native of the United States, a German, or an Irishman, went by the nickname "Frenchy." *Trial of Henry Wirz*, 510, 516. Jim Mallory may have been the soldier referred to by an anonymous veteran as having escaped and been recaptured five times. Free Lance, "Southern Prison Life," *NT*, 9 September 1882, 2. English prisoner James Gillespie, however, had a similar experience with his escape attempts. Casstevens, *"Out of the Mouth of Hell,"* 185–86, 190.

187 Marvel, *Andersonville*, 96–97; McElroy, *Andersonville*, 471–85.

188 Civil War pension file of Cassius M. Ellis, certificate 205157, RG 15, NARA; E. R. Ellis, *Biographical Sketches of Richard Ellis* (Detroit: W. Graham Print Co., 1888) 210.

189 John Burke, "Trials of a Prisoner," *NT*, 17 May 1923, 4; Albert J. Perry, *History of Knox County, Illinois: Its Cities, Towns and People* (Chicago: S, J. Clarke, 1912) 873.

190 Samuel Griswold, "Aunt Peny," in vol. 7 of *Confederate Reminiscences*, 43–45.

191 Memoirs of Hugh R. Snee, Andersonville National Historic Site.

192 Ed Gleeson, *Rebel Sons of Erin: A Civil War Unit History of the 10th Tennessee Infantry (Irish) Confederate States Volunteers* (Indianapolis IN: Guild Press, 1999) 309–10; "Escaped Federal Prisoner Arrested by a Woman," *Daily Columbus* (GA) *Enquirer*, 4 September 1864, 1; Daskam, *Adventures*, 11–35; memoirs of Daniel Bond, Newberry Library, Chicago IL; Luther S. Dickey, *History of the 103d Regiment, Pennsylvania Veteran Volunteer Infantry* (Chicago: L. S. Dickey, 1910) 88–89; Marvel, *Andersonville*, 223, 236, 300.

193 Dickey, *History of the 103d Regiment*, 88–89.

194 E. N. Gilpin diary, 23 April 1865, Manuscripts Division, Library of Congress, Washington DC.

195 Claim of John Wallace, commutation of rations claims, entry 139B, Records of the Commissary General of Prisoners, RG 249, NARA; Marvel, *Andersonville*, 221–22, 300. For the story of the *Sultana* see William O. Bryant, *Cahaba Prison and the Sultana Disaster* (Tuscaloosa: University of Alabama Press, 1990); Jerry O. Potter, *The Sultana Tragedy: America's Greatest Maritime Disaster* (Gretna LA: Pelican Publishing Company, 1992); and the *Sultana* records in Records of the Commissary General of Prisoners, RG 249, NARA.

196 Coulter, *Travels in the Confederate States*, 66, 152.

197 See, for example, the files of Theodore Bradley (Records and Pension Document file 704431) and Harlan P. Eggleston (Enlisted Branch file EAK-142-1869), Records of the Judge Adjutant General, RG 94, NARA. John B. Hotchkiss of Brooklyn NY escaped from Andersonville with a plan to escape to Cuba from a southern port as a sailor. Lost in the swamps, he became deranged and forgot his past. Hotchkiss did not recover until 1888, when he "awoke" upon reading a history of his family in New York. He had lived for decades as a prosperous plantation owner in Key West FL named John Schooner. "Curious War Stories," *Atlanta Constitution*, 28 April 1888, 2. For the story of amnesia victim William Newby, see Stuart McConnell, "The William Newby Case and the Legacy of the Civil War," *Prologue: The Quarterly of the National Archives* 30/4 (Winter 1998): 247–56.

198 "Lawrence LeBron, Grant's Trusted Scout."

199 Pension claim of John Bolton, application 431,853, certificate 553,473, widow's application 123,766, certificate 964,389, RG 15, and Names and some of the data taken from List of Prisoners Who Escaped, vol. 1, entry 109, RG 249, NARA; Grigsby, *The Smoked Yank*, 154. Lela Tindle, "Whatever Became of Boston Corbett?" *Civil War Times Illustrated* 30 (May–June 1991): 48–57; Boston Corbett file, WALZ-1325–1865, Enlistment Branch Records, RG 94, NARA. Samuel W. Ordell escaped from a marriage in 1911 when he sued for divorce on the grounds that his time at Andersonville was more pleasant than living with his wife's house pets. "35 Cats Drive Him to Sue," *The Washington Post*, 22 December 1911, 1.

CHAPTER THREE

200 An edited version of this essay appeared as "Guarding Andersonville: A Story of Georgians and the Civil War" in *The Historical Society of the Georgia National Guard Journal* 9 (Fall/Winter 2002/2003): 12–19.

201 L. M. Park, "Andersonville Prison," *Central Georgia Genealogical Society* 22/1 (January 2000): 14; *Trial of Henry Wirz* (Washington: Government Printing Office, 1868) 432; "Our Trip to Andersonville," *Albany* (GA) *Patriot*, 19 May 1864, 2. The service records of the guards have been microfilmed as *Compiled Service Records of Confederate Soldiers Who Served in Organizations From the State of Georgia* (National Archives microfilm M266). L. M. Park's file is on roll 132.

202 William Marvel, *Andersonville: The Last Depot* (Chapel Hill: University of North Carolina Press, 1994) 34, 50–51, 263; "Our Trip to Andersonville," *Albany* (GA) *Patriot*, 19 May 1864, 2. The 57th Georgia began the war in May 1862 as the 2nd Infantry Regiment, Georgia State troops, before becoming the 54th Georgia Confederate Volunteer Infantry and, in early 1863, the 57th. They surrendered at Vicksburg but, almost immediately, they received an exchange. In December 1863, some of its companies proved mutinous and threatened to escape to the North. Alexander A. Lawrence, *A Present for Mr. Lincoln: The Story of Savannah from Secession to Sherman* (Macon GA: Ardivan Press, 1961) 151–52. For examples of men from other units escorting new prisoners to Andersonville, see James Miller Wysor to George Washington Wysor, 7 August 1864, James Miller Wysor Collection, MSS 2 W9965 b, Virginia Historical Society, Richmond VA; and Robyn Williams Doyle, "Leonard Thompson Doyle," in vol. 9 of *Confederate Reminiscences and Letters, 1861–1865* (Atlanta: Georgia Division, United Daughters of the Confederacy, 1997) 37, and Irene Patterson, "William Henry Kitchens," in vol. 8 of *Confederate Reminiscences*, 83.

203 Marvel, *Andersonville*, 167; Ovid L. Futch, *History of Andersonville Prison* (Gainesville: University of Florida Press, 1968) 88, 94; C. B. Harkie file, *Compiled Service Records of Confederate Soldiers Who Served in Organizations From the State of Georgia* (National Archives microfilm M266, roll 530). Information on Col. Harkie also comes from Bruce Allardice, who is preparing to publish a book of biographies of Confederate colonels; also see Willard E. Wight, "Colonel Cyrus B. Harkie: A Troubled Military Career," in James I. Robertson, Jr., and Richard M. McMurray, eds., *Rank and File: Civil War Essays in Honor of Bell Irvin Wiley* (San Rafael CA: Presidio Press, 1976) 79–91.

204 Marvel, *Andersonville*, 21, 47–48, 219–20; *Trial of Henry Wirz*, 449; R. D. Chapman, "A Georgia Soldier, CSA," *Confederate Veteran* 38/9 (September 1930): 347–48, 472; Futch, *History of Andersonville Prison*, 54–56; John McElroy, *Andersonville: A Story of Rebel Military Prisons* (Toledo: D. R. Locke, 1879) 156–59, 191–92. The compiled service records of the 55th Georgia show that some of their number also worked as carpenters, called "mechanics," at erecting the buildings at Andersonville. See for example the J. H. Sullivan and George P. Sutherlin files in *Compiled Service Records of Confederate Soldiers Who Served in Organizations From the State of Georgia* (National Archives microfilm M266, roll 533).

205 Ambrose Spencer, *A Narrative of Andersonville* (New York: Harper & Brothers, 1866) 34–35; Marvel, *Andersonville*, 84; John W. Lynn, *800 Paces to Hell: Andersonville* (Fredericksburg VA: Sergeant Kirkland's Museum, 1999) 27–28, 140–41, 238–39.

206 *Trial of Henry Wirz*, 432. Allen Daniel Candler (1834–1910) served as lieutenant colonel and later colonel of the Fourth Georgia Reserves, after having been a private in the 34th Georgia Confederate Infantry Regiment. Although stationed at Andersonville, he would lose an eye at the Battle of Jonesboro on 1September 1864. Candler later served as congressman, secretary of state, governor, and compiler of historical records for Georgia. Lillian Henderson, comp., *Roster of the Confederate Soldiers of Georgia, 1861–1865*, 6 vols. (Hapeville: Longino & Porter, 1960) 3:824; Elizabeth H. Marshall, "Allen Daniel Candler," in Kenneth Coleman and Charles Stephen Gurr, eds., *Dictionary of Georgia Biography*, 2 vols. (Athens: University of Georgia Press, 1983) 2:162–63.

207 T. Conn Bryant, *Confederate Georgia* (Athens: University of Georgia Press, 1953) 89; Charles Fosdick, *Five Hundred Days in Rebel Prisons* (Blythe Dale MO: self-published, 1887) 61–63; Day, *Fifteen Months in Dixie*, 31–32; Marvel, *Andersonville*, 62–63.

208 Dr. David F. Cross, in "Why did the Yankees die at Andersonville?," *North & South Magazine* 6 (September 2003): 23–32, argues that hookworm proved especially deadly among the prisoners at Andersonville because of confinement in the southern climate.

209 Lynn, *800 Paces*, 295; Ezra Hoyt Ripple, *Dancing Along the Deadline*, ed. Mark A. Snell (Novato CA: Presidio Press, 1996) 42–43; Cross, "Why did the Yankees die at Andersonville?," 27–31.

210 William Burson, *A Race for Liberty* (Wellsville OH: G. W. Foster, 1867) 33; B. F. Jones, "Rebel Prisons," *National Tribune* (Washington DC) hereafter *NT*, 19 May 1904; Charles Richardson, *Story of a Private* (Milwaukee: George Richardson, 1897) 50.

211 "The Georgia Reserves Under Wirz," *Chicago Daily Tribune*, 6 March 1888, 1.

212 Day, *Fifteen Months in Dixie*, 31–32.

213 For the ages of the members of the garrison (15 to 18 and 45 to 50) also see *Trial of Henry Wirz*, 449; and L. M. White, "Reminiscences of the War Between the States," in vol. 6 of *Confederate Reminiscences*, 15.

214 Fosdick, *Five Hundred Days*, 26–27.

215 At least one instance exists of the children of guards from the Georgia Reserves marrying after the war, even though the families were from opposite ends of Georgia. Two guard accounts, those of James Ormond and B. L. McGough in the Civil War Miscellany Collection of the Georgia Archives, provide detailed information on Andersonville, as does the memoir of L. M. Parks. For more information on the guards, see chapter 7 of Lynn, *800 Paces*.

216 "A Gold Watch Presented to an Officer at Andersonville," *Athens* (GA) *Banner*, 26 April 1912, 8; Augustus C. Hamlin, *Martyriaor, Andersonville Prison* (Boston: Lee & Shephard, 1866) 53–54; William H. Smith diaries, vol. 1, MSS 13164, Special Collections, University of Virginia Libraries, Charlottesville VA. For a sample of letters like those described by Hamlin, see the T. J. Jackson letters in the Palmer Collection, Western Reserve Historical Collection, Cleveland OH. For examples of positive and long-term relations between prisoners and guards see Roy F. Jones, "Joe Carson," in vol. 9 of *Confederate Reminiscences*, 29; and D. C. Smith to W. D. Hammond, 11 October 1911, D. C. Smith Papers, AC 76323, Georgia Archives, Morrow GA.

217 Futch, *History of Andersonville Prison*, 86–88.

218 Wayne Dobson, "All Were Prisoners There," in *Andersonville: The Southern Perspective*, ed. J. H. Segars, (Atlanta: Southern Heritage Press, 1995) 150; *Trial of Henry Wirz*, 438; Marvel, *Andersonville*, 71. A roster of Furlow's battalion is in box 2, 3337–10, Record Group 22–1–75, Georgia Archives, Morrow GA.

219 U.S. War Department, *The War of the Rebellion: A Compendium of the Official Records Union and Confederate Armies*, 128 vols. (Washington DC: Government Printing Office, 1898–1911) ser. 2, vol. 7, pp. 552–53; Marvel, *Andersonville*, 285 n. 47.

220 Civilian visitors also stood between the cannons and the stockade.

221 For the weapons owned by Georgia civilians in 1864, see the original militia enrollment lists on microfilm in drawer 245, boxes 4–10, Georgia Archives, Morrow GA.

222 Marvel, *Andersonville*, 29, 50, 172–73; Edward F. Roberts, *Andersonville Journey* (Shippensburg VA: Burd Street Press, 1998) 43; Futch, *History of Andersonville Prison*, 56.

223 Arch Frederic Blakey, *General John H. Winder, CSA* (Gainesville: University of Florida Press, 1990) 178.

224 Five Confederate civilians were also buried at Andersonville prison. Deposition of Capt. S. C. Greene, 13 July 1866, *Benjamin B. Dykes v. United States*, United States Court of Claims, general jurisdiction #10703, RG 123, National Archives and Records Administration (NARA), College Park MD. Eventually the bodies received a transfer to Oak Grove Cemetery in Americus GA. The women of Americus paid for the removal with funds they had raised for a Confederate monument.

225 Lyman S. Shreeve, *The Hamlin Family* (Exira IA: self-published, 1902) 893.

226 *Trial of Henry Wirz*, 115, 438, 449; Harry G. Boyd, "Civil War Prisoners of War: A Study of the Changes in Disposition of Federal and Confederate Prisoners of War, Between the Shelling of Fort Sumter and the Surrender at Appomattox Courthouse," (Ph.D. diss., California State University, Fullerton, 1992) 159; Fosdick, *Five Hundred Days*, 26; Marvel, *Andersonville*, 21, 47–48, 215–16, 219–20; Futch, *History of Andersonville Prison*, 54–56; James L. Dunn to wife, 25 September and 5 November 1864, James Langstaff Dunn Collection, MSS 8301, Special Collections, University of Virginia Libraries, Charlottesville VA.

227 D. T. Chandler to R. H. Chilton, 5 August 1864, in *OR*, ser. 2, vol. 7, pp. 548–49, 552; David Williams, *Rich Man's War* (Athens: University of Georgia Press, 1998) 169–70; Winder to Howell Cobb, 9 July 1864, in Ulrich B. Phillips, ed., *The Correspondence of Robert Toombs, Alexander H. Stephens, and Howell Cobb* (Washington: American Historical Association, 1970) 644–45; Lynn, *800 Paces*, 206; Andersonville and unit files, Civil War Miscellany Collection, Georgia Archives, Morrow GA; *Trial of Henry Wirz*, 458; "Escape From Andersonville," *Atlanta Constitution*, 20 March 1891, 2.

228 Robert K. Sneden, *Eye of the Storm: A Civil War Odyssey*, ed. Charles F. Bryan, Jr., and Nelson D. Lankford (New York: Free Press, 2000) 253; Free Lance, "Southern Prison Life," *NT*, 5 August 1882, 2; John Worrell Northrop, *Chronicles From the Diary of a War Prisoner* (Wichita KS: Wining Printing, 1904) 72; John L. Ransom, *Andersonville Diary, Escape, and List of Dead* (New York: n. p., 1881) 65; Morgan E. Dowling, *Southern Prisons: Or Josie the Heroine of Florence* (Detroit: William Graham, 1870) 129–30; Marvel, *Andersonville*, 85; Lynn, *800 Paces*, 309; Sneden memoirs, vol. 5, p. 557, Virginia Historical Society, Richmond VA; William H. Smith diaries, vol. 1, 9 October 1964, MSS 13164, Special Collections, University of Virginia Libraries, Charlottesville VA.

229 Marvel, *Andersonville*, 198, 216, 219, 226; Robert Duncan Chapman, *A Georgia Soldier* (Houston: Robert L. Sonfield, Jr., 1994) 77–81; Francis Marion Blalock, "Some of My Experiences and Observations as a Southern Confederate Soldier," in vol. 17 of *Confederate Reminiscences*, 156–57.

CHAPTER FOUR

230 An earlier version of this essay appeared as "Limber Jim of Andersonville: A Note on Annotation" in *Documentary Editing* 24/3 (Summer 2002): 69–73.

231 Daniel J. Czitrom, in *Media and the American Mind* (Chapel Hill: University of North Carolina Press, 1982) discusses the growth of communication on the American media.

232 Ted and Hugh H. Genoways, eds., *A Perfect Picture of Hell: Eyewitness Accounts by Civil War Prisoners From the 12th Iowa* (Iowa City: University of Iowa Press, 2001) 6–8.

233 For the history of the Andersonville literary genre see Douglas Gibson Gardner, "Andersonville and American Memory: Civil War Prisoners and Narratives of Suffering and Redemption," (Ph.D. diss., Miami University, 1998).

234 Discussions of the history of false identity can be found in Karen Halttunen, *Confidence Men and Painted Women: A Study of the Middle-class Culture in America, 1830–1870* (New Haven: Yale University Press, 1982); Simon Worrall, *The Poet and the Murderer* (New York: Penguin and Putnam, 2002); John F. Kasson, *Rudeness & Civility: Manners in Nineteenth-century Urban America* (New York: Noonday Press, 1991); Kathleen De Grave, *Swindler, Spy, Rebel: The Confidence Woman in Nineteenth-century America* (Columbia: University of Missouri Press, 2002); Clive Cheesman and Jonathan Williams, *Rebels, Pretenders, & Imposters* (New York: St. Martin's Press, 2000); and John Q. Newman and Trent Sands, eds., *The Encyclopedia of Altered and False Identity* (San Diego: Index Publishing Group, 1996). Use of distance and multiple identities for crime occurred in the South by the 1830s. James Lal Penick, Jr., *The Great Western Land Pirate: John A. Murrell in Legend and History* (Columbia: University of Missouri Press, 1981) 5–6.

235 James H. Madison, "The Evolution of Commercial Credit Reporting Agencies in Ninteenth-century America," *Business History Review* 48/2 (Spring 1974): 164–86. Allan Pinkerton himself serves as a classic example of the man who escaped his past and repeatedly reinvented himself, as explained in James Mackay, *Allan Pinkerton: The First Private Eye* (New York: John Wiley & Sons, 1996).

236 A few of many examples, from *General Index to Pension Files, 1861–1934* (National Archives microfilm T287), include Peter Kiene (aka Keine), James McAnally (aka Nally), Jacques Roellinger (aka Jacques Cermann), and Wilson Jeffers (aka Jefferson Davis). For women assuming male identities before and during the Civil War see Elizabeth D. Leonard, *All the Daring of the Soldier: Women of the Civil War Armies* (New York: W. W. Norton, 1999) and DeAnne Blanton and Lauren M. Cook, *They Fought Like Demons: Women Soldiers in the American Civil War* (Baton Rouge: Louisiana State University Press, 2002).

237 Leo W. Faller and John L. Faller, *Dear Folks at Home*, ed. Milton E. Flower (Carlisle PA: Cumberland County Historical Society, 1963) 130; Melvin Grigsby, *The Smoked Yank* (1881; n. p., 1912) 116–17.

238 Grigsby, *The Smoked Yank*, 116–18; James Madison Page, *The True Story of Andersonville Prison* (New York: Neale Publishing, 1908) 102; Thomas O'Dea, *Andersonville Prison* (n. p., n. d.); Ezra Hoyt Ripple, *Dancing Along the Deadline*, ed. Mark A. Snell (Novato CA: Presidio Press, 1996) 33; J. S. Maltman, "Andersonville Prison," *Michigan University Magazine* 2/4 (Fall 1867): 347.

239 Quote in Basil Meek, *Twentieth Century History of Sandusky County* (Chicago: Richmond-Arnold, 1909) 920; William H. Smith diaries, vol. 1, 16 October 1864, MSS 13164, Special Collections, University of Virginia Libraries, Charlottesville VA. Wirz had given empty commissary barrels to the cook, James Duncan, to distribute to the prisoners for use in preventing wells from caving in and men from falling into the wells in the dark. William Marvel, *Andersonville: The Last Depot* (Chapel Hill: University of North Carolina Press, 1994) 90.

240 Herman A. Braun, *Andersonville: An Object Lesson on Protection* (Milwaukee WI: C. D. Fahsel, 1892) 40; *Trial of Henry Wirz* (Washington: Government Printing Office, 1868) 558–61; W. B. Hibbs, "Andersonville," *National Tribune* (Washington DC) (hereafter *NT*), 23 February 1888, 4; John Worrell Northrop, *Chronicles From the Diary of a War Prisoner* (Wichita KS: Wining Printing, 1904) 56. Guard J. A. Tigner remembered that Masons were among the prisoners allowed outside of the stockade until 4 P.M. each day, upon taking a Masonic oath not to escape. These men could trade for food and bring the provisions back with them into the stockade. "Excerpt From a Letter Written by J. A. Tigner Regarding Andersonville Prison" in vol. 9 of *Confederate Reminiscences and Letters, 1861–1865* (Atlanta: Georgia Division, United Daughters of the Confederacy, 1997) 244.

241 The street gangs of New York and the pre-Civil War Andersonville type of environment from which they emerged receives discussion in Herbert Asbury, *The Gangs of New York* (New York: Alfred A. Knopf, 1927).

242 Leroy L. Key, "Raiding in the Andersonville Prison," *New York Times*, 11 December 1864, 4; Henry C. Cox, "Six Months in Andersonville Prison," *Educational Bi-Monthly* 8 (April–June 1914): 293–94; James Burton diary (MSS 120), 22 May 1864, and James L. Hoster diary (MSS 7), p. 91, Special Collections, Woodruff Library, Emory University, Atlanta GA; Robert K. Sneden, *Eye of the Storm: A Civil War Odyssey*, ed. Charles F. Bryan, Jr., and Nelson D. Lankford (New York: Free Press, 2000) 220–22, 233–35.

243 For examples from the history of all of these illegal activities see Frank Browning and John Gerassi, *The American Way of Crime* (New York: G. P. Putnam's Sons, 1980).

244 Key, "Raiding in the Andersonville Prison"; Burton diary, 29 June 1864; William H. Lute, "The Raiders in Andersonville," *NT*, 18 December 1890, 4. Lute identified C. C. McCain of the 2nd Ohio Cavalry as a jury member in the trial of the raiders but, as shown in Appendix A, McCain does not appear on the jury list.

245 For Urban's/Dowd's account of the incident see John W. Urban, *Battle Field and Prison Pen* (Edgewood NJ: Edgewood Publishing, 1882) 327–31.

246 Hoster diary, 91–92, 94. As James Madison Page pointed out in *True Story of Andersonville Prison*, the federal government's campaign of vilification of Capt. Wirz continued after his execution to the point that many of the writers, including McElroy, rewrote history to leave out Wirz's role in suppressing the raiders.

247 *Daily Intelligencer* (Adrian MO), 6 December 1915, n. p.; Newspaper clipping from the *New York Mercury*, 20August 1865, in file Apz 479 (EB) 1865, entry 409, Records of the Adjutant General, Record Group (hereafter RG) 94, National Archives and Records Administration (NARA), College Park MD; "Death of `Hanging Judge," *The Washington Post*, 16 January 1916, MS1; J. J. Osborne, "Andersonville Raiders," *NT*, 23 September 1897, 2; William H. Lute, "The Raiders in Andersonville," *NT*, 18 December 1890, 4; Robert P. McRae, "The Andersonville Raiders," *NT*, 4 November 1890, 3; Faller and Faller, *Dear Folks at Home*, 128–129. Higginson acquired the name of "Romeo" from his ability to quote Shakespeare. For more information on Pete McCullough see Scott E. Sallee, "'Big Pete' McCullough: The Hanging Judge of Andersonville," *Blue & Gray* 22 (Summer 2003): 22–25.

248 John McElroy, *Andersonville: A Story of Rebel Military Prisons* (Toledo: D. R. Locke, 1879) 239; Michael Hileman memoirs in the possession of Harold D. Hileman and posted on the Web site EHistory; Key, "Raiding in the Andersonville Prison"; Ovid Futch, "Andersonville Raiders," *Civil War History* 2/4 (December 1956): 47–60; C. D. Bibbins, "Saw Raiders Hung," *NT*, 24 May 24, 1923, 7; Leverett C. Stevens, "A Forelorn Hope," in vol. 40 of *Military Order of the Loyal Legion of the United States*, (Wilmington NC: Broadfoot, 1997) 29–30; undated deposition of James Coon, Civil War pension of Hiram Grow, certificate 577301, Records of the Veterans Administration, RG 15, NARA; Faller and Faller, *Dear Folks at Home*, 130–31; unidentified memoir, Andersonville file, Civil War Miscellany Collection, Georgia Archives, Morrow GA. Contrary to the impressions made about what visitors see today, the graves of the raider leaders were unmarked and lost for many years. P. Craham, "Andersonville," *NT*, 16 May 1907, 6. A drawing of the execution of the raiders, by an Andersonville survivor, appears in Sneden, *Eye of the Storm*, 246. Sneden's original memoirs, at the Virginia Historical Society, also include detailed drawings of the gallows.

249 "The Eagle and the Wirz Trial," *Brooklyn Daily Eagle*, 9 October 1865, 2; Henry E. Olinger diary, 11 July 1864, William H. Smith diaries, vol. 2, MSS 13164, Special Collections, University of Virginia Libraries, Charlottesville VA.

250 "Execution at Andersonville," *NT*, 19 April 1923, 7; "The Eagle and the Wirz Trial," *Brooklyn Daily Eagle*, 9 October 1865, 2; Free Lance, "Southern Prison Life," *NT*, serialized on 5 August 1882, 2; 12 August 1882, 2; and 9 September 1882, 2; Thomas W. Cooker, "Another Reminiscence of Andersonville," *NT*, 21 December 1882, 2; *Trial of Henry Wirz*, 652–53; Sneden, *Eye of the Storm*, 234, 296; Marvel, *Andersonville*, 144.

251 Quoted in "The Eagle and the Wirz Trial," *Brooklyn Daily Eagle*, 9 October 1865, 2.

252 McElroy, *Andersonville*, 292; Ransom T. Powell, "Brave Little Red Cap," *NT*, 9 November 1882, 7; Charles F. Hopkins, "Hell and the Survivor," *American Heritage* 33 (October/November 1982): 84.

253 Testimony of George W. Fechter, trial of Henry Wirz, file MM2975, Records of the Bureau of Military Justice, RG 153, NARA; Robert Knox Sneden memoir, vol. 5, p. 540, Virginia Historical Society. Fechter testified at the trial of Henry Wirz that Jim Limber regularly brought into the camp eggs and other goods acquired from civilians and guards for sale to prisoners. For negative opinions of Fechter and Ellis see Marvel, *Andersonville*, 108–9.

254 Michael Regan, "Limber Jim," *NT*, 7 April 1887, 4.

255 James H. Buckley diary, Illinois State Historical Library; "Original Register of Federal Prisoners of War Confined at Andersonville, Ga. 1864–5," *Selected Records of the War Department Commissary General of Prisoners of War Confined at Andersonville, Georgia, 1864–65* (National Archives microfilm M1303, roll 1), Records of the Commissary of Prisoners, RG 249, NARA.

256 *Daily Intelligencer* (Adrian MO), 6 December 1915, n. p.; "Hanged For Being Hungry," unidentified 1890 newspaper article in Louis Manigault Scrapbook, Southern Historical Collection, University of North Carolina, Chapel Hill NC. Nichols's obituary also states that he was shunned by fellow prisoners for his role as the executioner. He was later one of the Michigan troopers paid for the capture of Jefferson Davis. Abel Wadsworth Payne was also eulogized as the executioner of the raiders. C. D. Bibbins, "Saw Raiders Hung," *NT*, 24 May 1923, 7.

257 See Leroy L. Key's narrative in McElroy, *Andersonville*, 471–85.

258 R. Randolph Stevenson, *The Southern Side; or, Andersonville Prison* (Baltimore: Turnbull Brothers, 1876) 140. The prisoners beat upon an Irishman for, while dispensing rations, clubbing a prisoner. Limber Jim may be the man standing on the ration wagon in a photograph made by Andrew J. Riddle. Marvel, *Andersonville*, 185.

259 W. B. Smith, *On Wheels and How I Came There* (New York: Hunt & Eaton, 1893) 228–29; Robert P. Black, "Another View," *NT*, 7 September 1916, 7; W. B. Hibbs, "Andersonville," *NT*, 23 February 1888, 4.

260 William H. Smith diaries, vol. 1, 11 December 1864, MSS 13164, Special Collections, University of Virginia, Charlottesville VA; testimony of George W. Fechter, *United States v. Henry Wirz*, file MM2975, Records of the Bureau of Military Justice, RG153, NARA.

261 George Plumleigh diary, 10 January 1865, Algonquin Historic Commission, Algonquin IL. None of the men identified as Limber Jim appear in the records of the prisoners of the 113th Illinois at Andersonville. Most, if not all of the men of this unit held at Andersonville were captured at Guntown MS on 10 June 1864.

262 Marvel, *Andersonville*, 96, 273–74, n. 10.

263 David Evans, *Sherman's Horsemen* (Bloomington: Indiana University Press, 1996) 268–69; Robert H. Kellogg, *Life and Death in Rebel Prisons* (Hartford CT: L. Stebbins, 1865) 243–44; H. A. M. Anderson to Wirz, 13 May 1864, Wirz correspondence, entry 10 (ch. 9, vol. 227), War Department Collection of Confederate Records, RG 109, NARA; Northrop, *Chronicles*, 63, 109–10; Peggy Scott Holley, "The 7th Tennessee Volunteer Cavalry: West Tennessee Unionists in Andersonville Prison," *West Tennessee Historical Society Papers* 42 (December 1998): 39–58; R. T. Powell to governor of Alabama, 30 September 1894, 24th Alabama file, regimental files, Alabama Department of Archives and History, Montgomery AL.

246 McElroy, *Andersonville*, 227; "The Andersonville Raiders," *NT*, 4 November 1897, 3.

265 McElroy, *Andersonville*, 227; Page, *The True Story of Andersonville Prison*, 113. Goss described Limber Jim with almost the same words. Warren L. Goss, *The Soldier's Story of His Captivity at Andersonville* (Boston: Lee and Shepard, 1867) 116. Even the physical descriptions seem to suffer from misidentification. The large, big built, Limber Jim seems to refer to the 6-foot 2-inch Leroy Key or perhaps to Peter "Big Pete" Aubrey. Other accounts describe Limber Jim as thin and long-limbed.

266 Frederick H. Dyer, *A Compendium of the War of the Rebellion* (Des Moines: self-published, 1908) 1076; Civil War pension of James McLaughlin, application 1298290, certificate 1148600, Records of the Veterans Administration, RG 15, NARA.

267 Hoster diary, 92.

268 Compiled service record of James McLaughlin, 1st Illinois Light Artillery, RG 94, NARA; Civil War pension of James McLaughlin.

269 Herman J. Peters, "Mercy of Wirz," *NT*, 10 March 1904, 3.

270 Meek, *Twentieth Century History of Sandusky County*, 920–21.

271 Curtis H. Terry, "Who Limber Jim Was," *NT*, 25 November 1897, 2.

272 Free Lance, "Southern Prison Life," *NT*, 5 August 1882, 2; Hoster, "Adventures of a Soldier," 92.

273 Dr. Karen Walker to author, 6 March 2002, in the author's possession, Hanceville AL, 20 September 2003; Powell, "Brave Little Red Cap," *NT*, 7 November 1882, 7; Grigsby, *The Smoked Yank*, 117; Albert Webster, Jr., "A Jaunt in the South," *Appleton's Journal* (13 September 1873): 324. President Jefferson and Varina Davis took in an abused mulatto orphan boy named Limber Jim. For an example of another "Limber Jim" see *United States v. Samuel Merrick, alias Limber Jim*, NRFF-21–3W51–319–5, National Archives Southwest Region, Fort Worth TX. Coincidently (?), a Mexican gambler and "disreputable person" named Rodolfo "Limber Jim" Buelna were killed in Hollister CA in 1882. "A Test Case," *Hollister Democrat*, 3 February 1882, 2.

274 *Trial of Henry Wirz*, 568–571. George W. Fechter presents another example of identity at Andersonville. Federal prosecutors at the trial of Henry Wirz and some writers since have questioned the credibility of Fechter, pointing out that, contrary to his testimony, no Fechter served in the federal Kentucky forces. Confederates under Maj. George M. Jesse, however, captured the 1st Kentucky Mounted Infantry (Col. Robert Morris), as Fechter stated, at New Castle KY on 21 September 1862, before the federal army could formally accept the regiment and create any muster rolls for it. George W. Fechter, born around 1839 in Baden, Germany, claimed to have worked as a coach maker in Cincinnati OH and Lexington KY before joining the 1st Kentucky. He does not, however, appear in the 1850 and 1860 federal censuses. By September 1865, he and his brother John lived in Quincy IL. George later lived in Alma KS; Colorado Springs CO; and Boise ID. Three dollar advertising notes from his Colorado Springs store are today rare collectibles. He died in Caldwell ID on 21 August 1892. *Trial of Henry Wirz*, 563, 565; O. E. Root, *Root's Quincy City Directory* (Quincy: Whig and Republican Office, 1866) 60; El Paso County CO, p. 422D, *Tenth Census of the United States (1880)* (National Archives microfilm T9, roll 90); "Finds First Copy of the Gazette," *Colorado Springs Gazette & Telegraph*, 3 February 1929, 5; obit, *Caldwell* (ID) *Tribune*, 10 September 1892, 1.

275 *Trial of Henry Wirz*, 510, 516, 557, 566; Marvel, *Andersonville*, 108–10, 191; John L. Ransom, *Andersonville Diary, Escape, and List of Dead* (New York: n. p., 1881) 46; Webster, "A Jaunt in the South," 324.

276 Powell, "Brave Little Red Cap," *NT*, 7 November 1882, 7; Daniel O'Connor, "Wirz's Villainies," *NT*, 6 December 1906, 6; "Original Register of Federal Prisoners of War Confined at Andersonville, Ga. 1864–5."

277 Sneden, *Eye of the Storm*, 212; Ripple, *Dancing Along the Dead Line*, 52.

278 John L. Jacobs, "Andersonville," *NT*, 22 January 1885, 3.

279 John W. Lynn, *800 Paces to Hell: Andersonville* (Fredericksburg VA: Sergeant Kirkland's Museum, 1999) 62; service record of Ambrose Spencer, 93rd New York, RG 94, NARA; "'Dead' For 51 Years, He Gets U. S. Position," *Atlanta* (GA) *Constitution*, 4 January 1916, 7.

280 James T. Davis, for example, reportedly died after reading his of son's death at Andersonville from a roster of the camp's dead. "Death from Broken Heart," *Brooklyn Daily Eagle*, 6 March 1866, 2.

281 William O. Bryant, *Cahaba Prison and the Sultana Disaster* (Tuscaloosa: University of Alabama Press, 1990) 101–8; Marvel, *Andersonville*, 244; "War Story of Soren Peterson," State Historical Society of Wisconsin, Madison WI; Lynn, *800 Paces*, 210–11.

282 Eugene Forbes, *Diary of a Soldier, and Prisoner of War in the Rebel Prisons* (Trenton NJ: Murphy & Bechel, 1865) 37; L. Foster to John A. Hix, 1 April 1865, *Union Provost Marshal's File of Papers Relating to Individual Civilians*, (National Archives micropublication M345, roll 196), Records of the Provost Marshal, RG 110, NARA.

283 J. E. Harrison, "Hell on Earth," *NT*, 24 March 1892, 4; "Curious War Stories," *Atlanta Constitution*, 28 April 1888, 2; Stuart McConnell, "The William Newby Case and the Legacy of the Civil War," *Prologue: The Quarterly of the National Archives* 30/4 (Winter 1998): 247–56.

284 *Cullman* (AL) *Progress*, 18 February 1886, 1; "Personated a Dead Man," *Brooklyn Daily Eagle*, 22 June 1890, 18; federal Civil War pension claims of Frederick Guscetti, certificates 70675 and widow 432343, and Jacques Roellinger, application 609780, Records of Veterans Affairs, RG 15, NARA.

285 Wirz to R. B. Thomas, 9 January 1865, Wirz correspondence; Free Lance, "Southern Prison Life," *NT*, 5 August 1882, 2; Northrop, *Chronicles*, 100–1. In April 1861, John Cunningham, John Cane, and Martin Hughs left Sumter County GA for Cincinnati OH. J. S. Lemmon remembered a prisoner from an Illinois battery and former school teacher in the South, perhaps in Georgia, raising morale at Christmas in Andersonville by eloquently denouncing the Confederates. B. Elmer O'Keeffe, ed., *The Search for Missing Friends*, 8 vols. (Boston: New England Historical Society, 1996) 5:253; Lemmon, "A Christmas in Andersonville," *NT*, 4 March 1886, 3. A Mary Rawson of Atlanta resettled in Iowa during the summer of 1864. Excerpts from her diary at the Atlanta History Center do not mention Andersonville, however. Micki Waldrop, Atlanta History Center, to author, 27 April 2001, in author's possession, Hanceville AL.

286 *Atlanta Consitution*, 29 June 1905, 11. A Pvt. Varnal Luce of Company D, 140th New York Volunteer Infantry, died at Andersonville of scorbutus on 20 September 1864. Jack Lundquist to author, 17 November, 2005, in author's possession, Hanceville AL.

287 Henry H. Rood, *History of Company "A" 13th Iowa Veteran Infantry* (Cedar Rapids IA: Daily Republican, 1889) 26–27; "Sketches of the 13th Iowa," in vol. 55 of *Military Order of the Loyal Legion of the United States*, 145–47; "Reunion's Biggest Day," *Nebraska State Journal* (Des Moines), 17 September 1897, n. p. Biographical information on Vincent F. Stevens comes from Randy Stevens of Troy MI. Vincent Stevens, as a hero of Shiloh, and Limber Jim, receive indirect support from a source appropriately enigmatic for the subject. A profane nonsense ballad of unknown origin called "Shiloh," has as part of its chorus: "Limber Jim, Shiloh." Other references to Limber Jim in the song also have no intelligible meaning. B. A. Botkin, *A Treasury of Mississippi River Folklore* (New York: Crown Publishing, 1955) 593–95; Harold Courlander, *Negro Folk Music, U. S. A.* (New York: Columbia University Press, 1963) 120–21. "Limber Jim" is the name of a character in other folk songs; see the discussion of this topic on "The Mudcat Café" Web site at http://www.mudcat.org.

288 Marvel, *Andersonville*, 35–38, 244–46.

289 Gayla M. Koerting, "The Trial of Henry Wirz and Nineteenth-century Military Law," (Ph.D. diss., Kent State University, 1995) 182–86; Gardner, "Andersonville and American Memory," 24–26, 234; George Parsons Lathrop, "The Bailing of Jefferson Davis," *The Century* 33/4 (February 1887): 636. For a discussion of the culpability of Wirz to the sufferings at Andersonville also see Robert E. and Katherine M. Morsberger, "After Andersonville: The First War Crimes Trial," *Civil War Times Illustrated* 13 (July 1974): 30–41; and D. Kent Fonner, "Villain or Victim? Henry Wirz was the Last Casualty of the Civil War," *America's Civil War* 1 (November 1988): 138.

CHAPTER FIVE

290 "Rev. William J. Hamilton sketch," *The Record: Official Organ of the Diocese of Louisville* (8 March 1884) 81. This newsletter was published in Louisville KY.

291 *All Hallows Report* (1856): 45–55; *Passenger Lists of Vessels Arriving in New York 1820–1897* (National Archives microfilm M237, roll 158), list 1147; David T. Gleeson, *The Irish in the South, 1815–1877* (Chapel Hill: University of North Carolina Press, 2001) 25–27, 36–37; Arthur S. Meyers, "'Come Let Us Fly to Freedom's Sky': The Response of Irish Immigrants in the South to Slavery During the Late Antebellum Period," *Journal of Southeast Georgia History* 7 (1989–1992): 20–39; Herbert Aptheker, *American Negro Slave Revolts* (1943; repr, New York: International Publishers, 1993) 327–28, fn. 6; James L. Dunn to wife, 22 December 1864, James Langstaff Dunn Collection, MSS 8301, Special Collections, University of Virginia Libraries, Charlottesville VA. For more on the Irish in the Old South, see Kieran Quinlan, *Strange Kin: Ireland and the American Revolution* (Baton Rouge: Louisiana State University, 2004).

292 Michael V. Gannon, *Rebel Bishop: The Life and Era of Augustin Verot* (Milwaukee: Bruce Publishing, 1964) 92; Howard Meriwether Lovett, "Macon in the War Between the States," *Confederate Veteran* 32/1 (January 1924): 52; William J. Hamilton file, Civil War Miscellany Collection, Georgia Archives, Morrow GA; "Blaine's Speech," *Athens* (OH) *Messenger*, 20 January 1876, 3.

293 *Trial of Henry Wirz* (Washington: Government Printing Office, 1868) 288–90.

294 "A Bit of Secret History," *New-York Times*, 14 October 1883, 2. Wirz supposedly arranged a release for a priest imprisoned in Macon, for which the Bishop in Savannah wrote him a letter of thanks. Presumably, that priest would have been Hamilton. "Sincere Praise for Wirz From Col. Jas. H. Fannin," *Atlanta Constitution*, 14 February 1909, M10.

295 Eliza Frances Andrews, *The War-Time Journal of a Georgia Girl, 1864–1865* (New York: D. Appleton, 1908) 77–78; Gannon, *Rebel Bishop*, 100n; An Old Prisoner, "The Case of Wirz," *Washington Chronicle* (Washington DC), 6 August 1865, 1. James Pike remembered that a Catholic priest entered Camp Oglethorpe three or four times to administer to dying federal officers. Confederate officials then banned the priest from the prison. "Stories Frequently Worth Telling of Experiences and Adventures in the Great National Struggle," *National Tribune* (Washington DC), 26 May 1887, n. p. Hamilton's banishment may have come as the result of a plot that the guards had uncovered whereby the officers at Macon planned to escape and release the enlisted men held at Andersonville.

296 Gannon, *Rebel Bishop*, 105; Lovett, "Macon in the War Between the States," 52.

297 Gannon, *Rebel Bishop*, 99–100, 104–7; Rita H. DeLorme, "Andersonville and Beyond: Reviewing the Career of Very Reverend Henry Peter Clavreul," *Southern Cross* (22 January 2004): 3.

298 Quoted in "The Eagle and the Wirz Trial," *Brooklyn Daily Eagle*, 9 October 1865, 2; William Marvel, *Andersonville: The Last Depot* (Chapel Hill: University of North Carolina Press, 1994) 140–41. Florida Methodist minister E. B. Duncan did conduct services with the prisoners at Andersonville twice. "A Methodist Minister's Visit to Andersonville," *NT*, 24 January 1884, 7; Ovid L. Futch, *The History of Andersonville Prison* (Gainesville: University of Florida Press, 1968) 61; Marvel, *Andersonville*, 163–64.

299 Peter J. Meaney, "The Prison Ministry of Father Peter Whelan, Georgia Priest and Confederate Chaplain," *Georgia Historical Quarterly* 71/1 (Spring 1987): 1–10, 19, 23–24. Whelan had the unique distinction of having been a prisoner of war while later administering to captives made of his former captors, to prison officer Henry Wirz, and to President Jefferson Davis in his captivity.

300 Gannon, *Rebel Bishop*, 104.

301 *Trial of Henry Wirz*, 291.

302 Rose Gibbons Lovett, *The Catholic Church in the Deep South: The Diocese of Birmingham in Alabama, 1540–1976* (Birmingham: n. p., 1980) 25; J. J. O'Connell, *Catholicity in the Carolinas and Georgia* (New York: D. & J. Sadlier, 1878) 565–66.

303 *Tenth Census of the United States (1880)* (National Archives microfilm T9, roll 141), Chatham County (GA) vol. 2, City of Savannah, p. 58, Records of the Bureau of the Census, Record Group 28, National Archives and Records Administration (NARA), College Park MD; *Proceedings of the 17th Annual Encampment of the Grand Army of the Republic: Department of Maine* (Lewiston ME: Journal Office, 1884) 79–80. Former Andersonville inmate Michael Dougherty wrote that Hamilton received the Congressional Medal of Honor on 23 January 1897. No record of his receiving such award has been found.

304 "Death of a Priest," *New-York Times*, 4 March 1884, 2; "Very Rev. W. J. Hamilton," *Daily Register* (Mobile AL), 4 March 1884, 2; "Rev. William J. Hamilton sketch."

CHAPTER SIX

305 An earlier version of this essay appeared as "A Day Captured at Andersonville Prison Camp: The Photographs of Andrew J. Riddle" in *Prologue: The Quarterly of the National Archives* 34/3 (Fall 2002): 212–17.

306 *Columbus* (GA) *Times*, 5 September 1864, 1.

307 Andersonville Cemetery file, Series S, Military Fortifications and National Cemeteries, War Department General and Special Staffs, Record Group (hereafter RG) 165, National Archives and Records Administration (NARA), College Park MD. Engle and Furlong photographed little more than what remained of the original stockade. The author of "Our Union Prisoners and Their Sufferings" in *Courier and Union* (Syracuse NY), 12 January 1865, 2, claimed to have seen a photograph of the hanging of the raiders at Andersonville. An N. C. Norman of Natchez MS offered a war time photograph of the interior of Andersonville for sale to the War Department in 1893. His letter and the photograph have not survived. "Andersonville," no. 367595, *Index to General Correspondence of the Record and Pension Office, 1889–1920* (National Archives microfilm M686, roll 7), Records of the Veterans Administration, RG 15, NARA.

308 For the problem of combining technical skill with business success in the antebellum iron industry of the period see Robert S. Davis, *Cotton, Fire & Dreams: The Robert Findlay Iron Works and Heavy Industry in Macon, Georgia, 1839–1912* (Macon: Mercer University Press, 1998) 44–47, 83–84.

309 John C. Craig, *Craig's Daguerreian Registry*, 3 vols. (Torrington CT: self-published, 1996) 3: 483; Ross J. Kelbaugh, *Directory of Maryland Photographers 1839–1900* (Baltimore: Historic Graphics, 1988) 43; *Macon* (GA) *Telegraph*, 22 August 1871, 10; *Macon* (GA) *Telegraph*, 24 March 1897, 9; Louise C. Barfield, *History of Harris County Georgia* (Columbus GA: self-published, 1961) 338; Mortality Schedules of the State of Maryland 1850–80, Baltimore County (1850), p. 152, Maryland Historical Society, Baltimore MD. For records about Andrew Riddle's likely family origins see New Castle County, Delaware, p. 57, *Fifth Census of the United States (1830)* (National Archives microfilm M19, roll 12); Baltimore MD, p. 84, *Sixth Census of the United States (1840)* (National Archives microfilm M704, roll 162); Baltimore MD, p. 96, *Seventh Census of the United States (1850)* (National Archives microfilm M432, roll 279); Columbus GA, p. 226, *Eighth Census of the United States (1860)* (National Archives microfilm M653, roll 132); Muscogee County, GA, p. 666, *Tenth Census of the United States (1870)* (National Archives microfilm T9, roll 159); and the will of John Riddle, Register of Administrations (1849–1852), p. 251, Baltimore County, Maryland State Archives, Annapolis MD. Kip Michael has a photograph of a "Josiah" or "Jonah" Riddle (the writing on the back is almost illegible) with a camera. It may be Andrew J. Riddle. Martha Mays, a slave who had been a wedding gift to Riddle from his father-in-law, identified him decades later as "Andrew Jackson Riddle." She was so young that she confused Riddle with his father-in-law, but she must have been referring to Riddle when she spoke of "artists what took purty pictures of fine ladies an' gent'men." Martha Mays interview in George P. Rawick, ed., *The American Slave: A Composite Biography*, 41 vols. (Westport CT: Greenwood Press, 1972–1979), supplement series 1, vol. 9, part 4, p. 1467.

310 "The Last Rite Tendered," *Macon* (GA) *Telegraph*, 24 March 1897, 2; *Compiled Service Records of Confederate Soldiers Who Served in Organizations From the State of Missouri* (National Archives microfilm M322, rolls 79, 145, 148, 188); deposition of A. J. Riddle, 26 May 1862, *Unfiled Papers and Slips Belonging to Confederate Compiled Service Records* (National Archives microfilm M347, roll 335), War Department Collection of Confederate Records, RG 109, NARA. No mention of any A. J. Riddle appears in Records of the Commissary of Prisoners, RG 249, NARA. The release of Andrew J. "Riddler," however, by exchange appears in Benjamin F. Butler to Robert Ould, 1 March 1864, in U.S. War Department, *The War of the Rebellion: A Compilation of the Official Records of the Union and Confederate Armies*, 128 vols. (Washington DC: Government Printing Office, 1898–1906) ser. 2, vol. 6, p. 1000.

311 Anne J. Bailey and Walter J. Fraser, Jr., *Portraits of Conflict: A Photographic History of Georgia in the Civil War* (Fayetteville: University of Arkansas, 1996) 3–4.

312 Turner files 1623 and 3288, *Case Files of Investigations by Levi C. Turner and Lafayette C. Baker, 1861–1866* (National Archives microfilm M797, rolls 48 and 88), RG 94, and Riddle to secretary of war, 3 April 1863, *Letters Received by the Confederate Secretary of War, 1861–1865* (National Archives microfilm M437, roll 114), RG 109, War Department Collection of Confederate Records, NARA.

313 Bailey and Fraser, *Portraits of Conflict*, 3–4; A. J. Riddle file, *Confederate Papers Relating to Citizens or Business Firms* (National Archives microfilm M346, roll 864); Andrew J. Riddle file, *Unfiled Papers and Slips Belonging to Confederate Compiled Service Records* (National Archives microfilm M347, reel 335); A. J. Riddle to secretary of war, 3 April 1863, *Letters Received by the Confederate Secretary of War, 1861–1865* (National Archives microfilm M437, roll 114), RG 109, NARA; "Riddle's Photographs," *Macon* (GA) *Telegraph*, 26 May 1866, 3; "The Last Rite Tendered," *Macon* (GA) *Telegraph*, 24 March 1897, 2.

314 James L. Nichols, *Confederate Engineers* (Tuscaloosa: Confederate Publishing Company, 1957) 88; Margaret E. Wagner, Gary W. Gallagher, and Paul Pinkelman, *The Library of Congress Civil War Desk Reference* (New York: Simon & Schuster, 2002) 347.

315 The recently discovered drawings of Robert Knox Sneden illustrates in detail many aspects of the prison that Riddle, with only his one day in the camp, missed; see Sneden, *Eye of the Storm: A Civil War Odyssey*, ed. Charles F. Bryan, Jr., and Nelson D. Lankford (New York: Free Press, 2000) and *Images From the Storm* (New York: Free Press, 2001).

316 William Marvel, "The Andersonville Artist: The A. J. Riddle Photographs of August 1864," *Blue & Gray Magazine* (August 1993): 18–23.

317 *Trial of Henry Wirz* (Washington: Government Printing Office, 1868) 411; *New York Times*, 24 March 1897. The judge advocate did introduce into the record a drawing of Andersonville prison by inmate Robert Sneden. *Trial of Henry Wirz*, 644.

318 *National Tribune* (Washington DC), 26 April 1883, n. p. Today, the National Archives and Records Administration have that copy. Other sets of the Riddle prints survive in the holdings of the Hargrett Rare Books and Manuscripts Library of the University of Georgia Libraries.

319 Robert H. Kellogg to George S. Godard, 23 February 1922, Robert H. Kellogg Collection, Connecticut Historical Society, Hartford CT.

320 Florida petitions, George Walker file, *Pardon Petitions and Related Papers Submitted in Response to President Andrew Johnson's Amnesty Proclamation of May 29, 1865 "Amnesty Papers"* (National Archives microfilm M1003, roll 15), RG 94, NARA; "Riddle's Photographs," *Macon* (GA) *Telegraph*, 19 October 1866, 3; "Riddle's Photographic Temple," *Macon* (GA) *Telegraph*, 9 April 1869, 3; "Pleasant Resort," *Macon* (GA) *Telegraph*, 27 May 1869, 3; 22 March 1897, 6; "The Last Rite Tendered," *Macon* (GA) *Telegraph*, 24 March 1897, 2; Anne K. Walker, *Backtracking in Barbour County: A Narrative of the Last Alabama Frontier* (Richmond VA: Dietz Press, 1941) 296–97; Credit report, Alabama, vol. 3, p. 148, (Barbour County), R. G. Dun & Company Collection, Baker Library, Harvard Business School, Cambridge MA.

CHAPTER SEVEN

321 Saul Levitt has the characters in his play *Andersonville Trial* discussing cannibalism but nothing on this subject appears in the trial transcript of the prosecution of Henry Wirz or in surviving newspaper accounts of the trial.

322 "Sketches of Life of B. L. McGough," *The Jackson Progress-Argus* (Jefferson GA), 1 July 1876, reprinted in *Confederate Reminiscences*, vol. 18, 125–28; *Compiled Service Records of Confederate Soldiers Who Served in Organizations From the State of Georgia* (National Archives microfilm M266, roll 174), B. L. McGough file, War Department Collection of Confederate Records, Record Group (hereafter RG) 109, National Archives and Records Administration (NARA), College Park MD.

323 William Marvel, *Andersonville: The Last Depot* (Chapel Hill: University of North Carolina Press, 1994) 56, 112, 174, 264.

324 *Trial of Henry Wirz* (Washington DC: Government Printing Office, 1868) 696.

325 Warren L. Goss, *The Soldier's Story of His Captivity at Andersonville* (Boston: Lee and Shepard, 1867) 59–60; pension file of Isaac N. Leonard, widow's application 471,291, Records of Veterans Affairs, RG 15, NARA.

326 "The Lady Prisoner," *Macon* (GA) *Telegraph*, 8 June 1864, 2; "Hotel de Castle Thunder," *National Republican* (Washington DC), 25 August 1864, 1; pension file of Isaac N. Leonard, widow's application 471,291, Records of Veterans Affairs, RG 15, NARA. A Mrs. Leonard appears in federal records as released at City Point VA, but the date of 21 August 1863 is one year too early. Slips on prisoners held in the CSA, entry 108, Records of the Commissary of Prisoners, RG 249, NARA.

327 *Eighth Census of the United States (1860)* (National Archives microfilm M429, roll 168), Chicago IL, Ward 10, p. 429, Records of the Bureau of the Census, RG 28, NARA; service record of Herbert Hunt, 61st Illinois Infantry Regiment, Records of the Adjutant General, RG 94, NARA; Jane Nash to author, June 2000, in author's possession, Hanceville AL. Herbert Hunt's prison record identified him in 1865 as born in Portland ME, age twenty-six, and five feet five inches tall, with light eyes, black hair, and fair complexion. H. Hunt, Slips on prisoners held in the CSA, entry 108, Records of the Commissary of Prisoners, RG 249, NARA.

328 Court case files A209 (1848), A626 (1849), A3344 (1857), A3346 (1857), A3347 (1857), A3440 (1857), A3470 (1857), A9792 (1876), A10406 (1877), and A0528 (1877), Herkimer County Clerk, Herkimer NY.

329 W. J. W. Kerr, "Sad Ending of a Wedding Trip," *Confederate Veteran* 23/6 (June 1915): 318. Kevin Frye understands that the Hunts were held in Castle Reed, a smaller stockade at Andersonville used for temporary imprisonments. Kevin Frye to author, 2 November 2003, in author's possession, Hanceville AL. A secondary source claimed that Dr. Kerr reported to the *Sumter Republican* on 14 July 1864 that Janie had disguised herself as a man to follow her husband into captivity. No such article has been found and it was likely a confused combination of the various tales of women at Andersonville. Kerr's service record identifies him only as the hospital steward. "Causes of Death at Andersonville," *National Tribune* (Washington DC), 16 December 1909, 5; W, J. W. Kerr file, *Confederate General Staff Officers and Non-Regimental Enlisted Men* (National Archives microfilm M331, roll 148).

330 Henry Wirz to provost marshal, 19 May 1864, Henry Wirz letter book, 18 May 1864 to 19 March 1865, p. 1, entry 10 (chapter 11, vol. 227), War Department Collection of Confederate Records, RG 109, "Specifically Exchanged," 8, 11, 28, and 29 April 1865, entry 70, box 2, Records of the Commissary of Prisoners, RG 249, NARA. An extensive but unsuccessful effort in several archives and libraries has been made to learn the details of the capture of the Hunts. Research has failed to locate records of any vessel captured at or near Fairfield NC at any time. The ships *Arrow* (civilian mail steamer contracted to the Army), *Emily* (civilian mail steamer contracted to the Army), and *Sea Bird* (civilian schooner hauling coal for the Navy) were captured by Confederate soldiers in the inland waterways of North Carolina in May of 1863, roughly the time that Dr. Kerr claimed that the Hunts were captured. Fifteen men under infantry Capt. John T. Elliott, and guided by infantry Capt. Willis B. Sanderlin, captured the steamers. Robert Stillery, and five other privates burned the *Sea Bird* after taking Capt. Scott and his crew as prisoners. Alexander C. Brown, "The Runaway Steamboat Caper," *The State* 45 (March 1978): 12–14; Clement A. Evans, ed., *Confederate Military History Extended Edition*, 17 vols. (Wilmington NC: Broadfoot Publishing, 1987) 12:269–70; Walter Clark, ed., *Histories of the Several Regiments and Battalions from North Carolina*, 5 vols. (Goldsboro NC: Nash Brothers, 1901) 5:17–18; "Disasters &c.," *Boston Shipping List*, 6 June 1863, 4. "The Situation," *New York Herald*, 28 May 1863, 5. The respective names of the captains and owners of the *Arrow* and *Emily* have not been discovered. Capt. Elliott and/or Capt. Sanderlin could have been the "Captain Ed. Lurrett" who captured the Hunts. In the Brown article (see above), Elliott was referred to incorrectly as "E. T. Elliott" and as named "Burress." Confederate records searched omit any reference to the Hunts or Morris before the Wirz letter and, contrary to Kerr's claims, the Hunts and Morris may have been captured during April 1864 when Plymouth NC fell to the Confederates. Seven civilian vessels, identities unknown, were sunk near Plymouth by the federal forces in an unsuccessful effort to try to impede the Confederate ram *Albemarle*. The Morris vessel may have also been captured by the federal navy, and Morris and the Hunts were being held in Plymouth when the Confederacy captured that town. Fairfield NC sits on shallow Lake Mattamuskett, which would have been a good place for hiding smuggling that was illegal both to the Confederate and United States governments.

331 William H. Smith diaries, vols. 1 and 2, MSS 13164, Special Collections, University of Virginia Libraries, Charlottesville VA; Jane Nash to author, June 2000, in author's possession, Hanceville AL. The date of the Hunts capture cannot be assumed based upon Janie Hunt giving birth. Wives sometimes accompanied husbands to sea, even when pregnant. Michael J. Crawford, "More than 'Rum, Buggary, and the Lash': Social History in American Naval Documents," *Documentary Editing* 27 (Summer 2005): 60–62.

332 "Dr. W. J. W. Kerr," *Confederate Veteran* 25/1 (January 1917): 31; Kerr, "Sad Ending of a Wedding Trip," 318.

333 Solon Hyde, *A Captive of War* (New York: McClure, Phillips & Co., 1900) 248–49; John Lewis Dance File, Civil War Miscellany Collection, Georgia Archives, Morrow GA; Ransom T. Powell, "Brave Little Red Cap," *National Tribune* (Washington DC), 16 November 1882, 7.

334 "Original Register of Federal Prisoners of War Confined at Andersonville, Ga. 1864–5," p. H-39 in *Selected Records of the War Department Commissary General of Prisoners of War Confined at Andersonville, Georgia, 1864–65* (National Archives microfilm M1303, roll 1), Records of the Commissary General of Prisoners, RG 249, NARA; Herbert Hunt file, *Union Provost Marshal's File of Papers Relating to Individual Civilians* (National Archives microfilm M345, roll 137); Nash to author, June 2000.

335 Herbert and Francis Jane Hunt are buried in unmarked graves in plot 169, with Herbert's parents, in the East Cemetery in Cromwell CT. Nash to author, June 2000, March 2005.

336 That no records have turned up of any attempt by Morris, his wife, or the Hunts to file a claim with the quartermaster general, Treasury, and Congress also implies that Morris acted as a private businessman, and not under government contract, when he, his ship, and the Hunts were captured by Confederates. If he sold wood directly to the federal government during the Civil War, the records of his sales are likely buried in the monthly returns of the individual quartermasters in Records of the Quartermaster General, RG 92, NARA. No index exists for these returns. Christopher Meekins, "Caught Between Scylla and Charybdis: The Civil War in Northeastern North Carolina," (MA thesis, North Carolina State University, Raleigh, 2001) 144–48. For a description of a proposal for such a venture, see P. F. Schliecker to Adm. D. D. Porter, 27 March 1865, *Subject File of the Confederate States Navy* (National Archives microfilm M1091, roll 45, frame 318), War Department Collection of Confederate Records, RG 109, NARA. Samuel Hazzard of New York, captain of the schooner *Jenny Hunter* was captured and imprisoned by the Confederacy on 6 February 1862 for his illegal trade. *[Communication From the Secretary of War, Enclosing a List of the Civilian Prisoners in Custody at Salisbury, North Carolina, Under Military Authority]* (Richmond: n. p., 1863) 5. As with Hunt's vessel, the official records are also silent on the capture of Hazzard's ship. George C. Mangan, James Schoff, and K. L. Shepard were held as prisoners by the Confederacy for "attempting to run the blockade without pass." Morning Report, Capt. G. P. Alexander, 18 September 1863, Department of Henrico Collection, MSS 3C7604a, section 13, folder 3, frame 879, Virginia Historical Society, Richmond VA.

337 The only prison record for John Morris is a slip in entry 142, RG 249, which reads "John Morris US Str." Eugene Forbes wrote that Morris had been captured at Plymouth NC (20 April 1864). Forbes may have been confused by the fact that Morris came to Andersonville with the Plymouth prisoners or, possibly, Hunt had been captured with Morris's ship a year before Morris himself became a prisoner at Plymouth, in separate incidents. The latter theory would explain why Morris wanted the Hunts interviewed as soon as he knew that they had been brought to Georgia. Wirz to provost marshal, 19 May 1864, Henry Wirz letter book, 18 May 1864 to 19 March 1865; Eugene Forbes, *Diary of a Soldier and Prisoner of War in the Rebel Prisons* (Trenton NJ: Murphy & Bechtel, 1865) 37.

338 Forbes, *Diary of a Soldier*, 37; L. Foster to John A. Hix, 1 April 1865, *Union Provost Marshal's File of Papers Relating to Individual Civilians* (National Archives microfilm M345, roll 196), Records of the Provost Marshal, RG 110, NARA; Caryl Darling, Herkimer County Historical Society, to author, 11 September 2000, in author's possession, Hanceville AL; court case files A9792 (1876), A10406 (1877), and A10528 (1877), Herkimer County Clerk, Herkimer NY.

339 Samuel Creelman, *Collections of a Coffee Cooler* (Pittsburgh: Pittsburgh Photo Engraving, 1890) 40–41; Dr. R. C. Gresham, "Reminiscences," in vol. 6 of *Confederate Reminiscences and Letters, 1861–1865* (Atlanta: Georgia Division, United Daughters of the Confederacy, 1995) 121–22; Marvel, *Andersonville*, 264–65, fn. 58; John W. Lynn, *800 Paces to Hell: Andersonville* (Fredericksburg VA: Sergeant Kirkland's Museum, 1999) 170–21; G. Wayne King, "Death Camp at Florence," *Civil War Times Illustrated* 12, no. 9 (January 1974): 38; "A Woman Soldier of the North," *New York Times*, 27 May 1934, pt. 6, p. 23; Virginia Revenel, "Florena Budwin Joined Husband in Army and Died as a Prisoner," newspaper article, 10 February 1957, Florena Budwin file, South Carolina Historical Society, Charleston SC; John Andrews to author, 21 February 2000, in author's possession, Hanceville AL. John H. Morris's wife Mary (never at Andersonville), coincidently (?), was born Mary Budlong.

340 Free Lance, "Southern Prison Life," *National Tribune* (Washington DC), 26 October 1882, 2.

341 Former Andersonville and Florence prisoner Morgan E. Dowling wrote such a work of fiction that he passed off as fact: *Southern Prisons: Or Josie the Heroine of Florence* (Detroit: William Graham, 1870)

342 Marvel, *Andersonville*, 264–65, n. 58; Frye to author, 10 November 2003, in author's possession, Hanceville AL.

343 Gresham, "Reminiscences," 121–22; Marvel, *Andersonville*, 264–65; Lynn, *800 Paces*, 170–71.

344 For the women prisoners of Castle Thunder see Sandra V. Parker, *Richmond's Civil War Prisons* (Lynchburg VA: H. E. Howard, 1990) 26–27; *New York Herald*, 30 January 1864, 4; *National Tribune* (Washington DC), 11 July 1889, n. p.; and *National Republican* (Washington DC), 25 August 1864, 1.

CHAPTER EIGHT

345 Modern studies on the realities of the effects of Sherman's campaigns include, among other works, Anne J. Bailey, *War and Ruin: William T. Sherman and the Savannah Campaign* (Wilmington DE: Scholarly Resources, 2003); Lee Kennett, *Marching Through Georgia: The Story of Soldiers and Civilians During Sherman's Campaign* (New York: HarperCollins, 1995); Michael Golay, *A Ruined Land: The End of the Civil War* (New York: John Wiley & Sons, 1999); and Joseph T. Glatthaar, *The March to the Sea and Beyond: Sherman's Troops in the Savannah and Carolinas Campaign* (New York: New York University Press, 1985).

346 For the burning of Columbia, see Marion B. Lucas, *Sherman and the Burning of Columbia* (College Station: Texas A&M University Press, 1976).

347 The correspondence is published in U.S. War Department, *The War of the Rebellion: A Compilation of the Official Records of the Union and Confederate Armies*, 128 vols. (Washington DC: Government Printing Office, 1880–1897), hereafter *OR*, ser. 1, vol. 39, pt. 2, pp. 414–22. One of the best examples of legend taking advantage of Sherman's reputation involved the alleged rape of Kate Nichols in Midway GA by Union soldiers during Sherman's occupation of nearby Milledgeville. Allegedly, the violation resulted in Mrs. Nichols's confinement in the state mental institution. The only shred of documentation of this story comes from a passage written and erased by Anna Marie Green from her memoirs after the Civil War. Nichols had been in the asylum, which happened to be located in Midway, even before the war. Records of her subsequent stays in the asylum made no mention of the rape but did diagnose her recurring condition as due to hereditary insanity. Her father had been an inmate before his death. Morton McInvale, "A Retreat From Tragedy," in vol. 2 of Olin Jackson, ed., *A North Georgia Journal of History* (Roswell GA: Legacy Publications, 1989–2000) 351–52, 360; medical case files, Central State Hospital, reel 350/18 and reel 350/20, Georgia Archives, Morrow GA.

348 Jane Singer, *The Confederate Dirty War: Arson, Bombings, Assassination and Plots for Chemical and Germ Attacks on the Union* (Jefferson NC: McFarland, 2005) 14, 19, 24.

349 Diary of Jasper Culver in the possession of Jan Therkildensen, Arvada CO; deposition of William Whipple, 26 July 1864, "Statements of Escaped Union Prisoners, Refugees, and Rebel Deserters," entry 4294, p. 26, Records of Continental Commands, Record Group (RG) 393, pt. 1, National Archives and Records Administration (NARA), College Park MD; Sherman to Ellen Sherman, 9 August 1864, in Sherman, *Sherman's Selected Correspondence*, ed. Books B. Simpson and Jean V. Berlin (Chapel Hill: University of North Carolina Press, 1999) 685.

350 Theodore P. Savas and David A. Woodbury, *The Campaign for Atlanta and Sherman's March to the Sea* (Campbell CA: Savas Woodbury, 1994) 36, 63–64, 246, 396; Arch Frederic Blakey, *General John H. Winder, CSA* (Gainesville: University of Florida Press, 1990) 186–90; David Evans, *Sherman's Horsemen* (Bloomington: Indiana University Press, 1996) 144–45, 161, 376; Richard M. McMurry, *Atlanta: Last Chance for the Confederacy* (Lincoln: University of Nebraska, 2000) 141, 146; John B. Hood, *Advance and Retreat* (New Orleans: Hood Orphan Memorial Fund, 1880) 215.

351 For the history of this cavalry campaign see Evans, *Sherman's Horsemen*.

352 Lee Kennett, *Sherman: a Soldier's Life* (New York: HarperCollins, 2001) 105–8, 146–47.

353 Kennett, *Marching Through Georgia*, 212.

354 Burke Davis, *Sherman's March* (New York: Random House, 1980), 66; Bailey, *War and Ruin*, 27; "Address by Colonel Charles D. Kerr," (1887), in vol. 26 of *Military Order of the Loyal Legion of the United States* (Wilmington NC: Broadfoot, 1991) 213–14; Charles Deal Kerr diary, Henry E. Huntington Library, San Marino CA; James C. Bonner, *Milledgeville: Georgia's Antebellum Capital* (Athens: University of Georgia Press, 1978) 192; Corydon E. Foote, *With Sherman to the Sea: A Drummer's Story of the Civil War* (New York: John Day, 1960) 218–19.

355 Free Lance, "Southern Prison Life," *National Tribune* (Washington DC), 19 August 1882, 2; Kennett, *Marching Through Georgia*, 261.

356 Testimony of Horatio B. Terrell in *Trial of Henry Wirz* (Washington DC: Government Printing Office, 1868) 173; William Marvel, *Andersonville: The Last Depot* (Chapel Hill: University of North Carolina, 1994) 211; Sherman to Ellen Sherman, 2 August and 9 August to Thomas Ewing, 11 August 1864, in Sherman, *Sherman's Selected Correspondence*, 680–81, 685, 690; Jacob Ritner, *Love and Valor: Intimate Civil War Letters of Captain Jacob and Emeline Ritner*, ed. Charles P. Larimer, (n. p., 2000) 364; Sherman to H. W. Halleck, 20 September 1864, *OR*, ser. 2, vol. 7, pp. 846–47, 851; William T. Sherman, *Memoirs of General William T. Sherman*, 2 vols. (New York: Appleton, 1875) 2:143; John Y. Simon, ed., *The Papers of Ulysses S. Grant*, 15 vols. to date (Carbondale: Southern Illinois Press, 1981–) 13:137n, 484n.

CHAPTER NINE

357 An edited draft of this essay appeared as "Yankee Gone South: The Georgia Odyssey of 'Colonel Spencer of Andersonville,'" *Georgia Historical Quarterly* 88/1 (Spring 2004): 50–65.

358 For the effects of such communication advances upon society see Daniel J. Czitrom, *Media and the American Mind from Morse to McLuhan* (Chapel Hill: University of North Carolina Press, 1982).

359 Karen Halttunen, *Confidence Men and Painted Women: A Study of the Middle-class Culture in America, 1830–1870* (New Haven: Yale University Press, 1982) 22–23, 31; John F. Kasson, *Rudeness & Civility: Manners in Nineteenth-century Urban America* (New York: Noonday Press, 1991) 109–11. On the conflict of failure in the nineteenth century, see Scott A. Sandage, *Born Losers: A History of Failure in America* (Cambridge: Harvard University Press, 2005).

360 Felix DeLaBraume, *Let Us Forgive, But Not Forget* (n. p., 1866) print. Federal deserter Felix Oeser, as Andersonville prisoner Felix DeLaBraume, did the first panoramic sketch of the camp, even while still a prisoner. In exchange for a pardon, he testified against Wirz too and used his drawing at the trial. *Trial of Henry Wirz* (Washington DC: Government Printing Office, 1868) 35–36; "Western Andersonville Survivors Association," Boston Corbett Collection, Kansas State Historical Society, Topeka KS; William Marvel, *Andersonville: The Last Depot* (Chapel Hill: University of North Carolina Press, 1994) 244–45. Thus a man guilty of fraud and perjury drew a depiction of Andersonville that contained at least one cameo of another fraud and fellow perjurer of the same trial, Ambroce C. Spencer.

361 Elias Child, *Genealogy of the Child, Childs, and Childe Families* (Utica NY: Curtiss & Childs, 1881) 117; Dorothic Bobbe, *De Witt Clinton* (Port Washington NY: Ira J. Friedman, 1962) 183; "De Witt as a Vituperator," *Hamilton* (OH) *Guidon*, 28 January 1875, 3.

362 John C. Miller, *Alexander Hamilton: Portrait in Paradox* (New York: Harper Brothers, 1959) 553–56; Jeffrey L. Pasley, *"The Tyranny of Printers": Newspaper Politics in the Early American Republic* (Charlottesville: University Press of Virginia, 2001) 266, 282. Thomas Eston Hemings, private of Company E of the 175th Ohio Infantry, an African-American grandson of Thomas Jefferson and Sally Hemings, spent time as a prisoner at Andersonville. He died on or about 1 January 1865 at Meridian MS while still a prisoner. Jack Lundquist to author, 28 June 2004, in author's possession, Hanceville AL.

363 *Trial of James Graham, before the Hon. Ambrose Spencer, Esq. for the Murder of Hugh Cameron, and Alexander M'Gillavrae: In Delhi, Delaware Co. July 14th, 1813* (Albany NY: J. Buel, 1814); Jay Gould, *History of Delaware County, and Border Wars of New York* (Roxbury NY: Keeny & Gould, 1856) 212–15.

364 Dumas Malone, ed., *Dictionary of American Biography* (New York: Charles Scribner's Sons, 1935) 9:443–45, 449–50.

365 "John Canfield Spencer," *The National Cyclopedia of American Biography*, 63 vols. (New York: James T. White, 1896) 6:6–7.

366 Works Projects Administration, "Annals of Cleveland, 1818–1935," 200 vols. (unpublished typescripts, 1938–1940), 25: 284; Oliver P. Chitwood, *John Tyler Champion of the Old South* (New York: D. Appleton-Century, 1939) 35–36, 281–84, 288, 292, 368 fn. 4; Robert Seager, *and Tyler too: A Biography of John & Julia Gardiner Tyler* (New York: McGraw-Hill, 1963) 224, 426.

367 "A Scrap of History," *Sandusky* (OH) *Clarion*, 26 August 1843, 2.

368 Stephen A. Douglas to Ambrose Spencer, 20 December 1857, Ambrose Spencer Collection, microfilm roll 199/25, Georgia Archives, Morrow GA; Gerald M. Capers, *Stephen A. Douglas: Defender of the Union* (Boston: Little, Brown, & Company, 1959) 6; Bob Buckeye, Middlebury College, to author, 17 October 2000, in author's possession, Hanceville AL.

369 Ontario County marriage records, Ontario County Historical Society, Canadaigua NY; Passenger list of the *Ontario*, 14 August 1833, *Passenger Lists of Vessels Arriving at the Port of New York, 1820–1894* (National Archives microfilm M237 roll 20); James P. Maher, *Index to Marriages and Deaths in the New York Herald, 1835–1850* (Baltimore: Genealogical Publishing Co., 1987) 113; *Savannah* (GA) *Morning News*, 23 November 1889, 8; John M. Baines, *Historic Hastings* (Hastings: F. S. Parsons, 1963) 404; Thomas B. Brett, unpublished history of Hastings, vol. 2, Hastings Library, East Sussex, England; Thronateeska Chapter, DAR, *History and Reminiscences of Dougherty County, Georgia* (Albany GA: self-published, 1924) 290. The Smithsonian American Art Museum Inventories of American Painting and Sculpture has identified two landscapes by "A. Spencer."

370 Capers, *Stephen A. Douglas*, 6; G. W. Morris to Ambrose Spencer, Jr., 27 June 1841, Ambrose Spencer Collection; Cuyahoga County OH, p. 251, *Sixth Census of the United States (1840)* (National Archives microfilm M704, roll 389); Works Projects Administration, "Annals of Cleveland," 21:64, 265, 288, 22:102, 253, 23 (pt. 1): 89, 128, 183.

371 Philip J. McFarland, *Sea Dangers: The Affair of the Somers* (New York: Schocken Books, 1985) 52–65, 269; Harrison Hayford, *The Somers Mutiny Affair* (Englewood Cliffs NJ: n. p., 1959) 3–4, 13; Works Projects Administration, "Annals of Cleveland, 1818–1935," 25:140; "What They Read," *Colorado Springs Gazette*, 20 October 1877, 3; Franklin B. Hough, *American Biographical Notes* (Albany NY: Joel Munsell, 1875) 372. A portrait of Philip Spencer appears in Hayward and Blanche Cirker, *Dictionary of American Portraits* (New York: Dover Publications, 1967) 580. Mackenzie was also a popular writer although he failed to write a book about the *Somers* mutiny, perhaps because he died in 1848. "Alexander Slidell Mackenzie," *National Cyclopedia*, 4:527–28. The trial of Philip Spencer received dramatization in "The Mutiny" episode on the CBS television program *JAG*. The *Somers* was named, appropriately as circumstances turned out, for Richard Somers, a naval officer killed under mysterious circumstances on a bomb ship in Tripoli Harbor during the war with the Barbary Pirates in 1804. James Tertius de Key, *A Rage for Glory: The Life of Commodore Stephen Decatur, USN* (New York: Free Press, 2004) 69.

372 Log of the U. S. sloop *Marion*, Naval Records Collection of the Office of Naval Records and Library, Record Group (hereafter RG) 45, National Archives and Records Administration (NARA), College Park MD; Commander Skinner to secretary of the Navy, 1 May 1846, *Letters Received by the Secretary of the Navy From Commanding Officers of Squadrons ("Squadron Letters")* (National Archives microfilm M89, roll 102); Hough, *American Biographical Notes*, 372; George A. Martin and Frank J. Metcalf, *Marriage and Death Notices From the National Intelligencer, 1800–1850*, microfilm edition (Washington DC: National Genealogical Society, 1976) 1938, 2065; *Onondaga* (New York State) *Standard*, 16 and 24 July 1815, 2. A false, but widely reprinted, report from the Ithaca newspaper announced that Ambrose's "only" sister died in a cannon explosion on 4 July near Syracuse. Ambrose's two sisters were actually "exemplary Christian ladies" and still living as late as 1876, the wife of Judge George W. Clinton of Buffalo and the first wife of Henry Morris, New York lawyer, respectively.

373 *Louisville* (KY) *Journal*, 26 December 1842, 2.

374 Testimony of Ambrose Spencer, general court martial of Henry Wirz, file MM2975, pt. 36, p. 2478, Records of the Judge Advocate General, RG 153, NARA.

375 "More on Snivley's and Warfield's Bands," *Sandusky* (OH) *Clarion*, 26 August 1843, 2; Republic of Texas pensions of William J. Cannen and William McMaster, rolls 207 and 229, Texas State Library and Archives Commission, Austin TX; Journal of Ambrose Spencer, Elias Viles Collection of Dairies of Indian Campaigns, Yale University, New Haven CT, p. 38–54; *Daily Georgian* (Savannah), 16 August 1843, 2; *Northern Standard* (Clarksville TX), 31 December 1842, 3; *Texas Telegraph & Register* (Houston), 23 August 1843, 1. For more on filibusters, see Robert E. May, *Manifest Destiny's Underworld: Filibusting in Antebellum America* (Chapel Hill: University of North Carolina Press, 2002).

376 Robert S. Davis, *Cotton, Fire, & Dreams: The Robert Findlay Iron Works and Heavy Industry in Macon, Georgia, 1839–1912* (Macon: Mercer University Press, 1998) 35–36, 38, 85, 106.

377 Tad Evans, *Milledgeville, Georgia, Newspaper Clippings (Southern Recorder)*, 12 vols. (Savannah: self-published, 1995–1997) 7:103; James C. Flanigan, *History of Gwinnett County Georgia*, 2 vols. (Hapeville GA: Tyler & Co., 1943) 1:95.

378 Eliza C. Ervin and Horace F. Rudisill, *Darlingtoniana: A History of People, Places and Events in Darlington County, South Carolina* (Columbia SC: R. L. Bryan, 1964) 198–99, 344–45; Albert G. Mackay, ed., *The Southern and Western Masonic Miscellany*, 2 vols. (Charleston SC: Walker & James, 1850) 1:197. An Ambrose Spencer did briefly attend the USMA in 1838 but that Ambrose was the son of Congressman John B. Spencer, only a kinsman of the Spencers discussed here. Register of Cadets, United States Military Academy, entry 237, Records of the Judge Adjutant General, RG 94, NARA; application of Ambrose Spencer, 200 (1838), *U. S. Military Academy Cadet Application Papers, 1805–1866* (National Archives microfilm M688, roll 117).

379 Darlington District SC, p. 327, Addison County VT, p. 165, *Seventh Census of the United States (1850)* (National Archives microfilm M432, rolls 851 and 920).

380 Petition of Agnes Spencer, 15 October 1861, Sumter County superior court minutes (1861–1869), pp. 142–44, microfilm roll 133/8, Georgia Archives, Morrow GA; John C. Spencer, will dated 10 July 1855, will book 15, pp. 325–34, Albany County Probate Court, Albany NY. The rest of the John Spencer's estate went to John's widow and two daughters; see footnote 372 above.

381 "Plains of Dora," *Daily Intelligencer* (Atlanta), 24 June 1859, 2.

382 Gordon B. Smith, *History of the Georgia Militia*, 4 vols. (Milledgeville GA: Boyd Publishing, 2000) 2:296–301.

383 Chatham County, Georgia, pp. 39, 79, Dougherty County GA, p. 549, *Eighth Census of the United States (1860)* (National Archives microfilm M653, rolls 115 and 120); William B. Williford, *Americus Through the Years: The Story of a Georgia Town and Its People, 1832–1975* (Atlanta: Cherokee Publishing, 1975) 76, 126, 449 fn. 21; deed, Agnes Spencer to Ambrose Spencer, 26 December 1862, deed book N (1859–1863), pp. 651–52, microfilm roll 132/6, Georgia Archives, Morrow GA; petition of Agnes Spencer, 24 December 1862, Sumter County superior court minutes (1861–1868), pp. 39, 200–1, microfilm roll 133/6, Georgia Archives, Morrow GA; deed, Ambrose Spencer to Robert L. Lawson, 17 March 1860, Chatham County deed book 3T (1860–1862), p. 154, roll 67/2, Georgia Archives, Morrow GA; Paul M. Pressly, "The Northern Roots of Savannah's Antebellum Elite, 1780s–1850s," *Georgia Historical Quarterly* 87/2 (Summer 2003): 158–99.

384 For a study of such "unionists", see Thomas G. Dyer, *Secret Yankees: The Secret Circle in Confederate Atlanta* (Baltimore: John Hopkins University Press, 1999).

385 Williford, *Americus Through the Years*, 75; Ambrose Spencer to secretary of war, 26 December 1861 and 9 February 1862, 9393–1862 and 11510–1862, *Correspondence Received by the Confederate Secretary of War, 1861–1865* (National Archives microfilm M437, rolls 22 and 29); *Compiled Service Records of Confederate Soldiers Who Served in Organizations From the State of Georgia* (National Archives microfilm M266, roll 188); *Compiled Service Records of Confederate Soldiers Who Served in Organizations From the State of Alabama* (National Archives microfilm M311, roll 74); certificate of Ambrose Spencer, 20 September 1864, 824-A-1863, *Correspondence Received by the Confederate Adjutant General, 1861–1865* (National Archives microfilm M474, roll 57).

386 Alphabetical Card File [of Confederate Records], Georgia Archives, Morrow GA; *Compiled Service Records of Confederate Soldiers Who Served in Organizations From the State of Georgia* (National Archives microfilm M266, rolls 73, 74, 141, 145).

387 Thomas M. Owen, *History of Alabama and Dictionary of Alabama Biography* (Chicago: S. J. Clarke, 1921) 1606–1607; Sarah Van V. Woolfolk, "George E. Spencer: A Carpetbagger in Alabama," *Alabama Review* 19/1 (January 1966): 41–52; Hough, *American Biographical Notes*, 371–72.

388 Testimony of Ambrose Spencer, general court martial of Henry Wirz; William Marvel, *Andersonville: The Last Depot* (Chapel Hill: University of North Carolina Press, 1994) 230, 302–3; Lewis S. McGuire to Littleton P. Dorman, 19 December 1866, deed book (1863–1869), pp. 452–53, microfilm roll 132/7, Georgia Archives, Morrow GA. General U. S. Grant issued a pass to a Mr. (or Mrs.) Spencer and servant to return to Georgia on 7 January 1863. Spencer file, *Union Provost Marshal's File of Papers Relating to Individual Civilians* (National Archives microfilm M345, roll 254).

389 A. C. Spencer to adjutant general, 20 September 1863, Mark Blandford to James A. Seddon, 19 November 1864, 824-A-1863, 3473-B-1864, *Letters Received by the Confederate Adjutant and Inspector Generals, 1861–1865* (National Archives microfilm M474, rolls 57, 98); same to secretary of war, 22 July 1864, 13-A-1864, *Letters Received by the Confederate Secretary of War* (National Archives microfilm M437, roll 146); Ambrose Spencer file, *Confederate Papers Relating to Citizens or Business Firms* (National Archives microfilm M346, roll 970); *Compiled Service Records of Confederate Soldiers Who Served in Organizations From the State of Georgia* (National Archives microfilm M266, roll 188).

390 *New York Times*, 4 August 1865, 1; order of N. P. Chipman, 17August 1865, document 454325, Records and Pensions Manuscripts, Records of the Adjutant General, RG 94, NARA. That Ambrose Spencer wrote the articles is confirmed by his statement in the articles of his having been the foreman of the Sumter County grand jury in the last days of the war. Sumter County superior court minutes (1861–1868), p. 393, microfilm roll 133/8, Georgia Archives, Morrow GA.

391 Marvel, *Andersonville*, 194–95, 244; order of N. P. Chipman, 17August 1865, document 454325, Records and Pensions Manuscripts, Records of the Adjutant General, RG 94, and testimony of Ambrose Spencer, general court martial of Henry Wirz, file MM2975, pt. 36, pp. 2453–2496, RG 153, NARA. Ambrose made no effort to receive a federal pardon required for the restoration of his citizenship. The pardons are in *Pardon Petitions and Related Papers...Amnesty Proclamation of May 29, 1865* (National Archives microfilm M1003) and are indexed in Carolyn M. Rowe, *Index to Individual Pardon Applications From the South, 1865–1898* (Pensacola: self-published, 1996).

392 Williford, *Americus Through the Years*, 75–76, 100.

393 N. P. Chipman to Spencer, 25 March 1866, Ambrose Spencer Collection; "The Andersonville Prison," *Brooklyn Daily Eagle*, 27 July 1866, 2; Ovid L. Futch, *History of Andersonville Prison* (Gainesville: University of Florida Press, 1968) 140.

394 Appointment papers, Ambrose C. Spencer, Records Relating to the Appointment of Federal Judges, Marshals, & Attorneys, Records of the Department of Justice, RG 60, NARA; J. Holt to [?], 10 March 1866, in U.S. War Department, *The War of the Rebellion: A Compilation of the Official Records of the Union and Confederate Armies*, 128 vols. (Washington DC: Government Printing Office 1880–1901) ser. 2, vol. 7, pp. 887–88; *Augusta Chronicle*, 4 September 1866, 2; Spencer to Hamilton Fish, 18 March 1869, *Letters of Application and Recommendation, Grant Administration* (National Archives microfilm M968, roll 57); *Edward's Annual Directory to...the City of Chicago* (Chicago: Richard Edwards, 1870) 780; John David Brandenburg and Rita B. Worthy, *Index to Georgia's 1867–1868 Returns of Qualified Voters and Registration Oath Books (White)* (Atlanta: self-published, 1995) 445; Cook County IL, p. 440B, *Ninth Census of the United States (1870)* (National Archives microfilm M593, roll 207).

395 Milo Erwin, *The History of Williamson County, Illinois* (Marion IL: n. p., 1876) 109–11; Edgar F. Raines, Jr., "The Ku Klux Klan in Illinois, 1867–1875," *Illinois Historical Journal* 78 (Spring 1985): 29; *U.S. v. Veach, et. al.*, case 2008, U.S. District Court of Southern Illinois, National Archives—Great Lakes Region, Chicago IL.

396 *Missouri-Statesman* (Columbia), 28 April 1876, 2; *People's Tribune* (Jefferson City MO), 19 April 1876, 2; *State Journal* (Jefferson City MO), 5 May 1876, 4; marriage book D (1868–1881), p. 181, Cape Girardeau County Circuit Court, Cape Girardeau MO.

397 *State v. Jeffers*, court records book D, n. p., Osage County Circuit Court, Linn MO; *Missouri Statesman*, (Columbia), 28 April 1876, 2, 24 November 1876, 1; *State Journal* (Jefferson City MO), 5 May 1876, 2; *Chicago Tribune*, 14 April 1876, n. p.; *History of Cole, Moniteau, Morgan, Benton, Miller, Maries, and Osage Counties* (Chicago: Goodspeed Publishing, 1889) 660; *New York Times*, 28 April 1876, 4. Wilson John Jeffers had enlisted in the 18th Illinois Infantry under the name of "Jefferson Davis." After his release from prison, he spent time in an asylum, married in Missouri, moved to Oregon, and died in 1902. His account of his complicated and colorful life, given in his pension application, did not include any mention of his murder conviction and bigamy. Civil War pension of Wilson J. Jeffers, certificate 920530, and Civil War widow's pension Clara L. Jeffers, certificate 573940, Records of the Veterans Administration, RG 15, NARA.

398 *State Journal* (Jefferson City MO), 28 April 1876, 5; *New York Times*, 26 April 1876, 5.

399 *State Journal* (Jefferson City MO), 28 April 1876, 5.

400 Williford, *Americus Through the Years*, 449, fn. 21; *Savannah* (GA) *Morning News*, 23 November 1889, 8; Rocky Mountain News (Denver CO), 3 August 1897, 10.

CHAPTER TEN

401 An earlier draft of this essay appeared as "'The Devil's Advocate': O. S. Baker and the Henry Wirz/Andersonville Military Tribunal" in *Journal of Southern Legal History* 10/1, 2 (January 2002): 25–57.

402 Gayla M. Koerting, "The Trial of Henry Wirz and Nineteenth-century Military Law," (Ph.D. diss., Kent State University, 1995) 103, 108.

403 Saul Levitt, *The Andersonville Trial* (New York: Dramatists Play Service, n. d.) 16. For federal investigations of suspicious persons in the Washington DC area, see *Case Files of Investigations by Levi C. Turner and Lafayette C. Baker, 1861–1866* (National Archives microfilm M797), Records of the Adjutant General, RG 94, NARA.

404 In the handwriting of the period, the letters "S" and "L" looked very similar.

405 Levitt, *The Andersonville Trial*, 16. Levitt apparently chose the name for his character from T. Otis Baker (born about 1844 in Maryland), a Baltimore attorney of the 1870s. Baltimore MD, p. 559, *Ninth Census of the United States (1870)* (National Archives microfilm M593, roll 575), Records of the Bureau of the Census, Record Group (hereafter RG) 29, National Archives and Records Administration (NARA), College Park MD; *Wood's Baltimore City Directory* (Baltimore: John W. Woods, 1871) 34. Louis Schade, Baker's co-counsel, had opposed a war to end slavery. Koerting, "The Trial of Henry Wirz," 107–8.

406 See, for example, Koerting, "The Trial of Henry Wirz," 108; Edward F. Roberts, *Andersonville Journey* (Shippensburg VA: Burd Street Press, 1998) 112; and John W. Lynn, *800 Paces to Hell: Andersonville* (Fredericksburg VA: Sergeant Kirkland's Museum, 1999) 325.

407 Critics claimed that General Winder never bothered to even see the interior of the stockade. Winder, however, suffered "gangrene of the face" from his exposure to the prison and his physician ordered him not to return to the interior of the stockade. Lynn, *800 Paces*, 120.

408 For the background of Henry Wirz see William Marvel, *Andersonville: The Last Depot* (Chapel Hill: University of North Carolina Press, 1994).

409 Ovid L. Futch, *History of Andersonville Prison* (Gainesville: University of Florida Press, 1968) 23, 25–26, 90–92; "Major Wirz at Andersonville," *Confederate Veteran* 28/7 (July 1920): 276. Wirz was also regarded as highly efficient before he worked at Andersonville; see the undated petition in his compiled service record *Compiled Service Records of Confederate General and Staff Officers and Non-Regimental Enlisted Men* (National Archives microfilm M331, roll 271); War Department Collection of Confederate Records, RG 109, NARA; and Maj. E. Griswold to J. B. Benjamin, 13 May 1863, Confederate States of America, MS 13,744 (Pickett papers), vol. 35, applications for passports, Library of Congress.

410 Quoted in James A. Mowris, *A History of the 117th Regiment, NY Volunteers* (Hartford CT: Case, Lockwood and Company, 1866) 286.

411 Roberts, *Andersonville Journey*, 48. For Andersonville prison slang in popular usage see George E. Shankle, *American Nicknames: Their Origin and Significance* (New York: H. W. Wilson, 1955).

412 Futch, *History of Andersonville Prison*, 20, 22, 25, 90; Lynn, *800 Paces*, 32; *Trial of Henry Wirz* (Washington DC: Government Printing Office, 1868) 99.

413 U.S. War Department, *The War of the Rebellion: A Compendium of the Official Records Union and Confederate Armies*, 128 vols. (Washington DC: Government Printing Office, 1898–1911) ser. 2, vol. 7, p. 622; Roberts, *Andersonville Journey*, 48.

414 For a sampler of defenses of Wirz by former prisoners of Andersonville see *Facts and Figures vs. Myths and Misrepresentations Henry Wirz and Andersonville* (Atlanta: Georgia Division UDC, 1921), a copy of which is in the Andersonville file of the Civil War Miscellany Collection, Georgia Archives, Morrow GA; also see "Union Soldier Defends Memory of Wirz," *Atlanta* (GA) *Constitution*, 3 December 1905, M9.

415 Roberts, *Andersonville Journey*, 100; Koerting, "The Trial of Henry Wirz," 178–79. *Grand Traverse Herald* (Grand Traverse MI), 22 September 1865, 2, reported that watches Wirz had stolen from prisoners were recovered from a G. T. Garrison, reportedly Wirz's agent. The same paper also claimed that a woman who had lost a son at Andersonville, and had another who had gone insane there, tried to attack Wirz at the trial.

416 "Execution of Wirz," *Brooklyn Daily Eagle*, 11 November 1865, 2.

417 "Andersonville: A Story of Southern Prisons," *Waukesha* (WI) *Feeeman*, 25 March 1880, 2.

418 Thomas F. Curran, "General Orders No. 100," in vol. 3 of David S. and Jeanne T. Heidler, eds., *Encyclopedia of the American Civil War* (Santa Barbara CA: ABC-CLIO, 2000) 819; John R. Cronin, "Rules of War," in vol. 3 of Richard N. Current, *Encyclopedia of the Confederacy* (New York: Simon & Schuster, 1993) 1352–53; Gary J. Bass, *Stay the Hand of Vengeance: The Politics of War Crimes Tribunals* (Princeton: Princeton University Press, 2000) 28–36; Aryeh Neier, *War Crimes* (New York: Random House, 1998) 12–14.

419 "Sincere Praise for Wirz From Col. Jas. H. Fannin," *Atlanta* (GA) *Constitution*, 14 February 1909, M10; Marvel, *Andersonville*, 241.

420 Koerting, "The Trial of Henry Wirz," 98–103, 168; Robert G. H. Kean, *Inside the Confederate Government: The Diary of Robert Garlick Hill Kean*, ed. Edward Younger (New York: Oxford University Press, 1957) 228; *The Trial of Henry Wirz*, 805. Similar criticisms have been made of the current system of military justice by tribunal. Edward T. Pound, "Unequal Justice," *U.S. News & World Report* 133 (16 December 2002): 19–22, 24–30.

421 Undated letter in Henry Wirz file, James Hughes Collection, Bancroft Library, Indiana University, Bloomington IL. Well-funded Confederate agents were active after the war. Did they hire Denver, Hughes & Peck to defend Davis and the others but then withdraw their support when Wirz remained as the only named defendant? For how Confederate naval officer James A. Semple used the $86,000 in gold entrusted to him see Robert Seager, *and Tyler too: A Biography of John & Julia Gardiner Tyler* (New York: McGraw-Hill, 1963) 518–19, and for information on thousands of dollars more hidden in Florida for use as needed by former Confederates, see Arch Frederic Blakey, *General John H. Winder, CSA* (Gainesville: University of Florida Press, 1990) 203. Louis Schade would circulate stories that Wirz was offered a pardon if he would implicate Jefferson Davis and others in the deaths of the prisoners at Andersonville. The already dying Henry Wirz, if he received such an offer, declined it. Lynn, *800 Paces*, 342–43. His enemies could have raised suspicions about promises of support for his families in America and Europe because he did not implicate others in the Andersonville tragedy.

422 James William Denver to Mrs. S. C. Deaver, 13 August 1865, Andersonville/Wirz Collection, Rare Books and Special Collections, University of Notre Dame, South Bend IN. Denver, Colorado is named for James William Denver.

423 Births, Marriages, and Deaths, Orleans MA, microfilm rolls 0778357 and 0778358, Genealogical Society of Utah, Salt Lake UT; Susan E. Roser, *Mayflower Marriages* (Baltimore: Genealogical Publishing Company, 1990) 188; Revolutionary War pension claim of Benoni Baker, W14237, *Revolutionary War Pension and Bounty-Land Warrant Application Files, 1800–1900* (National Archives microfilm M804, roll 114), Records of the Veterans Administration, RG 15, NARA. Boys born of mothers who died in childbirth often received the name "Benoni" (Hebrew for "son of my sorrow"), from the first name given to the Biblical Benjamin, the son of Jacob. Despite the unsupported claim that Benoni and his children were Quakers, they appear, as does Obadiah Baker Jr., as members of the First Church in Orleans MA. "Records of the First Church in Orleans, Formerly the First Church in Eastham, Mass.," *Mayflower Descendant* 13 (1911); 93, 14 (1912): 137.

424 Peterson to Obadiah S. Baker, 20 May 1849, copy provided by Robert Eugene Haynes; Worcester County MA, p. 73, *Seventh Census of the United States (1850)* (National Archives microfilm M432, roll 344), RG 29, NARA; *Centennial History of the Town of Millbury, Massachusetts* (Millbury: n. p., 1915) 142. Baker may have been preparing to try to enter the Worcester Medical College or Harvard Medical College. His father and brothers were listed as boot makers in the 1850 census of nearby Mendon, Worchester County MA, p. 308, *Seventh Census of the United States (1850)* (National Archives microfilm M432, roll 344) RG 49, NARA. Different vital records in Orleans also show his father Obadiah, Sr. (1792–1869) as a farmer and a miller.

425 *Warren Journal* (Belvidere NJ), 19 May 1863; original marriage record of Obadiah S. Baker and Sarah Matlock Van Voy, in author's possession, Hanceville AL; Roll of attorneys, Municipal Archives of New York, New York City; Edwin G. Burrows and Mike Wallace, *Gotham: A History of New York to 1898* (New York: Oxford University Press, 1999) 706.

426 Burrows and Wallace, *Gotham*, 967–68; *New York Times*, 30 July 1858, 3; *New York Times*, 25 August 1858, 1; *Annie L. McCarron v. Orrin S. Baker*, #31553, December 1874, Circuit Court of St. Louis, Missouri State Archives, Jefferson City MO. Baker did not advertise his services, and therefore provided no information on his background, in newspapers, city directories, or national directories of attorneys. No information on his legal training has turned up in the various records of his admission to the bar.

427 *Austin Roe v. Obadiah S. Baker* (1857) and *Daniel B. Pierson v. Obadiah S. Baker* (1860), County Clerk and Clerk of the Supreme County, New York County Court House.

428 New York City, 20th Ward, p. 234, *Eighth Census of the United States (1860)* (National Archives microfilm M653, roll 817), RG 29, NARA; Los Angeles County, Enumeration district 47, Sheet 8, *Twelfth Census of the United States (1900)* (National Archives microfilm T623, roll 89), RG 29, and Civil War pension claim of Orin S. Baker, certificate 457,627, RG 15, NARA; New York, vol. 377 (New York City), p. 130, R. G. Dun & Company Collection, Baker Library, Harvard Business School.

429 *Trial of Henry Wirz*, 695; Baker to Johnson, 25 June 1861, papers of Andrew Johnson, manuscripts division, Library of Congress; *Continental Monthly Devoted to Literature and National Policy* 4 (July 1863): 51–56; O. S. Baker to Sarah Baker, 4 July 1863, copy provided by Robert Eugene Haynes, Seattle WA.

430 Orrin S. Baker to Sarah Baker, 8 and 29 June 1862, copies provided by Robert Eugene Haynes, Seattle WA; *Norfolk* (VA) *Union*, 12 June 1862; Spencer Wilson, "Experiment in Reunion: The Union Army in Civil War Norfolk and Portsmouth, Virginia" (Ph.D. diss., University of Maryland, 1973) 100–1.

431 District 6, *Internal Revenue Assessment List for Virginia, 1862–1866* (National Archives microfilm M793, roll 4), Records of the Internal Revenue Service, RG 58, compiled service record of Orin S. Baker, 16th Virginia Infantry, *Compiled Service Records of Volunteer Union Soldiers who Served in Organizations from the State of Virginia* (National Archives microfilm M398, roll 2), RG 94, and H. Sutcliffe to Capt. Smith, 13 January 1864, *Union Provost Marshal's File of Papers Relating to Individual Civilians* (National Archives microfilm M345, roll 14), Records of the Provost Marshal, RG 110, NARA; *The Union Army*, 8 vols. (Washington: Federal Publishing Company, 1908) 2:306; Wilson, "Experiment in Reunion," 100–1, 119, 126, 128, 133–35, 187–88; Ludwell H. Johnson III, "Blockade or Trade Monopoly?: John A. Dix and the Union Occupation of Norfolk," *Virginia Magazine of History* 19/93 (January 1985): 54–78.

432 Kenneth W. Munden and Henry Putney Beers, *The Union: A Guide to Federal Archives Relating to the Civil War* (Washington DC: National Archives, 1989) 113–14; Andrew Boyd, *Boyd's Washington and Georgetown Directory* (Washington DC: Andrew Boyd, 1865) 426; Arlington County Minute Book, 1862–1866, pp. 229, 237, Arlington County Court House VA; Division 1, District 3, *Internal Revenue Assessment List for the District of Virginia, 1862–1866* (National Archives microfilm M793, roll 3), RG 58, NARA.

433 O. S. Baker to Secretary of War, 20 June and 15 August 1865, vol. 147 (1863 and 2422) *Letters Received by the Secretary of War: Registered Series, 1801–1870* (National Archives microfilm M221, rolls 279–80), Records of the Secretary of War, RG 107, NARA; 9th Division, *Internal Revenue Assessment List for the District of Columbia, 1862–1866* (National Archives microfilm M760, roll 7), RG 58, NARA.

434 Koerting, "The Trial of Henry Wirz," 108.

435 *New York Times*, 31 August 1865, 1.

436 See Lewis L. Laska and James M. Smith, "'Hell and the Devil': Andersonville and the Trial of Capt. Henry Wirz, CSA, 1865," *Military Law Review* 68 (Spring 1975): 77–132; Louis Fisher, "Military Tribunals: a Sorry History," *Presidential Studies Quarterly* 33 (September 2003): 484–508; and Marouf Hasian, Jr., *In the Name of Necessity: Military Tribunals and the Loss of American Civil Liberties* (Tuscaloosa: University of Alabama Press, 2005). For the procedures of the Roman Inquisition see Michael White, *The Heretic and the Pope* (New York: William Morrow & Company, 2002). The procedures in the Wirz trial, however, also bear a striking similarity to those employed in such famous early English trials as that of Sir Walter Raleigh in 1603 for treason and of John Law in 1694 for murder. Giles Milton, *Big Chief Elizabeth* (New York: Farrar, Straus and Giroux, 2000) 257–58; Janet Gleeson, *Millionaire: The Philanderer, Gambler, and Duelist who Invented Modern France* (New York: Simon & Schuster, 1999) 53–56. Members of the modern military of the United States receive some protection from this type of "justice" through the military's use of civilian military criminal investigative organizations.

437 Joseph Holt to E. M. Stanton, 13 November 1865, in *OR*, ser. 3, vol. 5, p. 493.

438 *Trial of Henry Wirz*, 723–29.

439 Koerting, "The Trial of Henry Wirz," 72–86; Roberts, *Andersonville Journey*, 111; Dayton Pryor, *The Beginning and the End: The Civil War Story of Federal Surrenders Before Fort Sumter and Confederate Surrenders After Appomattox* (Bowie MD: Heritage Books, 2001) 376.

440 *Trial of Henry Wirz*, 532–35; *Washington* (DC) *Chronicle*, 24 September 1865, 1.

441 "Wirz Trial Adjourned," *New York Times*, 15 September 1865, 1; "A Bit of Secret History," *New York Times*, 14 October 1883, 2.

442 "Diary of Henry Wirz," *New York Times*, 15 November 1865, 1.

443 Roberts, *Andersonville Journey*, 104–34; Koerting, "The Trial of Henry Wirz," 152, 171–74, 200.

444 Koerting, "The Trial of Henry Wirz," 108.

445 "Wirz Trial," *Washington* (DC) *Chronicle*, 1 October 1865, 1; *Trial of Henry Wirz*, 526–27, 595; Kean, *Inside the Confederate Government*, 230.

446 "Wirz Trial," *Washington* (DC) *Chronicle*, 27 August 1865, 1; "Wirz Trial," *Washington* (DC) *Chronicle*, 15 October 1865, 1; *Trial of Henry Wirz*, 594, 695, 702.

447 John D. Lawson, *American State Trials*, 17 vols. (St. Louis: F. H. Thomas Law Book Company, 1917) 8:691; *New York Times*, 29 August and 15 September 1865.

448 "Wirz Trial," *Washington* (DC) *Chronicle*, 24 September 1865, 1.

449 Roberts, *Andersonville Journey*, 132–33.

450 *Trial of Henry Wirz*, 702–5.

451 Roberts, *Andersonville Journey*, 109, 111–13, 115–16.

452 [no title], *Daily National Intelligencer* (Washington DC), 11 November 1865, 1; "Execution of Wirz," *New York Times*, 11 November 1865, 1. The Swiss consul general, John Hitz, (coincidently the future uncle of J. Edgar Hoover) tried to obtain a pardon for the Swiss-born Wirz. John Hitz to [?], 10 November 1865, Bar E 2300, dispatch 240, Bundesarchiv, Bern, Switzerland.

453 Roberts, *Andersonville Journey*, 131, 133, 139–41; unidentified 1865 newspaper clipping, Louis Manigault scrapbook, Southern Historical Collection, University of North Carolina at Chapel Hill, Chapel Hill NC; Robert E. and Katherine M. Morsberger, *Lew Wallace: Militant Romantic* (New York: McGraw-Hill, 1986) 194. Wirz and Tennessee guerrilla Champ Ferguson were the only persons executed for war crimes in the Civil War. *Harper's Weekly*, 11 and 25 November 1865, pp. 716, 748–49. For Ferguson's circumstances see Thurman Sensing, *Champ Ferguson: Confederate Guerilla* (Nashville: Vanderbilt University Press, 1942).

454 O. S. Baker to secretary of war 10 and 25 October 1865, 16 February 1866, vol. 151, B2627, B2671, C2321, *Register of Letters to the Secretary of War, 1861–1870* (National Archives microfilm M22, roll 124), RG 107, NARA; James W. Duncan file, *Compiled Service Records of Confederate Soldiers who Served in Organizations From the State of Louisiana* (National Archives microfilm M320, roll 150), War Department Collection of Confederate Records, RG 109, NARA.

455 [no title], *Washington* (DC) *Chronicle*, 8 October 1865, 1; court martial file of James W. Duncan (MM-3895), Records of the Judge Advocate General, RG 153, NARA; O'Bryne Family Papers, folder 13, collection 1294, Georgia Historical Society, Savannah GA. James W. Duncan was born in Wheeling VA around 1840 and worked as a clerk in New Orleans when the war began. After his escape, he and his wife Alice moved to Philadelphia PA where they still resided and he worked as a confectioner as late as 1880. According to researcher Dennis W. Brandt, Duncan lived in Pittsburgh in the 1890s, where he testified in the pension claims of former Andersonville prisoners. James W. Duncan, compiled service record; James W. Duncan file, Records and Pension File 534029, RG 94, NARA; Marvel, *Andersonville*, 247; Philadelphia, p. 333C, *Tenth Census of the United States (1880)* (National Archives microfilm T9, roll 1183), RG 29, NARA.

456 George Parsons Lathrop, "The Bailing of Jefferson Davis," *The Century* 33 (February 1887): 636; Koerting, "The Trial of Henry Wirz," 196–201. Some recent scholars have argued that the military commission that tried the Lincoln conspirators failed to prove, or even uncover, the very real conspiracy of Confederate officials that it sought to expose. See William A. Tidwell, James O. Hall, and David W. Gaddy, *Come Retribution: The Confederate Secret Service and the Assassination of Lincoln* (Jackson: University Press of Mississippi, 1988).

457 Koerting, "The Trial of Henry Wirz," 48–49. In *Ex parte Quirin*, the Supreme Court ruled that a group of German saboteurs could be tried by military commission because the Constitution did not require trial by jury for crimes against the rules of war. In that instance; however, Congress had authorized the president to conduct such trials. The issues around the trial of the German saboteurs find in-depth discussion in Louis Fisher, *Nazi Saboteurs on Trial* (Lawrence: University Press of Kansas, 2003).

458 "The Captain Wirz Trial," *New-York Times*, 3 November 1918, pt. 3, p. 7; "Wirz Case Cited Against Ex-Kaiser," *New-York Times,* 21 January 1919, 6. Also see *American and German War Ordeals—A Contrast: The Trial of Captain Henry Wirz for War Crimes* (St. Louis: N. Jones, 1917).

459 For a history of publications of the Wirz trial see Douglas Gibson Gardner, "Andersonville and American Memory: Civil War Prisoners and Narratives of Suffering and Redemption," (Ph.D. diss., Miami University, 1998) 24–26. For an example of the modern debate on the Wirz trial, see "Controversy—Partisan Comments on Andersonville," *Blue & Gray Magazine* 3 (December–January, 1985–1986): 22–37.

460 A. E. Zucker, *The Forty-Eighters: Political Refugees of the German Revolution of 1848* (New York: Columbia University, 1950) 336; "Editor Schade Dead," *Washington Post*, 26 February 1903, 3; Lynn, *800 Paces*, 364; Koerting, "The Trial of Henry Wirz," 202–9; also see Norton P. Chipman's article "The Captain Wirz Case" in the *New York Times*, 29 December 1918.

461 Richmond Banks file, James Hughes Collection; Robert S. Davis, "The Georgia Odyssey of the Confederate Gold," *Georgia Historical Quarterly* 86/4 (Winter 2002): 569–86.

462 By the time of the Wirz's trial, Reinhard had struck out on his own. [Advertisement], *Daily Morning Chronicle* (Washington DC), 25 August 1865, 1.

463 Committee of Publication, *Records of the Columbia Historical Society*, 5 vols. (Washington: The Society, 1902) 5:272; *Spencer v. Martin*, Law Case Files, 1863–1934, case file 3100, entry 60, General Term Minutes, Supreme Court of the District of Columbia, vol. 1, pp. 225, 227, 229, vol. 4, pp. 31, 41, Records of the District Court of Columbia, RG 21, NARA; *New York Times*, 13 September 1867, 1; newspaper clippings, January 1869, microfilm reel 13, frames 280–88, papers of Elizabeth Cady Stanton and Susan B. Anthony, Library of Congress.

464 *Annie L. McCarron v. Orrin S. Baker*, #31553, December 1874, Circuit Court of St. Louis, Missouri State Archives, Jefferson City MO.

465 Ibid.

466 Ibid. As Annie L. Baker, age thirty and born in Pennsylvania, she appears as a housekeeper in the household of Henry L. Patterson in the 1880 federal census of St. Louis. An Edith I. Baker, age six and whose father was born in Massachusetts, is also in the household, presumably the daughter of Orrin Baker and Annie McCarron born in December 1873. St. Louis, St. Louis County, p. 209A, *Tenth Census of the United States (1880)* (National Archives microfilm T9, roll 720), RG 29, NARA. Annie L. McCarron Baker continued to live in the St. Louis area as a maid and housekeeper. She died in March 1931 at City Hospital in St. Louis. Her daughter Edith apparently had no issue. Patricia Walls Stamm to author, 29 January 2004, in author's possession, Hanceville AL.

467 Copy of check provided by Robert Eugene Baker, Seattle WA. No information has been found on exactly what Orrin S. Baker did to earn $1,000 and a Thanksgiving dinner from Adams. The legal work may have concerned the expansion of Adams's Turkish baths or the unspecified reasons for closing his original bath. J. A. Dacus and James W. Buel, *A Tour of St. Louis, or Inside the Great City* (St. Louis: self-published, 1878) 325; George F. Adams, *The Turkish Bath Handbook* (St. Louis: n. p., 1881) 201.

468 *Annie L. McCarron v. Orrin S. Baker*, #31553, December 1874, Circuit Court of St. Louis, Missouri State Archives, Jefferson City MO.

469 *Todd v. Germania Fire*, 1 MO App 472 (1876), Eastern District Appellate Court, *Barnum v. Bobb*, 68 MO 619 (1879), State Supreme Court, *O. S. Baker vs. Samuel Engler and Charles B. Roberts*, #30138, October 1874, *O. S. Baker v. J. D. Brooks*, #25192, April 1873, Circuit Court of St. Louis, Missouri State Archives, Jefferson City MO; *Business Directory of San Francisco and Principal Towns of California and Nevada* (San Francisco: L. M. McKenney, 1877) 320; Alameda County, Enumeration District 12, p. 43, *Tenth Census of the United States (1880)* (National Archives microfilm T9, roll 62), RG 29, NARA.

470 *Los Angeles City Directory* (Los Angeles: W. H. L. Corran, 1887) 93; *Los Angeles City Directory* (Los Angeles: Corran, 1890)107–8; *Yale Seventy-Seven: Their Lives and Letters* (New Haven: n. p., 1892), 18–19; Ronald L. Mendell and Timothy B. Phares, *Who's Who in Football* (New Rochelle NY: Arlington House, 1974) 25; *Who's Who in the Pacific Southwest* (Los Angeles: The Times-Mirror, 1913) 22.

471 Patient register, Napa Hospital, Napa, California; *San Francisco* (CA) *Call*, 16 July 1889; Civil War pension claim of Orin S. Baker, certificate 457,627, RG 15, NARA; *Yale Seventy-Seven*, 18. Sarah claimed Orrin's body but no record has survived of his place of burial. Son Charles, an invalid, died in 1898; daughter Lesbia in 1941; and son Eugene in 1942. They are buried with Sarah (d. 1914) at Rosedale Cemetery in Los Angeles. Lesbia married and later divorced Dr. Robert William Haynes. She also became a member of the Friday Morning Club, an organization of socially progressive women founded by Massachusetts suffragette Caroline Maria Severance. Lesbia's brother-in-law, social reformer Dr. John Randolph Haynes, controlled the Los Angeles city water works and southern California politics for decades. (He had a connection to another lawyer, his patient Clarence Darrow.) Her son, Robert Eugene Haynes, pioneered aviation and radio manufacture in the United States.

CHAPTER ELEVEN

472 This article was used in Robert E. L. Krick, *Staff Officers in Gray* (Chapel Hill: University of North Carolina Press, 2003).

473 Billy Townsend, *Camp Lawton: Magnolia Springs State Park* (Atlanta: Georgia Department of Natural Resources, 1975) 22–3; Douglas O. Gardner, "Prisoners in War," in vol. 3 of David S. and Jeanne Heidler, eds., *Encyclopedia of the American Civil War* (Santa Barbara CA: ABC-CLIO, 2000) 1572; Gayla M. Koerting, "The Trial of Henry Wirz and Nineteenth-century Military Law" (Ph.D. diss., Kent State University, 1997) 197–98.

474 Cooper County, Missouri, p. 76, *Seventh Census of the United States (1850)* (National Archives microfilm M432, roll 398), Records of the Bureau of the Census, Record Group (hereinafter RG) 29, National Archives and Records Administration (NARA), College Park MD.

475 Credit report, Virginia, vol. 13, p. 142, R. G. Dun Collection, Baker Library, Harvard Graduate School of Business Administration, Cambridge MA. For the story of William Walker's filibusters, see Albert Z. Carr, *The World and William Walker* (New York: Harper & Row, 1963); Brady Harrison, *Agent of Empire: William Walker and the Imperial Self in American Literature* (Athens: University of Georgia, 2004); and Rudy Wurlitzer, *Walker* (New York: Harper & Row, 1987).

476 Application for a commission, file Virginia A81, entry 261, applications for commissions, Records of the Secretary of War, RG 107, NARA; D. W. Vowles to John B. Floyd, 10 April 1858 and Floyd to Vowles, 12 April 1858, file V8; *Letters Received by the Secretary of War, 1861–1870* (National Archives microfilm M567, roll 593), Department of the Army, RG 107, NARA.

477 Marion County, Missouri, p. 678, *Eighth Census of the United States (1860)* (National Archives microfilm M653, roll 632), RG 29, NARA; Arthur W. Hafner, *Directory of Deceased American Physicians 1804–1929*, 2 vols. (Chicago: American Medical Association, 1989) 2:1605; Paul G. Anderson, Washington University School of Medicine, to author, 27 February 1998, in author's possession, Hanceville AL.

478 W. N. M., "Capture of Lexington, Missouri by Price's Army," *Southern Bivouac* 3/3 (November 1884): 107.

479 Compiled service record of D. W. Vowles, *Compiled Service Records of Confederate State and Non-Regimental Enlisted Men* (National Archives microfilm M331, roll 255), War Department Collection of Confederate Records, RG 109, NARA; R. I. Holcombe, *History of Marion County Missouri* (1884; repr., Hannibal: Marion County Historical Society, 1979) 932; Albert Castel, *General Sterling Price and the Civil War in the West* (Baton Rouge: Louisiana State University Press, 1968) 55; Elizabeth Bethel, *Preliminary Inventory of the War Department Collection of Confederate Records, Record Group 109* (Athens GA: Iberian Press, 1994) 9; U.S. War Department, *The War of the Rebellion: A Compendium of the Official Records Union and Confederate Armies*, 128 vols. (Washington DC: Government Printing Office, 1898–1911) ser. 2, vol. 3, pp. 896–97; Janet B. Hewett, ed., *Supplement to the Official Records*, 96 vols. (Wilmington NC: Broadfoot, 1996) pt. 2, vol. 38, pp. 475, 489, 495; *Quincy* (IL) *Whig*, 14 and 15 August 1919, 2. For information on men from Illinois in the Confederate army see Ed Gleeson, *Illinois Rebels* (Carmel: Guild Press of Illinois, 1996) xiii-xv.

480 Frances H. Casstevens, *George W. Alexander and Castle Thunder: A Confederate Prison and Its Commandant* (Jefferson NC: McFarland & Company, 2004) 93; Compiled service record of D. W. Vowles, *Compiled Service Records of Confederate State and Non-Regimental Enlisted Men* (National Archives microfilm M331, roll 225); *Reports on Prisoners, 1864*, (Chapter 9, vol. 229), entry 10, War Department Collection of Confederate Records, RG 109, NARA.

481 Arch Fredric Blakey, *General John H. Winder, CSA* (Gainesville: University of Florida Press, 1990) 185.

482 John W. Lynn, *800 Paces to Hell: Andersonville* (Fredericksburg VA: Sergeant Kirkland's Museum, 1999) 47, 56, 68, 74–75, 78, 81, 146, 263, 266, 303, 357, 361; Marvel, *Andersonville*, 28, 79, 212, 235. Novelist MacKinlay Kantor repeated an error from a prisoner's account of misidentifying Capt. Vowles as Lt. Boyce, in chapter 55 of the Pulitzer Prize-winning novel *Andersonville*. He also wrote of Winder being intimidated by the "gentleman" commandant of Camp Lawton and wanting to remove him from command!

483 The Robert Knox Sneden Collection, Historical Society of Virginia has the largest amount of material on Camp Lawton, including several drawings; see Sneden, *Eye of the Storm: A Civil War Odyssey*, ed. Charles F. Bryan, Jr., and Nelson D. Lankford (New York: Free Press, 2000) 260–63, and Sneden, *Images From the Storm*, ed. Charles F. Bryan, Jr., and Nelson D. Lankford (New York: Free Press, 2001) 223–28. None of the official records of Camp Lawton survives. Henry Putney Beers, *The Confederacy* (Washington DC: National Archives Trust, 1986) 252. The site of Camp Lawton is today part of Magnolia Springs State Park.

484 Free Lance, "Southern Prison life," *National Tribune* (Washington DC), 9 September 1882, 2.

485 Townsend, *Camp Lawton*, 1–23; Ovid L. Futch, *History of Andersonville Prison* (Gainesville: University of Florida Press, 1968) 77; Lonnie R. Speer, *Portals to Hell: Military Prisons of the Civil War* (Mechanicsburg PA: Stackpole Books, 1997) 278–79; George A. Rogers and R. Frank Saunders, Jr., "Camp Lawton Stockade, Millen, Georgia, CSA," *Atlanta Historical Journal* 25 (Winter 1981): 81–94; Beers, *The Confederacy*, 54; *Trial of Henry Wirz* (Washington: Government Printing Office, 1868), 326–27. For an account of the prisoners paying bribes to be placed on the exchange list at Millen, see Magnus Tait, *My Rebel Prison Life* (n. p., 1888) 16.

486 Marvel, *Andersonville*, 246–47; court-martial file of James W. Duncan, file MM3895, Records of the Judge Advocate General, RG 153, James W. Duncan file, Records and Pension File 534029, RG 94, NARA.

487 *Quincy* (IL) *Whig*, 14–15 August 1919; *Register of Officers and Agent...Service of the United States on the Thirtieth of September, 1877* (Washington: Government Printing Office, 1878) 8; *Index (Soundex) to the Federal Population Census Schedules for Illinois (1900)* (National Archives microfilm T1043, roll 443), RG 29, NARA; advertisement, *Indiana County Gazette* (PA), 17 May 1899. Vowles's brother Newton worked for many years in Washington as a real estate agent. For the Vowles family in Washington, see the volumes of William H. Boyd, *Boyd's Directory of the District of Columbia* for 1875 through 1878. The pardon petitions appear in *Pardon Petitions and Related Papers...Amnesty Proclamation of May 29, 1865* (National Archives microfilm M1003), RG 107, NARA, and have an index in Carolyn McGough Rowe, *Index to Individual Pardon Applications From the South, 1865–1898* (Pensacola FL: self-published, 1996).

488 *The New York Times Index Vol. 7. No. 3 July–August-September 1919* (New York: New York Times, 1919) 379.

APPENDIX A

489 A private Samuel Hooper, musician of Company H, Eighth Pennsylvania Cavalry survived Andersonville.

490 See chapter 10.

491 See chapter 4.

492 A petition signed by these sergeants is copied into "Statements of Escaped Union Prisoners, Refugees, and Rebel Deserters," entry 4294, Records of Continental Commands, Record Group 393, pt. 1, National Archives and Records Administration (NARA), College Park MD.

493 John W. Urban wrote his account of this incident in *Battle Field and Prison Pen* (Edgewood NJ: Edgewood Publishing, 1882).

494 Charles W. Ross was the alias used by George W. Fechter of the First Kentucky Mounted Infantry, as explained by Fechter in his testimony in the trial of Henry Wirz. *Trial of Henry Wirz* (Washington DC: Government Printing Office, 1868) 568–71.

495 See Peter J. Meaney, "The Prison Ministry of Father Peter Whelan, Georgia Priest and Confederate Chaplain," *Georgia Historical Quarterly* 71/1 (Spring 1987): 1–24.

INDEX